The Virtuous Barrel

How to Transform Corporate Scandals into Good Businesses via Behavioral Ethics

Alexandre Di Miceli da Silveira

Copyright © 2018 Alexandre Di Miceli da Silveira

All rights reserved.

ISBN-13: 9781728669083

Table of Contents

1. What is behavioral ethics? 1
Part 1: We overestimate our ethical behavior 10
2. Human, all too human I: limited rationality and cognitive biases 17
3. Human, all too human II: Stages and dynamics of our decision-making process 34
Part 2: Most of the wrong things are done by good people 46
4. The pressures of those who are part of our daily lives 50
5. The pressures of our organizational environment..72
6. The pressures of the institutional context in which we are embedded 94
7. The time factor and the gradual change in our ethical standards...................112
8. Ethical blind spots and the danger of rationalizations 127
The Ford Pinto Case: The dramatic outcome of a limited framing of reality...................136
The AB InBev model: success story or dangerous context for ethical blindness? 140
Part 3: Core Implications of Behavioral Ethics Findings for Sound Management and Governance 154
9. Business scandals are not caused by a few bad apples 154
10. Rules and controls have limited efficacy and can generate dangerous side effects....166
A caveat: some companies do not want to improve ethical behavior for real 176
Part 4: Solutions to Promote Ethics in Business 179
11. What can I do to avoid becoming ethically blind? Defensive strategies at the personal level 179
12. What should be done to avoid ethical blindness in my organization? The role of culture 198
13. What should be done to avoid ethical blindness in my organization? The role of leadership 222
Excerpt of the Ethical Leadership at Work by Kalshoven, Hartog, and De Hoogh 244
Excerpt of an Indicator to Measure Ethical Awareness...................................245
Part 5: A Final Message 249
14. Toward a new paradigm for sound organizations: culture, leadership, and purpose as the foundation for business success in the twenty-first century 249
References...277
Annex. Behavioral ethics measuring instruments..304
About the Author 322

Tables

Table 1. Organizational types according to "Reinventing Organizations" 262

Figures

Figure 1. Two Cognitive Processes of Our Mind: The Rider and the Elephant Metaphor. 20
Figure 2. Stages of our decision-making process...40
Figure 3. Moral balance: Our mental scoreboard that computes right and wrong behaviors. 40
Figure 4: Asch Experiments: evidence of the power of peers over our judgment. 58
Figure 5. A simple exercise to illustrate our framing of reality. 127
Figure 6. The "tunnel" as a metaphor for our framing of reality. 130
Figure 7. The "beach" as a metaphor of the complete reality. 131
Figure 8. The process of ethical fading that leads to ethical blindness................135
Figure 9. Ford Pinto and the risks of a limited framing of reality. 137
Figure 10. Governance, Leadership and Culture as Inseparable Elements to Achieve a Higher Purpose 273

All websites referred to in the endnotes were accessed on September 30th, 2018.

"To my wife Angela, whose encounter led me to the process of personal transformation that made this book possible."

Preface

> *"Helping businesses to perform just a little better, just a little more ethically, is arguably the most important project humanity can undertake."*
> Jonathan Haidt (1963–)[1]

Companies play a key role in our society.[2] They can create value for all stakeholders through innovative products for their clients, good career options for employees, business opportunities for suppliers, revenues for the government, and financial returns for debt and equity investors. This collective prosperity depends, however, on the quality of the decisions made by the managers and employees, including from the ethical point of view.

Since the early 1990s, a movement demanding companies to improve their "corporate governance" has gained traction around the world.[3] Initially, the movement aimed at making firms more responsible and transparent to their investors. Over the years, the list of better governance practices has been enlarged with the inclusion of social and environmental demands toward a broader set of stakeholders. As a result, many investors today require companies to adopt appropriate environmental, social, and governance (ESG) standards so they can be eligible for investments.

At the end of the day, sound corporate governance means creating an organizational culture in which executives and employees want – by themselves – to behave ethically, comply with the norms, and make decisions in the best long-term interest of the organization.[4] A key concern in the business world nowadays is whether this goal is indeed being achieved.

There have been significant advances since the inception of the movement for better governance in the corporate world. Stakeholder expectations on the role of companies in society has grown substantially in the past decades, along with stricter regulations demanding higher business standards in most countries.

This has led, in turn, to significant changes in the way businesses around the world are run. Compared with the early 2000s, for example, most companies now have more sophisticated incentive and control systems in place as well as more active and professional boards of directors. In addition, as we shall see later, there are now many good examples of companies adopting innovative practices to better deal with their impact on society and foster healthier relationships with their key stakeholders.

On the other hand, despite noteworthy managerial efforts of many companies more attuned to the social values and demands of the twenty-first century, the reality is that people everywhere are still witnessing serious unethical breaches in the business world. These immoral and, in most cases, illegal wrongdoings take many forms, such as corporate corruption, financial fraud, tax evasion, price-fixing, environmental crimes, violation of human and workers' rights, etc.

Corporate scandals have been recurring in developed and developing countries. In the United States, for instance, the 2000s were marked by a wave of accounting frauds in 2001–2002 epitomized by the Enron and Worldcom collapses, the stock option backdating scandal in 2005,[5] and the breakdown of systemically critical financial institutions such as Bear Sterns and Lehman Brothers leading to the 2008 global crisis.[6] In addition, major high-profile malfeasances involving rich-country companies include the payment of large-scale bribes (e.g., Siemens in 2006,[7] Alstom in 2014,[8] and Rolls-Royce in 2017[9]), money laundering (e.g., Olympus in 2011[10] and HSBC in 2012[11]), ecological disasters motivated by poor governance practices (e.g., BP oil spill in 2010),[12] the rigging of the London interbank offered rate (Libor) by several UK banks (e.g., Barclays and UBS in 2012),[13] the cheating of emissions tests to illegally pollute the environment (e.g., Volkswagen in 2015 and Fiat–Chrysler in 2017),[14] and the creation of millions of fake customer accounts (e.g., Wells Fargo in 2016).[15]

In the developing world, corporate bribery and corruption are still rampant. This has been amazingly exemplified by the colossal Operation "Lava Jato" ("Car Wash," its police code name) in Brazil. Launched in 2014, this investigation is considered by many the largest corruption scandal in history.[16] Initially focusing on overpriced contracts between private construction firms and Petrobras (a state-owned oil company), the investigation uncovered a web of political and corporate kickbacks in hundreds of public-work contracts of a dozen countries in Latin America and Africa.

The figures are impressive: over 200 executives and politicians have been arrested in Brazil alone, including 14 CEOs of the largest private groups of the country.[17] The case also ended up with the biggest leniency agreement ever in a bribery case. In December 2016, Odebrecht then the largest construction group in Latin America – and Braskem (its petrochemical arm) agreed to pay a record penalty of $3.5 billion as part of a plea bargain with US, Swiss, and Brazilian prosecutors to terminate the accusations. In the agreement, Odebrecht recognized the payment of $3.3 billion in grafts between 2006 and 2014 to more than 1,000 politicians and officials from Latin America and Africa.[18]

At a time of great discussion on sustainability issues, a key theme for our collective survival, Brazil also recently offered another example of the dire consequences of poor management and governance. In November 2015, a huge dam operated by Samarco – a joint-venture of mining giants BHP Billinton and Vale – collapsed. The waste killed 19 people and devastated historical cities, rivers, and valleys. Prosecutors filed homicide charges against 21 top executives from the three companies involved, including board members and Samarco's former CEO. According to the investigation, several problems related to the dam's structure had been brought to senior managers years before.[19] An internal corporate memo circulating months before the collapse, for example, warned that up to 20 people could die in the event of dam rupture.[20] The official conclusion of the investigation was that there was a deliberate "prioritization of profits in detriment of safety practices for the people and environment."[21]

All these episodes caused great economic value destruction as well as huge environmental and social harm. They also showed that, for many companies, the adoption of sound corporate governance practices has been used more as marketing tools than as a genuine business approach based on solid principles and long-term relationship-building.

Recent corporate scandals have also contributed to a widespread erosion of public trust in business. A 2013 survey conducted by Edelman Institute with 31,000 people from 26 countries, for example, found that only 18% of respondents trust business leaders to tell the truth and make ethical and moral decisions.[22] Another survey ranked business leaders as one of the three lowest respected professions, along with politicians and real estate agents.[23] This lack of trust in executives is also observed within companies. In a survey conducted in 2016 with 33,000 employees from 28 countries, only 24% of employees believed that their CEOs exhibit ethical behavior.[24] As summarized by an editorial of the *Academy of Management Journal*, "Business is often seen as a consumer of trust rather than a generator of trust."[25]

In consequence of this breakdown in trust, a growing number of people have become increasingly cynical and disenchanted with the business world. One of the best evidences on this comes from a 2017 survey conducted in 155 countries by the Gallup Institute. It found that only 15% of employees worldwide are engaged with their jobs – meaning they are highly involved in and enthusiastic about their work and workplace –, while 85% are not engaged or actively disengaged. According to Gallup, the lower productivity resulting from this condition generates worldwide losses of approximately $7 trillion.[26]

It is critical, therefore, to reflect on the following question: Why do these colossal episodes of corporate mismanagement stemming from unethical and illegal decisions still take place after decades of debates on corporate governance as well as increased regulations demanding better management and governance in the business world?

Are these cases the fault of some (very few) "evil" people? Or do they simply reflect that human beings are intrinsically (and hopelessly) "evil"? These are usual responses people give when questioned on the causes of recent corporate scandals.

The first answer is known as the "rotten apples" line of reasoning. That is, these scandals would have been caused by a few malicious people acting in a rational and dishonest way, usually at the top of organizations.

At the other extreme resides the second answer. In this case, the problem would be the alleged "evil nature" of human beings. For advocates of this view, there would be no way to avoid such scandals because they would be the inevitable consequence of our fundamentally selfish and individualistic "human nature." In this regard, one research with experts on corporate malfeasance concluded that "Employees in corrupt organizations perceive human beings as evil. That is, all individuals play unfair ... and that is why employees expect everyone to behave corruptly."[27]

In view of the obvious failure of the traditional approach to corporate governance in preventing business scandals based on the old carrot and stick paradigm, I have started investigating alternative perspectives that could ensure genuinely well-governed companies. This effort led me to the emerging field of behavioral ethics.

In my view, this field is probably the most promising approach to understand what is going on in the business world as well as to find solutions to promote sound management and governance practices. This book is the outcome of years of research and discussions with academics and business leaders from various countries on these issues. As a result, it connects state-of-the-art research to concrete business cases.

From the academic perspective, this book was only possible due to the work of pioneering researchers in the field of behavioral ethics. Among the leading authorities on this subject, who provided the conceptual basis for this work, stands out professors Guido Palazzo, Ulrich Hoffrage, Max Bazerman, Ann Tenbrunsel, Jonathan Haidt, Muel Kaptein, Linda Treviño, Robert Prentice, Francesca Gino, and Dan Ariely. In particular, the concepts of "ethical blindness," originally formulated by Palazzo and Hoffrage and of "bounded ethicality" developed by Bazerman and Tenbrunsel, served as the theoretical backbone for this book.[28]

The text is divided into five parts. In the first two, I describe the central elements of behavioral ethics, a multidisciplinary-field based on social psychology, neuroscience, and other cognitive sciences. This will allow us to see that the typical answers given to explain current corporate wrongdoings, i.e., the "rotten apples" and the "selfish nature" arguments, are insufficient and generally incorrect.

My goal is to demonstrate that the vast majority of corporate misconduct is the result of a collective process of "ethical fading" taking place within the firms. This process leads many well-intentioned people with good values – like you or me – to behave in an unethical or even illicit way (or at least to become silent observers of improper actions by others).[29]

This loss of sensitivity to the implications of our acts or omissions, in turn, tends to generate a central concept for this book called "ethical blindness." People become ethically blind when they behave unethically while perceiving their actions – at least at that very moment – as correct, justifiable, or defensible.

Before going further, it is worth noting that looking for a deeper understanding of the dynamics that caused recent corporate scandals obviously does not exempt the individuals involved from their legal and moral responsibilities. These people, particularly those in leadership positions, usually have their share of blame for their acts, as they have actively contributed to build or reinforce the perverse organizational context leading to ethical blindness. On the other hand, because these individuals have also been influenced by this very same context and its typical pressures, the solution to prevent corporate transgressions clearly goes far beyond the mere conviction or replacement of specific individuals.

It is also important to highlight that people do not necessarily respond in the same way to the same circumstances due to their unique mix of nature and nurture. Certain individual characteristics may influence the propensity toward misconduct. Research shows, for example, that women, older people, more conscientious individuals, and those under a lower level of stress are generally less likely to behave dishonestly.[30] In contrast, certain personality traits also seem to make some individuals more prone to unethical conduct. In the case of Brazilian state-owned company Petrobras, for example, authorities found that a midlevel executive named Pedro Barusco received about $100 million in bribes over nearly two decades. During his testimony, he said: "I started receiving bribes in 1997. It was a personal initiative, totally mine."[31]

There are, therefore, some individuals willing to do anything to maximize their power or wealth. However, there is ample evidence that these "rotten apples" are not sufficient to explain the magnitude and extent of the corporate problems we have been witnessing. In fact, as I will demonstrate throughout this book, major business scandals only occur when unethical practices are supported – tacitly or explicitly – by ordinary people like us.

This means that the greatest risk for sound management and governance standards does not come from a few bad apples but from those with good values who start to rationalize their behaviors or to become silent observers as a result of cognitive biases, day-to-day pressures, and a perverse temporal dynamic.

Having a correct understanding of what is really going on in the way businesses are run is critical to find correct answers to the current faults in the corporate world. As a consequence, the third and fourth parts of the book offer a set of solutions to prevent ethical blindness taking place at the individual and organizational levels.

These solutions are intended to help companies to develop a healthy ethical culture under the guidance of conscious leaders. They go far beyond increasing rules, controls, or the implementation of compliance programs – traditionally recommended but clearly insufficient initiatives to promote sound corporate governance for real.

The fifth and last part of the book, in turn, reflects on current practices in the business world from a broader perspective with the goal of presenting new paradigms for successful management and governance in the twenty-first century. This section shows how current scandals originate from a common thread, i.e., the adoption of a problematic approach to corporate governance based on the idea that the role of managers is to maximize shareholders' wealth (particularly in the short term). It is this outdated mindset on the role of business in society, completely misaligned with the structural changes and the *zeitgeist* of this new century, that has led to the recent large-scale episodes of corporate wrongdoings.[32]

The profound technological, economic, and social changes we are going through, of which current corporate misconducts are only a reflection, will lead us to a new paradigm on what healthy management and governance means. It is quite likely that the new model for business success in the twenty-first century will be based on three central elements: the pursuit of a higher purpose, conscious leadership, and an ethical culture that awakens the best out of people.

In order to evolve into a better society, it is imperative that companies should be led by executives who routinely ponder on the broader implications of their actions and are able to exhibit high empathy in their decisions.[33] It is out of this deep reflection that these leaders will be able to make decisions based on sound ethical principles that align their companies to the common good. As pointed out by Professor Jonathan Haidt in the quote opening this preface, improving the ethical behavior in the business world – going way beyond the mere focus on complying with regulations – is plausibly the main global challenge of our time. If successful, we will manage to create a much better world for us and our descendants. This is the aim of this book. Have a good reading!

---

[1] Source: Forbes Magazine Interview. 02/03/2016. Will Your Ethics Hold Up Under Pressure? Available at https://www.forbes.com/sites/roncarucci/2016/02/03/will-your-organizations-ethics-hold-up-under-pressure/#72abebf75532

[2] An example of the relevance of business for society comes from a 2016 study by Global Justice Now. It concluded that, out of the world's 100 largest economic entities, 69 are companies and only 31 are countries. The study also noted that the revenues of the ten largest companies are bigger than the GDP of most countries in the world. Source: Global Justice Now. 2016 Countries vs. Corporations dataset. Available at http://www.globaljustice.org.uk/sites/default/files/files/resources/corporations_vs_governments_final.pdf

[3] Corporate governance refers to the way by which businesses are directed, incentivized and controlled, including its explicit and tacit rules. Publications on this field such as corporate governance codes usually focus on the relationships between shareholders, board of directors and the senior management team.

[4] Subject to the public interest when company interests conflict with the public interest.

[5] A paper by Lie (2005) shows that around 2,000 US companies have altered the dates of their executives' stock option plans to dates immediately before sharp increases in stock prices. This practice substantially increased their managers' compensation, leading to an investigation by the SEC (Securities and Exchange Commission). More than 130 companies have been identified as practicing improper backdating, resulting in the firing or resignation of more than 50 senior managers.

[6] In just five years from 2002 to 2007, federal prosecutors in the United States secured convictions against more than 200 CEOs, 50 CFOs, and 120 vice-presidents. In addition, from 2008 to 2015, twenty of the world's biggest banks have paid more than $235 billion due to a series of misdeeds ranging from fines for manipulation of interest rates to compensation of deceived customers. Sources: Soltes (2016: 41) and http://graphics.thomsonreuters.com/15/bankfines/index.html, respectively.

[7] New York Times. 12/20/2008. At Siemens, bribery was just a line item. Available at http://www.nytimes.com/2008/12/21/business/worldbusiness/21siemens.html

[8] New York Times. 12/22/2014. Alstom to plead guilty and pay US a $772 million fine in a bribery scheme. Available at https://www.nytimes.com/2014/12/23/business/alstom-plead-guilty-bribery-us-justice-department.html

[9] BBC News. 01/18/2017. Rolls-Royce apologises after £671m bribery settlement. Available at http://www.bbc.com/news/business-38644114

[10] Bloomberg Businessweek. 02/16/2012. The Story Behind the Olympus Scandal.

Available at https://www.bloomberg.com/news/articles/2012-02-16/the-story-behind-the-olympus-scandal

[11] Bloomberg. 07/03/2013. HSBC Judge Approves $1.9B Drug-Money Laundering Accord. Available at https://www.bloomberg.com/news/articles/2013-07-02/hsbc-judge-approves-1-9b-drug-money-laundering-accord

[12] Reuters. 11/13/2014. US judge upholds BP 'gross negligence' Gulf spill ruling. Available at https://www.reuters.com/article/us-bp-spill/u-s-judge-upholds-bp-gross-negligence-gulf-spill-ruling-idUSKCN0IY01320141114

[13] BBC News. 12/19/2012. UBS fined $1.5 billion for Libor rigging. Available at http://www.bbc.com/news/business-20767984

[14] The New York Times. 05/19/2017. Fiat Chrysler to Modify 100,000 Vehicles After Accusations of Emissions Cheating. Available at https://nyti.ms/2rzJGIz

[15] CNN Money. 08/31/2017. Wells Fargo uncovers up to 1.4 million more fake accounts. Available at http://money.cnn.com/2017/08/31/investing/wells-fargo-fake-accounts/index.html

[16] The Guardian. 06/01/17. Operation Car Wash: Is this the biggest corruption scandal in history? Available at https://www.theguardian.com/world/2017/jun/01/brazil-operation-car-wash-is-this-the-biggest-corruption-scandal-in-history

[17] The figures are available at http://lavajato.mpf.mp.br/. Other impressive outcomes of Operation Car Wash are worth mentioning: 1,765 court proceedings; 881 search warrants and seizures; 881 search warrants and seizures; 101 preventive arrests; 111 temporary arrests; 340 requests for international cooperation with 43 countries; 163 plea bargain agreements; 10 leniency agreements with companies; 177 convictions in the lower court, totaling 1,753 years.

[18] Financial Times. 12/28/2016. A Brazilian bribery machine. Available at https://www.ft.com/content/8edf5b2c-c868-11e6-9043-7e34c07b46ef. The Economist. 12/22/2016. Brazil's gargantuan corruption scandal goes global. Available at https://www.economist.com/news/21712445-american-authorities-reach-record-bribery-related-settlement-two-huge-companies. Valor Econômico. 12/21/216. Odebrecht e Braskem firmam maior acordo de leniência dos EUA. Available at http://www.valor.com.br/politica/4814985/odebrecht-e-braskem-firmam-maior-acordo-de-leniencia-dos-eua

[19] The investigation carried out by Brazilian federal prosecutors is available at http://www.mpf.mp.br/mg/sala-de-imprensa/docs/denuncia-samarco

[20] G1/Globo. 10/20/2016. MPF denuncia 22 pessoas e quatro empresas por desastre em Mariana. Available at http://g1.globo.com/minas-gerais/desastre-ambiental-em-mariana/noticia/2016/10/mpf-denuncia-26-pessoas-por-rompimento-da-barragem-da-samarco.html

[21] Folha de São Paulo. 10/20/2016. Procuradoria denuncia 21 pessoas sob acusação de homicídio em Mariana. Available at http://www1.folha.uol.com.br/cotidiano/2016/10/1824611-procuradoria-denuncia-21-pessoas-por-homicidio-em-tragedia-de-mariana.shtml

[22] Edelman Trust Barometer 2013. Annual Global Study. Available at https://www.edelman.com/news-awards/2013-edelman-trust-barometer-finds-crisis-leadership

[23] Frank Luntz. 2016. The Attitudes and Priorities of the Snapchat Generation. Available at http://static.politico.com/bc/7c/c808106e44eaa8855a3a12553bb7/snapchat-generation-

release.pdf

[24] Another survey conducted by the Gallup Institute in the US showed that the public trust on big companies reached a historic low of 18% in 2016, up from 30% ten years earlier. Sources: 2017 Edelman Trust Barometer. Available at http://www.edelman.com/trust2017/; 2016 Edelman Trust Barometer – Employee Engagement. Available at http://www.edelman.com/insights/intellectual-property/2016-edelman-trust-barometer/state-of-trust/employee-trust-divide/. Gallup – Confidence in Institutions. Available at http://www.gallup.com/poll/1597/confidence-institutions.aspx

[25] Hollensbe et al. (2014: 1227).

[26] Gallup's 2017 State of the Global Workplace Report. Available at https://www.gallup.com/workplace/238079/state-global-workplace-2017.aspx. According to Gallup Institute, the active disengagement of employees costs the US economy about $500 billion a year. Another survey, conducted by Steelcase Inc in 2016 with 12,480 people from 17 countries, came up with a similar conclusion. Only 13% of employees said to be highly committed and satisfied with their companies, while more than a third expressed to be completely demotivated and disengaged. Source: Steelcase 2016 Global Report. Engagement and the Global Workplace. 2016. Available at https://info.steelcase.com/global-employee-engagement-workplace-report#introduction (access in 01/08/2018).

[27] Campbell and Göritz (2014: 302). These experts included former CEOs of corrupt organizations, ombudsmen, police officers, and investigative journalists.

[28] Palazzo et al. (2012), and Bazerman and Tenbrunsel (2011).

[29] "Values" can be defined as "principles" or "motivators" that we consider important to guide our lives. For a holistic view of the concept of values, see Woodward and Shaffakat (2016).

[30] Robertson et al. (2016), Decety (2016), Ryan (2016), Sommer et al. (2014), Jia et al. (2014), Steffensmeier et al. (2013), Cumming et al. (2012), Haselhuhn and Wong (2011), Decety et al. (2011), Ones et al. (2007), and Dawson (1997).

[31] UOL – Universo online. 10/03/2015. Comecei a receber propina em 1997 por iniciativa pessoal, diz delator. Available at https://noticias.uol.com.br/politica/ultimas-noticias/2015/03/10/comecei-a-receber-propina-em-1997-por-iniciativa-pessoal-diz-barusco.htm

[32] *Zeitgeist* is a German word that can be defined as "the defining spirit or mood of a particular period of history as shown by the ideas and beliefs of the time". Source: English Oxford Living Dictionary.

[33] According to Baron-Cohen (2012: 18), empathy can be defined as our ability to identify what someone else is thinking or feeling and to respond to their thoughts and feelings with an appropriate emotion. The author also argues that evil deeds (such as unethical actions) can be simply seen as the absence of empathy, exacerbated by negative environmental factors and a genetic component.

The Virtuous Barrel:
How to Transform Corporate Scandals into Good Businesses via Behavioral Ethics

1. What is behavioral ethics?

> *"The only difference between saints and sinners is that every saint has a past while every sinner has a future."*
> Oscar Wilde (1854–1900)[1]

The quote above from acclaimed writer Oscar Wilde captures very well the spirit of the emerging field of "behavioral ethics."[2] This recent topic, based on sciences such as social psychology, sociology, behavioral economics, and neuroscience, aims to address two major questions:[3]

1. How do people actually behave when they are exposed to ethical dilemmas?
   and,
2. Why do ordinary people (or simply "good people") do bad things, often without being fully aware that they are acting against their own values?

These questions represent a new perspective for the field of ethics. The traditional approach, prescriptive and based on philosophy, aims to discuss and inform people how they should behave. Behavioral ethics, in contrast, simply attempt to understand what factors might lead well-intentioned people to act in unethical and sometimes even illicit ways. This subject, thus, seeks to understand how people do actually behave, instead of how they should behave.[4]

The traditional approach to ethics is grounded on theories that assume people are rational and fully reflect on their actions. The two major theses, widely debated in ethics courses, are the deontology of Immanuel Kant and the utilitarianism of Jeremy Bentham and John Stuart Mill.

The deontological approach argues that the morality of an action should be based on the adherence to universal principles as well as on the impossibility of violating the fundamental rights of human beings to achieve any purpose. In other words, it is a principles-based approach, in which the ends never justify the means, and where each human life is invaluable (not being acceptable to use rational computations to deal with it).[5]

The utilitarian approach, in turn, judges an action in terms of its consequences. According to this view, the most correct decision is the one that benefits the greatest possible number of people and leads to the greater collective well-being. Importantly, this should be the case even for decisions that could take people's lives or violate other principles. Utilitarianism, therefore, is a consequence-based approach in which the ends justify the means.[6]

The normative discussion about ethics based on theories such as deontology and utilitarianism is certainly very important. After all, how can we judge people's conduct without a guidance that establishes *ex-ante* what is ethical or unethical?

On the other hand, behavioral ethics also has a relevant and well-defined scope: to analyze, mostly through experiments with real people, how individuals behave when they are subjected to ethical dilemmas. For the business world, the field plays a key role by shedding light on the situational and psychological factors that encourage or discourage ethical behavior in the workplace.

If knowledge on normative ethics would be enough to effectively improve human behavior, then individuals with high expertise on its concepts such as ethics professors would probably behave more ethically than the rest of the population. Curiously, though, scientific evidence shows that not even ethicists tend to behave systematically better when compared with others.

This was demonstrated by a series of papers led by philosophy professor Eric Schwitzgebel.[7] For one of his works, he went to libraries from universities all over the

The Virtuous Barrel:
How to Transform Corporate Scandals into Good Businesses via Behavioral Ethics

United States and concluded that ethics books were 50% to about twice as likely to be missing than books from other areas of philosophy comparable in terms of age and popularity.[8] In another research, he concluded that ethics professors did not behave better than professors from other fields in any of eight activities having a moral dimension, e.g., blood and organ donation, election attendance, vegetarianism, payment of academic societies membership fees, replying to student emails, and even the frequency of staying in touch with one's mother.[9] Ethics professors seem to agree with Schwitzgebel's results. In another research, he asked participants of the annual conference of the US Association of Philosophy to anonymously compare the moral behavior of ethicists to that of both philosophers of other fields and non-academics of similar social background.[10] At the end, the majority of respondents agreed with the idea that ethicists do not behave, on average, better than non-ethicists.

The central message from these papers is clear: Studying ethics from a strictly intellectual point of view will not necessarily make people behave more ethically.[11] In fact, the opposite can occur, i.e., studying ethics from a rational and normative perspective can make individuals more prone to use rhetoric to justify their preferred courses of action, thus increasing the chance of unethical behaviors.

This view is endorsed by Mary Gentile, professor of ethics at the University of Virginia. She argues that the traditional training on ethics, centered on the discussion of complex dilemmas using ethical reasoning models developed by philosophers has led to a sort of "ethics fatigue" among executives, who tend to view these intellectual debates as tedious exercises.[12]

Gentile also observes that many executives learn how to use these normative theories to justify any decisions they want to make, including those that lead to their own benefit. As a result, when faced with an ethical conflict, practitioners may first decide what they want to do and only then select the model of ethical reasoning that best supports their choice ... exactly the opposite of what we intend to achieve with the study of ethics.[13]

Psychologist Jonathan Haidt, a professor of ethics at New York University and founder of EthicalSystems, a multidisciplinary initiative that brings together leading researchers on behavioral ethics, made a similar criticism.[14] For him, traditional ethics trainings fail to effectively change people's conduct because they are based on mid-twentieth-century theories, e.g., Lawrence Kohlberg's theory of moral development,[15] assuming that people are fully rational, when in fact they are not. In contrast, he developed a social-intuitionist model that argues that our moral judgment primarily results from an intuitive and automatic process usually (but not always) followed by reasoning.[16]

The modern view on ethics, therefore, is that people behave virtuously when they are moved not only by reason but essentially by intuition, emotion, and empathy. Countless research in the fields of neuroscience and social psychology has corroborated this claim. These areas have shown that our morality has evolved for the sake of promoting cooperation in large groups, a critical ability to our evolutionary success.

The development of morality, in turn, has led to biological changes in our species that raise emotions when faced with ethical dilemmas. In many cases, consequently, it is the measurable physiological discomfort we feel that prevents us from acting dishonestly.[17] Thus, emotions play a key role in restraining our unethical behavior, and it is not possible to talk about ethics from a strictly rational perspective.[18]

Before moving forward, it is important to make a brief digression on the concept of ethics. Although the normative discussion of what is right or wrong is not the focus of this book – which aims to show why and under what circumstances we may act contrary to our own values and initial intentions – the box below helps us understanding this conception.

> *Since we are talking about ethics...*
>
> *Ethics can be understood through the lens of our relationships. It represents the values, principles, and norms of conduct that guide our relations with our relatives, friends, society, sentient creatures, and the planet.*

The Virtuous Barrel:
How to Transform Corporate Scandals into Good Businesses via Behavioral Ethics

To behave ethically, we must reflect on the impacts and potential harm we may cause with our actions. This will lead us to systematically question ourselves on "what is the right thing to do?".

Adopting norms of coexistence to guide our exchanges with the world make us transcend our individual perspective and adjust our self-interest to a wider social perspective.

Ethics, therefore, go beyond our egocentrism: They always involve some personal sacrifice resulting from our relationships so that we can live better collectively. As one apocryphal phrase says: "no pain, no ethics."

Ethics are critical for us to evolve into a more prosperous society. They determine how we live together and how we interact with others without harming them. Among the harms we may cause with our actions or omissions are physical damages (e.g., causing an accident); emotional or psychological damages (e.g., short-term emotional problems arising from humiliations that can evolve to lasting psychological traumas); financial damages (e.g., taking advantage of the lack of knowledge of others); and, reputational damages (e.g., disclosing the weaknesses of others, whether true or not).

Although some people unfortunately see ethics as an old and "out of fashion" issue, the topic is actually even more important nowadays.

This assertion comes not only by the fact that people tend to be less and less influenced by religion (which historically has been in charge of determining what is morally right), but also because our twenty-first century society is characterized by elements that foster thoughtless and questionable behaviors. These elements include the existence of uncertain "rules of the game," people overloaded with information and activities, a constant need for quick decisions, a difficulty of establishing long-term relationships, extreme competitiveness, a crisis of guidance and values, consumerism, and hedonism.

Our contemporary society increasingly needs, therefore, effective rules of coexistence, cooperation, communion, and connection with the world. Thus, we need to embed ethics into our daily lives, starting from the daily choices about what we eat, wear, and how we have fun.

The definition of what constitutes an unethical decision is another important issue on ethics discussions. For many scholars, an unethical behavior can be defined as a conduct that violates society's accepted moral norms (such as cheating, stealing, lying, taking undue credit, etc.). To a large extent, unethical behaviors also overlap with illegal acts because the law should represent the agreement of society about what constitutes an acceptable behavior.

Notwithstanding, recent conceptual developments, such as the moral foundations theory proposed by psychologist Jonathan Haidt, added new layers of complexity to this discussion by arguing that there are six innate moral foundations upon which cultures develop their various moralities: care/harm, fairness/cheating, loyalty/betrayal, authority/subversion, sanctity/degradation, and liberty/oppression.

To find out if something we are doing (or intending to do) is unethical or not, some authors propose using the so-called "publicity test": Would you feel comfortable by seeing your decision on the cover of a newspaper? (One variant of this argument asks if you would feel good in explaining what you intend to do in a letter to your mother.)

Finally, it is also worth making a distinction between ethics and morality, two related concepts that are commonly used interchangeably. Ethics usually have a more secular and universal nature: They represent the distinction between right and wrong conduct based on questioning, reflection, and introspection. Morality, in turn, frequently has a more religious and cultural connotation: It represents the concept of right or wrong according to what is prescribed by sacred texts or moral codes (this interpretation on the relationship between ethics and morality is obviously not consensual among scholars, with other views being accepted).

After this conceptual digression on normative ethics, let us return to its behavioral aspect. This strand represents a new way of comprehending the conduct of people in organizations. While the traditional approach assumes that it is enough to classify people as "good" or "bad" according to their character, i.e., expecting that those with "good character" will always act ethically, behavioral ethics departs from the premise that most transgressions derive from both the psychological complexities of human beings and the powerful effects of the contexts of which they are part.

As a result, this new way of understanding questionable behaviors assumes that the situation and the belief system to which people are subject are the main determinants of their behavior, instead of their character or disposition. As pointed out by Harvard Business School professor Eugene Soltes, author of a book based on interviews with dozens of convicted senior managers involved in the most significant corporate scandals in history "[to judge executives' unethical actions], we have to imagine ourselves

The Virtuous Barrel:
How to Transform Corporate Scandals into Good Businesses via Behavioral Ethics

surrounded by their norms and immersed in their culture – not just in the present but in the past as well ... we have to see ourselves as being shaped by the experiences they faced throughout their careers, not by those we face in our own."[19]

To improve ethical conduct, thus, we must go beyond the view that human beings always act in a rational and calculated way. It is necessary to analyze the impact of their psychological processes, contextual pressures, and temporal dynamics. This is what will help us, in turn, to create environments in which ethical conduct is easy-to-do, automatic, and customary.

Albeit recent, the field of behavioral ethics has already reached two major conclusions based on numerous experiments with thousands of individuals. Although somewhat uncomfortable to fathom, these findings are essential for us to evolve toward de facto well-run organizations.

What are these conclusions? Are you ready?

---

[1] Source: A Woman of No Importance (Act 3). Available at http://genius.com/Oscar-wilde-a-woman-of-no-importance-act-3-annotated

[2] Among the academic papers detailing the field of behavioral ethics, stand out Robertson et al. (2016), Irlenbusch e Villeval (2015), Langevoort (2015), Kluver et al. (2014), Prentice (2014), Bazerman e Gino (2012), De Cremer et al. (2010), Rupp et al. (2011), Salvador and Folger (2009), and Treviño et al. (2006).

[3] According to Robertson *et al.* (2016: 6, 43-44), neuroscience research aims to relate the brain activity to human cognition, emotions, and behavior. The area uses five main techniques for its inferences: electroencephalography (EEG – based on changes in the electrical activity of the brain), functional magnetic resonance imaging (fMRI – based on changes in cerebral blood flow or metabolism), transcranial magnetic stimulation and transcranial direct
current stimulation (TMS and tDCS – based on temporary inhibition or stimulation of specific brain areas or functions), hormones (measures of hormone concentration in saliva or blood), and implicit biological measures (measurements of pupil dilatation, skin conductance, etc.).

[4] In academic jargon, the traditional approach to ethics presents a normative or prescriptive approach for this field, while behavioral ethics adopts an empirical or descriptive approach.

[5] For Kant, attitudes such as murder, theft and lies should be absolutely forbidden, even in cases where acting in this way could lead to greater collective happiness. Source: Kant, I. (1998). Critique of Pure Reason Ed. Cambridge University Press.

[6] The famous ethical dilemma of the "runaway trolley" illustrates the difference in approach of the two key theories of normative ethics. In this dilemma, suppose there is a trolley running loose the railway tracks. Ahead, there are five people tied up on the tracks unable to move. The trolley is headed to go straight for them. You are standing next to a lever and have the possibility of avoiding

this tragedy. If you pull the lever, the trolley will switch to a different track. However, you observe that there is one person also tied up on the side track. Would you pull the lever and save five people, thus diverting the trolley onto the side track where it would kill one person instead? The vast majority of people tend to respond that they would pull the lever in order to save the life of the five people. Doing this means acting according to Bentham's utilitarianism: what matters is the consequence, that is, the action that results in the greatest happiness for the maximum of people. Now imagine the same situation as before: a runaway trolley will hit five unaware workers standing on the rails. This time, you are on a bridge under which the trolley will pass, and you can only stop it by placing something very heavy in front of it. You see a very fat man carrying a heavy backpack next to you. The only way to stop the trolley is to push him over the bridge and onto the track, killing him to save the five people. Would you push this person to the railroad? From a logical perspective, there is no difference between this dilemma and the previous one: we continue to discuss the possibility of exchanging the life of one individual for the life of five other people. Curiously, though, about 70% of people in this case say they would not push the individual. Why does this happen? In a seminal study, Greene et al. (2001) showed that, although based on the same logic, the second variant of the train dilemma activates areas of the brain associated with emotion. This led the authors to create the "dual process theory of moral judgment," which argues that our brain has two competing subsystems for moral reasoning: an intuitive and emotional-based one associated with deontological options; and, a rational-based one associated with utilitarian options. This thesis would explain, therefore, why we tend to be inconsistent with ethical principles in dilemmas such as the runaway trolley. In addition, another recent study by Kahane et al. (2015) found that people who favor a utilitarian view of sacrificing one person to save others tend to be more lenient with moral transgressions and have less difficulty in hurting others in their daily lives.

[7] Schwitzgebel and Rust (2014a), Schwitzgebel and Rust (2014b), Rust and Schwitzgebel (2013), Schwitzgebel et al. (2012), Schwitzgebel and Rust (2010), Schwitzgebel (2009) and Schwitzgebel and Rust (2009).

[8] Schwitzgebel, E. (2009).

[9] Schwitzgebel and Rust (2014a).

[10] Schwitzgebel and Rust (2009).

[11] Again, this does not mean that the normative approach to ethics is unimportant. Since there can be no empirical research without a conceptual basis to support it, it is not possible to assess people's ethical behavior without a normative approach that establishes *ex-ante* what is ethical or unethical. On the other hand, empirical studies observing the factors that influence how people make decisions with ethical implications can help us to rethink key issues such as free will, responsibility, and intentionality. This, in turn, can lead to a reformulation of current normative ethics theories. This constant feedback between the two approaches helps us moving forward in the field of ethics. For a deeper discussion on this, see Orlitzky (2016), Greene and Cohen (2004), and Greene (2014).

[12] Gentile (2010, preface).

[13] Gentile (2010, preface). Another critique on traditional ethics trainings comes from Soltes (2016: 313), who argues that "perversely overconfident in their capabilities after such training, they [the executives] may pay even less attention to their decisions out of the mistaken belief that they will be able to successfully resolve them in the future".

[14] For more on this initiative, see http://www.ethicalsystems.org/content/who-we-are

[15] Kohlberg's theory (1969) classifies people into three levels of moral development, each one of them divided into two sub-stages.

[16] Haidt (2012: 105-106).

[17] For more on this, see Garrett et al. (2016). This remarkable study, which concluded that our brain becomes increasingly less sensitive to unethical behavior, is detailed in Chapter 7.

[18] Haidt (2001). Damasio (1994) also corroborates this view by showing how individuals suffering from trauma in brain regions associated with their emotions find it extremely difficult to make ethical decisions. More recently, Bzdok et al. (2012) concluded that brain areas related to empathy are an active part of moral decisions, thus endorsing the relevance of our intuitive-emotional capacity for ethical behavior.

[19] Soltes (2016: 329).

Alexandre Di Miceli da Silveira

Part 1: We overestimate our ethical behavior

> *"To act well, it's not enough to have good values. You have to understand the chains of causes and effects."*
> Yuval Harari (1976–) [1]

The first major conclusion from the experiments in the field of behavioral ethics is that we have a strong tendency to overestimate our ethical conduct. That is, we often do not realize that there is a gap between how ethical we would like to be and how ethical we really are.

To illustrate this outcome, I have personally conducted a survey with 197 senior executives – mostly directors and members of the C-Suite – who attended courses for board members in Brazil. These upper senior executives are on average 51 years old and answered the questions anonymously.[2]

Inspired by a similar exercise created by Max Bazerman from Harvard Business School and Ann Tenbrunsel from the University of Notre Dame, I initially asked them: "Are you currently satisfied with your day-to-day ethical behavior?" Subject to a binary option, 97% of the executives said "yes."[3]

Because there was very little variation in the answers, I then proceeded to ask additional questions: "From 0 to 100, how ethical do you think you are compared with the average citizen of the population?" The subjects were informed that 0 (zero) corresponded to the least-ethical person in the country's population, 100 corresponded to

The Virtuous Barrel:
How to Transform Corporate Scandals into Good Businesses via Behavioral Ethics

the most ethical person, and 50 stood for an ethical behavior similar to the average citizen of the population.

The chart below presents the individual responses.

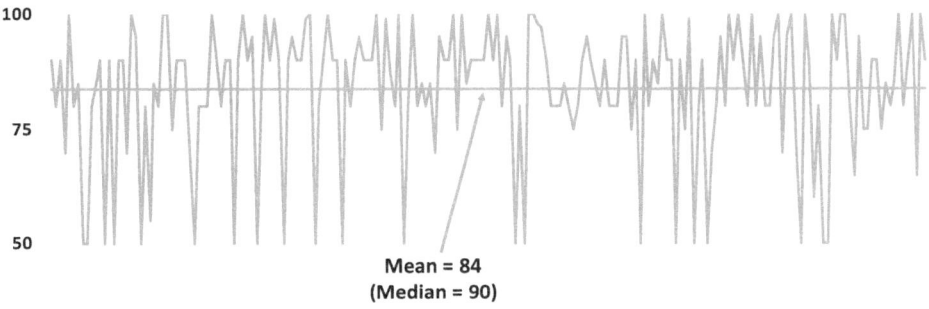

Chart 1. How ethical you are compared with the average citizen of the population?

As depicted in Chart 1, no senior executive self-scored him or herself less than 50. In fact, 32 subjects answered 100, claiming to be the most ethical person in Brazil's population of over 200 million people. Overall, the mean was 84 and the median 90. This obviously reveals the huge self-confidence on their ethical behavior compared with that of the "ordinary" citizen.

I also asked executives to compare themselves with other employees from their companies – in theory, a more homogeneous group composed of individuals socially closer to respondents than the average citizen of the population. In this case, I asked: "Compared with the people working in your company, how ethical do you think you are?" The answers are presented in Chart 2.

Chart 2. How ethical you are compared with the people of your company?

As shown above, the results were qualitatively the same. The median was 85 and the median remained at 90. In addition, 28% of the senior executives claimed to be the most ethical individuals of their organization. As shown in Chapter 4, this is a highly unlikely result, as research shows that power tends to reduce our empathy and undermine our ethical behavior.

The big exception came from an individual at the bottom right of the chart who answered just 10. A reflection on this "outlier" leads to two possibilities: either he or she did something serious that day at his or her firm (perhaps better not to be aware of to avoid being an accomplice), or this individual simply made a mistake in his or her response, scoring 10 in the survey instead of 100.

Finally, I also asked senior executives how ethical their companies are compared with those of their peers. The chart (not displayed to save space) was similar to the previous charts. The average score was 84, and the median remained at an astounding 90, indicating

The Virtuous Barrel:
How to Transform Corporate Scandals into Good Businesses via Behavioral Ethics

that more than half of executives believe their companies are among the top 10% ethical companies of the market.

Interestingly, it is noteworthy that several respondents of this survey worked for companies involved in Brazil's huge Car Wash corruption scandal and were now taking part in corporate governance courses as an effort to improve their company's ethical standards. Thus, not even working in companies involved in scandals has made executives less optimistic about the ethical behavior of their organizations...

For comparison purposes, similar surveys in the United States have yielded nearly identical results, with the average ranging from 75%–80%, while another US research found that 84% of the people considered themselves to be morally correct and honest.[4]

The summary of the first conclusion of behavioral ethics, therefore, is that we have a strong tendency to fall short of our ethical standards: In general, we tend to consider ourselves to be more virtuous, honest, trustworthy, fairer, and more supportive than the average person. In reality, though, the best predictor of how we will indeed behave seems to be how we predict others will behave in a given circumstance.

Many scientific studies have empirically corroborated this assertion.[5] One study asked 270 participants to judge themselves and the average person on 30 personality traits reflecting three core dimensions of social perception: morality, competence, and sociability.[6] Virtually all individuals inflated their moral qualities. In particular, the magnitude of this "positive illusion" was much greater in morality issues than in those who are desirable but do not have a moral quality (such as determination, intelligence, etc.). The authors' conclusion is that "Most people consider themselves paragons of virtue; yet few individuals perceive this abundance of virtue in others."[7]

Another study, curiously entitled "Behind Bars but Above the Bar," found that even prisoners consider themselves to be morally superior than most people.[8] This research, carried out with convicted offenders at a prison in the south of England, asked inmates to compare themselves against two groups, i.e., other prisoners and members of the community, on nine pro-social characteristics such as kindness, morality, honesty, generosity, and law abidingness. Although serving sentences for violence, robbery, burglary, and drug trafficking (among other offenses), prisoners rated themselves better than individuals from the two comparison groups on all traits except for "law abidingness." In particular, they rated themselves as more moral, more kind, more self-controlled, more compassionate, more generous, more trustworthy, and more honest. In the case of law abidingness, despite being imprisoned exactly for violating the law, inmates considered themselves equal (but not worse) than the average member of the community.

Our overconfidence about our ethical conduct creates an illusion of moral superiority that may make us complacent about our behavior. This is dangerous because it can lead us to behaving unethically justified by the conviction that, deep down, we are good and honest people.

Consequently, one of the main consensuses among social psychologists is that we are intrinsically moralistic, judgmental, and righteous, and our behavior is often inconsistent and contradictory. We have, therefore, a strong propensity to the so-called "moral hypocrisy."[9]

Examples of moral hypocrisy abound in daily news. One instance comes from Emilio Odebrecht, patriarch of the huge construction group bearing his name involved in the largest documented case of corporate corruption in history. In May 2015, he wrote a column in a newspaper strongly disapproving bribery. In the text, the businessman stated that "Corruption is a serious problem and must be treated with respect to the law," and that it is urgent "to get rid of both briberies and mismanagement, because these two plagues drain wealth, taxpayer money and moral values." To conclude, he emphasized that "Tackling corruption is necessary ... because the cause that binds all of us is to build a better country for future generations."[10] A year and a half later, Emilio was sentenced to four years under house arrest thanks to the Operation Car Wash. In 2017, he confessed

The Virtuous Barrel:
How to Transform Corporate Scandals into Good Businesses via Behavioral Ethics

in a testimony that slush funds in his company "have always existed, since my father's time."[11]

It's not all bad news, though. we have a great "ethical potential" because the vast majority of people, with the exception of a few psychopaths scattered in the population (more details on Chapter 9), indeed want to make a positive contribution to society and do no harm to others.[12]

To fulfill our "ethical potential," the first (great) step to take is to be humble and opened to accept the limitations of our mind and to recognize the power that the context may have over our judgments. Professor Eugene Soltes endorse this statement. After carrying out conversations with dozens of white-collar criminals, he concluded that "In our own small ways, we are all susceptible to making the same mistakes as these former executives. Appreciating our lack of invincibility – our inherent weakness and frailty – offers us the best chance of designing the appropriate mechanisms to help manage these limitations ... it's only when we realize that our ability to err is much greater than we often think it is that we'll begin to take the necessary steps to change and improve."[13]

Before detailing the process leading to ethical blindness, it is important to comprehend the reasons behind the inflated perception of our ethical behavior. We will see that this distorted perception of reality is the outcome of typical features of our cognitive system that generate the so-called cognitive biases as well as of the stages and dynamics for our decision-making.

To understand these issues in depth, let's go to the next chapter.

---

[1] Source: The New York Times. 03/19/2018. What's Next for Humanity: Automation, New Morality and a 'Global Useless Class'. Available at https://nyti.ms/2GKewac

[2] 78% of respondents were men; 22% women.

[3] Bazerman and Tenbrunsel (2011: 1).

[4] Bazerman and Tenbrunsel (2011), and Aquino and Reed II (2002).

[5] Tappin and McKay (2016), Guenther and Timberlake (2012), Zell and Alicke (2011), Messick and Bazerman (1996), Taylor and Brown (1988), and Messick et al. (1985).

[6] Tappin e McKay (2016). Curiously, the authors did not find a significant relationship between the illusion of moral superiority and participants' self-esteem.

[7] *Ibid*: 2.

[8] Sedikides et al. (2014).

[9] In his book on the reasons why people have polarized views on issues such as religion and politics, Haidt (2012: Introduction, XXIII) concluded: "the take-home message of the book is ancient. It is the realization that we are all self-righteous hypocrites".

[10] Folha de São Paulo. 08/12/2016. Emílio Odebrecht vai cumprir 4 anos em prisão domiciliar na Lava Jato. Available at http://www1.folha.uol.com.br/poder/2016/12/1839414-emilio-odebrecht-vai-cumprir-4-anos-em-prisao-domiciliar-na-lava-jato.shtml; Folha de São Paulo. 03/05/2015. Emílio Odebrecht: Uma agenda para o futuro. Available at http://www1.folha.uol.com.br/opiniao/2015/05/1623461-emilio-odebrecht-uma-agenda-para-o-futuro.shtml

[11] Folha de São Paulo. 13/03/2017. Sempre existiu caixa dois, diz Emílio Odebrecht à Justiça. Available at http://www1.folha.uol.com.br/poder/2017/03/1866042-sempre-existiu-caixa-dois-diz-emilio-odebrecht-a-justica.shtml

[12] See Aquino e Reed (2002) for further evidence on this claim.

[13] Soltes (2016: 9; 329-330).

2. Human, all too human I: limited rationality and cognitive biases

> *"Let us not forget that the reasons for human actions are usually incalculably more complex and diverse than we tend to explain them later, and are seldom clearly manifest."*
> Fyodor Dostoyevsky (1821–1881)[1]

When we become aware via the news of a new case of corporate malfeasance, there is a strong tendency to assume that the individuals involved in these episodes carefully calculated the benefits and costs of their decisions before acting. In other words, we tend to assume that these wrongdoings are the consequence of malicious people with lack of character deliberately opting for dishonesty.

However, our tendency to think that dishonest people always act in a cold and rational way is not supported by the experiments in the field of behavioral ethics. On the contrary, as we shall see, research shows that most of the wrong things are done by ordinary individuals who, instead of being guided by deliberative reasoning based on ethical principles, simply got carried away by the circumstances without proper consideration of the consequences of their actions.

This is also the conclusion of Eugene Soltes in his book *Why They Do It*. After interviewing dozens of convicted senior managers, he noticed that "Many people claim that executives make decisions through explicit cost-benefit calculation ... this explanation seems at odds with how these former leaders made choices that eventually led them to prison."[2] One of his examples comes from Scott London, a former senior partner at KPMG convicted for providing illegal information of his client companies to a friend. According to the accountant, "At the time this was going on, I just never really thought about the consequences ... The money was nominal ... I will lose my CPA license. None of these things were going through my mind ... I never once thought about the costs versus rewards."[3]

Based on a deep analysis of similar cases, Soltes concluded that "Many [executives] were not mindfully weighting the expected benefits against the expected costs ... I didn't see this. Instead, I found that they expended surprisingly little effort deliberating the consequences of their actions. They seem to have reached their decisions to commit crimes with little thought or reflection. In many cases, it was difficult to say that they had ever really 'decided' to commit a crime at all."[4]

This is also the finding of Joris Luyendijk, a trained anthropologist who interviewed around 200 London-based bankers in the aftermath of the 2008 global financial crisis. He concluded that "Yes, there is a lot of greed in the City, as there is elsewhere. But if you blame all the scandals on individuals you imply that the system itself is fine and all we need to do is to smoke out the crooks .... I am convinced that were we to pack off all the employees in the City to a desert island and replace them a quarter of a million people, we would see in no time the same kind of abuse and dysfunctionality. The problem is the system."[5]

To accept the argument that most unethical acts are committed by those who did not deeply ponder on the pros and cons of their actions from a utilitarian perspective, it is first necessary to understand how people actually make decisions. Until the end of the twentieth century, the prevailing idea was that our judgments are the outcome of an elaborate deliberative system. Consequently, we could be able to be fully rational most of the time, except for the moments in which we would be under the strong effect of emotions.[6] Actually, though, this is a wrong and outdated view.

The modern view on our decision-making process, based on countless research in the field of applied psychology starting in the 1970s and now widely accepted in the scientific community nowadays, demystified the idea of full rationality. The research has shown that our reasoning is rather limited and that our decisions are strongly influenced by our (often distorted) perception of reality. As a result, our decisions are, to a large extent, predictable but not rational.

Systems 1 and 2

According to Daniel Kahneman, the first psychologist to win a Nobel Prize in economics in 2002,[7] our mind can be understood by a metaphor dividing it into two components, the so-called Systems 1 and 2.

System 1 operates quickly, automatically, and intuitively, virtually without requiring any effort or energy expenditure. If you hear the sentence "coffee with ...," for example, you will think of "milk" immediately, before it ends. System 1 makes the vast majority of our day-to-day decisions, such as completing this sentence or driving a car on an empty street. Most of the time, therefore, we simply operate on "autopilot."

System 2, in turn, is much slower, logical, and deliberative, requiring more concentration and substantial energy expenditure of our body. If I show you the calculation "24 x 17," you will have to focus in order to find its result. During this time, research shows that your pupils will dilate, your heart rate will accelerate, and your blood pressure will increase, among other physiological changes. System 2, therefore, makes the decisions that require more mental effort, such as resolving this calculation or parking the car in a tight spot.

The rider and the elephant

> *"The reasoning process is more like a lawyer defending a client than a scientist seeking truth."*
> Jonathan Haidt (1963–)[8]

A similar and more playful way to understand how we process information is via the metaphor of the "rider and the elephant." According to its creator Jonathan Haidt, our mind is divided into two cognitive processes: intuition and reasoning.[9]

The "rider" represents our processes based on reason, i.e., our explicit, conscious, and deliberative reasoning. Because it depends on language, the rider is much more recent in evolutionary terms, being located in the prefrontal cortex region of our brain.

The "elephant," in turn, represents our intuition. It is our gut feeling that reacts almost instantaneously to anything we are exposed to, such as ideas, people, or situations, and it may or may not include emotions.[10] The elephant is independent of language and much older in evolutionary terms, being located in the limbic system of our brain.

The figure below illustrates the rider and the elephant metaphor.

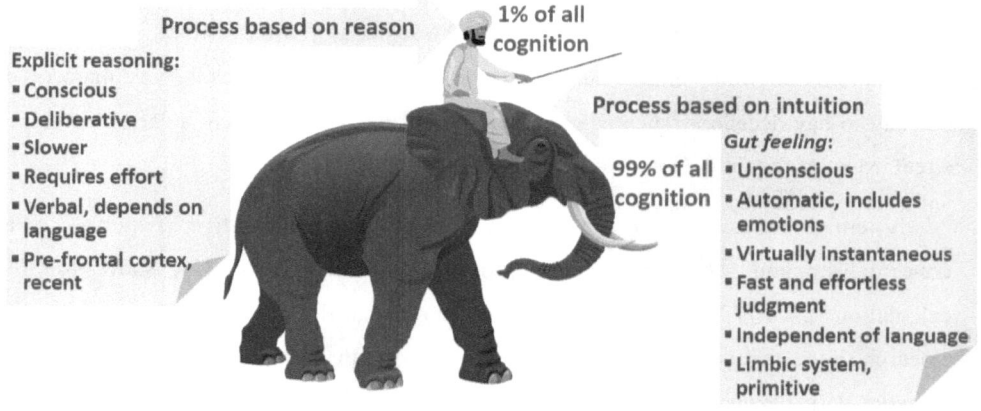

Figure 1. Two Cognitive Processes of Our Mind: The Rider and the Elephant Metaphor.
Source: Adapted from Haidt, J. (2006). *The Happiness Hypothesis: Finding Modern Truth in Ancient Wisdom.* **Basic Books.**

According to Haidt, several experiments show that the elephant dominates the rider, determines our habits, and makes the vast majority of our decisions. This conclusion endorses eighteenth-century philosopher David Hume's view that "reason is the slave of passions."[11]

We have a strong tendency, therefore, to immediately judge what is presented to us based on our intuition. Frequently, it is only after this judgment that we seek to find arguments and explanations to justify the decisions we have already made. Thus, even when we convince ourselves that we are applying a reflective reasoning to find the truth, we are often just searching for evidence to support our immediate intuitive judgment.

From an evolutionary perspective, this is the main role of the rider: to act as a sort of "internal lawyer" or "public relations officer" specialized in creating explanations for the decisions we make viscerally.

Metaphors of our decision-making process and ethical behavior

There is a direct relationship between the metaphors illustrating the inner workings of our mind and our ethical behavior. Unlike the traditional view, which argues that people who act dishonestly always do so after rationally weighing the pros and cons of their decisions, the reality is that many unethical behaviors are the outcome of automatic, thoughtless decisions.

In this sense, it is always important to highlight that ethics are, to a large extent, the result of awareness, reflection, and consideration of impacts on other people. Thus, the more we get carried away by the impulses of the "elephant" (or "System 1"), the less likely it is that we will be able to analyze a decision from an ethical perspective and make the decision in accordance with our values. The more impulsive our behavior, the less reflected it is. Consequently, potentially worse our ethical conduct will tend to be.

This does not mean, however, that our visceral reaction should be neglected and that we should only seek to act "rationally." Intuition plays a key role in the quality of all our decisions, including from the ethical standpoint. In many situations, for example, we feel there is something wrong in going ahead with a particular course of action, even when it is legal and apparently defensible from the technical perspective.[12] Neuroscientist Antonio Damasio, one of the main authorities on the relation between brain and body, states: "Feelings do not only reveal the dark side of reason: they help us making decisions that are good to us."[13]

Every good decision, including those with ethical implications, should be based on the agreement of our Systems 1 and 2 or, alternatively, of the rider and the elephant. It is essential, therefore, to put the two modes of thinking, i.e., reason and intuition, to dialogue and reach a consensus before our decisions.[14]

Heuristics and cognitive biases

" ."

Friedrich Nietzsche (1844–1900)[15]

Because the rider (or System 2) requires a lot of energy from our bodies, we try to make the most use of the elephant (or System 1). To make quick and almost effortless decisions, our intuitive system makes use of the so-called "heuristics." These are "rules of thumb" or "cognitive shortcuts" that we unconsciously developed to make quick decisions in the complex environment in which we live.

Heuristics are useful on most occasions. However, because they are affected by our emotional motivations and limited ability to process information, these rules of thumbs can lead us to make systematically wrong judgments in predictable ways.[16] Let's take the so-called "availability heuristic" as an example. It stems from our tendency to evaluate the probability of occurrence of an event based on the ease with which examples of similar events come to our minds. What do you think is most likely: Dying in a plane crash or by hot tap water? Being killed by a dog attack or by falling off your couch? At least in the United States, the right answer to the two questions has been the second option.[17]

Because many people tend to recall remarkable episodes associated with the first alternative in both questions (air crashes and dog attacks), we are prone to attribute an inflated likelihood of occurrence to these events.[18]

Heuristics are not just an intellectual curiosity. In the case of the availability heuristic, people, companies, and even countries may come to prioritize wrong issues due to a distorted perception of reality. The survey "The Perils of Perception" carried out by Ipsos Moris Institute in 2015 corroborates this assertion.[19] The institute interviewed more than 25,000 people from 33 countries. One of the questions was: "What is the percentage of

The Virtuous Barrel:
How to Transform Corporate Scandals into Good Businesses via Behavioral Ethics

the population of your country that you believe to be an immigrant?" In the case of the United States, respondents believed there are 33% of immigrants in its population, while the true figure is only 14%. Looking at all questions, the Institute calculated an "index of ignorance" based on the distance between people's perception of reality and the real figures. Mexico topped the list, and Latin-American countries occupied five out of the 10 top spots (Mexico, Brazil, Peru, Colombia, and Argentina). At the other end, South Korea exhibited the lowest level of ignorance. Thus, the argument that the world in our head is not a precise replica of reality seems to be even truer in some countries than in others.

Although useful for helping to save time and brain energy, heuristics can generate so-called "cognitive biases." Biases are predictable and systematic errors arising from our personal beliefs and preferences. They result from our distorted framing of reality and can lead us to make irrational decisions.

We are subject to numerous biases, both at the individual as well as at the collective level. Over the past decades, more than 170 cognitive biases that may impair our judgment have been cataloged.[20]

Cognitive biases can lead us to make wrong decisions not only from a technical point of view but also from the ethical standpoint. The following are examples of some of the most common cognitive biases, including their ethical implications.

Self-serving bias

We have a strong propensity to analyze a situation and to remember it from a perspective that unduly favors us.

A survey in the United States exemplifies this bias.[21] In one version of the poll, a group of people answered the following question: If you are sued by someone else and ultimately you win the case, would it be fair for the person who sued you to pay your legal expenses? About 85% of the respondents agreed with this idea.

Another group, in turn, answered a slightly different version of the question: If you sue someone else, and you ultimately lose the case, would it be fair for you to pay the other person's legal expenses? In this case, only 44% agreed with this idea, although it refers to the same concept as that of the previous question.

The self-serving bias aims to protect and enhance our self-esteem. It causes our minds to unconsciously process and absorb the information that is advantageous to us and, at the same time, to ignore or even erase from memory the information that is not good.

One consequence of this bias is that our judgments tend to be inevitably affected by our self-interest and personal preferences, especially when the decision at stake is important, and there is high uncertainty about the facts. It is also worth noting that this distorted perception of reality takes place even when we have the best of intentions and really strive to act fairly and impartially.[22]

Another outcome of the self-serving bias is that we tend to ascribe successes to our talent and efforts and impute failures to the circumstances or other people. This bias, thus, inflates the perception of our individual competence as well as makes us less prone to criticism.[23] There is also a serious ethical implication at stake because our tendency to unfairly judge credits or errors related to a decision may inadvertently harm the lives of others.

Egocentric bias
We tend to have an inflated perception of our personal contribution to any collective endeavor. For example, consider the following question: What is the percentage of good ideas of your work team generated by yourself? Research conducted after the completion of projects shows that the sum of the percentages in a group can easily exceed 100% when members are individually asked about their personal contributions.[24]

The same applies to personal life. In a classic research, married couples were asked to separately assess their individual roles in several household chores, such as preparing breakfast, cleaning, and shopping. In this case, self-allocated responsibility oscillated around 150% when summed together.[25]

The egocentric bias is also present in the way we assess the performance of the groups to which we belong. In joint ventures, for example, we tend to believe that the contribution of our company to the success of the venture is much greater than that of the other partner firms.

Thus, because we focus too much on our own efforts and too little on others, the perception of our personal contribution to group efforts is often greater than objective reality can sustain. The egocentric bias can even lead us to mentally reconstruct the past for the sake of increasing the role we had in a certain circumstance.[26] This bias, therefore, also has a relevant ethical implication because it can lead us to unfairly allocate the credits of collective initiatives.

Max Bazerman and Ann Tennbrusel, authors of a book detailing our cognitive biases and its ethical implications, describe an additional problem deriving from the egocentric bias.[27] According to these authors, evidence shows that learning about this bias makes us more attentive to its manifestation in other people but not in ourselves. In other words, we only recognize that others are egocentric, i.e., an egocentric interpretation of the egocentric bias.

Confirmation bias

We tend to assign more importance to information that confirms our beliefs or initial opinion on a certain subject. Corroborating this assertion, research shows that we tend to spend twice as much time to actively seek information that supports our point of view than on finding facts that contradict it.[28]

Peter Drucker, a leading management guru of the twentieth century, noticed this bias after decades as a consultant for large organizations. In his words, "People simply do what everyone is far too prone to do anyhow: look for the facts that fit the conclusion they have already reached. And no one has ever failed to find fact he is looking for."[29]

Research in the US showed that the confirmation bias manifests itself even from the neurological perspective.[30] During the US presidential election of 2004, scientists analyzed the brain activity of 30 partisans through functional magnetic resonance imaging (fMRI). Half of them described themselves as strongly Republican, while the other half self-declared as strongly Democrats. During the experiment, voters were expected to assess statements in which both candidates, Republican George W. Bush and Democrat John Kerry, clearly contradicted themselves.

As predicted, Republican voters proved to be as critical of Democratic candidate Kerry as Democratic voters were of Bush, the Republican candidate. At the same time, none of them unfavorably evaluated the contradictory statements of their own candidates.

The most interesting results, however, came from the fMRI exam. Scientists noted that the area of the brain most closely associated with reasoning (i.e., the dorsolateral prefrontal cortex) was virtually inactive during the experiment. On the other hand, they observed the following areas as remaining active during the exercise: the orbital frontal cortex, responsible for processing emotions; the anterior cingulate, involved in the resolution of conflicts; the posterior cingulate, related to moral judgments; and the ventral striatum, an area related to reward or relief activated by successful equilibration to an emotionally stable judgment.

Therefore, reasoning about the facts presented by the candidates was completely secondary to the emotional power of standing with their party. This, in turn, led participants to create justifications to sustain their political convictions. This kind of evidence shows that the effect of confirmation bias is likely to be even greater on emotionally charged issues such as politics and religion.

The ideological polarization currently observed in social networks, therefore, is at least partially driven by this bias: It is very pleasant, even from the physiological standpoint, to relate to people who reinforce our worldview by saying that our beliefs are correct, while it is unpleasant to be exposed to opinions that contradict our beliefs.

The Virtuous Barrel:
How to Transform Corporate Scandals into Good Businesses via Behavioral Ethics

A 2015 study investigating the behavior of more than 10 million U.S. Facebook users corroborated this belief.[31] The paper, published in the prestigious journal *Science*, concluded that the social network is a true box of resonance for our ideas: of all links visited by people with a more liberal orientation, only 24% challenged their way of thinking. In the case of the news accessed by conservatives, just 35% of the content cut across their ideological affiliation.[32]

Individuals with better education or higher intellectual capacity are not immune to the confirmation bias. On the contrary. There is evidence that people with a high IQ (intellectual quotient) are more likely to create justifications that confirm their initial opinions, thus reinforcing the problem.

Confirmation bias shows, therefore, that we are very good at challenging other's people points of views but not our own. This leads to a serious ethical implication: By being prone to unfairly criticize potentially valuable ideas from other people that are contrary to our beliefs, we may inadvertently end up demotivating or harming them.

Optimism or overconfidence bias

Optimism and overconfidence are two of the most documented biases in the literature. They are interrelated and are present, to a greater or lesser extent, in almost everyone. A curious survey conducted with 1,000 respondents in the United States demonstrates the extent of this bias. In this poll, 87% of survey takers claimed to believe they would go to heaven, while only 79% said they believed that Mother Teresa of Calcutta would also make it.[33]

Exhibiting a high degree of optimism and overconfidence can lead us to overestimate the prospects of our initiatives as well as to underestimate its risks. These biases generate a kind of "illusion of control" about the outcomes of our activities, even when we do not have any control over the various factors having an impact on them.

One of the most interesting findings in the field of behavioral corporate finance, for instance, is that entrepreneurs tend to be systematically more optimistic and overconfident than the general population.[34] This is an intuitive result because these individuals must be optimistic by definition to start a new company (often against the odds).

Although optimism can have positive consequences, as in the decision to enter seemingly unpromising markets that end up being profitable, this bias can also lead to excessive investments or borrowing that result in severe value-destruction. This assertion is exemplified in the box below. It describes the case of HRT, a Brazilian oil company run by an excessively optimistic CEO. The case demonstrates the dangers of the absence of effective checks and balances in organizations led by highly biased people.

Optimism and overconfidence: The case of oil company HRT

HRT is an oil company that did its initial public offering (IPO) in 2010. At the time, the company was in a pre-operational stage. That is, the firm was just a set of drilling projects, with no revenues.

The company was founded by Marcio Rocha Mello, chairman of its board of directors and CEO at the time of the IPO. As its founder and controlling shareholder, the decision-making power at HRT clearly gravitated around Mr. Mello.

In an interview to Brazilian magazine Capital Aberto in May 2011, Mr. Mello expressed clear signs of the biases of optimism and overconfidence:

"...I have the power to answer any question, warns the CEO ... We will be one of the largest oil companies in the world!"

"...I have all the answers. Is it the map of the riches beneath the Earth, clear in your mind? Mello confirms..."

"...People come here and ask me what problems we may have to achieve our goals; what are our challenges. I answer: none!"

"...At that point of the interview, Mello had said that he never got sick during his life, that he makes all decisions in a millisecond and never makes mistakes in business..."

"...I demand from myself to be the best. But I am humble!"

The Virtuous Barrel:
How to Transform Corporate Scandals into Good Businesses via Behavioral Ethics

HRT's IPO was a huge success. The company raised around US$1.5 billion, mostly from institutional investors, with its shares initially quoted at around $14. Months later, its shares peaked at around $25, and HRT's market value reached $6 billion.

A few months later, however, its heavy investments in the Amazon region and Africa began to show they would hardly pay off. A year after the IPO, the company still had not found a single drop of oil.

Two years after the peak in market value, the HRT shareholders, led by foreign funds, started to publicly demonstrate their dissatisfaction with Mr. Mello. Initially, they joined forces to elect board members and try to replace him as chairman of the board. The mere announcement that shareholders were getting together to change the board's leadership raised share prices by 33% in two days.

Shareholders succeeded in replacing Mello as chairman of the board at the end of April 2013. Just 11 days after the shareholders' meeting, Mello resigned as chairman of the board. On the same day, HRT shares rose almost 11%.

Earlier in April 2017, the company was still in a difficult situation, with its shares quoted at only 50 cents, 98% down its peak six years before (HRT is currently called PetroRio). Clearly, Mello's exaggerated optimism did not work out. For investors, this case shows the importance of having effective checks and balances to mitigate decisions made by excessively biased individuals.

Actually, the overall impression of the HRT case is that investors were actually the most overconfident ones by putting their money in the hands of founder Mello.

Applied to the field of behavioral ethics, the overconfidence bias leads us to overestimate the power of our own good intentions. In an experiment on sexual harassment, for instance, a group of women was asked how they would respond to inappropriate job interview questions posed by a male interviewer (such as if they had a boyfriend). Although 70% predicted that they would refuse to answer the sexist questions or terminate the interview, none of them did so when actually placed in a realistic job interview.[35]

In-group favoritism bias

Our primitive "elephant" always prefers what is perceived as familiar and secure. As a result, we have a strong tendency to support and favor opinions from people who belong to our group, compared with views from those perceived as out of our circle. It is important to note that the idea of "group" goes beyond our relatives or work team, encompassing those who belong to our religion, race, or gender.

Research has confirmed our preference for people with whom we have any kind of similarity. One study, for example, revealed that individuals exhibited a higher degree of cooperation in a prisoners' dilemma game with people whom they believe to share the same birthday date.[36] Another paper noticed that we are even disproportionately likely to marry others whose first or last names resemble our own.[37]

Our preference for what is familiar manifests itself even in our consumption and career decisions. In the first case, surveys show that people whose names start with the letter C (like Carol) are more likely to opt for Coca-Cola, while those starting with the letter P (like Peter) tend to choose Pepsi-Cola.[38] Research conducted in the United States also shows that people whose names begin with letter D have a greater likelihood of becoming dentists, while those with names starting with G have a greater chance of moving to states beginning with the same letter, such as Georgia.[39]

The main ethical implication of implicit favoritism of in-group members is that, by giving preference to those perceived as belonging to our group, we can inadvertently discriminate against and harm people of social out-groups – especially those belonging to minorities.[40] Actually, the problems of prejudice and racism may be more related to an unconscious affection for the people belonging to our group than due to a negative and conscious attitude toward people outside our circle.

In the business world, the in-group favoritism bias has a serious ethical implication because it is directly linked to the difficulty of increasing the access of women to top management positions. In the case of boards of directors, for instance, the appointment of

The Virtuous Barrel:
How to Transform Corporate Scandals into Good Businesses via Behavioral Ethics

new members usually derives from a process that is more relational and subjective than technical and objective. As a result, there is a natural tendency of those holding top positions to nominate people who are demographically or ideologically like them.

---

[1] Source: Fyodor Dostoevsky. The Idiot (Vintage Classics). Knopf Doubleday Publishing Group. 2012: 484. Part Four.

[2] Soltes (2016: 6).

[3] *Ibid*: 99.

[4] *Ibid*: 6.

[5] Luyendijk (2015: 253-254).

[6] The concept of "rationality" means that we are able to process all the information available to solve a problem (even if very complex) in an objective, complete, fact-based and unbiased way – without the influence of the environment or other people. It also means that at the end of this process, we will always be able to consistently choose the option that maximizes our personal utility. The concept of emotions, in turn, refers to our primary feelings: anger, fear, disgust, joy, sadness, contempt, surprise and disappointment.

[7] Kahneman carried out his pioneering studies on behavioral economics during the 1970s with his colleague Amos Tversky. With the death of Tversky in 1996, Kahneman ended up receiving the Nobel Prize in Economics alone. Among his seminal works, stand out Tversky and Kahneman (1973) and Kahneman and Tversky (1979). In 2011, Kahneman summarized his forty years of research in an international bestseller entitled "Thinking, fast and slow".

[8] Source: Haidt (2001: 820).

[9] Haidt (2006) e Haidt (2013).

[10] It is here that the intuitionist approach of psychologists such as Haidt differs from the classic paradigm of reason vs. emotion. For them, although all emotions express themselves automatically, there are many intuitive and automatic reactions in our mind that do not manifest themselves as emotions.

[11] Full quote: "Reason is and ought only to be the slave of the passions, and can never pretend to any other office than to serve and obey them". David Hume (1711-1776).

[12] In this sense, the modern view in the field of medicine is that the concept that there is an "imperial brain" commanding our whole body is wrong. In fact, our body is also filled with neurons (there are about 100 million neurons in the intestines alone), as well as there is a constant bidirectional communication between brain and body, including for decision-making. Source: Mente Cérebro Magazine, 286: 21-22. "How the brain helps heal the body".

[13] Interview to Mente Cérebro Magazine, n. 286: 47. "Feelings are made of emotions".

[14] The need to unite the cognitive and emotional aspects of our decisions is not new to Chinese philosophy. The word Xin, for example, simultaneously serves to denote the concepts of heart and mind. Source: http://languagelog.ldc.upenn.edu/nll/?p=14807

[15] Source: Friedrich Nietzsche. §483. Human, All Too Human.

[16] The busier and hurried we are and the more experience we have in a certain activity, the greater will be the likelihood that we will make use of the intuitive system 1 for our decisions.

[17] In 2016, nobody died in a crash of a United States-certificated scheduled airline, while burns from hot tap water resulted in about 100 deaths per year (mostly young children and seniors). In the

second question, the probability of dying from falling off furniture in your own house is nearly thirty times greater than dying from a canine attack! Sources: http://health.usnews.com/health-news/news/articles/2013/03/31/hot-tap-water-may-pose-scalding-hazard; https://www.forbes.com/sites/danielreed/2016/12/28/in-the-last-7-years-you-were-more-likely-to-be-run-over-by-a-car-than-to-die-in-an-airline-crash/#76b9a297428a; http://study.com/academy/lesson/availability-heuristic-examples-definition-quiz.html

[18] The "ease" with which similar examples come to our mind depends, in turn, on three factors: the frequency of exposure (e.g., media coverage), the emotional intensity of this episodes (e.g., personal experiences), and temporal proximity (more recent events are assigned a greater weight).

[19] Source: Perils of Perception 2015. Ipsos Mori Institute. Available at https://www.ipsos-mori.com/researchpublications/researcharchive/3664/Perils-of-Perception-2015.aspx

[20] The link http://en.wikipedia.org/wiki/List_of_cognitive_biases provides a list of more than 170 cognitive biases.

[21] Stephen Budiansky, Ted Gest, & David Fischer. 1995. How Lawyers Abuse the Law. US News and World Report January 30th; 50-56.

[22] As an example, an auditor stated the following during a testimony to the US SEC (Securities and Exchange Commission) in 2000: "We are professionals that follow our code of ethics and practice by the highest moral values. We would never be influenced by our own personal financial well-being versus our professional ethics". According to Moore et al. (2006), this statement reflects an embarrassing ignorance about the impact of the self-serving bias on our personal decisions. The auditor's full testimony is available at https://www.sec.gov/rules/proposed/s71300/testimony/shamis1.htm

[23] Curiously, our judgment tends to reverse when we evaluate others: in this case, we tend to ascribe other people's success to the circumstances and their failures to their own personal deficiencies.

[24] Caruso et al. (2006).

[25] Ross and Sicoly (1979).

[26] Although bearing some resemblance to self-serving bias, egocentric bias is different because people also tend to consider themselves overly responsible for the negative outcomes of the group to which they belong. This bias shows how we attach greater weight to what we do in relation to other people belonging to our group under all circumstances, including the negative ones.

[27] Bazerman e Tenbrunsel (2011: 56).

[28] Hart et al. (2009). Some papers refer to confirmation bias by the term congeniality bias.

[29] Source: Drucker. P. 2008. The Essential Drucker: The Best of Sixty Years of Peter Drucker's Essential Writings on Management. Ed. HarperBusiness. Chapter. 17.

[30] Westen et al. (2006). Other papers also show that people seeing the same political debate or football match will have different perceptions depending on their initial personal preferences.

[31] Bakshy et al. (2015).

[32] The researchers also concluded that the biggest culprit for our limited exposure to attitude-challenging content is not Facebook's news feed ranking algorithm, but rather the individual choices of users themselves.

[33] 1997 US News and World Report study. Available at http://www.nytimes.com/2013/01/26/your-money/tips-for-making-decisions-and-sticking-to-them.html. This survey is also cited by Gino (2013) in her book "Sidetracked: Why Our Decisions Get Derailed and How We Can Stick to the Plan".

[34] Invernizzi et al. (2017) and Koellinger et al. (2007).

[35] Woodzicka and LaFrance (2001).

[36] Miller et al. (1998).
[37] Jones et al. (2004). Haidt (2006) describes other interesting examples related to this issue in his book.
[38] Brendl et al. (2005).
[39] Pelham et al. (2002).
[40] The so-called implicit association test developed by non-profit organization Project Implicit® shows how most of us is full of prejudices, especially regarding people who are not part of our social group. More information at https://implicit.harvard.edu/implicit/

Alexandre Di Miceli da Silveira

3. Human, all too human II: Stages and dynamics of our decision-making process

> *"If you tell the truth you don't have to remember anything."*
> Mark Twain (1835–1910)[1]

In addition to our limited rationality and distorted perception of reality, the inflated perception of our ethical behavior is also the result of the stages and dynamics of our decision-making process.

Let's start with the first point. Our decisions can be divided into three moments: planning (pre-decision), action (the actual moment of the decision), and evaluation (post-decision).[2] In each situation, there is usually tension between doing what is best for us (what "I want to do") and doing what we believe is the correct behavior for a harmonious coexistence with the world (what "I ought to do").

What "I want to do" corresponds to the impulsive decision that is most pleasurable or personally advantageous to us in that situation. What "I ought to do," in turn, corresponds to the more reflected action based on the principles and values we intend to uphold for a cooperative life in society.

A simple example of a traffic situation demonstrates how this process occurs. Imagine you need to make a left turn on an avenue with three lanes during your commute to work in a day that you're particularly tight on time. There is only one lane available for conversion, while the others are used by vehicles that continue straight ahead. However, there is a long line of cars on the left lane for conversion. What "I ought to do" is obviously going to the end of the line just like all other vehicles. However, to avoid

The Virtuous Barrel:
How to Transform Corporate Scandals into Good Businesses via Behavioral Ethics

spending time queueing like everyone else, it may be tempting to go forward through the center lane and make the conversion at the very last moment, cutting the line by jumping in front of a vehicle in the left lane. This often represents what "I want to do." How do you think you would act in such situation?

Pre-decision: The planning

Before making decisions, almost everybody plans to act ethically. This is the moment in which the "rider" is in charge, and we have a broader, long-term, and deontological (principle-based) view of our actions: "I should behave ethically, and that is how I am going to conduct myself!"

In the traffic situation of the previous section, we all believe (or intend to believe) that we would respect the norms by queueing just like the other drivers. The problem, though, is that research shows that we have a strong tendency to make wrong predictions of our behavior in social situations.[3]

A paper compared, for example, people's forecast of their behavior during negotiations with their actual performance when they were indeed bargaining. Researchers concluded that there was a complete disconnection between negotiators' forecasts and their actual behaviors. In their words, "Negotiators may think they will fight fire with fire, think they will be lions that roar, but in the end, they are merely mice that whimper."[4]

Action: The moment of decision

When faced with the situation itself, a conflict arises between what we "ought to do" and what "we want to do." The "want self," which represents the visceral reaction of our "elephant," often takes over and dominates our thoughts at this point. As a result, all the principle-based and long-term view we displayed in the beginning usually ends up becoming a narrow and short-term view focused on the immediate gain or pleasure.

The "heat of the moment" can also increase the likelihood of deviating from our values and principles by preventing us from perceiving the wider consequences of our actions. Implicitly, it works as if we tell ourselves: "I do not realize the ethical implications of this decision, so I'll do what's best for me." Moving back to the traffic example, this impulse could lead us to avoid the line on the left and follow the central lane until jumping in front of a queueing vehicle at the time of conversion.

In cases of corruption and organizational fraud, something similar may occur. The vast majority of people firmly believe they would always act in line with what they "ought to do." That is, they act according to their morals, ideas, and values. In many cases, though, individuals end up behaving differently when things actually happen, subdued by their immediate gain or pleasure.

Post-decision: The evaluation
As we distance ourselves from our thoughtless decision, the ethical implications of our actions start to come to our minds with increasing intensity. It is at this moment that an uncomfortable feeling often arises between the ethical image we have of ourselves and our actual conduct.

This state of psychological stress resulting from the internal contradiction between our values and our actual behavior is called "cognitive dissonance." Psychologist Lou Festinger coined this term after conducting several experiments in the 1950s.[5] In a classic study, he found that participants who received $1 to perform an extremely boring exercise rated the activity as more enjoyable than those who received $20 to do the same task. According to Festinger, people who received $1 did not want to admit that they had been part of such a tedious exercise for so little. As a result, they chose to create a truth for themselves that the task had been nice in order to show internal psychological consistency. His experiments, therefore, showed how the quest to eliminate our cognitive dissonance can lead us to self-deceive ourselves without even realizing it.

The Virtuous Barrel:
How to Transform Corporate Scandals into Good Businesses via Behavioral Ethics

In the business world, cognitive dissonance can be represented by the gap between a manager's genuine desire to behave honestly and his or her unethical (or even illegal) actions in the exercise of his or her professional position.

Cognitive dissonance causes irritation, stress, and reduces energy. To cope with it, we go through a process called "moral disengagement" by which we deactivate our moral self-regulatory processes so that we end up persuading ourselves that our questionable conduct was acceptable.[6] At this point, the so-called "rationalizations" come into play. These are the justifications for dubious behaviors we tell ourselves through the use of seemingly rational arguments to avoid being seen as the bad guys of our own narrative.

Rationalizations, which are one of the main mechanisms of moral disengagement, can take many forms. For instance, we may come to portray an unethical behavior as something that serves a greater purpose, misrepresents the harmful consequences of our behavior, and even dehumanizes or blames the victims of our unethical actions (Chapter 8 details our main rationalizations).[7]

Our mind has an incredible ability to rationalize improper behaviors. The greater the cognitive dissonance, the greater is the motivation to rationalize our conduct to make it more tolerable. In the simple traffic example discussed in this chapter, we could justify our unethical deed based on rationalizations such as: "it was only today that I acted like this," "I was late," "everybody does it," or "this did not hurt anyone."

In addition to the rationalizations, we have developed a series of memory biases designed to protect our self-esteem and minimize our cognitive dissonance.[8] Our minds are so malleable and selective that we are even able to unconsciously distort the memories of our decisions to feel better. There is evidence, for example, that we remember in more detail the situations in which we behaved ethically than those in which we acted in a questionable way, a process called "motivated forgetting."[9]

One of the main works in this area was published in 2016 with the appropriate title "Memories of Unethical Actions become Obfuscated over Time."[10] Based on nine different experiments with more than 2,100 participants, the researchers concluded that, after engaging in dishonest behavior, individuals' memories of their actions become increasingly obscured due to the psychological distress and discomfort caused by such misdeeds. In one experiment, for example, volunteers participated in 10 rounds of a coin-toss task in which they could lie to increase their pay. Two weeks later, they were asked to remember details of the coin-toss task and of another event that occurred in the same day (e.g., their dinner that night). Researchers observed that the greater the amount of cheating on the coin-toss task, the lower the quality of participants' memories about the experiment (the memory concerning the dinner on the same day, though, was not affected). The conclusion was the same for several variants of the experiment performed with different groups. The authors named this process "unethical amnesia," a situation in which memories of our past unethical behavior become less clear, less detailed, and less vivid over time than memories of ethical actions (or of actions unrelated to ethics). For them, ethical amnesia is the main reason why people are more likely to repeat dishonest acts over time.[11]

The results of this and other similar papers show, therefore, that we continually act as a sort of "revisionist historians" of our acts in order to preserve our positive self-image. In other words, our plastic and selective mind often allows us to have the best of worlds: We manage to maximize our personal gains (in the traffic example, doing the conversion without queuing) while, at the same time, keeping intact our positive self-image ("I should have behaved ethically. Well … on second thought, that's how I indeed have acted!").

In the jargon of psychologists, this is the outcome of the so-called "self-concept maintenance theory."[12] This approach argues that we are often divided between two competing motivations: gaining from cheating versus maintaining our positive self-concept as honest persons. As a result, we tend to solve this motivational dilemma by finding a balance in a way that we behave dishonestly enough to profit from the situation but honestly enough to maintain our positive self-view as decent individuals.

The Virtuous Barrel:
How to Transform Corporate Scandals into Good Businesses via Behavioral Ethics

As Eugene Soltes observed after interacting with senior executives convicted for creating Ponzi schemes: "None of the former executives I spoke with saw himself as a fraud... the person they saw in the mirror was successful, entrepreneurial, and ambitious. They didn't see themselves as the kind of people who created fraudulent enterprises. Most victims of deception are easy to spot... but the individuals perpetrating these schemes were also victims of a sort – victims of their own self-deception."[13]

Many recent experiments corroborate this idea. They show that the vast majority of people inflate their performance to increase their pay. This dishonesty, though, goes only up to a certain point, from which it would be difficult to keep maintaining a positive concept of themselves (in general, studies show that the average magnitude of dishonesty ranges between 10% to 20% of legitimate claims).[14]

In short, we try to look fair and honest not only in front of others but also to ourselves.[15] This makes us more likely to perform small unethical deeds of easy rationalization, as they allow us to earn undue benefits without harming the positive image we have of ourselves.[16]

People who say they can sleep with a "clean conscience" after dishonest acts, therefore, can often be telling the truth, although that does not mean they have behaved honestly. The figure below illustrates our decision-making process. It shows how we can get out of a decision involving a situation in which we acted reprehensibly with the conviction that "ethics indeed is what matters."

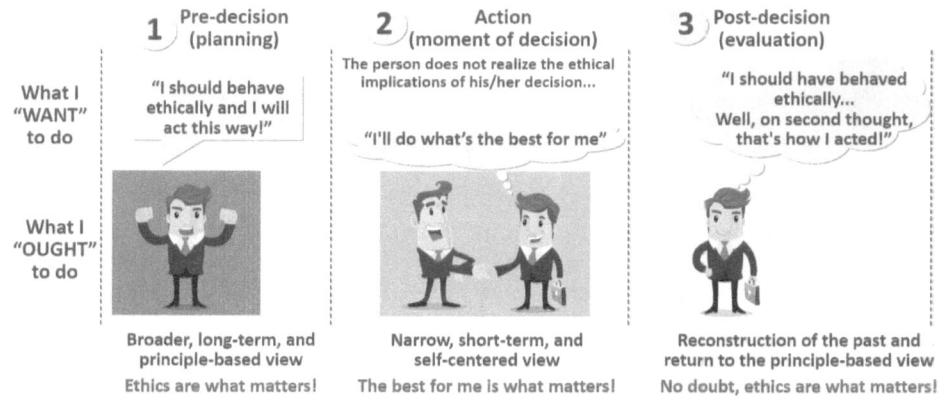

Figure 2. Stages of our decision-making process.
Source: Adapted from Bazerman, M., Tenbrunsel, A. 2011. *Blind Spots*. Princeton University Press.

In addition to the temporal inconsistencies that often prevent us from being as ethical as we desire to be, another issue makes it difficult for us to always exhibit proper conduct: Our ethical behavior tends to be dynamic and volatile rather than being always just "good" or "bad." According to psychologists, we have a kind of mental scoreboard that counts our good and bad deeds for the sake of achieving a "moral balance."[17] The figure below illustrates this concept.

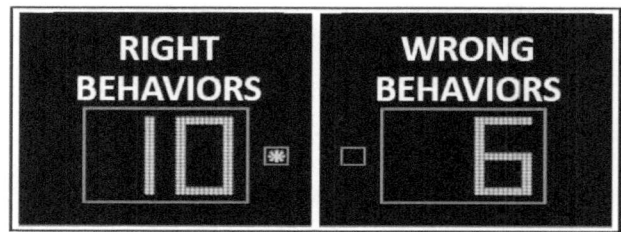

Figure 3. Moral balance: Our mental scoreboard that computes right and wrong behaviors.

Moral balance is divided into two aspects: moral compensation and moral licensing.

When we act below our ethical standards, we tend to feel bad and try to compensate for our bad behavior with good deeds. As a result, we actively look for an opportunity to do something good in order to regain the balance of our mental scoreboard. This is called moral compensation or moral cleansing.[18]

The need to compensate for our bad behaviors may occur in a curious way: One study, for example, divided participants into two groups. In one, participants were asked to recall in detail an ethical action from their past and to describe any related feelings or emotions they experienced. The other group, in turn, was asked to recall an unethical act. Both groups then engaged in a word completion task in which they converted word fragments into meaningful words. One of them, for instance, was W_ _H. In this case, the full word could be "wish" or "wash." Participants who recalled an unethical deed generated much more cleansing-related words (in this case, "wash") than those who recalled an ethical deed. At the end of experiment, participants were also offered a choice between an antiseptic wipe and a pencil as a free gift. In this case, those who recalled unethical acts were twice more likely to pick the antiseptic wipe (67%) than those who recalled ethical deeds (33%).[19]

In another study, the researchers intended to check if physical cleansing was indeed able to "wash away" our sins. This time, they asked all participants to describe a previous unethical behavior. Afterward, some of them were asked to cleanse their hands with an antiseptic wipe, while others were not given this option. At the end, all completed a survey to assess their current emotional state. As expected, participants who cleansed their hands after the unethical recall reported feeling better (e.g., less guilty, less embarrassed) compared with those who did not. According to researchers, there is a clear association between ethical and physical cleanliness: Threats to moral purity activate a need for physical cleansing, which can relieve moral emotions related to the wrongdoing (the term "get your hands dirty" really seems to have an unconscious meaning to all of us).[20]

The concept of moral compensation applies not only for individuals but also for legal persons. It is usual, for example, to observe companies involved in serious environmental or human rights issues investing more in sustainability and corporate responsibility initiatives as an attempt to cleanse their sins.[21] Scientific evidence supports this claim.[22]

A study of 3,000 US companies over 15 years, for instance, concluded that firms tend to engage in corporate social responsibility (CSR) with the purpose of offsetting corporate social irresponsibility such as tax problems, controversial investments, or environmental fines.[23] Specifically, the researchers observed that, when companies do more "harm," they also do more "good." This result was particularly strong in industries in which social irresponsibility tends to be subject to greater public scrutiny, such as the chemical, pharmaceutical, and the automobile industries. According to the authors, companies tend to use CSR strategically as a marketing tool to compensate for the negative effects of irresponsible misconducts.

Another paper on this field analyzed 4,500 companies over 19 years. It also concluded that firms' CSR initiatives seems to trail their social irresponsibility. They also found that CSR has worked to a large extent as a way for companies to reduce the costs to society stemming from irresponsible practices without having to pay them in full.[24] In this case, however, researchers observed that this "penance mechanism" is not effective at compensating for the negative economic effects of socially irresponsible conducts.

There is also the other side of the coin. When we do something good, we may feel a surplus on our mental scoreboard. This may give us a feeling that we are entitled not to live up to our own ethical standards. This is called "moral licensing."[25] Moral licensing is dangerous because it suggests that it is precisely when we are feeling good about our conduct that we are in greater danger of behaving unethically.

Research found, for instance, that people act less altruistically after purchasing green products than after buying conventional products.[26] Even more worryingly, a second related experiment showed that "green" consumers became more likely to cheat and steal than buyers of conventional products. According to the authors, purchasing green products provides a sort of moral credential that can produce the counterintuitive effect of fostering selfish and unethical behaviors.[27]

The Virtuous Barrel:
How to Transform Corporate Scandals into Good Businesses via Behavioral Ethics

Another research with the suggestive title "When Sunlight Fails to Disinfect" shows how disclosing the conflicts of interest we are subject to can also generate a dangerous moral license.[28] In this study, participants were assigned the role of either "estimators" or "advisors." Estimators were asked to assess actual sale prices of four houses. They were given an information packet containing a photo of the house, a map of its location, and basic information about the property. Advisors, in turn, were required to advise estimators on the sale prices of the houses.

Advisors had a significant informational advantage over estimators. They received all the information estimators had, plus information on recent sale prices, tax-assessed values of comparable neighborhood homes, and the tax-assessed value . This made them sort of "experts" on the issue (similarly to investment advisors, stock analysts, lawyers, etc.). Estimators were aware of advisors' informational advantage and were given suggested sale prices on an "advisor's report" before making their estimates.

In an initial condition of the experiment ("no conflict of interest"), advisors were paid the same as estimators. In this variant, they were relatively accurate in their appraisals: advisors' mean suggestion across houses was around $204,000, only $14,000 more than the mean sale price of $190,000.

The researchers then created a new version of the experiment ("conflict of interest, without disclosure"), in which advisors were paid based on how high their estimators' appraisals were compared with the actual sale price. In this condition, advisors' mean suggestion across houses jumped to around $236,000.

The most interesting results came from the third version of the experiment ("with conflict of interest, with disclosure"). In this case, advisors would still be paid based on the upward inaccuracy of estimators. However, this time they were required to inform estimators in advance about their conflict of interest.[29] Under this condition, advisors' mean suggestion across houses reached around $255,000, almost $20,000 more than when they did not have to disclose their conflicts of interest.

More importantly: while in the conflicted condition "without disclose" estimators ended up making mean estimates of around $221,000 across the four houses, their mean estimates in the conflicted condition "with disclosure" increased to almost $230,000. This means that the disclosure did not compensate for the damaging effects of the conflicts of interest (actually, it resulted in mean estimates more than $8,000 higher than the correct sale prices).

This study demonstrated two perverse effects of the so-called "full disclosure" in the jargon of market practitioners. To experts, full disclosure confers a dangerous moral license by leaving them morally free to offer even more biased opinions than they would initially make due to their conflicts of interests. For those who depend on the advice of conflicted experts, full disclosure can worsen their choices, thus ending up in larger financial losses.

The scientific evidence on moral licensing makes it clear that good behavior today is no guarantee of good behavior tomorrow. Thus, people should aim toward understanding how their past behavior influences their future decisions in order to avoid succumbing to the tendency of playing a zero-sum game from the ethical standpoint.

---

[1] Source: Twain, Mark. Notebook entry, January or February 1894, Mark Twain's Notebook, ed. Albert Bigelow Paine (1935). Available at https://en.wikiquote.org/wiki/Mark_Twain

[2] These steps are described by Bazerman and Tenbrunsel (2011).

[3] This is in fact another cognitive bias, called "planning fallacy". More information at https://en.wikipedia.org/wiki/Planning_fallacy

[4] Diekmann et al. (2003: 673).

[5] Brehm e Festinger (1957).

[6] For more on moral disengagement, see Welsh et al. (2014), Detert et al. (2008), and Bandura (1990).

[7] Bandura (1990: 27).

[8] The link https://en.wikipedia.org/wiki/List_of_memory_biases describes a full list of these biases.

[9] Kouchaki e Gino (2016), Anderson e Hanslmayr (2014) e Shu et al. (2011).

[10] Kochaki e Gino (2016: 6166).

[11] One study of the research asked participants to remember unethical actions they had

The Virtuous Barrel:
How to Transform Corporate Scandals into Good Businesses via Behavioral Ethics

committed or that others had committed. In this case, people remembered with less clarity their unethical acts, but continued to remember with high clarity the dishonesty of others.

[12] Mazar et al. (2008), and Ariely, D. (2008).

[13] Soltes (2016: 257).

[14] Ayal e Gino (2011), and Gino et al. (2009).

[15] Touré-Tillery e Fishbach (2012) provide interesting evidence on this.

[16] Still according to this theory, the greater the ambiguity of a situation, the greater is the propensity to rationalize our actions in order to maximize our personal benefit.

[17] Nisan (1990) developed the first conceptual model on "moral balance".

[18] Tetlock et al. (2000).

[19] In a variant, participants were told to hand-copy a short story written in the first person. The story described either an ethical deed (helping a co-worker) or an unethical act (sabotaging a co-worker). Afterwards, they were asked to rate the desirability of various products on a 1-7 scale. Researchers then observed that those asked to copy the unethical story increased the desirability of cleansing products (such as soaps, disinfectants, etc.) as compared to other products (such as juices, CD cases, etc.).

[20] Zhong et al. (2006: 1452).

[21] In Enron's notorious case, Kenneth Lay, its Chairman of the Board, used to spend most of his time on charity events. Oftentimes, the greatest offender can be the greatest philanthropist!

[22] Kang et al. (2016), Kotchen and Moon (2012), and Heal (2005).

[23] Kotchen and Moon (2012).

[24] Kang et al. (2016).

[25] Merritt et al. (2010), Sachdeva et al. (2009), and Zhong et al. (2009).

[26] Mazar and Zhong (2010). Curiously, the authors observed that people acted more altruistically after being exposed to green products than after being exposed to conventional products (probably because of the activation of social responsibility and ethical conduct norms associated with these products). So, the mere exposure to green products and the purchase of such products seem to lead to significant different behavioral consequences.

[27] Ibid: 494.

[28] Cain et al. (2011).

[29] Advisors were required to provide estimators with the following handwritten disclosure: "As an advisor, I am required to inform you that I am paid based on how high your estimate of the property sale price is relative to the actual sale price".

Part 2: Most of the wrong things are done by good people

> *"The sad truth is that most evil is done by people who never make up their minds to be good or evil."*
> Hannah Arendt (1906–1975)[1]

The second major conclusion of behavioral ethics is that most of the wrong things are done by ordinary people, i.e., by individuals with no malicious intent nor any relevant personality disorder such as lack of empathy. In other words, the findings of behavioral ethics suggest that most of us may end up committing unethical behaviors given the right circumstances.

It is difficult for us to accept that this argument is true. Most people have been educated to think that bad things are done by "bad people" while "good people" do virtuous things. However, most of us have not been educated to believe that people of "good character" can do bad things.

In addition, social psychology has also shown that we are prone to the so-called "fundamental attribution error": When we see someone doing something unusual, our first reaction is to judge his or her behavior by discarding the circumstances and assuming he or she did it on purpose due to his or her personal traits. For example, if someone cuts us off while driving, our first thought can be "what an idiot" instead of considering the possibility that the driver is rushing someone to the hospital. Likewise, when we hear about a corporate malfeasance in the business world, we tend to take for granted that the outcome was created by a few malicious individuals.[2]

The Virtuous Barrel:
How to Transform Corporate Scandals into Good Businesses via Behavioral Ethics

Good people can do bad things because they gradually become "ethically blind," in the sense that they fail to fully understand the consequences of their behaviors at the time of their actions. As a result, they simply come to think that what they are doing is right or at least justifiable.

According to professors Guido Palazzo, Franciska Krings, and Ulrich Hoffrage, who first coined this term, ethical blindness can be defined as the temporary inability of a decision maker to see the ethical dimension of a decision at stake. The professors argue that this phenomenon can be understood along three aspects. The first is that people deviate from the values and principles they have tried to live up to in the past. The second is that ethical blindness is a temporary and context-bound state. This means that, for reasons related to the circumstances, individuals are not able to use their moral reasoning for deciding. However, when the situation changes, they are likely to once again practicing their original values and principles. The third is that ethical blindness is unconscious, in the sense that individuals are either unaware to be deviating from their values or are not able to access those values when deciding.[3]

As a result, people who become ethically blind only acquire a clearer dimension of the implications of their actions afterward and would not want to repeat them if they had another perspective of reality at that time.[4] Not coincidentally, many people involved in corporate scandals are shocked by their own behavior when the context changes, coming to the public with statements such as: "I could not realize how I deviated from my values at that moment."[5]

Ethical blindness is the consequence of a process called "ethical fading." This process represents the gradual loss of ethical discomfort by individuals with good values. In the words of professors Ann Tenbrunsel and David Messick, who pioneered this concept, ethical fading is the process "by which the moral colors of an ethical decision fade into bleached hues that are void of moral implications."[6] As a result of this series of steps, individuals end up becoming silent observers of improper actions or even actively contributing to questionable behaviors in their workplace.

Ethical fading generally develops as follows: We initially feel that something is wrong with certain practices we see or are compelled to do. In this situation, we initially feel strong tension between the implications of these behaviors and our personal values. Over time, however, we tend to become less and less sensitive to these practices, i.e., the stress becomes less intense and moral concerns begin to disappear. The process continues, in small steps, until we completely lose sight of the ethical dimension of our actions or omissions. After a certain point, we stop questioning ourselves. Transgressions that initially generated internal dilemmas come to be seen as normal or even defensible. At this point, we have become ethically blind.[7]

Ethical blindness results from a combination of three factors: distorted perception of reality, contextual pressures, and a perverse temporal dynamic.

Let's start with how we frame reality. As described in Chapter 2, we all interpret the world around us through our own lenses, creating a "mental frame" or unique reality based on our life experiences, educational background, and cognitive biases. As the writer Anaïs Nin said, "We don't see things as they are, we see things as we are."[8]

The problem, though, is that our perception of reality can be narrowed or even distorted after interacting with various contextual pressures. According to robust scientific evidence on behavioral ethics, pressures in our social context that can undermine our ethical judgment are composed of three main layers:
- The immediate context (our daily work life);
- The organizational context (the culture and practices of the organization we work for); and,
- The institutional context (the environment in which our organization is embedded).

In the following chapters, I will detail each one of these layers of contextual pressures as well as the elements related to the temporal dynamics that may impair our ethical judgments. Afterward, we will return to the discussion of our distorted perception of reality, thus concluding this second part of the book with a complete overview of the process leading to ethical blindness.

---

[1] Source: Arendt. H. 1978. The Life of the Mind (1), Thinking. Available at https://en.wikiquote.org/wiki/Hannah_Arendt

[2] On the other hand, when we cut someone off in traffic, we usually convince ourselves that we had to do so. For more on the fundamental attribution error (also known as the correspondence bias), see http://ethicsunwrapped.utexas.edu/glossary/fundamental-attribution-error

[3] Palazzo et al. (2012, 325).

[4] Authors like Bazerman and Tenbrunsel (2011) employ the term "bounded ethicality" instead of the concept of ethical blindness. According to them, bounded ethicality represents the systematic and predictable ways in which people make decisions without realizing the implications of their behavior. Chugh et al. (2005) is probably be the first paper to have coined the term "bounded ethicality".

[5] This was also one of the conclusions of Soltes (2016: 304): "Many of the executives I spoke with did not perceive the harm associated with their choices at the time they were making them. It's only with the benefit of hindsight that the detrimental effects of their conduct became clear to them."

[6] Tenbrunsel and Messick (2004: 224).

[7] This argument is based on a rationale carried out by Bazerman and Tenbrunsel (2011: 69-71).

[8] Source: Anaïs Nin. 1961. The Seduction of the Minotaur, p. 124. There is a dispute over the authorship of this quote. For some, it comes from the Talmud, the sacred book of the Jews. For a discussion on this, see "Seeing things: The Internet, the Talmud and Anais Nin," Crane e Kadane (2008).

4. The pressures of those who are part of our daily lives

> *"The most unpardonable sin in society is independence of thought."*
> Emma Goldman (1869–1940)[1]

The first layer of contextual pressures that may affect our ethical behavior is the immediate context in which we are inserted. There are three main aspects related to the circumstances of our daily lives that can increase the likelihood of ethical blindness:

- The pressure of authority;
- Peer pressure; and,
- The self-imposed pressure due to our professional role.

The pressure of authority

> *"Blind belief in authority is the greatest enemy of truth."*
> Albert Einstein (1879–1955)[2]

The pressure coming from hierarchical superiors is probably the most powerful force that can affect our ethical judgment. From childhood, we are indoctrinated to obey and please figures representing authority such as parents and teachers. Years later, this obedience is reinforced in organizations. It is important to note that the tendency to obey authority figures comes not only from fear but also from the will to please and to show that we are competent.

According to social learning theory, we discover how to behave in a certain situation by noticing others' behaviors and attitudes and their outcomes.[3] Individuals that are

The Virtuous Barrel:
How to Transform Corporate Scandals into Good Businesses via Behavioral Ethics

observed are called models. We are particularly likely to follow influential models who are more relevant for us and symbolize the norms of conduct of the group to which we belong to. In companies, senior leaders as C-level executives and board members embody the behavior to be noticed and imitated, i.e., they represent the organization's standards, what is in fact important and accepted in this environment.

Numerous experiments demonstrate how pressure from authority figures may lead us to follow orders in a thoughtless way, often against our principles. In two different studies, for example, employees ended up discriminating against black people and foreigners in a personnel-selection process after being told by superiors to behave this way.[4] In another study, 22 night nurses received a call by a fake physician who described himself as "Dr. Smith."[5] He asked them to see if they had a drug named "astroten." When the nurses checked the stock, they could see that the maximum dosage was supposed to be 10mg. After reporting to the "doctor" that the drug was available, they were told to administer 20mg of the drug to a patient ("Dr. Smith" justified the request by saying he was in a hurry and would sign the authorization form when he came to see the patient later on). The medication was not real, though the nurses thought it was. If the nurses opted to administer the drug, they would have broken three hospital rules: they were not allowed to accept instructions over the phone, the dose was double the maximum threshold allowed, and the medicine was unauthorized because it was not on the ward stock list. Incredibly, 21 out of the 22 nurses tested (95%) were easily influenced into executing the order. Curiously, when other nurses from the same hospital were asked to discuss what they would do in a similar situation, all but one said they would not comply with the order under any circumstances.

The most famous experiment on the power of authority was conducted by psychologist Stanley Milgram in the 1960s.[6] Milgram's work produced dramatic results by showing that about two-thirds of ordinary people would apply a lethal shock of 450 volts to another individual just because a scientist asked them to do so. The next box details this experiment, considered by many the most impressive in the history of social psychology.

Milgram's experiments and the power of authority

Stanley Milgram's famous experiments with electric shocks in the 1960s are probably the best example of our tendency to obey authorities under certain circumstances in a thoughtless way.

After the Second World War, the famous Nuremberg trials took place. The main defense argument used by Nazi officials in the trial was that they were only "following orders." Many psychologists were intrigued in understanding how highly civilized and well-educated German officers could have committed so many atrocities.

In 1961, Stanley Milgram, a Yale professor, began a series of tests to investigate whether the context could lead individuals to blindly obey authority figures, even if by doing so they would harm other people.

The idea was simple: A community member was asked to volunteer in a scientific experiment of memory and learning through a newspaper ad in exchange for a symbolic compensation of $4. Upon arrival, the volunteer was introduced to a "scientist" and to another "community member" (actually, both actors). The volunteer was informed that he or she was going to participate in a study designed to investigate the effect of punishment on learning.

One participant would be the "teacher," while the other would be the "learner." The draw was rigged, so that volunteers always ended up being the "teachers" and the confederate the "learner." Then, both the teacher and the scientist conducted the learner into a room. The learner was seated in a sort of electric chair with his arms strapped and his wrist attached to an electroshock machine.

The Virtuous Barrel:
How to Transform Corporate Scandals into Good Businesses via Behavioral Ethics

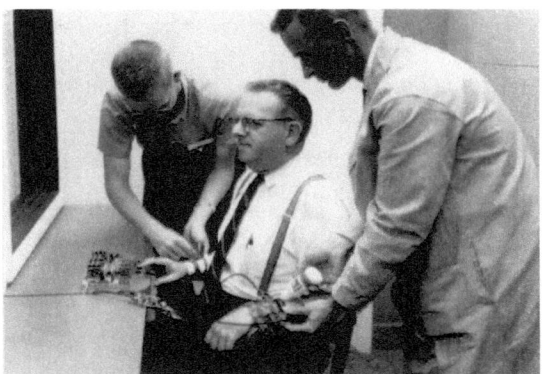

Milgram experiments: Dramatic evidence of the power of authority over our ethical judgment. (from left to right: volunteer/teacher, actor/learner and lab scientist).

The actor/learner was subject to a memory test applied by the volunteer/teacher. At each error of the learner, the teacher was required to apply an electric shock of increasing intensity: starting at 15V, with increments of 15V until a hypothetical limit of 450V. The shock generator machine had a voltage scale with labels indicating its danger, from "slight shock" for 45V shocks, to "danger: severe shock" for shocks above 400V (the label "XXX" was marked below the maximum 450V shock).

The actor had a well-defined script. At 75V, he grunted. At 120V, he complained loudly. At 150V, he said his heart was bothering him and demanded to be released from the experiment. At 225V, he started kicking the wall separating him from the volunteer. At 345V, when the machine's caption pointed to "extreme shocks," he issued agonizing screams of pain. At 405V, when the caption indicated "potentially lethal" shock, the actor stopped responding. At this moment, the "scientist" would tell the volunteer that the absence of answers should be interpreted as a wrong answer, thus asking him to continue applying the shocks. At 450V, the lethal electrical shock, the study would end.

If the volunteer expressed interest in leaving the experiment, the research protocol established that the "scientist" would ask him to proceed through four sentences: (i) "please, continue"; (ii) "the experiment requires you to continue"; (iii) "it is essential that you continue"; and, iv) "you don't have other choice, you must continue." If the volunteer still showed interest in leaving the experiment, then the test would be stopped.

Before carrying out the research, Milgram believed that the level of obedience in the United States would be much lower than that of Germany due *to its culture being supposedly more opened to questioning. He submitted the experimental design to several psychologists. On average, psychologists estimated that people would stop around 140V and that only one in 1,000 volunteers would apply the lethal shock of 450V.*

The results were impressive: no volunteers gave up before 300V and 26 of the 40 participants (65%) went until the end by inflicting 450V shocks. Most people, therefore, would have applied a lethal shock to an innocent person simply because they were told to do so by a scientific authority. It is worth noting that the compensation to participate in the experiment was fixed and paid in advance (irrespective of the magnitude of the shock applied).

Milgram's studies were replicated with more than 1,000 people in various contexts and countries, yielding qualitatively similar results. Men and women exhibited statistically similar rates of obedience, with women usually showing higher levels of stress during the experiment. Although widely publicized in the 1960s and 1970s, these impressive results fell into relative oblivion after research ethics committees banned replications of the experiment due to the potential psychological problems inflicted on volunteers.

After interviewing the participants, Milgram concluded that we have a nature intrinsically linked to loyalty that lead us to obey authority in most circumstances. For Milgram, we go through a so-called "agency shift" in which we forego our rationality and values to satisfy the expectations of authorities to reach a better outcome for the group.

In these circumstances, we would suspend our autonomy and simply come to see ourselves as instruments of a greater authority. In Milgram's words: "The essence in obedience consists in the fact that a person comes to view himself as an instrument for carrying out another person's wishes, and he therefore no longer regards himself as responsible for his actions ... The disappearance of a sense of responsibility is the most far-reaching consequence of submission to authority."

People interviewed by Milgram after the tests even showed some satisfaction in being loyal to the authority. When asked why they had behaved in such way, many volunteers simply replied that they had "given their word" or felt a "duty of loyalty" to the scientist.

The overall result of the experiments on the influence of authority, including the classic Milgram experiment described above, is that most people would go against their own values and principles if they were driven by someone seen as a legitimate leader to behave in a questionable way.[7] In other words, the vast majority of people tend to obey to

The Virtuous Barrel:
How to Transform Corporate Scandals into Good Businesses via Behavioral Ethics

authorities under certain circumstances, including in the performance of reprehensible acts.

The pressure of authority that melts away people's morality tends to be even more relevant in highly hierarchical structures, as is the typical case in the corporate world. Take, for example, the case of Petrobras, the Brazilian oil company involved in a huge corruption scandal. One of the key players in the wrongdoings was its senior manager in charge of supply-chain named Paulo Roberto Costa. After being promoted to the C-Suite, Mr. Costa replaced all managers immediately reporting to him. In the first meeting with his team, he reminded everyone that "the music has changed, and whoever does not dance according to the music will be out." According to a former manager reporting to him, the message was clear: "Whoever did not obey would not have a position in his department."[8]

Another example comes from Odebrecht, the private construction company involved in the same corruption scandal. In early 2017, a group of 77 senior executives entered into a plea bargain with prosecutors. Afterward, many of these executives declared to be upset with Odebrecht's former CEO, Marcelo Odebrecht. They believed it was unfair to include their names in the list of corruptors because, in their view, they were only "following orders" on decisions involving bribes to politicians.[9]

A third example comes Banco Panamericano, a Brazilian bank listed on the stock exchange that announced a massive fraud of around $2.5 billion (half of its total assets) at the end of 2010. In an interview to a local newspaper, the former chairman of its board of directors Luiz Sandoval was asked how he learned about the fraud. He said that the CEO and the CFO (later convicted as the main architects of the malfeasance) have told him at a meeting that the bank had suffered massive losses from "errors of accounting parameterizations." Because Sandoval did not know what this alleged practice was about, he called the bank's leading accountant. Shortly after arriving, the accountant started telling him about the fraud. Sandoval then questioned, "Do you know this is illegal? It is illicit?" To which the accountant replied: "Yes, sir. But I did it because I got orders from the CFO."[10]

These examples corroborate the conclusions of sociologist Robert Jackall in his superb book *Moral Mazes* about the world of managers at large US corporations. He observed that one of the golden rules to survive in this particular environment is that subordinates must never contradict their boss's judgment in public. In his view, violation of this admonition "is thought to constitute a kind of death wish in business, and one who does so should practice what one executive calls 'flexibility drills,' an exercise 'where you put your head between your legs and kiss your ass goodbye.'"[11]

At the end of his analysis, Jackall summarized the fundamental rules of corporate life in five warnings, all related to the dangers of authority pressure: "(1) You never go around your boss; (2) You tell your boss what he wants to hear, even when he claims he wants dissenting views; (3) If your boss wants something dropped, you drop it; (4) You are sensitive to your boss's wishes, so you anticipate what he wants; (5) Your job is not to report something your boss does not want reported, but rather to cover it up. You do what your job requires, and you keep your mouth shut."[12]

It is essential to constantly monitor ourselves, therefore, in order to do not risk suspending our ethical judgment to obey or please our hierarchical superiors. As highlighted by Muel Kaptein in his book *Workplace Morality*, "One way of steeling yourself against submitting to improper requests is not to see responsibility as a fixed quantity… if you do something because another person tells you to, you are still responsible for the decision to comply with the request. Shirking responsibility is by definition irresponsible."[13]

Peer pressure

> *"It takes a great deal of courage to stand up to your enemies, but even more to stand up to your friends."*
> J. K. Rowling (1965–)[14]

The Virtuous Barrel:
How to Transform Corporate Scandals into Good Businesses via Behavioral Ethics

Peer pressure from co-workers or other team members is the second element of the immediate context that may increase the risk of ethical blindness.

Throughout our evolution, we developed an innate tendency to go along with the group and often to behave as part of a herd.[15] This claim comes from the "multilevel selection theory," which argues that our genes came down to us not only because some individuals outcompeted their neighbors but also because some groups outcompeted neighboring groups.[16] Contemporary evidence of this idea in the business world comes from a statement of a treasury director at a global financial institution, who said that "Bankers work in teams, and the ethics is: you are with us or you are against us ... This is about tribal bonding, about belonging and sticking to your mates."[17]

This propensity to display team spirit is positive in order to increase social cohesion and the adherence to the formal and informal norms of the organization. However, group pressure can also lead us to switch off our moral judgments and end up behaving in ways we would normally not agree with.[18]

This argument was corroborated by an in-depth research of employees working for corrupt organizations. It concluded that "team spirit" and "security" were the two main values they shared with peers.[19] As the authors point out, "Employees need to stick together, which increases group coercion. Through this coercion, employees face higher pressure to follow group norms."

In another related survey, this time focusing on the finance industry, the author argues that "to an important degree, the financial world is not populated by people willfully doing evil but by conformists who have simply stopped asking questions about right and wrong. Things are going rather well for them and, in their bubble, they are exposed to likeminded people."[20] Unethical behaviors, therefore, often result from our readiness to follow conventions for the sake of avoiding problems, even at the expense of our own values.

The classic experiments carried out by Solomon Asch in the 1950s demonstrated the huge power of peers over our judgment.[21] In these studies, a volunteer was asked to answer a simple test of visual accuracy, as illustrated in Fig. 4. Volunteers were required to look at the left line and indicate which of the three lines on the right was equal to it in length (as you can easily see, the right answer in this example is letter C).

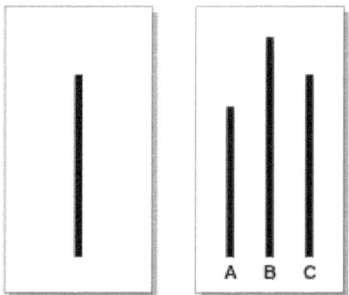

Figure 4: Asch Experiments: evidence of the power of peers over our judgment.

To assess to what extent the participant was influenced by the group's opinion, he was surrounded by several other "volunteers" (actually, all actors). In some cases, the confederates intentionally gave clearly wrong answers. In the Fig. 4, for example, sometimes all erroneously stated that the correct answer would be letter A.

Asch conducted the experiment with hundreds of people. He found that about 75% of individuals gave at least one wrong answer after 12 rounds, while more than half of the volunteers gave incorrect answers in more than 50% of the rounds. Impressively, 5% gave wrong answers in every round of the experiment.

The researcher interviewed the participants afterward, asking why they had given clearly wrong answers. Two main reasons emerged. Some claimed to have gone along with the group because they no longer believed in their own perception ("if everyone sees, then it must be true"). Others, in turn, argued to be aware they were giving the wrong answer. However, they preferred erring along with the others to fit in than giving right answers and staying out of the group. Regardless of the quality of the responses, all participants also reported feeling strong pressure to decide in line with peers.[22]

More recently, the influence of peers on our ethical behavior was demonstrated in a curious experiment detailed in the box below.[23]

The Virtuous Barrel:
How to Transform Corporate Scandals into Good Businesses via Behavioral Ethics

A recent experiment on peer influence over our ethical behavior

In a recent experiment carried out by researchers Francesca Gino, Shahar Ayal, and Dan Ariely, participants received a sheet of paper with 20 "task matrices." Each matrix was composed of nine cells as in the three examples below:

1.26	4.57	2.49
3.41	9.24	7.48
2.52	6.34	8.64

2.84	7.53	3.48
6.12	5.39	4.56
1.93	9.37	3.88

5.62	1.19	6.17
9.34	3.53	2.44
7.61	4.82	8.81

The participants were instructed to "solve" as many matrices as possible in five minutes by finding two numbers adding up to 10 (in the first matrix on the left, for instance, the numbers would be 2.52 and 7.48).

At the end of the experiment, participants would receive $0.50 per matrix solved. Thus, they could receive up to $10 if they correctly found each pair of numbers for all 20 matrices.

In the initial condition of the experiment (the "control condition"), there was no opportunity to cheat. After five minutes, individuals simply handed the test to the experimenter, who checked how many matrices each participant had solved and paid the amount due. In this situation, participants were able to solve seven matrices on average, receiving a payment of $3.50.

Next, researchers created a variant called the "shredder condition." At the end of the five minutes, participants were asked to count the number of matrices they had correctly solved, write this number on an answer form, shred their matrix worksheet in a shredding machine placed in the corner of the room, pay themselves based on their answer form, and then leave the room (in this case, the experimenter just kept reading a book to show that he was not monitoring the participants).

In this variant, where dishonesty was obviously possible and the likelihood of punishment null, the number of matrices solved quickly rose from seven to 12, and participants earned on average $6.

In order to investigate what would happen if people saw others blatantly cheating, researchers then created a new condition for the study, named "in-group-identity."

In this case, a professional actor pretended to be another participant taking the test. This condition followed the same procedure as of the shredder

> *condition, with one difference: About only one minute after the start of the experiment, the actor stood up and said: "I've solved everything!"*
>
> *Participants obviously knew that it would be impossible to solve all 20 matrices in such a short time. The researcher then told the actor to shred the answer form, take the $10 out of the envelope, and just walk away. The actor then grabbed the $10 and left the room smiling under the astonished eyes of the other participants.*
>
> *By observing this negative example, participants exposed to this peer-based condition claimed having solved 15 matrices on average, three more than in the shredder condition and more than double the control condition.*
>
> *This study suggests, therefore, that peer influence is likely to be an important factor in unethical behavior: By seeing that dishonest behavior is socially acceptable, people tend to feel free to cheat even more.*

Our propensity toward conformity tends to be even stronger when we are surrounded by work colleagues or friends as well as when we are asked to decide on more subjective and ambiguous issues (just as is the case of many business decisions with ethical implications).

In the corporate world, where people relate to each other on a daily basis, and issues are much more complex than in the Asch experiment, the pressure for everyone to show cohesion with their peers is obviously much greater.[24] In a survey with over 2,000 corporate executives in the United States, for example, nearly half reported working for organizations where they regularly feel the need to conform, while more than half said that people in their organizations do not question the status quo.[25]

It is noteworthy that many companies actually seek to actively strengthen conformity as a valuable asset of the organization. In the middle of the last century, for example, IBM's then-CEO James Watson tried to create the so-called IBMers: ideally "interchangeable" executives who were supposed to wear the same clothes, receive the same training, and adopt similar behavioral habits.[26] More recently, a book named *Final Accounting* about Arthur Andersen (the accounting firm that collapsed in the early

2000s) reported that the company had a powerful set of social norms aimed at transforming new graduates who entered the firm into true "androids."[27]

Other companies also strive to build a strong "culture of consensus," which tends to prompt individuals (especially junior employees) to adjust their opinions over time to conform with the majority. Nietzsche described the risk of such approach very well by stating that "a young man can be most surely corrupted when he is taught to value the like-minded more highly than the differently minded."[28]

Self-imposed pressure due to our professional role
The third factor of the immediate context that can undermine our ethical judgments is the least observed one: the pressure we impose on ourselves due to the expectations of our position.

When we adopt a different ethical conduct depending on the professional roles we undertake, we engage in a concept called "role morality."[29] This mindset is potentially dangerous because it may lead to a feeling that our professional position grants us a kind of "special permission" to behave unethically, even if such behavior would be reprehensible in other circumstances. As a result, we may end up applying ethical standards in our professional lives that diverge from those applied in our personal lives.

In the business world, role morality may lead executives to act in a way they would consider unethical if acting solely for their personal benefit. However, because they are acting on behalf of their organizations, they come to see the same behaviors as acceptable. According to research, people working in large corporations tend to have an even greater propensity to differentiate their personal values from those prevailing in their workplace.[30]

Sociologist Robert Jackall observed this phenomenon after interviewing dozens of managers of big corporations over many years. He concluded that "bureaucratic work causes people to bracket, while at work, the moralities that they might hold outside the workplace or that they might adhere to privately and to follow instead the prevailing morality of their particular organizational situation."[31] He also quotes a former vice president of a large company who declared that "What is right in the corporation is not what is right in a man's home or in his church. What is right in the corporation is what the guy above you wants from you. That's what morality is in the corporation."[32]

One of the most impressive experiments on how people tend to drastically change their behavior due to the social role assigned to them was carried out by psychologist Philip Zimbardo in the early 1970s.[33] In his classic study, detailed in the box below, volunteers began to display cruel behaviors toward other participants just because they were required to play the role of prison guards in a role-playing exercise simulating prison life.[34]

> *The Stanford Prison experiment and the power of the social role over our behavior*
>
> *Aiming to investigate whether social roles can induce people to change their behaviors, psychologist Philip Zimbardo devised a role-playing exercise at Stanford University simulating prison life in which some young people would be assigned the role of guards or prisoners for a few days.*
>
> *His initial motivation was to understand whether the widely reported brutality of prison guards was the result of an allegedly sadistic personality trait ("bad people" opting to follow this profession) or if it had more to do with the role expected by society and the environment in which they were inserted (the situational aspect deriving from the power of context).*
>
> *Zimbardo converted the basement of Stanford's psychology department into a false prison. Seventy-five volunteers enrolled in exchange for a $15 per day compensation to participate in the experiment. Twenty-four were selected (all were subject to personality tests aimed to eliminate those with psychological or criminal history or drug abuse). A draw defined those who would become "guards" or "prisoners" during the experiment.*
>
> *The initial idea of the study was to assess the evolution of the behavior of the "guards" during the 15 days it was supposed to last. Were they going to start behaving in a cruel way?*
>
> *The results were dramatic. Participants – both guards and prisoners – ended up changing their behavior dramatically, gradually failing to distinguish reality from their roles in the role-playing. The guards began to physically and psychologically torture the prisoners, often with refinements of*

sadism (see figure below). Several prisoners went through serious emotional disturbances. One had to leave the experiment after displaying uncontrollable explosions of screaming, crying, and anger. A (real) priest was even called in to help mitigate the prisoners' psychological distress.

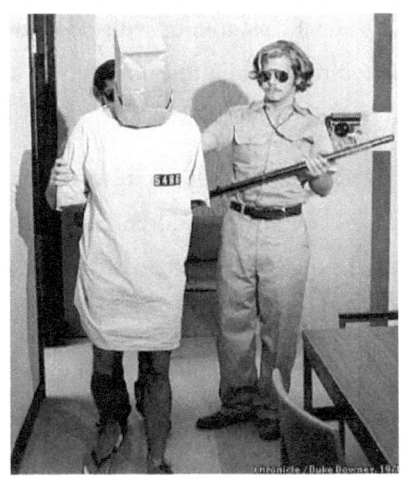

The Stanford Prison experiment: A dramatic example of how our social role can influence our behavior

Instead of the expected 15 days, Zimbardo had to terminate the experiment on the sixth day before he completely lost control of the situation. The researcher only made that decision after his wife Christina Maslach, also an emeritus professor of psychology, persuaded him that all protocols had been violated and that he could not go on. The psychologist later acknowledged that he did not begin to realize how far he had gone in the experiment: "I was already thinking more like the prison warden than as a scientist."

The central conclusion of the study is that people tend to quickly adjust themselves to the social role expected of them. In the specific case of prison guards, the results obviously suggest that their behavior is much more a product of situational factors than of their personality.

The Stanford Prison experiment, therefore, demonstrated the powerful impact of a bad environment on ordinary people. Many were permanently traumatized. A phrase from one of the "guards" of the experiment sums up very well the ethical blindness they started to exhibit: "While I was there as a guard, I did not feel any remorse or guilt. Only months later, after reflecting, I realized what I had done."

More recently, another experiment published in the prestigious journal *Nature* corroborates the power of role morality by showing how much the professional self-image can influence individual behavior.[35] In this research, carried out with 128 employees of a large international financial institution with around 12 years of experience in the industry, executives acted much more dishonestly just by having their professional image as "bankers" reinforced before the study.

For half of the executives (the so-called "control group"), researchers asked general questions about their personal lives, such as how many children they had and what were their main hobbies. The purpose of these questions was to highlight their personal identity as ordinary citizens prior to the experiment.

For the other half (the "experimental group"), researchers asked questions related to their professional lives, such as how much time they worked every day, what were their positions, and their main daily activities at the bank. In this case, the goal was to emphasize their professional identities as "bankers."

Participants were then taken to an isolated room where they were asked to flip a coin 10 times and anonymously report the results in a computer. They knew that they would receive $20 for each tail reported.

Statistically, the mean number of tails reported for each group should fluctuate around 50%. This is exactly what happened with the "control group." People who were reminded of their personal identity reported on average 51.6% of successful coin flips, a figure statistically similar to the expected 50% of a binomial distribution. Thus, bank employees were honest under normal circumstances.

The most interesting thing occurred to the individuals reminded of their professional identity before the test. In the "experimental group," the percentage of successful coin flips rose to around 60%, a much greater figure than what was supposed to be randomly obtained. Thus, individuals started to behave dishonestly simply because they were reminded right before the test that they were executives from the financial industry.

The Virtuous Barrel:
How to Transform Corporate Scandals into Good Businesses via Behavioral Ethics

In the experimental group, researchers also noted that 8% of participants claimed to have obtained 10 "tails" in a row in order to pocket the maximum $200 earnings. This virtually impossible statistical outcome was not reported by anyone from the control group. After having their professional identities highlighted right before the test, therefore, some executives left aside any ethical concerns and began to behave like true *homo economicus*.[36]

According to authors, the overall conclusion of their research is that "the prevailing business culture in the banking industry favors dishonest behavior and thus has contributed to the loss of the industry's reputation." On the other hand, the positive news is that researchers also acknowledged that "differently from the perception of the public opinion, we observe that bank executives tend to behave honestly in a control condition."

This important experiment demonstrates how the position we hold can change our self-perception and, consequently, influence our behavior. In a book on white-collar crimes, for example, many executives involved in illicit acts saw themselves primarily as "problem-solvers." As a result, they simply believed that their role was to solve any kind of problem with ingenuity, even circumventing the rules if necessary. As Robert Jones, a former executive convicted for financial fraud, pointed out: "You have a career of being able to find solutions, being successful … I worked in the industry for 20 years, and we always figured stuff out. We always did well … you have to understand, it comes from a career of trying to find solutions to things. We never grew up with someone saying you can't do it and therefore you're not going to hit a number."[37]

This sort of reasoning, therefore, generates interesting reflections related to the current business scandals aired in the news, such as:
- What is the expected behavior of an executive in charge of commercial negotiations: to win contracts at any cost?
- What is the role of a CFO: being rude, cost-cutting, insensitive to impacts on employees' lives?

- What is the role of a CEO: to make trade-offs among stakeholders in the name of maximizing shareholders' wealth?
- What is the expected behavior of a good executive: to be a problem-solver without ethical considerations?

Everyone should deeply reflect on the pressures related to the behavioral expectations of their positions. This will help us to know if, at the end of the day, we are acting according to our values and beliefs or if we are just being prisoners of a role. Actually, the self-imposed pressure due to the professional role is the backdrop of a central issue in corporate governance debates: What is the expected role of a good business leader?

The other side of the coin: the risks of power

> *"Power tends to corrupt and absolute power corrupts absolutely."*
> John Dalberg-Acton, Lord Acton (1834–1902)[38]

The perception we have of our power is another key aspect related to our social role that may impair our ethical judgment. Because one of the major consensuses among business experts is that ethical behavior in organizations depends to a large extent on the integrity and example of its leaders, this issue is particularly relevant to ensure proper corporate governance. Evidence shows, however, that establishing a decent ethical tone at the top is more difficult than it looks.

Numerous research demonstrates that power tends to unconsciously change our behaviors by making us less empathic, more aggressive, and more hypocritical from a moral standpoint.

In the case of empathy deficit, a senior HR manager at a large international bank corroborated this finding by saying that "The easier it is to fire someone, the easier it is for top managers to lose empathy. Humans become numbers very easily for them. They lose empathy."[39] In the case of aggressiveness, a curious experiment found that people with more expensive cars (a symbol of their social status) are much more likely to disrespect pedestrians and honk in a belligerent way than drivers of lower status cars.[40]

The Virtuous Barrel:
How to Transform Corporate Scandals into Good Businesses via Behavioral Ethics

The relationship between aggressiveness and power is also well observed in the business world.[41] Dick Fuld, the former CEO of US investment bank Lehman Brothers whose collapse triggered the 2008 global financial crisis, is a clear example of this profile: His nickname was "Gorilla" due to his highly intimidating posture. Because Fuld led the bank with an iron fist until its insolvency, his profile also fits very well with a paper that concluded that powerful individuals become more aggressive when they feel they are incompetent in their domain of power.[42] As legendary Russian writer Fyodor Dostoyevsky articulated two centuries ago, "The more incompetent one feels, the more eager he is to fight."[43]

In addition to increased aggressiveness, other scientific experiments concluded that:
- More powerful people tended to impose strict moral standards on other people at the same time as they are more prone to practice less decent moral behavior. Compared with the powerless, the powerful condemned other people's cheating more, while also cheating more themselves and were stricter in judging other people's moral transgressions than in judging their own transgressions.[44]
- Upper-class individuals behaved more unethically than lower-class individuals. Relative to lower-class people, upper-class individuals were more likely to break the law while driving, exhibit unethical decision-making tendencies, take valued goods from others, lie in a negotiation, cheat to increase their chances of winning a prize, and, endorse unethical behavior at work.[45]
- Upper-class individuals were more likely to favor utilitarian choices in ethical dilemmas as well as being more prone to take resources from one person for the sake of benefiting others in an allocation task due to their lower empathy for the person whose resources were taken.[46]
- Participants with a higher sense of power experienced less distress and less compassion and exhibited greater autonomic emotion regulation when confronted with another participant's suffering.[47]
- Higher social class is associated with increased entitlement and narcissism. Upper-class individuals reported greater psychological entitlement, narcissistic

personality tendencies, and were more likely to behave in a narcissistic fashion by opting to look at themselves in a mirror.[48]

The results of these studies make it clear that the challenge of maintaining high ethical standards tends to be much greater for business leaders. Curiously, this is recognized even by offenders themselves. In his personal agenda, seized during the Car Wash operation in Brazil, former Petrobras C-level executive Paulo Roberto Costa (mentioned earlier in this chapter) had an ironic handwritten note that said: "Ending corruption is the ultimate goal of those who have not yet come to power."[49]

When we come to occupy powerful positions, we run the risk of starting to see ourselves as someone unique who must be subject to different standards than those under our supervision. As a result, we may unconsciously see ourselves above others and lower our ethical standards accordingly.

This issue is detailed by professor Muel Kaptein.[50] In his view, this happens because power feeds the image of the rules being less applicable to the influential person himself. After all, supervision requires distance, and he or she does not belong to the party being supervised. In the jargon of psychology, power tends to increase our "moral hypocrisy."

Not everything, however, is bad news. Research has revealed that the effect of power on moral hypocrisy depends on the legitimacy of the power: When the position of power is denied a sense of entitlement, and the powerful feel his or her position as illegitimate, researchers observed that the moral-hypocrisy effect was reversed, with the undeserved powerful becoming stricter in judging his or her own behavior than in judging others' conduct.[51]

From the point of view of sound management and governance, this implies that managers should see their role as having a larger and socially important implication than just making money for shareholders. By elevating the responsibility of business leaders as individuals who ultimately should serve society, we increase the chance that they will have a humbler perception of themselves, thus fostering humility instead of hypocrisy.

The Virtuous Barrel:
How to Transform Corporate Scandals into Good Businesses via Behavioral Ethics

---

[1] Source: Emma Goldman. Anarchism and Other Essays. 1910. Ch. 2: Minorities Versus Majorities. Available at http://theanarchistlibrary.org/library/emma-goldman-anarchism-and-other-essays

[2] Free translation from the original: "*Autoritätshörigkeit ist der größte Feind der Wahrheit*". Source: Albert Einstein. Letter to Jost Winteler, 07/08/1901. Available at http://www.aphorismen.de/zitat/118921

[3] Social learning theory was developed by Albert Bandura in the 1960s. It argues that learning is a cognitive process that occurs within a social context and through direct observation and instruction, not necessarily requiring reinforcements and rewards. In his classic studies, Bandura showed that children exposed to an aggressive model reproduced considerably more aggressive behaviors toward a Bobo doll than children not exposed to the aggressive example. For more information, see Bandura and Walters (1963), Bandura (1969), and Bandura and Walter (1977).

[4] Brief et al. (1995), and Petersen e Dietz (2000).

[5] Hofling et al. (1966). A summary is available at McLeod (2008).

[6] Milgram (1963), Milgram (1965), and Milgram and Gudehus (1978).

[7] Milgram's experiments have been recently replicated out of the academic world to check if people's behavior had changed substantially fifty years after the original experiment. The results were not encouraging. In a 2009 replication carried out by BBC, nine of the twelve participants (75%) were until the very end by applying the lethal shock on the volunteer (the link https://vimeo.com/89396290 shows the video of this experiment). In another 2009 replication by France Télévision as part of a program called *jeu de la mort*, over 90% of the participants applied the supposedly lethal shock to other people, including a Jewish participant whose grandparents had been killed in a concentration camp during World War II! (The video for this program is available at https://youtu.be/6gsKGyMZ_Q4)

[8] Paduan (2016, p. 203).

[9] Folha de São Paulo. 02/13/2017. Desde delação, Marcelo Odebrecht enfrenta mágoa de antigos colegas. Available at http://www1.folha.uol.com.br/poder/2017/02/1858157-desde-delacao-marcelo-odebrecht-enfrenta-magoa-de-antigos-colegas.shtml

[10] Estado de São Paulo. 12/25/2010. O vice-presidente de finanças do banco mandou o contador maquiar o balanço. Available at http://economia.estadao.com.br/noticias/geral,o-vice-presidente-de-financas-do-banco-mandou-o-contador-maquiar-o-balanco,658184

[11] Jackall (1988: 20).

[12] *Ibid*: 110.

[13] Kaptein (2013 : 48).

[14] Source: https://www.goodreads.com/quotes/993937-there-are-all-kinds-of-courage-said-dumbledore-smiling-it

[15] Acting in conformity with the group was a winning strategy in our early days, when humans lived in small numbers and survived as hunter-gatherers. The video available at https://youtu.be/BgRoiTWkBHU illustrates in a funny way the extent of our strong tendency to replicate the behavior of others surrounding us.

[16] Kluver et al. (2014: 153, 154). As pointed out by the authors "the key implication of this work for researchers in behavioral ethics is that humans may have inherited a suite of biobehavioral adaptations and tendencies conducive to acting in the interest of groups, above and beyond what might be expected…".

[17] Luyendijk (2015: 236, 238).

[18] Based on fMRI scans, Cikara et al. (2014) concluded that the part of our brain that makes

moral judgements is less active when we're in a group.

[19] Campbell and Göritz (2014: 305).
[20] Luyendijk (2015: 220).
[21] Asch (1955), Asch (1956), and Levine (1999).
[22] According to Asch (1956), the factors that increased the percentage of people's conformity with the group were: the size of the group (the more people, the greater the tendency towards conformity), the difficulty of the task (the more complex the task, the greater the conformity), and the status of the other people of the group (the higher the perceived status, the greater the conformity). On the other hand, the factors that reduced conformity were the following: the lack of unanimity (a single dissident greatly reduced the degree of conformity with the group), and the possibility of giving anonymous responses.
[23] Gino et al. (2009).
[24] This applies not only to group decisions, but also to the way of dressing, talking, behaving, etc.
[25] Harvard Business Review. 24/10/2016. Let your workers Rebel. By Francesca Gino. Available at https://hbr.org/cover-story/2016/10/let-your-workers-rebel
[26] See link http://www.ozy.com/flashback/from-ibm-to-google-the-birth-of-company-culture/37176 for further details on IBMers.
[27] See link http://www.nytimes.com/2003/02/23/business/book-value-a-culture-turned-against-itself-at-andersen.html for further details.
[28] Source: Friedrich Nietzsche. The Dawn of the Day, 1911, p. 262 (trad. John McFarland Kennedy). Ed. The MacMillan Company.
[29] For more on role morality, see Andre (1991), Werhane and Freeman (1999), Gibson (2003), and Radtke (2008).
[30] For a compilation of this evidence, see Jackall (1988).
[31] Jackall (1988: 6).
[32] *Ibid*: 6.
[33] Haney et al. (1972), Haney et al. (1973), and Zimbardo (2007).
[34] The original videos of Zimbardo's experiment are available at https://youtu.be/sYtX2sEaeFE, https://youtu.be/uTdttd7XTfQ e https://youtu.be/fQnOkmvigi0 . The seminal article describing the experiment was written by Haney et al. (1973). A recent summary can be found at McLeod (2016).
[35] Cohn et al. (2014).
[36] The concept of *homo economicus* was originally coined by critics of John Stuart Mill's 1836 work on political economy. It assumes that human beings always: make perfectly rational decisions; think exclusively in maximizing their own personal economic gains; and, are interested in breaking the rules if the applicable penalty multiplied by the probability of being caught is lower than the expected benefit of a dishonest act. *Homo economicus* is a standard assumption of most neoclassical economic models.
[37] Soltes (2016: 189).
[38] Source: Historical Essays and Studies, by John Emerich Edward Dalberg-Acton. (1907). Appendix, p. 504. Available at https://en.wikiquote.org/wiki/John_Dalberg-Acton,_1st_Baron_Acton
[39] Luyendijk (2015: 98).
[40] While drivers of lower status cars took an average of five seconds to honk, luxury car drivers honked in about two seconds! For more information, see Diekmann et al. (1996).
[41] It is unclear, though, whether power leads people to become more aggressive or whether our current corporate environment makes it easier for more aggressive people to reach the top.

[42] Fast e Chen (2009).
[43] Source: https://quotes.thefamouspeople.com/fyodor-dostoevsky-1441.php
[44] Lammers et al. (2010).
[45] Piff et al. (2012).
[46] Côté et al. (2013).
[47] Van Kleef et al. (2008).
[48] Piff (2014).
[49] UOL, coluna de Leandro Mazzini. 21/09/2014. Em agenda, Paulo Roberto Costa ironiza pobre e corrupção. Available at http://colunaesplanada.blogosfera.uol.com.br/2014/09/21/em-agenda-paulo-roberto-costa-ironiza-pobre-e-corrupcao/
[50] This issue is addressed in greater depth by Kaptein (2013: 53).
[51] Lammers et al. (2010).

5. The pressures of our organizational environment

> *"If people are good only because they fear punishment, and hope for reward, then we are a sorry lot indeed."*
> Albert Einstein (1879–1955)[1]

The second layer of contextual pressures that can impair our ethical judgments comes from the organizational context, i.e., the environment created by the company through its practices and culture. Evidence shows that three organizational aspects may foster unethical behaviors:

- Unrealistic or unidimensional goals that take people to the limit to achieve them as well as promote a "tunnel vision" of their role;
- Excessive internal competition reinforced by a "winner-take-all" performance evaluation system that induces individuals to do everything to survive and not being seen as a failure; and,
- A language full of euphemisms or metaphors of war or games, which tends to mitigate the feeling that wrong things impacting real people are being made.

Unrealistic or unidimensional goals

> *"Morals go out of the window when the pressure is on. When the responsibility is there, and you have to meet budgetary numbers, you can forget about morals. Circumstances overrule morals."*
> Steven Hoffenberg, former CEO (1945–)[2]

The Virtuous Barrel:
How to Transform Corporate Scandals into Good Businesses via Behavioral Ethics

Setting hard-to-reach goals for employees and executives for the sake of promoting better organizational performance has become a standard practice in today's corporate world.

However, to begin with, unrealistic goals can worsen productivity rather than improve it. By realizing that their goals are not feasible, people are likely to become discouraged rather than more motivated. Overly ambitious goals can also lead executives to take excessive risks to achieve them. In this case, the individual can perceive him or herself in a kind of game where it is worth risking everything instead of simply accepting a "sure loss."

In addition to being potentially unproductive, setting unrealistic goals may induce executives to do anything to meet them in order to not lose their jobs or harm their careers. Science corroborates the argument that the pressure to hit unattainable targets dramatically increases the likelihood of unethical and even illicit actions.[3] One study, for example, found that high performance goals led to a hypercompetitive, individualistic mindset coupled with adversarial social behaviors.[4] In another paper, based on a laboratory experiment with 154 participants, the researchers found that those with unmet goals were more likely to engage in unethical behavior, particularly when they fell just short of reaching their goals.[5] Interestingly, the authors also observed that this relationship held for goals with and without economic incentives.

In addition, a recent study analyzed the impact of establishing consecutives goals, a common practice in organizations in which the completion of an existing goal is followed by the assignment of a new one.[6] In this case, the researchers found that setting consecutive high goals can increase unethical behavior through depletion of our self-regulatory resources. According to the study, "Our results suggest that when organizations consistently set aggressive performance targets for employees and appear to care more that the numbers were achieved than how the numbers were achieved, they may be creating an environment in which employees will both be highly depleted and highly tempted to cheat in order to reach the goal."[7]

This is exactly what happened with Wells Fargo, a US bank subject to a huge scandal in 2016.

To begin with, the bank enjoyed a remarkable reputation for sound management until its wrongdoings came to light. It emerged largely unscathed from the 2008 financial crisis and ranked first in market capitalization among all US banks. In 2015, Wells Fargo ranked seventh on Barron's list of most respected companies and 22nd of Fortune's world's most admired firms.[8] The bank also proudly held itself apart from its New York peers and regularly touted its "culture of caring."[9]

Scratch below the surface, though, and the reality was not so shiny. The bank developed a system in which employees were assigned excessively ambitious goals for cross-selling, a business tactic in which existing customers are sold additional products. These goals included opening new accounts and selling credit cards. According to one report, district managers discussed daily sales for each branch and for each employee four times a day, some going as far as setting daily and hourly sales targets.[10] If the branch did not reach its targets, the shortfall was added to the next day's goals. One area president, for instance, used to tell employees to "do whatever it takes" to sell.[11] Goals were constantly updated, while shaming and threats of terminations by managers in case of missing sales goals were commonplace.[12]

Wells Fargo's cut-throat sales culture tied compensation to hitting unattainable targets. Moreover, employees were only rewarded by their ability to meet sales targets without considering how those goals were met.[13] Because they could not keep up with these goals, many simply started creating fictitious accounts and credit cards on behalf of their customers.

In an amazing demonstration of the power of a toxic culture, this behavior has become widely disseminated in the organization: the bank disclosed in 2016 that no less than 5,300 employees from 6,000 branches opened about 1.5 million unauthorized deposit accounts as well as falsified 565,000 credit card applications over several years.[14]

The Virtuous Barrel:
How to Transform Corporate Scandals into Good Businesses via Behavioral Ethics

In August 2017, an outside review commissioned by the bank found an additional 1.4 million unauthorized accounts, boosting fake-accounts estimate to staggering 3 million.[15]

In April 2017, Wells Fargo's board of directors published the results of an independent investigation based on interviews with more than 100 former and current employees and on the analysis of more than 35 million documents.[16] The report identified the bank's sales incentives programs and performance management measures as the primary drivers of the wrongdoings. According to the document, "The root cause of sales practice failures was the distortion of the bank's sales culture and performance management system, which, when combined with aggressive sales management, created pressure on employees to sell unwanted or unneeded products to customers and, in some cases, to open unauthorized accounts." Concerning the bank's leadership, the investigation also concluded that "The senior leadership of the bank failed to appreciate that their sales goals were too high and becoming increasingly untenable. Over time, even as senior regional leaders criticized the increasingly unrealistic sales goals, the bank's senior management tolerated it as a necessary by-product of a sales-driven organization."

It is also worth mentioning the revelation of another major ethical breach at Wells Fargo after its scandal emerged. A study concluded that, while female financial advisers were less likely than their male counterparts to engage in misconduct, the bank regularly punished female employees more harshly than its male advisers. Specifically, the authors found that female financial planners at Wells Fargo were 27% more likely to experience a "job separation" following unethical behavior relative to male advisers.[17]

At the end, Wells Fargo fired its then-chairman and CEO along with 5,300 employees, entered into a $185 million settlement with federal regulators, and committed to completely change its culture and incentive system by eliminating sales goals for retail bankers as well as redesigning branch-level incentives to emphasize customer experience.[18]

Another relevant case linking ethical problems to unrealistic goals took place at the Brazilian branch of Santander, a Spanish bank. In March 2017, prosecutors filed a public civil suit against the financial institution asking for a compensation of BRL460 million (around $150 million) for collective moral damages. According to the investigators, the bank has adopted an organizational model based on stressful management and moral harassment aimed at reaching excessively high financial goals.[19] In their view, these practices harmed employees' health and ended up in losses to the public treasury. Specifically, the prosecutors estimate that sick leaves of people who fell ill due to the bank's management system have cost around $30 million to the government's social security system.[20]

According to the lawsuit, Santander adopts overly high targets that are constantly increased as well as keeps employees under threat of dismissal in the case of not meeting the goals. This, in turn, would have also harmed consumers – who would eventually have ended up being victims of "compulsory" cross-sales or other illegal practices.[21] In order to validate their claim, public prosecutors carried out a survey with employees from several Santander branches. In one of the branches, for example, 88% of the employees said they were subject to unrealistic productivity targets, 77% reported that those who do not meet the targets have been threatened with dismissal, 66% felt under excessive pressure and were intimidated by their managers for hitting the numbers, 55% said that trying to meet their goals was harming their health and social life, and 100% reported feeling anxious about their work as well as felt constantly nervous, tense, and worried.

The more ambitious the goals, therefore, the greater the likelihood of misconduct. This is particularly dangerous when employees receive ambiguous messages from the organization, such as "I want you to reach your goals at any cost" and "I want you to always act according to our code of ethics." When these messages conflict, reaching the goals tends to prevail, even if through questionable behaviors. Thus, it is essential for leaders to clearly signal to employees the real priority of the organization.

The Virtuous Barrel:
How to Transform Corporate Scandals into Good Businesses via Behavioral Ethics

Another problem related to the incentive system arises when an organization establishes unidimensional goals solely based on meeting specific financial indicators, such as a certain return on investment, sales margin, revenues growth, etc. Having only a specific number to reach induces individuals to a sort of "tunnel vision" which, in turn, tends to make them insensitive to the ethical implications of their actions.[22] As summarized via research on corporate corruption, "The exclusive focus on financial results is an important characteristic of unethical cultures."[23]

A good example comes from oil company OGX, one of the six companies listed on the stock exchange belonging to the extinct empire of Brazilian mega-entrepreneur Eike Batista (in 2011, Mr. Batista became the seventh richest person in the world with a fortune of $30 billion). Around 90% of OGX executives' total compensation was linked to the company's stock price, a speculative indicator by definition.[24] Correspondingly, instead of focusing on managing the company, its executives directed their efforts toward managing market expectations to maximize their earnings. Obviously, this had also become an invitation to unethical behaviors. Afterward, regulators uncovered that bad news about the company were omitted while executives sold their stocks at inflated prices.[25] In addition, managers used to disclose exaggerated projections of future oil revenues for the sake of exercising their stock option plans.[26] In the end, although the oil company collapsed in 2013 without generating any economic value throughout its history, dozens of its top executives pocketed millions of dollars during the brief period in which its stocks remained artificially high. To put a figure on it, at least 10 senior executives of OGX pocketed between $35 million and $100 million, while dozens of others received between $1 million and $35 million.[27]

In a unidimensional incentive system, therefore, individuals tend to only focus on the specific indicator ("the number") they should meet to be well assessed. This, in turn, is likely to lead them losing sight of the whole.[28] Unconsciously, the end starts to justify the means, and executives begin to tell themselves something like: "My role is just to hit that number; everything that does not relate to my goal is off my radar."[29]

A 2016 survey of 2,825 executives from 62 countries corroborates this claim by finding that 42% of respondents would justify unethical behaviors to meet financial targets.[30] This was also the conclusion of a study based on interviews with experts who had first-hand contact with employees of fraudulent organizations. According to the authors, corrupt companies share an underlying assumption that the end justifies the means manifested by the value of "results orientation." This exclusive focus on outcomes is disconnected from ethical values and tends to enable employees to facilitate corruption.[31] The focus on outcomes also has two practical consequences. The first is that, in the process of rationalization, employees fail to question organizational or work goals. The second is that it undermines employees' moral standards, allowing them to engage in corruption without feeling guilty. As one interviewee pointed out, "Well, I have to reach these results, and nobody is interested in how I do it; it is just important that I reach them."[32]

The singular focus on hitting financial targets, a prevalent practice today in most companies, is a result of the old "carrot and stick" mentality. This obsolete mindset assumes that the only thing that motivates human beings is a monetary reward. Recent research, however, demonstrates that our most powerful source of incentive comes from intrinsic motivation, which is the natural tendency to seek to expand our skills and to look for challenging situations because of our own volition – not to fulfill social obligations or to obtain some external reward. According to this literature, intrinsic motivation is increased when we feel we have greater autonomy (the ability to be self-directed), mastery (the ability to become increasingly competent in something), and purpose (the sense of doing something meaningful aligned with the common good) in the workplace.[33]

Several studies have also shown that the excessive emphasis on extrinsic motivators, such as bonuses, rewards, and other monetary incentives, destroys people's intrinsic motivation. This "crowding-out effect"[34] occurs because the work starts to be perceived as something inherently bad, which always requires a reward.

The Virtuous Barrel:
How to Transform Corporate Scandals into Good Businesses via Behavioral Ethics

So, although well-intentioned, simplistic incentive systems based on one-dimensional goals can often produce negative side-effects, including poorer performance and more unethical deeds. It is crucial, therefore, to reflect on how people will respond to the incentives created. Ideally, business leaders should design a system with multiple and achievable goals in which people actively participate in setting their own goals.

Excessive internal competition reinforced by a "winner-takes-all" performance evaluation system

"To the winner, the potatoes!"
Machado de Assis (1869–1904)[35]

Another common practice in many companies nowadays is to foster huge internal competition among employees. For advocates of this idea, the pursuit of the best individual outcome would lead to the survival of the fittest and the maximum economic efficiency for the company, emulating Adam Smith's famous "invisible hand" for the economy.

Evidence shows, however, that fostering excessive internal competition can lead to poorer performance as well as to increased unethical behavior, particularly when it elicits fear and anxiety.[36] In the case of Wells Fargo, for example, the bank created a competitive atmosphere by frequently ranking the performance of individuals, branches, and regions. As shown by Azish Filabi and Bharathy Premachandra, authors of a report about the scandal, these rankings circulated bank-wide, creating significant pressure to outperform peers and shaming of those who fell short. In their view, "For many, this meant that selling more than your colleagues was a prerogative and failing to do so meant penalization, transfer and even termination."[37]

In the academic arena, a recent experiment entitled "Does Competition Enhance Performance or Cheating?" told volunteers they would participate in a game with two distinct modalities: a "competitive" treatment, where individuals had to compete against each other for payment and only one person in each six-member group got paid, and a "noncompetitive" condition, where payment depended only on the individual's own performance.[38] In the competitive situation, researchers observed that individuals cheated more, particularly those who were less capable of solving the task at hand. Thus, instead of getting participants to improve their performance to maximize earnings, the competitive situation simply encouraged them to cheat on others. Worse still, participants' overall performance in the competitive treatment was actually slightly inferior than in the noncompetitive condition.

In the business world, encouraging excessive competition through "carrots" such as status, promotions, or compensation has often been an invitation to poor long-term performance or wrongdoings. The box below details the case of Sears, a US retail firm, as one of the clearest examples of the pernicious consequences when internal competition is pushed to the detriment of internal cohesion among employees.[39]

> *The Sears case: The problems of a culture that emphasizes internal competition*
>
> *Based on Bloomberg Businessweek "At Sears, Eddie Lampert's Warring Division Models Adds to the Troubles," and The New York Times "The Incredible Shrinking Sears" articles.*
>
> *Every year, the presidents of Sears business units make a pilgrimage to the company headquarters in Chicago. There, they ask Eddie Lampert, its CEO and chairman of the board, for money. (Having started his career on the risk arbitrage desk at Goldman Sachs, Mr. Lampert is now a reclusive hedge fund manager living in a $38 million mansion in Florida.)*
>
> *Because he doesn't like to fly, Mr. Lampert attends these meetings via videoconference from his home. He leads from afar and reportedly sets foot at Sears headquarters no more than twice a year, seldom meeting personally with executives.*
>
> *Mr. Lampert acquired ownership control of Sears in 2005 through a buyout in which he ended up with 55% of its shares. Since 2008, he separated Sears into 30 business units. Each has its own CEO, board of directors, and financial statements. In practice, the company has been transformed into a set of autonomous silos competing for revenues and resources. (A similar strategy is used at some hedge funds, where different teams compete with one another for scarce resources.)*

The Virtuous Barrel:
How to Transform Corporate Scandals into Good Businesses via Behavioral Ethics

Mr. Lampert believes that his model, based on extreme internal competition, will generate the best outcome for Sears: "If the company's leaders act selfishly, they would run their divisions in a rational manner, boosting overall performance."

In practice, however, this management model has been extremely harmful. The company has been ravaged by infighting, as divisions fiercely battle for everything from scarce financial resources to space in stores.

One former executive described, for example, that managers would tell their sales staff not to help customers in adjacent sections, even if someone asked for help. Another executive, interviewed by Bloomberg, said that the model has created a "warring tribes" culture: "If you are in a different business unit, then we are in two competing companies ... Cooperation and collaboration do not exist there."

Lampert's model, which privileges people who act selfishly, has created rival factions, with negative impacts for Sears. Each unit has started to think only of its profit, failing to consider the collective outcome for the company. "Turf wars sprang up over store displays. No one is willing to make sacrifices such as reducing prices to boost store traffic (which would benefit other divisions)."

Internal competition has reached such a degree that executives started bringing laptops with screen protectors to meetings, so their colleagues couldn't see what they were doing.

Until earlier 2018, Lampert's management model proved to be disastrous. Since acquiring control of the company 13 years earlier, Sears' revenues dropped from $49 billion to around $20 billion. 175,000 people lost their jobs. The company's cash reached the lowest level in 20 years. Less than 1% of revenue has been allocated to investments, a ratio up to four times lower than the average among industry peers. Stocks plummeted an incredible 97%, from around $115 in June 2005 to a paltry $3.6 in January 2018. Its market capitalization collapsed accordingly, from $15 billion to less than a quarter of a billion ($226 million).

The prospects are also not good. As exemplified by the selling of 266 properties for $3 billion in 2015 (now having to pay rent on real estates it once owned), Sears has been kept afloat largely by putting up for sale its most valuable assets. As a result, as The New York Times pointed out at the end of 2017, "Sears is now on analysts' short list of most-likely-to-go-bankrupt retailers."

The Sears case demonstrates the dangers of a management style that encourages internal competition to the detriment of cohesion and cooperation. In addition to creating a paranoid environment in which people prioritize their short-term personal agendas, a culture of aggressiveness incites arrogance and pride, thus increasing the chance of unethical behaviors.

Another practice leading to excessive internal competition is the implementation of an evaluation system that categorizes employees as "successful" or "failed." This "winner-takes-all" arrangement in which individuals ranked as top performers are disproportionately rewarded, and those considered low performers are weeded out or ostracized, is dangerous, as it creates a toxic atmosphere of struggle for survival in which the success of a colleague often means your own individual failure.

One of the most striking examples of the pernicious effects of such a Darwinian environment comes from Enron, the US energy company that went bankrupt in 2001 and is still considered the most iconic corporate governance scandal in history. Its performance evaluation system, called performance review committee (PRC), is detailed below.[40]

> *The Enron Case: A performance evaluation system that promotes a Darwinian environment*
>
> *Based on McLean and Elkind's (2004) book The Smartest Guys in the Room: The Amazing Rise and Scandalous Fall of Enron*
>
> *Enron CEO Jeffrey Skilling had a Darwinian view of life and how the world worked. For him, money was the only thing that motivated people. At Enron, Skilling implemented a performance evaluation system called the performance review committee (PRC). This system aimed at releasing what he believed to be people's natural instinct for the "survival of the fittest."*
>
> *The PRC established that individuals were annually graded from 1 to 5 based on the opinion of all the people they worked with (a 360-degree assessment). At the end of this harsh one-day process, the 10% to 15% individuals with the worst ratings (the low-performers) were required to be fired, while the top 10% received millionaire bonuses (the company used to*

The Virtuous Barrel:
How to Transform Corporate Scandals into Good Businesses via Behavioral Ethics

> *buy several Ferraris that were given to the best assessed as part of their award).*
>
> *Skilling used to say that this brutal method of "ranking and yanking" was Enron's "main internal process." The CEO also recognized that the company's culture was rough and aggressive.*
>
> *In an interview, an Enron trader proudly stated that "If I'm on the way to my boss's office to talk about my compensation and if I have to step on somebody's throat on the way to double it? Well, I would stomp on the guy's throat. You know that, that's how people are here."*
>
> *In addition to stimulating all kinds of unethical behavior, the PRC became a flawed process. Aiming to be well-assessed, many executives began making deals with colleagues to get good grades and to jointly assign bad grades to teammates they disliked. Other managers, in turn, started to produce fictitious profits. It was worth everything not to be considered a "failure" in this system.*
>
> *Instead of fostering meritocracy, therefore, Enron's PRC created a politicized workplace with excessive internal competition, bordering on paranoia in some divisions. Enron's outcome is known by everyone: The company went bankrupt in 2001 after disclosing numerous illegal operations to inflate earnings for the sake of enabling its executives pocketing millions in stock-option plans.*

Enron's PRC is a perfect example of the problems generated by Darwinian evaluation systems. To begin with, these systems usually fail to create a meritocratic environment. In fact, the opposite is often true: Because the results (for better or worse) of these one-off evaluation events are seen as decisive for everyone's career, these systems tend to create a highly politicized workplace.

In addition, these winner-takes-all schemes create an internal atmosphere primarily characterized by fear and terrorism. To survive in this environment and not be considered a "loser," people are induced to behave in ways that are extremely harmful to a company, such as obeying any requests from superiors without question, acting in conformity with the rest of the organization (even when they do not agree with certain practices), and being silent about ethical problems they see on a daily basis. This has been well summarized by Professor David Mayer of University of Michigan who argued that "If you let a winner-take-all mentality dominate your culture, it's amazing what people become comfortable with in the name of competition."[41]

This outcome is particularly true for less competent executives. Because they know they will have a very small chance of succeeding by sticking to the rules, it is more likely that these individuals will be dishonest with colleagues, customers, and other stakeholders in order to avoid a "certain loss." A recent research corroborates this assertion. After conducting an experiment in which participants could make use of illegitimate tools to improve their results, researchers concluded that "Poor performers significantly increase their cheating behavior under competition, which may be a face-saving strategy or an attempt to retain a chance of winning."[42]

Despite producing serious side effects, Enron's PRC is still a source of inspiration for many corporations. One example comes from the financial industry. After interviewing about 200 finance executives from the City of London, investigative journalist Joris Luyendijk observed that "Every year, prestigious top banks fire the worst-performing staff – no matter how much profit was made. It is called 'the cull,' the same term used when infected cattle have to be destroyed. Every six months everybody gets to evaluate their colleagues' performance in 360-degree reviews."[43] The author also notes that "A system like this makes office politics very important. You need to say hello to the right people at the right time. Team members are also in competition for a better ranking in the review. As you would expect, friends will give friends good reviews."[44]

Another example comes from Amazon, the world's largest online retailer. In 2015, *The New York Times* talked to more than 100 of the company's past and current executives to draw a picture of its culture.[45] One of the company's practices is the "anytime feedback tool," an appliance that allows employees to praise or criticize colleagues directly to management. All team members are ranked, and those who stay in the bottom should be fired every year. This evaluation system has created a perverse incentive. According to the article, many executives said the device has become a space for intrigue and scheming. Some described making secret pacts with colleagues to bury

The Virtuous Barrel:
How to Transform Corporate Scandals into Good Businesses via Behavioral Ethics

the same person at once or to praise one another lavishly. Others, in turn, declared feeling sabotaged by negative comments from unidentified colleagues with whom they could not defend themselves.

During Amazon's annual performance evaluation event, company managers said they were often forced to fire talented people in order to meet quotas established by the forced ranking system. One of the strategies adopted, according to the interviewees, was to choose a "sacrificial lamb" in order to protect more essential team members from dismissal. As one former marketing manager at Amazon reported: "You learn how to diplomatically throw people under the bus … It's a horrible feeling."

Instead of a winner-takes-all Darwinist system, leaders should focus on creating a culture that emphasizes solidarity, trust, cohesion, and cooperation among all employees.[46] This is what creates long-term value for companies and makes them more productive, with lasting positive effects for society. This view is corroborated by numerous scientific evidences showing that the ability to cooperate is the key factor for the evolutionary success of all kinds of human groupings (such as companies) and even of whole species such as ours.[47] As attested by a group of experts in organizational behavior, "Designing systems to promote ethical behavior requires more than attending to the treatment of individuals in organizations. It may also require behaviors that appeal to our evolved tendency to lose ourselves in the process of sustaining a moral community capable of acting together as one."[48]

One of the leading references in this area of organizational behavior is Adam Grant, professor at Wharton University.[49] His research with over 30,000 people across industries around different world cultures has shown that people can be classified into three groups: "givers," "matchers," and "takers." The first group collaborates with others without expecting immediate retribution ("what can I do for you?"). The second group is pragmatic and seeks to maintain an even balance between giving and taking ("what can one do for the other?"). The third group, in turn, is completely self-serving in its social interactions ("what can you do for me?").[50]

After carrying out 38 studies with more than 3,600 work units worldwide, Grant observed that "givers" tend to appear more frequently among worst performers. This occurs because they spend a good deal of time helping others, which ultimately gives them less time to stand out individually. Collectively, though, "givers" are essential because their personal sacrifice makes their organization better. According to Grant, there is a clear relationship between the frequency of giving behavior in a team or an organization and better performance in various metrics such as profitability, customer satisfaction, employee retention, and even lower operating expenses.[51]

Implementing winner-takes-all performance evaluation systems fosters an environment of greater individualism, which harms the "givers" and benefits the "takers" of the organization. The key to business success, according to Grant, is exactly the opposite: to create a culture where collaboration is the norm, "takers" are eliminated, and "givers" can thrive.[52] He argues that most organizations go in the wrong direction with respect to incentive systems because "the greatest untapped source of motivation is a sense of service to others; focusing on the contribution of our work to other people's lives has the potential to make us more productive than thinking about helping ourselves."[53]

Language full of euphemisms or analogies of war or games

> *"Don't you see that the whole aim of Newspeak is*
> *to narrow the range of thought?"*
> George Orwell (1903–1950)[54]

One of the main recent conclusions of cognitive sciences is that the vocabulary we use not only reveals but also influences our world view and the way we behave. As a result, the third element associated with the organizational context that can propel unethical action is the least observed of all, i.e., the language that permeates an organization.[55]

The power of language over our decisions was demonstrated in an experiment in which researchers followed the reactions of two groups.[56] One group was told they would participate in the "Wall Street Game," while for the other the exercise was labeled the

The Virtuous Barrel:
How to Transform Corporate Scandals into Good Businesses via Behavioral Ethics

"Community Game." The two activities were identical: They involved the familiar prisoner's dilemma in which participants must decide whether to "cooperate" or "defect." Although the exercise was similar, the results for the two groups were completely different. While about 70% of those selected for the "Wall Street Game" adopted a selfish stance, around two-thirds of the participants in the "Community Game" chose cooperation.[57]

For the corporate world, this result shows that the language used by business leaders can shape the cultural values of their organizations and, consequently, influence employee behaviors. According to Guido Palazzo and Ulrich Hoffrage, professors at the University of Lausanne, three kinds of language usually employed at many companies are particularly dangerous from the ethical standpoint.[58]

The first is the frequent use of euphemisms. In the famous corruption scandal involving Siemens in the past decade, bribes were referred to as "NA," a German abbreviation for "*nützliche aufwendungen*" (meaning "useful money"), while the middlemen used to graft government officials to secure contracts were named "business consultants."[59] Enron described the millions of dollars paid as bribes in India as "funds to educate Indians."[60] HSBC referred to a huge fine of $1.9 billion for drug money laundering as "regulatory and law enforcement matters."[61] Some large global financial institutions labeled pending fines for recent scandals as "legacy issues" requiring "customer redress."[62] In Brazil's Operation Car Wash, the construction company Odebrecht even created a specific department for paying bribes, called the "Structured Operations Division."[63]

In other cases, fraudulent practices are called "creative accounting" or "financial engineering"; customer abuse becomes "mis-selling"; evading taxes becomes "tax optimization with tax-efficient structures"; firing people to improve the bottom line becomes "making the organization lean" or "downsizing"; environmental pollution is named "issuing externalities," and so on.[64] In the case of the financial industry, this was summarized in the book *Swimming with Sharks* based on hundreds of interviews with

London-based bankers: "The vocabulary available to people in finance is stripped of terms that could provoke an ethical discussion. Hence the biggest compliment in the City is 'professional.' It means moral beliefs are for home."[65]

By mitigating the feeling that wrong things are being made, euphemistic labeling tends to normalize and legitimize unethical behaviors, which send a powerful subliminal message to employees akin to "to the extent that you can disguise your unethical deeds, we will accept them and even implicitly encourage them."

The other types of dangerous vocabulary from the ethical standpoint are the frequent use of metaphors of war or gaming. Both create narrow perspectives of reality, making it more difficult for people to notice the consequence of their actions on other people.

One study based on views of experienced experts on corrupt organizations, for instance, concluded that people working at these firms usually perceive themselves to be fighting in a war.[66] Half of the interviewees quoted war metaphors to describe work circumstances in corrupt organizations, including comments such as "People at my company are soldiers" and "We have to kill to eat ... when you are in the middle of the battle, you are trying to defeat the enemy." The authors concluded that "Corrupt organizations perceive themselves as a military force rather than as an ordinary company" and that its employees "See competing organizations as enemies that need to be defeated to secure the continuity of their own company."[67]

Interviews carried out by another research also noted that global banks make abundant use of militaristic terms: A lucrative deal is described in the market as "rape and pillage," a team working for months on a deal is called a "special forces unit," and bankers used to say that in the world of finance it is "have lunch or be lunch."[68] Guido Palazzo and Ulrich Hoffrage offer additional examples of these risky vocabularies by using the case of Lehman Brothers, the US investment bank that collapsed in 2008.[69] The institution adopted a war language full of testosterone. Its employees used to say that the bank was run by a "junta of platoon officers" where traders were daily dispatched to the

The Virtuous Barrel:
How to Transform Corporate Scandals into Good Businesses via Behavioral Ethics

"frontline of a war zone" spending most of the time "in combat" firing their "financial cannons."

The militaristic jargon loads the environment with stress, pressure, and fear. From the ethical perspective, it is dangerous because it conveys a tacit message that the rules of "peacetime" are no longer valid and that the company is in an extreme situation where everything is allowed to survive. Everyone outside the organization is perceived as an enemy, and those inside start to believe they were allowed to do anything to "win" and even that this is their duty because they are supposedly in a "kill or die" situation.

Gaming metaphors were also common at Lehman Brothers. Traders liked to say they were in the "mortgage game," that the market was a "big casino" and that it was necessary to have the "instinct of a gambler." By comparing the environment in which they worked to a game, they created the illusion of acting in an artificial universe where there were no real consequences of potential losses. That is, they acted as if they were inside a big videogame disconnected from reality in which they could not seriously harm "flesh and bone" people, such as retirees of the pension funds who were among their main clients.

Abuse of euphemisms or metaphors of war or games, therefore, is not a good sign. They alter employees' perceptions and, consequently, their work attitudes. For business leaders, the message is clear: If the organization changes the way people communicate, it also changes the way its members think and work. This applies not only for bad behaviors, as in the cases presented, but also potentially for good outcomes.

---

[1] Source: Albert Einstein, "Religion and Science," New York Times Magazine, 9/11/1930.
[2] Source: Soltes (2016: 272). Steven Hoffenberg was the former chairman and CEO of Towers Financial Corporation, a factoring company who became one of the largest Ponzi schemes in history. In 1997, he was sentenced to 20 years in prison for defrauding around $475 million of thousands of investors.

³ Barsky (2008) developed a conceptual model explaining how setting performance goals can induce unethical behavior. In addition, Ordoñez et. al (2009) reviewed the downsides of goal-setting. The authors drew a parallel between goal-setting and prescription strength medications. They say that, if overprescribed, goal-setting can lead to serious side-effects, including a "narrow focus that neglects non-goal areas, a rise in unethical behavior, distorted risk preferences, corrosion of organizational culture, and reduced intrinsic motivation".

⁴ Poortvliet and Darnon (2010).

⁵ Schweitzer et al. (2004).

⁶ Welsh e Ordóñez (2014).

⁷ *Ibid*: 86. Actually, there is scientific evidence that the mere fact of imposing performance goals on employees is enough to negatively affect their moral standards and increase the propensity for unethical behavior. As an example, Schweitzer et al. (2004) show how an easy-to-reach goal without any pecuniary reward proved sufficient to increase the dishonesty of participants in an experiment, compared to a situation in which individuals were only encouraged to "do their best".

⁸ Barron's 2015 ranking: https://www.barrons.com/articles/apple-tops-barrons-list-of-respected-companies-1435372737; Fortune's 2015 ranking http://fortune.com/worlds-most-admired-companies/2015/wells-fargo-22/

⁹ Under pressure: Wells Fargo, misconduct, leadership and culture. January 2018. By Bharathy Premachandra and Azish Filabi. Available at http://www.ethicalsystems.org/content/under-pressure-wells-fargo-misconduct-leadership-and-culture

¹⁰ Darden Ideas to Action. Wells Fargo and the Public's Withdrawal of Trust. 06/09/2017. By Luann J. Lynch and Carlos Santos. Available at https://ideas.darden.virginia.edu/2017/06/wells-fargo-and-the-publics-withdrawal-of-trust/

¹¹ *Ibid.*

¹² Under pressure: Wells Fargo, misconduct, leadership and culture. January 2018. By Bharathy Premachandra and Azish Filabi.

¹³ *Ibid.*

¹⁴ Actually, as pointed out by Bharathy Premachandra and Azish Filabi, the fraudulent practices were first brought to the attention of Wells Fargo's senior management back in 2011. However, they were systematically downplayed as minor isolated incidents caused by a few bad apples. Thus, leadership (consciously or unconsciously) opted to remain in denial. Source: Under pressure: Wells Fargo, misconduct, leadership and culture. January 2018. By Bharathy Premachandra and Azish Filabi.

¹⁵ Bloomberg. Wells Fargo Boosts Fake-Account Estimate 67% to 3.5 Million. 08/31/2017. Available at https://www.bloomberg.com/news/articles/2017-08-31/wells-fargo-increases-fake-account-estimate-67-to-3-5-million

¹⁶ Independent Directors of the Board of Wells Fargo & Company Sales Practices Investigation Report. 04/10/2017. Available at https://www08.wellsfargomedia.com/assets/pdf/about/investor-relations/presentations/2017/board-report.pdf

¹⁷ Egan et al. (2017).

¹⁸ The New York Times. 09/16/2016. Wells Fargo Scandal May Be Sign of a Poisonous Culture. Available at https://nyti.ms/2kjjqhK. It is worth noting, though, that less than a year later another crisis emerged at the bank. This time, an internal report disclosed that more than 800,000 people who took out car loans from Wells Fargo were charged for auto insurance they did not need, and some of them were still paying for it at the time of the announcement. The expense of the unneeded insurance, in turn, pushed roughly 274,000 customers into delinquency and resulted in almost 25,000 wrongful vehicle repossessions. Source: The New York Times. 07/27/2017. Wells

The Virtuous Barrel:
How to Transform Corporate Scandals into Good Businesses via Behavioral Ethics

Fargo Forced Unwanted Auto Insurance on Borrowers. Available at https://nyti.ms/2h7Boak

[19] ACP-0000342-81.2017.5.10.0011, 3ª Vara do Trabalho de Brasília – DF. The lawsuit can be accessed at https://pje.trt10.jus.br/consultaprocessual/pages/consultas/ConsultaProcessual.seam

[20] A survey of pension benefits granted to Santander's employees showed that payments due to mental disorders corresponded to 37.3% of the bank's total paid benefits in 2015. Source: MPT Notícias. 04/11/2017. Santander processado em R$460 mi por assédio e estresse. Available at http://portal.mpt.mp.br/

[21] UOL Notícias, blog do Sakamoto. 04/07/2017. Por lucrar com estresse de bancários, Santander é processado em R$460 mi. Available at https://blogdosakamoto.blogosfera.uol.com.br/2017/04/07/por-lucrar-com-estresse-de-bancarios-santander-e-processado-em-r-460-mi/ .

[22] The tunnel vision metaphor can be understood as follows: by focusing only on our specific goals, we begin to look only at the light at the end of the tunnel. All the rest, including the ethical consequences of our decisions, becomes dark and irrelevant.

[23] Campbell and Göritz (2014: 309).

[24] According to Leo (2014: 207), each C-level officer at OGX earned an average of BRL1 million in salary plus BRL9 million in company stocks in 2010.

[25] According to Cuadros (2016: 46-47, 215), some OGX executives even sold shares from their stock option plans (that could only be exercised in a future date) with a large discount to an investment bank in order to pocket some money as quickly as possible. Still according to the author, when the investment bank realized the despair of the executives to sell their shares at a big discount, one of its funds set up a large short position in OGX shares, which allowed the institution to make a huge profit.

[26] Leo (2014: 207-208).

[27] Ironically, the chief of investor relations (CIRO) left OGX shortly before the most important announcement of its history: in June 2012, the company finally disclosed that its oil reserves were much smaller than expected. He sold his shares two months earlier, pocketing $60 million during his five years tenure at the company. Source: Revista Exame. 03/19/2014. Todos os homens de Eike. Available at http://exame.abril.com.br/revista-exame/edicoes/1061/noticias/todos-os-homens-de-eike

[28] According to Barsky (2008), unidimensional goals can increase unethical behavior by leading individuals to concentrate their mental resources on goal attainment rather than on moral standards. Consequently, their narrowed focus can lead them to experience lower levels of moral awareness.

[29] It is worth mentioning that evaluating people solely based on the meeting certain indicators can also induce them to the so-called "incentive gaming," a practice of manipulation of indicators.

[30] EY Global Fraud Survey 2016. Available at http://www.ey.com/Publication/vwLUAssets/ey-global-fraud-survey-2016/$FILE/ey-global-fraud-survey-final.pdf

[31] Campbell and Göritz (2014: 303). In addition, the authors report that the value "results orientation" connects to other important values such as "success" and "need for security". Their overall conclusion is that the underlying

assumption ''the end justifies the means'' is the key characteristic of a corrupt organizational culture.

[32] *Ibid*: 302.

[33] Many books compile scientific evidence of the critical importance of fostering intrinsic motivation, including Pink (2011), Thomas (2009), Sansone and Harackiewicz (2000), and Deci and Ryan (1985).

[34] Frey and Jegen (2001) developed the first theory on the crowding-out of intrinsic motivation. For more information on this, see Ryan and Decy (2000a), Ryan and Decy (2000b), and Frey (1994).
[35] Source: Quincas Borba, Capítulo VI. 1891.
[36] Steinhage et al. (2015).
[37] Under pressure: Wells Fargo, misconduct, leadership and culture. January 2018. By Bharathy Premachandra and Azish Filabi. Page 9.
[38] Schwieren and Weichselbaumer (2010).
[39] Information on Sears case was taken from: Bloomberg Businessweek. 7/11/2013. At Sears, Eddie Lampert's Warring Division Models Adds to the Troubles. Available at http://www.businessweek.com/articles/2013-07-11/at-sears-eddie-lamper:s-warring-divisions-model-adds-to-the-troubles; and, The New York Times. 08/11/2017. The Incredible Shrinking Sears. Available at https://nyti.ms/2uOeTsH
[40] Information on Enron's PRC system come from McLean and Elkind (2004) book.
[41] The Building Blocks of Business Ethics. 8/10/2015. Available at https://michiganross.umich.edu/alumni/dividend/fall2015/building-blocks-business-ethics .
[42] Schwieren and Weichselbaumer (2010: 241).
[43] Luyendijk (2015: 88).
[44] *Ibid*: 89.
[45] The New York Times. 8/15/2015. Inside Amazon: Wrestling Big Ideas in a Bruising Workplace. Available at https://nyti.ms/2k1fqlS
[46] The focus on competition rather than on cooperation stems from a misunderstanding by many business leaders of Darwin's concept of natural selection. Darwin sought to clarify his view on this issue in his book "The Descent of Man" by stating that: "A tribe including many members who, from possessing in a high degree the spirit of patriotism, fidelity, obedience, courage, and sympathy, were always ready to aid one another, and to sacrifice themselves for the common good, would be victorious over most other tribes; and this would be natural selection". Source: Charles Darwin. The Descent of Man, 1871, chapter 5. Available at https://ebooks.adelaide.edu.au/d/darwin/charles/d22d/chapter5.html
[47] These scientific researches are summarized in the books by Nowak (2013), and by Nowak and Highfield (2011). Among the papers finding similar results, stand out Rand and Nowak (2013), Nowak (2006), and Qin et al. (1995).
[48] Kluver et al. (2014: 157).
[49] The next paragraphs were constructed based on Grant's (2013) book as well as on his talk at the TED event "are you a giver or a taker?," available at https://www.ted.com/talks/adam_grant_are_you_a_giver_or_a_taker
[50] After analyzing more than 30,000 people around the world, Grant found that 19% of people are "givers," 25% "takers," and 56% "matchers". It is also worth noting that psychopaths are necessarily "takers," although not all "takers" are necessarily psychopaths.
[51] The researcher also found that "givers" exhibit greater variability of individual performance, being more frequent among the individuals with better performance.
[52] In his research, Grant noted that that the negative impact of a "taker" on a culture is usually double to triple the positive impact of a "giver".
[53] The New York Times. 3/27/2013. Is Giving the Secret to Getting Ahead? Available at http://nyti.ms/10LrYjQ
[54] Orwell, George. (1949). 1984. Chapter 5. Available at https://ebooks.adelaide.edu.au/o/orwell/george/o79n/chapter1.5.html

The Virtuous Barrel:
How to Transform Corporate Scandals into Good Businesses via Behavioral Ethics

[55] Bickerton (2017).

[56] Liberman et al. (2004).

[57] There is evidence that our morality changes just by speaking in a foreign language. A study by Costa et al. (2014) showed, for instance, that people tend to exhibit a more utilitarian and less deontological (principle-based) behavior when subjected to ethical dilemmas in a language that is not the individual's native language. Another paper, by Geipel et al. (2015), showed that people who read stories in a foreign language were much more likely to view certain behaviors as less morally wrong than when they were reading them in their own language. According to the researchers, we operate in a more deliberative and rational way when we speak in a foreign language (using more our "system 2"). This tends to make our moral judgments less loaded with visceral and emotional reactions, leading to a more utilitarian perspective.

[58] Course "Unethical Decision Making," Coursera. Professors Guido Palazzo and Ulrich Hoffrage. Week 3. Available at https://www.coursera.org/learn/unethical-decision-making

[59] The New York Times, 12/20/2008. At Siemens, Bribery Was Just a Line Item. Available at https://nyti.ms/2jE03A6; The Guardian, 9/18/2013. Siemens and the battle against bribery and corruption. Available at https://www.theguardian.com/sustainable-business/siemens-solmssen-bribery-corruption

[60] Center for the Advancement of Public Integrity. (2016). What do Corrupt Firms have in Common? Available at http://www.law.columbia.edu/public-integrity/integrity-brief-series.

[61] Luyendijk (2015: 170).

[62] *Ibid*: 170.

[63] Folha de São Paulo, 22/03/2016. Odebrecht tinha 'departamento' de propina no Brasil, diz Lava Jato. Available at http://www1.folha.uol.com.br/poder/2016/03/1752707-odebrecht-tinha-departamento-de-propina-no-pais-diz-lava-jato.shtml

[64] According to Luyendijk (2015: 89), a senior investment banker from the City of London said that his department colleagues who had suddenly been fired were always referred to as having resigned: 'it sounds better, he said with a shrug'.

[65] Luyendijk (2015: 107).

[66] Campbell and Göritz (2014).

[67] *Ibid*: 299-300. The authors also note (p. 302) that "the perception of war is an external pressure that allows employees to keep their positive image of their organization because the organization apparently needs to win the war to ensure employees' jobs."

[68] Luyendijk (2015: 104).

[69] Course "Unethical Decision Making," Coursera. Professors Guido Palazzo and Ulrich Hoffrage. Week 3. Available at https://www.coursera.org/learn/unethical-decision-making

6. The pressures of the institutional context in which we are embedded

> *"The social universe has no 'natural laws' ... This means that assumptions that were valid yesterday can become invalid and, indeed, totally misleading in no time at all."*
> Peter Drucker (1909–2005)[1]

The third layer of pressures that can affect our ethical behavior comes from the institutional context where individuals and companies are embedded. Before addressing the main aspects related to this macro environment, it is important to make a brief digression to align the concept of "institutional context."

Institutions correspond to the "rules of the game" that permeate our social, political, and economic relations,[2] i.e., what we take for granted in our lives and what is normal for a certain society. Institutions can be formal or informal. Examples of the first group are the codified rules created to govern our relationships, such as the laws. The second, in turn, corresponds to social traditions and norms, including how people interpret and follow the rules.

Understanding the institutions of which we are part of is important because they are the backdrop for our worldview, including our perception of what constitutes appropriate or inappropriate behavior.[3] For example, if a particular institutional environment is too permissive regarding the violation of rules, then it will help to normalize unethical behaviors.

The Virtuous Barrel:
How to Transform Corporate Scandals into Good Businesses via Behavioral Ethics

Three main factors from the institutional environment tend to affect ethical behavior in the corporate world:

- The culture of the country where companies and individuals are ingrained;
- The dogmas of executive education that shape managers' worldview; and,
- The behavior of industry peers.

Culture of the country

The culture of the country where one is raised may affect his or her perception of morality and, consequently, ethical behavior. It is quite intuitive to assume, for example, that the same company with offices in Colombia, France, South Africa, and Japan can be subject to different levels of employee compliance to its policies.

There is scientific evidence supporting the assertion that people living in environments more conducive to corruption tend to disrespect the rules more frequently.[4] Researchers Raymond Fisman and Edward Miguel conducted one of the most interesting studies in this area.[5] They analyzed parking ticket violations committed by 1,700 UN diplomats from 149 countries between 1997 and 2002. During that period, these authorities knew in advance that all parking tickets would be waived because of their diplomatic immunity. Many seem to have taken advantage of this exemption because diplomats received a total of 150,000 fines during the five years under analysis.

The key result of the study was quite intuitive: Diplomats from more corrupt nations received far more fines than those from less corrupt nations.[6] At the top of the list were Kuwait, Egypt, Chad, and Sudan. Every diplomat from Kuwait, for instance, received an average of 246 parking tickets. At the other end were countries such as Japan, Norway, Sweden, and Canada. Diplomats from these countries did not receive a single fine over the five-year period, even knowing beforehand that their parking violations would be waived.[7]

Another study with similar results was published in 2015.[8] In partnership with the US International Revenue Service, the researchers analyzed 25,000 corporate tax audits for over 10 years. The researchers found that foreign-controlled companies whose owners have come from countries with higher corruption norms evade more taxes in the United States.[9] The authors also analyzed the behavior of US-based firms after the implementation of several enforcement measures in the mid-2000s designed to increase tax compliance. Remarkably, they noted that these enforcement efforts were less effective in reducing tax evasion by companies whose owners were from corrupt countries. According to the authors, their results present a real challenge to regulators because they show that firms subject to higher corruption norms are less likely to respond to increased enforcement of the rules.

The idea that people coming from more corrupt environments tend to be more prone to unethical actions has also been corroborated by experiments conducted across multiple countries. One of these studies was published by researchers Abigail Barr and Danila Serra.[10] After carrying out experiments with 195 students from 34 different countries, they observed a strong positive correlation between the level of corruption in the country where undergraduate students grew up (measured by Transparency International) and their level of cheating in a bribery game.[11] The study corroborates the view that the persistence of corruption can be seen as a result of an institutional logic more prominent in some countries that reinforces certain patterns of behavior considered as expected and normal.

In 2016, a paper published at journal *Nature* corroborated this view. In this research, Simon Gächter and Jonathan F. Schulz asked 2,568 young volunteers from 23 countries to take part in a very simple game. They should roll a die twice and report the result of the first roll. They got $1 if they reported a one; $2 if they reported two; and so on, up to five. However, if they reported a six, they would not earn anything. Researchers could not see the true results and paid volunteers based on what they said. If all participants were honest, then the average claim would be $2.5. If everyone was dishonest, then all would have claimed $5. They also developed an index of the "prevalence of rule violations" (PRV) based on country-level data on corruption, tax evasion, and fraudulent politics. In the end, the authors found that participants living in societies with high PRV had a much better chance of bending the rules of the game to maximize their gain than those living in low PRV countries. As an example, people from high PRV countries demanded an average payment of $3.53, significantly above the average payment of $3.17 for participants from other countries. According to the authors, their findings show that "Corruption and fraud are things going on in the social environment all the time, and it's plausible that it shapes people's psychology, what they can get away with. They begin to tell themselves something like: 'It's okay! Everybody does it around here!'"[12]

The dogmas of executive education

> *"A social discipline such as management deals with the behavior of people and human institutions. Practitioners will therefore tend to act and to behave as the discipline's assumptions tell them to."*
> Peter Drucker (1909–2005)[13]

Institutions create belief systems that drive individuals to follow an established set of practices and interpretations. A very strong belief system, however, has a dark side: It creates unquestioned dogmas or ideologies with no room for criticism or alternative views.

In the business world, several doctrines currently taught at most business schools are like such dogmas. Among them are standout ideas, e.g., markets are efficient ("market prices are always correct!"), individuals should act in a self-interested way to maximize economic well-being ("the invisible hand of the market turns our egoism into a good thing for everyone!"), mergers and acquisitions are positive for society ("they increase companies' efficiency and, as a result, they generate a better result for us all!"), and, that the market is always able to properly self-regulate itself ("the less state regulation and the smaller the size of government, the better for society!").

For the field of business ethics, two ideologies widely diffused by executive education programs tend to foster ethical blindness by promoting amoral behavior, i.e., shareholder value maximization and the concept of *homo economicus*.

The first dogma departs from the premise that the company is a mere financial asset or money-making machine owned by shareholders. As a result, the central mission of executives would supposedly be to maximize stockholder wealth. The second assumes that human beings always act rationally in order to maximize their own personal utility. Accordingly, our only goal in any social interaction or other circumstance would be to achieve the greatest gain for ourselves.

Let's start with shareholder value maximization (SVM). Despite being the most powerful ideology in the business world today, the concept of SVM is relatively recent. This idea was developed in the 1970s based on texts by economists of the so-called Chicago School, most notably Milton Friedman and Michael Jensen. Friedman, for instance, wrote a famous article in which he argued that the moral responsibility of managers is to conduct business in accordance with shareholder predilections, which generally means making as much money as possible.[14]

Because of this view, widespread in the business world after Jack Welch's rise to the helm of GE in 1981, a well-governed and well-managed company came to be seen as one in which the interests of executives and shareholders are aligned to maximize its market value. Consequently, a "good executive" was remodeled into the one who produces the greatest possible financial outcome for shareholders.

In practice, however, the unreflective pursuit of this ideology has serious limitations. A growing literature, based on empirical data, provides compelling evidence that running companies with the aim of maximizing their stock price might lead to severe side effects for all corporate constituencies, including:[15]

- Managerial myopia, with the generation of long-term liabilities to be borne by society;
- Underinvestment, due to the increased "financialization" of companies;[16]

The Virtuous Barrel:
How to Transform Corporate Scandals into Good Businesses via Behavioral Ethics

- Managerial focus on managing market expectations for the sake of maximizing equity-based pay;
- Opportunistic behavior of shareholders seeking short-term gains in mergers and acquisitions;
- Increased income inequality within companies and at the societal level;
- Increased job insecurity, stress, and lack of purpose in the organizational environment;
- Encouragement of amoral behavior and ethical blindness;
- Deterioration of long-term firm performance; and,
- Recurrent production of systemic crises with worst long-term outcomes for capital markets, the environment, and investors.

The collapse of a huge dam in Brazil operated by a company named Samarco, a joint-venture of mining giants BHP Billinton and Vale, is a tragic example of the negative effects following the relentless quest to maximize shareholder returns.[17]

Samarco had built a dam called Fundao in 2008. Soon after its inauguration, the dam began presenting structural flaws that obliged the company to halt its operation for about a year in April 2009. According to the investigation conducted by Brazilian public prosecutors, the company's board of directors opted for a series of "patches" instead of implementing a definitive solution that would require more investments and halt its operation for a longer time. Because these structural problems were never fully resolved, it is very likely that they have aggravated the failures leading to the dam's collapse years later.[18]

In 2013, an independent group composed of renowned consultants in the analysis of dams, called the Independent Tailings Review Board (IRTB), found that the Fundao dam had clear signs that its internal drainage was already insufficient. However, according the prosecutors, "When the rupture occurred, almost two years after the IRTB recommendations, not even the reinforcement of the shoulder drain was complete. And, in the meantime, Samarco's operations continued as usual, including an elevation of the dam so it could receive more mud."[19]

Samarco kept making use of several interim solutions while seeking at the same time to maximize its production. As an example, his board of directors asked the senior management team in 2013 to "increase sales to take advantage of the current favorable market conditions" as well as "to seek maximum efficiency in production bottlenecks."[20]

In April 2014, the board asked the management team to expand the volume of production without increasing costs. In the same meeting, in which there was no record of any discussions about the concerns raised by the IRTB, the board approved the payment of BRL2 billion (around $900 million at the time) in dividends to shareholders. In the words of the public prosecutors who carried out a deep investigation of the case, "Production, profit, dividends, money were more important and urgent."[21]

In August 2014, the engineering team at Samarco discovered several cracks in the dam. An external consultant made several recommendations after finding that the cracks characterized serious signs of a pre-rupture process. In November, the IRTB reinforced its worries, demanding Samarco to prioritize the solutions suggested by the consultant. However, the company did not follow the recommendations and opted instead to keep increasing the volume of waste.[22] In July 2015, just four months before the dam collapsed, Samarco employees detected a number of anomalies related to the dam's stability, including the so-called "upwelling" (a water leakage) at the bottom.[23]

In November 2015, the collapse of Fundao dam finally took place. The 40 million cubic meters tsunami of iron ore and silica waste buried a city called Bento Gonçalves. Nineteen people died and 256 were injured; this included a huge death toll of domestic and wild animals (including endangered species). Lagoons and important rivers, such as the historic Rio Doce, were contaminated, and at least 240 hectares of Atlantic forest were degraded.[24]

There was no lack of financial resources for Samarco to avoid this tragedy. In 2014, the company had achieved the best financial result in its history, with a gross turnover of

The Virtuous Barrel:
How to Transform Corporate Scandals into Good Businesses via Behavioral Ethics

BRL7.6 billion (around $3.4 billion, a 5% increase over 2013) and net income of BRL2.8 billion (around $1.3 billion). Despite the huge profits, management continued to announce in its reports the implementation of a policy aimed at "reducing production costs," "enhancing the efficiency of the process," and "increasing productivity gains."[25]

Samarco's management philosophy has led the company to cut the budget from key safety areas, including dam management. According to public prosecutors, dam safety expenses were reduced by 41% in real terms between 2012 and 2015, a period in which the company's production increased substantially and the problems with Fundao only worsened.[26]

In addition, the investigations also uncovered that a plant belonging to Vale (the mining giant who was one of Samarco's controlling shareholders) used to throw waste secretly into the dam since its inauguration. According to investigators, Vale's mud was critical for the elevation of the reservoir level, accounting for about 27% of all volume deposited on the Fundao dam between 2008 and 2015.[27]

The complete analysis of Samarco's failure led public prosecutors to conclude categorically that "The excessive quest for the increase in production, materialized in successive projects of expansion of the plants executed at a high speed, contributed to the collapse of the dam … the defendants opted for a business policy that prioritized economic gains at the expense of safety practices for the environment and for those potentially affected, assuming all the risks of causing deaths."[28]

In addition to Samarco's tragic episode, GE – once the symbol of the movement for shareholder value creation in the early 1980s – is also an important example of the long-term negative outcomes following an incessant focus on maximizing stock prices.[29]

The company suffered a complete restructuring after its iconic CEO Jack Welch took office in 1981.[30] Willing to please the market as part of his priority to raise GE stock prices, Mr. Welch implemented the whole set of prescriptions embedded in the shareholder value paradigm: severe downsizing, closure or selling of less profitable units, series of spin-offs and acquisitions, adoption of stock options plans, implementation of a

Darwinian performance evaluation system, and systematic meeting of stock analysts' quarterly earnings estimates for 29 quarters in a row.[31]

GE also went through an intense process of "financialization" in which it became increasingly dependent on the financial industry through GE Capital, its finance arm. It was an opportunistic strategic change: Mr. Welch himself acknowledged that GE turned to the world of finance just because it seemed to be an easy way to make money.[32] The company borrowed cheaply due to its triple-A credit rating, thus becoming America's biggest private issuer of short-term debt.[33]

At the end of Welch's two-decade tenure, results could not seem better. The company's market capitalization rose from $14 billion to $470 billion in December 2000, making GE the then-most-valuable company in the world. At that point, GE Capital represented 41% of its profits.[34] Welch was so celebrated that Fortune named him the "manager of the century" in 1999.[35]

The long-term outcome of Welch's business model, though, only began to become clear afterward. On the eve of the 2008 global financial crisis, GE Capital assets peaked at a half trillion dollars (a similar figure to that of the Lehman Brothers). With the eruption of the crisis, its fragility became clear. GE capital could not roll over around $72 billion on commercial papers. The firm reached a point in which it had to receive a government bailout of $60 billion in guarantees for its debt. Since then, the era of easy profits has gone and GE Capital became a burden.

In what was considered by *The Economist* magazine "a landmark in American capitalism,"[36] Welch's successor Jeffrey Immelt finally announced in April 2015 that GE was going to sell its finance arm.[37] According to the publication, "Mr. Immelt has finally stamped his mark on GE, in a way that is damaging for the reputation of Mr. Welch."[38]

The outcome for GE long-term stockholders since its move toward the tenets of shareholder value maximization is disappointing. The company had a market capitalization of $114 billion in early October 2018, about one-quarter its market value

The Virtuous Barrel:
How to Transform Corporate Scandals into Good Businesses via Behavioral Ethics

18 year before back in 2000. It also no longer boasts its longstanding AAA credit rating.[39] From the whole period from January 1981 to October 2018, GE stock rose at a rate about 50% lower than the S&P 500 index. In addition, because the company stock is much riskier than the market portfolio, a "fair" return to its shareholders should have been much higher to compensate for its increased risk.

The negative consequences for GE's shareholders due to the structural shifts under Mr. Welch's tenure are even more serious than low risk-adjusted stock returns. GE's corporate identity has been severely harmed after a frantic period of M&A activity of around $100 billion only in the 2000 decade. In the past 20 years, it is reasonable to say that the company was treated as a sort of portfolio of short-term financial assets. Traditional areas also seem to have lost the ability to innovate what once was the hallmark of the company. *The Economist* summarized the current market skepticism with the once revered company by saying that "by announcing the closure of GE's financial arm, Jeffrey Immelt has only won half of the battle to save the company."[40] In June 2017, Mr. Immelt was replaced by John Flannery under the promise of carrying out a major turnaround at the company. Barely a year later, in October 2018, Mr. Flannery was also ousted after not being able to restore confidence among investors.[41]

Previously seen as a corporate role model around the world, GE teaches important lessons for companies obsessed with maximizing shareholder returns at any cost. Sooner or later, the impact of a narrow vision for the business will be felt by the shareholders themselves.[42]

Despite its obvious problems, the idea that executives' primary responsibility is to maximize "shareholder value" continues to be taught and promoted by most business schools around the world. As pointed out by business journalist Duff McDonald in his book *The Golden Passport* on the inner workings of Harvard Business School, "When students enter business school, they believe that the purpose of a corporation is to produce goods and services for the benefit of society. When they graduate, they believe that it is to maximize shareholder value."[43]

The ideology is still strongly defended by many executives questioned for their ethical behavior. An example comes from Goldman Sachs, the US investment bank subject to several lawsuits over the years due to wrongdoings. Soon after the outbreak of the 2008 financial crisis, its CEO Lloyd Blankfein came out publicly to defend the bank's approach, even claiming that they were just "doing God's work."[44]

The second ethically dangerous and widely diffused doctrine is the idea that human beings behave (or at least should behave) as *homo economicus*. In this sense, agency theory (one of the main theories of corporate governance) assumes that people:[45]

- Make perfectly rational decisions;
- Think exclusively in maximizing their own personal economic gains;[46] and,
- Are always interested in breaking the rules if the expected benefit of a dishonest act is greater than the applicable penalty multiplied by the probability of being caught.[47]

The widespread adoption of the *homo economicus* mindset creates many problems from an ethical standpoint. To begin with, it treats various immoral behaviors in the business world as something acceptable as long as the person is acting "rationally to maximize his or her personal interest." Moreover, as a self-fulfilling prophecy, the dissemination of this concept in business schools may induce individuals to behave this way because they begin to see such behavior as "expected" or even "correct" from the perspective of rationality.

Let's take the example of economics students. Numerous researches show that students tend to be less cooperative and more selfish in lab experiments.[48] Although there is evidence that part of this result stems from a "selection effect" of the course, which tends to attract less "pro-social" people, this does not necessarily mean that economics students have an intrinsically worse morality than other human beings. In fact, these papers also show that pupils are subject to a strong "indoctrination effect" during their course, being taught that the *homo economicus* behavior is an appropriate model to be

The Virtuous Barrel:
How to Transform Corporate Scandals into Good Businesses via Behavioral Ethics

emulated by rational people (e.g., it is usual for these students to take exams in which the "correct" answer is the one that maximizes their personal gain).

The biggest problem with the *homo economicus* concept, however, is that it is simply a misleading idea about human nature.[49] Over tens of thousands of years of our evolution, we have developed an inner sense of morality that allowed us to live and work in highly cohesive groups. This only happened because the best survival strategy for our ancestors was to suppress selfishness and self-interest that would be good for the individual but bad for the group.[50] Societies and markets, therefore, have always depended fundamentally on trust, collaboration, and morality to function properly.

Not surprisingly, hundreds of experiments carried out in recent decades with human beings in real situations have shown that most people tend to act cooperatively to reach the best collective outcome, particularly on behalf of their groups.[51] In addition to the abundant evidence that most people prefer to show symbiotic behavior based on reciprocity and altruism, studies in the field of neuroscience have also shown that we actually take pleasure in doing so.[52] As recognized even by Luigi Zingales, a professor at the traditionally orthodox-oriented University of Chicago and former president of the American Finance Association, "The traditional assumption of '*homo economicus*' started to crumble when confronted by the evidence."[53]

So, the idea that we behave as *homo economicus* may be useful for the construction of mathematically beautiful theoretical models by orthodox economists, but it is limited and often incorrect when confronted with reality. In fact, the relentless and sole quest for the best personal outcome as advocated by this dogma tends to be more a pathological exception than a rule of our behavior.

Several papers have also demonstrated that people tend to exhibit a more prosocial behavior when an adequate social context is created.[54] As mentioned by Lynn Stout, a former corporate law professor at the University of Cornell, it all depends on having our consciousness "activated." According to her, three main factors that trigger people's conscience with the purpose of fostering an unselfish prosocial behavior are:[55]

1. Instructions from authority;
2. Reciprocity, that is, beliefs about others' prosocial behavior; and,
3. Empathy, that is, the magnitude of the perceived benefits of one's actions to others.[56]

There is, therefore, a very clear relationship between the mental models executives learn in business schools and the decisions they end up making as managers. Teaching executives that their role is to maximize shareholder wealth leads them to frame their decisions solely based on its economic costs and benefits without any ethical considerations. Similarly, indoctrinating managers that we are mere *homo economicus* leads them to think only of themselves without considering the collective interest of their organizations and society.

This view was very well-summarized by professor Sumantra Ghoshal, who argued that "Hundreds of thousands of executives who attended business courses have learned the same lessons ... by propagating ideologically inspired amoral theories, business schools have actively freed their students from any sense of moral responsibility."[57] Martin Parker, author of the book *Shut Down the Business School,* endorses this statement by saying that "if we teach that there is nothing else below the bottom line, then ideas about sustainability, diversity, responsibility and so on become mere decoration. The message that management research and teaching often provides is that capitalism is inevitable, and that the financial and legal techniques for running businesses are a form of science. This combination of ideology and technocracy is what has made business school into such an effective, and dangerous, institution."[58]

Thus, to improve business ethics for real, it is critical to seriously rethink what is taught to students and practitioners in business schools.

Behavior of industry peers

The third broader factor that may impair executives' ethical judgment involves the standard practices of the business world, particularly in their industry. Companies tend to

The Virtuous Barrel:
How to Transform Corporate Scandals into Good Businesses via Behavioral Ethics

follow the formal and informal norms adopted by their peers. It is common for executives, for instance, to justify their behavior based on the argument that "It's how things are done in my industry."

The similarities among industry peers stem from factors such as coercion (e.g., requirement to prepare the same reports, adoption of similar organizational structures); mimicry (e.g., tendency to copy others, especially success stories); and, prescription (e.g., executives subject to the same ideologies, frequent turnover of professionals within the same industry, business practices shared in industry-related events).

The Operation Car Wash offers an interesting example of how companies tend to replicate the behavior of their peers. More than 20 construction firms participated in this huge criminal scheme, including Brazil's five largest contractors.[59] Many of them ended up creating a cartel with the goal of replacing real competition by bid rigging in government procurement processes.

According to federal prosecutors, bid prices were set in secret meetings in which the construction firms defined who would secure the contract and what price it would be. The cartel even crafted a regulation simulating the rules of a football league to determine how the public contracts would be distributed.[60]

---

[1] Source: Drucker. P. 2008. The Essential Drucker: The Best of Sixty Years of Peter Drucker's Essential Writings on Management. Ed. HarperBusiness. Cap. 6

[2] According to North (1990), one of the main authors in this area, "Institutions are the rules of the game in a society or, more formally, are the humanly devised constraints that shape human interaction".

[3] According to authors such as Harari (2014), we live in an "imagined reality" composed of a set of collectively-created fictions (such as states and religions) which are manifested by our traditions, beliefs and social values.

[4] Gächter and Schulz (2016), Dimant and Schulte (2016), DeBacker et al. (2015), Arnold et al. (2007), Banuri and Eckel (2012), and Curtis et al. (2012).

[5] Fisman and Miguel (2007).

[6] The level of corruption of the diplomats' country of origin was measured by an indicator provided by Transparency International. The positive impact of the country's corruption on the number of parking tickets remained statistically significant after researchers controlled for various factors, such as the country's average income, diplomats' salaries, fixed effects related to the

country's geographic region, etc.

[7] Since 2002, US authorities were allowed to confiscate the diplomatic plates of vehicles that received more than three parking tickets. As a result, the number of violations dropped dramatically (a 98% reduction!), especially for diplomats who used to receive more fines. According to the authors, this shows that both cultural norms and law enforcement are important determinants of the level of corruption.

[8] DeBacker et al. (2015).

[9] This result was particularly pronounced for small companies.

[10] Barr e Serra (2010).

[11] The authors did not find significant results for a sample of foreign graduate students living and studying at Oxford University. In their view, graduate students that spent a longer period in the UK may have undergone a secondary socialization which influenced their individuals' norms, values and beliefs related to corruption. The data supported their argument by showing that the time spent in the UK was associated with a decline in the propensity of an individual to engage in bribery during the experiment.

[12] Gächter e Schulz (2016). The researcher's statement was made in an interview for The Atlantic Magazine. Source: The Atlantic Magazine. Corruption Corrupts. 03/09/2016. Available at https://www.theatlantic.com/science/archive/2016/03/corruption-honesty/472779/

[13] Source: Drucker. P. 2008. The Essential Drucker: The Best of Sixty Years of Peter Drucker's Essential Writings on Management. Ed. HarperBusiness. Chapter. 6

[14] Many forget, though, two central aspects of Friedman's texts: its historical context, in the climax of the Cold War and the need to reaffirm belief in the free market; and, his caveats, such as his view that the manager's moral duty is to maximize profits was only when executives "…conformed to the basic rules of the society, both those embodied in law and embodied in ethical custom."

[15] In an interview to Soltes (2016: 242), Andrew Fastow, the former CFO of Enron convicted for fraud, summarized the side-effects deriving from the focus on stock price maximization by saying that: "My intentions were good. I was trying to do what was the best for Enron, but the way we as a company defined success was incorrect. We defined success by reported earnings and the stock price. We were not defining it as increasing economic value". In addition, Silveira (2015a) details the empirical literature on the negative side-effects resulting from the relentless focus on shareholder value maximization.

[16] According to Van der Zwan (2014), financialization refers to the web of interrelated process – economic, political, social, technological, cultural, etc. – through which finance has extended its influence beyond its traditional role as provider of capital for the productive economy into realms of social life. One of the branches in this literature deals with the financialization of the modern corporation. In this case, it analyzes the increasing financial orientation of non-financial corporations.

[17] Information describing the Samarco case has been entirely taken from the legal proceedings brought by Brazil's Federal Public Prosecutors against Samarco, its administrators and its controlling shareholders. The lawsuit has been prepared as a result of the investigations following the collapse of its dam. The full version of the lawsuit is available at http://www.mpf.mp.br/mg/sala-de-imprensa/docs/denuncia-samarco. .

[18] Federal Public Prosecutors lawsuit: 180.

[19] This legally required independent committee, made up of independent consultants of national and international renown, was set up to evaluate issues related to dams and tailings disposal. See Federal Public Prosecutors lawsuit: 165-169.

The Virtuous Barrel:
How to Transform Corporate Scandals into Good Businesses via Behavioral Ethics

[20] Samarco's corporate risk manual, in effect since at least October 2011, already listed the risk of "critical failure in the dam operation process". In the field "event description," the document stated that "this risk includes both the disruption of the geotechnical structure itself and the operational disruptions that may occur in the day-to-day operations, causing critical interruptions." The document was impressively accurate: in the "health and safety" column, about 20 people were expected to die in the event of a collapse of the Fundao dam, almost exactly the number of victims of the tragedy afterwards (19 deaths). See Federal Public Prosecutors lawsuit: 181-186.

[21] Federal Public Prosecutors lawsuit: 119-120.

[22] Federal Public Prosecutors lawsuit: 135-138.

[23] Federal Public Prosecutors lawsuit: 159-160.

[24] Samarco, its administrators and controlling shareholders were sued for environmental and criminal crimes. Environmental crimes included pollution offenses against fauna and flora, cultural heritage, and environmental management. Criminal offenses included flooding, collapse, homicide and personal injury.

[25] Federal Public Prosecutors lawsuit: 191-192.

[26] One of the clearest examples of the cost reduction policy was observed in the item "Consulting and Technical Assistance". The proposed budget for 2015 predicted the optimization of consulting services by replacing external consultants for Samarco employees in order to reduce the value of project services. This proposal clearly contradicted ITRB recommendations to reinforce Samarco's Geotechnics team, considered by the experts as inexperienced and without sufficient qualification to deal with the complexity of Fundao.

[27] Federal Public Prosecutors lawsuit: 55.

[28] Federal Public Prosecutors lawsuit: 191-192.

[29] The GE case is based on Silveira (2015a).

[30] In August 1981, Jack Welch gave his first speech entitled "Growing fast in a slow-growth economy". For many, this speech is considered the initial landmark of the shareholder value movement.

[31] According to Soltes (2016: 146-147), "GE practice of earnings management would later be deemed as illegal by the SEC…Some of the earnings management practices that leaders at GE trumpeted as being accepted also turned out to be fraudulent. GE was charged with misleading investors by employing a variety of noncompliant accounting practices that allowed it to avoid missing analysts' forecasts."

[32] According to The Economist "its easy earnings were a form of corporate opium that the firm was addicted to". The Economist. Banking on de-banking. 04/18/2015. Available at http://www.economist.com/node/21648681/.

[33] According to The Economist, because GE was not considered a bank by regulators, it was allowed even thinner capital buffers than many lenders had. Source: The Economist. General Electric: Back to Business. 04/18/2015.

[34] Source: The Economist. Electric shock: GE breaks up. 04/10/2015. Available at http://www.economist.com/node/21642356.

[35] Source: http://archive.fortune.com/magazines/fortune/fortune_archive/1999/11/22/269126/index.htm

[36] Source: The Economist. General Electric: Back to Business. 04/18/2015.

[37] GE plan is to shrink its finance arm to below 10% of profits by 2018, restraining it to the traditional role of providing credit for customers of GE products.

[38] Source: The Economist. Electric shock: GE breaks up. 04/10/2015.

[39] On 10/06/2018, General Electric company long-term credit rating was A2 from Moodys and

A from Standard & Poor's. Source: http://www.ge.com/investor-relations/fixed-income-investors

[40] Source: The Economist. Banking on de-banking. 04/18/2015. Available at http://www.economist.com/node/21648681/. Interestingly, The Economist made several compliments to Welch when he retired from the company in 2000. Among other compliments, the publication stated that "...it is American firms' Welchian willingness to take hard decisions that has given American business its current pre-eminence."; and, that "It is this relentlessness that makes GE both so successful and so hard to copy." Source: The Economist. The house that Jack built. 09/16/1999. Available at http://www.economist.com/node/239557

[41] Source: CNN Money. GE unexpectedly removes its CEO. 09/30/2018. Available at https://edition.cnn.com/2018/10/01/business/general-electric-ceo-flannery-culp/index.html

[42] Ironically, even Jack Welch recognized the potential side effects of the focus on shareholder value maximization. In an interview for the Financial Times in the aftermath of 2008 global crisis, the executive said that managers should not set share price increases as their overarching goal and that "shareholder value is a result, not a strategy... Your main constituencies are your employees, your customers and your products... On the face of it, shareholder value is the dumbest idea in the world." Source: Financial Times. 02/12/2009. "Welch condemns share price focus."

[43] McDonald (2017). Because the number of Fortune 500 chief executives who earned their business degrees at Harvard Business School (HBS) is three times the total from the next most popular business school (Wharton School at the University of Pennsylvania), it is hard to overstate HBS influence on corporate America. Not coincidentally, HBS hired Michael Jensen, the architect of the principal-agent theory that underpins the concept of shareholder value maximization in the 1980s. Source: The New York Times. 04/10/2017. Book Pins Corporate Greed on a Lust Bred at Harvard. Available at https://www.nytimes.com/2017/04/10/business/dealbook/11-andrew-sorkin-harvard-business-school.html

[44] Source: The New York Times. 11/09/2009. Blankfein Says He's Just Doing 'God's Work'. Available at http://dealbook.nytimes.com/2009/11/09/goldman-chief-says-he-is-just-doing-gods-work/?_r=2

[45] Agency theory was formulated by Jensen and Meckling (1976). The theory is basically concerned in creating the most efficient contract to align the interests of one party (the "agent") with those of another (the "principal") in situations where the principal concedes authority to the agent to act on his or her behalf. Bringing this very simple concept to the business world, it created a clear prescription: because the theory assumes that shareholders are the owners of companies, it argues that they should be seen as principals who have delegated their decision-making power to managers, their allegedly agents. The theory underlying premise is that agents are rational and utility maximizers. As a result, it predicts that managers will not necessarily act in the best interests of shareholders. The solution to this "agency problem," in turn, would be the establishment of costly incentives and monitoring to ensure the alignment of interests between agents and principals.

[46] Economists usually argue that the maximization of a person's utility function does not necessarily translate into the maximization of its economic wealth. However, they also usually omit the fact that the vast majority of economic models depart from this equivalence in their construction. As a result, although in theory utility does not corresponds to monetary outcomes, this is assumed in most economic models. On this issue, Stout (2012: 26) points out that "Sometimes advocates for economic analysis try to soften homo economicus' sharp corners by arguing that people seek to maximize not their own material wealth but their "utility," and may get utility from helping others, following ethical rules, and so forth. I have explained at length elsewhere how this stratagem robs economic analysis of usefulness and reduces it to a tautology with no predictive power."

The Virtuous Barrel:
How to Transform Corporate Scandals into Good Businesses via Behavioral Ethics

[47] This prediction is largely based on the classical paper of Nobel Prize winner Gary Becker (1968).

[48] Bauman and Rose (2011), for example, found that economics students are less generous in giving than students from other courses at the University of Washington. They also noted that voluntary donations from students in other areas drop significantly after being exposed to microeconomics courses. A similar result was found by Frey and Meier (2003) with economics students at the University of Zurich. Frank and Schulze (2000), in turn, have noted that economics students are more likely to accept bribery offers, while Rubinstein (2006) found that they have a greater propensity to place profit maximization as a more important criterion than the well-being of workers. These studies demonstrate how economics courses in the past decades have neglected the essence of economics as a moral science whose ultimate goal must be to improve our overall well-being.

[49] For a discussion on this, see Kluver et al. (2014). The authors describe three views of human nature in increasing level of psychological accuracy of human behavior: homo economicus, homo heuristicus, and homo duplex. The homo heuristicus advances the rational and selfish concept of homo economicus by acknowledging the influence of the unconscious mind and our systematic biases. However, according to the authors, homo heuristicus view cannot fully explain the pervasive human desire to feel connected to and immersed within groups. As a result, they propose the concept of homo duplex, which describes human beings as moving back and forth between two very different ways of being: a lower (individualistic) level, and a higher (ego-free, collectively-oriented) level. For them, the balance between these selfish and groupish tendencies influences the ethical profile of the organization in complex ways.

[50] For more on this, see Harari (2014), Nowak e Highfield (2011), Wilson (2010) e Wilson (1975).

[51] For references on dozens of studies that corroborate this statement, see Silveira (2015b).

[52] Kosfeld et al. (2005).

[53] Kosfeld et al. (2005).

[54] Silveira (2015b) describes several papers supporting this statement.

[55] Zingales (2015: 1).

[56] Fischer et al. (2013) analyzed the effect of nine rituals on prosocial behavior. They found that ritualistic synchronized activities can indeed increase prosocial activity among group members. Thus, developing organizational rituals can be viewed as another factor that "activates" people's conscience.

[57] Ghoshal (2005: 75-76).

[58] Source: The Guardian. 27/04/2018. Why we should bulldoze the business school. Available at https://www.theguardian.com/news/2018/apr/27/bulldoze-the-business-school

[59] website G1 – Globo. 07/07/2016. 6 das 10 maiores empreiteiras tiveram executivos presos na Lava Jato. Available at http://g1.globo.com/politica/operacao-lava-jato/noticia/2016/07/6-das-10-maiores-empreiteiras-tiveram-executivos-presos-na-lava-jato.html

[60] Source: official Lava Jato operation website: http://lavajato.mpf.mp.br/entenda-o-caso

Alexandre Di Miceli da Silveira

7. The time factor and the gradual change in our ethical standards

> *"The least initial deviation from the truth is multiplied later a thousand-fold."*
> Aristotle (384AC–322AC)[1]

In previous chapters, we have seen how contextual pressures can affect our worldview and thereby undermine our ethical judgment. However, there is still a central component to understand how ethical blindness takes place. That element is time.

The time can affect our ethical behavior in three ways:

- As an element of pressure that leads to thoughtless decisions: lack of time leads us to decide quickly, often without fully understanding the ethical implications of our actions;
- As an element that consolidates organizational routines: certain organizational practices become increasingly difficult to change over time, especially in the case of companies once acclaimed as successful businesses; and,
- As an element that leads to gradual and imperceptible changes in our concept of "normal": time changes individuals and organizations slowly, creating a "new normal" may can lead to corruption and other unethical behaviors.

Time as an element of pressure that leads to thoughtless decisions

> *"When you are under time pressure for a decision, you need to follow intuition."*
> Daniel Kahneman (1937–)[2]

The Virtuous Barrel:
How to Transform Corporate Scandals into Good Businesses via Behavioral Ethics

Practicing good ethical conduct depends on our ability to reflect about the consequences of our actions and to control our self-interested impulses. The less time we have to decide, the greater is the possibility of making decisions on autopilot based on our intuitive processes. Consequently, the greater is the likelihood of unethical behaviors.

Using the concepts of our decision-making process described in Chapter 2, the intense pace of corporate life to which most people are subject restricts our cognitive resources. This, in turn, induces individuals to rely on decision strategies metaphorically illustrated by the "elephant" or "system 1."

A classic study shows in a dramatic way how time as an element of pressure can lead to making thoughtless decisions.[3] In this experiment, seminary students (who were studying for ordination as clergy) were told they had to prepare to give a lecture on the parable of the Good Samaritan in another building located one block away. As is well known, this parable of the Bible portrays a situation in which a Samaritan is the only person to help a stranger asking for help.

On their way to the other building, an actor was lying on the floor asking for help. For the so-called "control group," there was no time pressure. That is, at the end of the one hour allowed to prepare for the lecture, the researchers asked seminary students to move to the other building as planned. In this group, everyone offered help to the stranger grunting with pain.

For the other half of the participants (the "experimental group"), the researchers included time pressure. After only about 30 minutes, they informed the participants that the plans had changed and they should go immediately to the other building under penalty of missing the lecture. In this group, only 10% of the seminary students offered help to the man lying on the floor: 90% simply ignored the call for help despite going to give a lecture on the importance of helping strangers (in the rush to go ahead, some even stepped over the stranger). This experiment demonstrates how time pressure can lead us to ignore many important things, including the consequences of how our actions affect other people.

There is still another important aspect about time pressure that should be highlighted: It can lead us to physical and mental depletion that also may lead to unethical behavior. Because sound ethical conduct depends to a large extent on our ability to resist temptations and control our selfish impulses, many studies show a clear relationship between overloaded minds and dishonesty.[4]

One of these papers, entitled "too tired to tell the truth," separated 84 individuals into two groups.[5] One group was required to write a short essay without using words containing either the letters A and N (a difficult task that causes mental depletion); the other group was told to write the essay without using the letters Z and X (an easy assignment not causing mental exhaustion). Participants were then asked to solve "task matrices" similar to those described in Chapter 4.[6] The researchers found that people initially subjected to mental depletion defrauded the test at a magnitude 65% higher than the control group. They concluded that "When self-control has been weakened by depletion of its resources, selfish and dishonest behavior may readily ensue."[7]

Sleep deprivation is another relevant factor associated with mental exhaustion that can significantly impair our ethical behavior. Several studies corroborate this claim.[8] One of them analyzed the effect of two nights of sleep deprivation on our moral judgments.[9] Initially, 26 well-rested volunteers were subjected to a series of 30 moral dilemmas.[10] Each contained a proposed solution, to which participants had to indicate whether they considered it "appropriate" or "inappropriate."

One of the dilemmas, for example, reads as: "You are a doctor. You have five patients, each of whom is about to die due to a failing organ of some kind. You have another patient who is healthy. The only way that you can save the lives of the first five patients is to transplant five of this young man's organs (against his will) into the bodies of the other five patients. If you do this, the young man will die, but the other five patients will live. Is it appropriate for you to perform this transplant in order to save five of your patients?"

Subsequently, volunteers were submitted to 53 hours of continuous wakefulness. At the end of the period of sleep deprivation, the researchers asked participants the same moral dilemmas presented in the beginning of the study. The results were impressive. The number of highly questionable solutions participants considered "appropriate" for the ethical dilemmas almost doubled.[11] This means that individuals have become much more likely to accept morally questionable courses of action, as exemplified by the example above. The damaging effect of sleep deprivation was corroborated by magnetic resonance imaging tests. This analysis showed a substantial reduction in the activity of participants' medial prefrontal cortex, a region associated with the formation of our moral judgments.

A central implication of these studies for the business world is that organizations fostering a nerve-racking and unbalanced routine on their employees tend to be more prone to ethical problems.

An interesting example comes from the case of Santander bank, as described in Chapter 5, in which its Brazilian subsidiary was sued for adopting a management model based on stress and unrealistic goals.[12] As part of the case file, prosecutors included the results of a survey with employees from bank branches aimed to assess the psychological impacts of this managerial approach.[13] The results were frightening. In one of the branches, for instance, 43% of employees stated that they have considered ending their lives, 86% reported sleeping badly and having difficulty to think clearly and making decisions, 43% declared to feel that their lives are useless, 100% were feeling sad and have cried more than usual, and 33% have regularly taken medicines for anxiety in the previous six months.

The Santander example is not restricted to emerging markets. Interviews with bankers working in the United Kingdom described a similar situation. According to a book on the prevalent culture at large financial institutions "The process [to become a 'blinkered banker'] starts with the hours. For years, you are permanently sleep-deprived while spending every waking hour in the office ... Particularly in deal-making, which demands 'pulling an all-nighter': you work until 7 a.m., take a taxi home to shower and change, and then take the same taxi back to the office."[14] This lifestyle was corroborated by a former treasury director of a large London-based financial institution. He reported that "There wasn't any time for self-reflection. I ended up drinking huge amounts. Alcohol is a quick mood changer; it stops you from thinking and dulls you down."[15]

The comparison of the scientific results assessing the impact of mental depletion on honesty with the highly stressful reality experienced in many organizations clearly shows, therefore, that the current business environment is unfortunately a perfect match for ethical blindness.

To conclude, mental exhaustion and stress make it difficult to integrate the emotional and cognitive aspects of a decision, a critical requirement for making sound moral judgments. As a result, when we are consumed, our decisions become more impulsive and focused on minor technical aspects. It is as if our "moral muscle" gets weary, leading us to succumb to the impulses and temptations in these moments of weakness.[16] So, we must be careful not to get too tired or stressed in order to remain honest.

Time as an element that cements organizational routines

> *"It's particularly difficult to change course when the things that get you in trouble are the things that are also the source of your strength."*
> Jared Diamond (1937–)[17]

Time is also an element that reinforces organizational routines. Many business practices and decisions become increasingly systematized and predictable over time. There is a positive side to this. Standard practices are useful for simplifying our lives and facilitating decision-making as well as for providing us with a sense of stability and identity.

Routines, however, have a dangerous side. They tend to reinforce our worldview, be it correct or not. In the business world, companies tend to move toward an "architecture

The Virtuous Barrel:
How to Transform Corporate Scandals into Good Businesses via Behavioral Ethics

of simplicity" manifested by an increasingly homogeneous and narrow perception of reality by its executives.[18] This leads managers to operate on "autopilot" through processes that disconnect them from reflection and may give rise to ethical blindness. In opposition to the well-known concept of mindfulness, Harvard University professor of psychology Ellen Langer describes this state as "mindlessness," i.e., the inability to notice new things and to be sensitive to context and perspective.[19]

This state of mindlessness is fostered in managerial life, as it usually consists of a set of well-established routines carried out in an uncritical way. Actually, this was even used as part of the defense arguments of Dennis Kozlowski, the former CEO of Tyco sentenced to more than eight years in prison for improperly receiving around $100 million in unauthorized bonuses. He described his routine of signing documents in the following way: "I signed everything, but it was the same thing that I had been doing since 1976 ... I had the company tell me what it was, and I signed it. So, how's that criminal?"[20]

Another practical example of how the routines and habits cultivated by managers can lead to improper business practices comes from Andrade Gutierrez, a large Brazilian construction group who agreed to pay around $350 million in fines as part of a plea bargain deal with prosecutors. In his testimony to justice, its former CEO Otávio Azevedo said that the payment of bribes was seen within the company as "something natural," a mere "commercial cost added in the composition of the budget of our works."[21]

A third demonstration of the dangers of thoughtless routines comes from Odebrecht's "Structured Operations" division, which was considered by Bloomberg as "perhaps the farthest-reaching, most efficient corruption machine in modern business."[22] In a report by the *Financial Times*, corruption became so routinized that this division had its own computer system detailing the amounts to be paid, the people who would receive the bribes, and the black market bankers called *doleiros* ("dollar men") in charge of making the payments.[23] It was in this system that a low-profile secretary named Maria Tavares, who had been at Odebrecht for decades, began her workday by inputting the details of the bribery payments booked for that week.[24] The payroll included politicians and other public authorities of a dozen of countries in Latin America and Africa. A former Odebrecht senior manager estimates that the department paid around $3.3 billion in bribes between 2006 and 2014, with cash payments reaching around $15 million in a single day.[25] The sophistication reached such a point that Odebrecht set up a true "one-stop shop" by buying a bank in Antigua where corrupt officials could open accounts and receive the money directly.[26]

Routines are created as the outcome of the experience and repetition of our decisions over time. In particular, it is even more difficult to change entrenched habits when the company was recognized, at least for a while, as a "successful" organization. In this case, customs evolved over the years through positive feedback: The more success the company had, the more people believed they were doing the right thing.[27]

Brazilian oil company Petrobras endorses this assertion. The company was involved in a massive scandal that led it to write off $17 billion in 2015 due to losses from corruption and overvalued assets. Before that, though, it experienced a golden period from the mid-2000s until 2008. During this time, motivated by the euphoria of international investors with Brazil and the sharp increase of oil prices (from $28 to $97 per barrel), Petrobras market capitalization soared to almost $300 billion, becoming the third most valuable company in the world in 2008. In addition, the oil company also managed to raise $70 billion in 2010, the world's largest capitalization at the time.

These huge numbers, coupled with its gigantic investments and several acquisitions, reinforced the view inside the firm that the spurious relationships with contractors and politicians were "natural" practices for a state-owned company of its size and simply part of a game that could not be changed. The view that wrongdoings had become routine at the top of the organization was acknowledged by its C-level officer Paulo Roberto Costa, one of the main executives involved in the scandal. In an interview before being arrested, he was asked if Petrobras was indeed a rich source of funding for election campaigns due

The Virtuous Barrel:
How to Transform Corporate Scandals into Good Businesses via Behavioral Ethics

to its thousands of contracts per year with private constructors. Mr. Costa then replied: "But it has always been like this, it is still like this, and it will continue to be like this at Petrobras."[28]

Later, the federal judge in charge of the case summed up the situation by asserting in his sentence that "Bribes had become routine, and those involved did not even know anymore why they were paid or why they were received ... When corruption is systemic, kickbacks are paid routinely and viewed by participants as the rule of the game, something natural and not abnormal that reduces the moral costs of crime."[29]

The ethical blindness reinforced by the perception of success, therefore, makes it difficult to change old and established practices that have been useful in the past. The risk becomes even greater when an organization faces a disruptive future. In times of drastic changes in the external environment, thus, the routines of the past become a trap.

Because people tend to dislike change, when members of an organization feel that the system to which they belong to is under threat, they sense that their own identity is also in danger. As a result, they often tend to strengthen their habits and routines with tooth and nail, even if they have proved to be a failed course of action for an external observer.

Drastic changes in the external environment have led to the collapse not only of large companies but also of entire civilizations. After studying in his book *Collapse* how societies fail or succeed, for instance, the anthropologist and historian Jared Diamond concluded that many civilizations, when faced with a crisis, tended to reinforce their old habits in response to threats instead of changing their way of living.[30] This tendency to follow established patterns of behavior even in response to dramatic environmental shifts was called "active inertia" by professor Donald Sull. In his view, because organizations get stuck in the modes of thinking and working that brought success in the past, they simply try to accelerate all their tried-and-true activities. As a result, in trying to dig themselves out of a hole, they just deepen it.[31]

Executives must be careful, therefore, so that their companies do not become stuck in a scenario in which only a small range of alternatives is perceived as possible. This is an invitation not only to ethical blindness but to the very demise of the organization.

The time that leads to gradual and imperceptible changes

> *"It's easier to hold to your principles 100% of the time than it is to hold to them 98% of the time."*
> Clayton Christensen (1952–)[32]

Unethical actions are also the outcome of a process of moral disengagement that unfolds over time through gradual and imperceptible changes. Almost no one, and probably no organization, simply decides to commit a serious transgression from day to night. Our perception of what is "normal" is what unconsciously changes, and most people simply do not notice the gradual erosion of their ethical standards.[33] As a result, a sequence of small breaches may escalate into larger violations over time.

A remarkable work published in 2016 in the prestigious journal *Nature* shows how our brain becomes less sensitive to everything we are exposed to, including to our own dishonest behavior.[34] The research, entitled "The Brain That Adapts To Dishonesty," analyzed the activation in the amygdala of individuals participating in a behavioral task in which they were given repeated opportunities to act dishonestly (the amygdala is a critical region for the processing of emotions such as fear or anxiety). Researchers observed that, in the beginning, participants exhibited dishonest behaviors of small magnitude that were always accompanied by a strong reaction in their amygdala. However, as the experiment proceeded, and as participants repeated their dishonest behaviors in order to increase their personal gain, this region of the brain became less and less sensitive. In other words, the amygdala simply adapted to unethical behaviors, responding less and less emotionally to them. Interestingly, researchers also noted that the decrease in the signal emitted by this region proved to be an excellent predictor of increased dishonesty of participants in the future. This means that, based on the extent of decrease of amygdala activation, the authors were able to predict with high accuracy if

The Virtuous Barrel:
How to Transform Corporate Scandals into Good Businesses via Behavioral Ethics

participants were going to behave dishonestly in subsequent rounds of the experiment. According to the researchers, "Our results uncover a biological mechanism that supports a 'slippery slope': what begins as small acts of dishonesty can escalate into larger transgressions."[35]

Because change typically happens at a slow pace and on a small scale, i.e., one short step at a time, it may go unnoticed, just like the "boiling frog" fable.[36] This happens because the reference point for our today's decision is not an imaginary moral point from years ago when we were still acting with 100% integrity. The anchor for our today's decision is our yesterday's decision. So, if the transgression is only a little bigger than yesterday's, the "ethical delta" remains acceptable, and we will keep moving toward increasingly unethical courses of action.[37]

The gradual change in the perception of what is normal is the result of the so-called "shifting baseline."[38] A group of researchers observed this phenomenon in 2005 after interviewing three generations of fishers from Mexico's Gulf of California where fish populations have declined steeply over the last 60 years.[39] For each generation, the number of species and the amount of fish they remembered from their first fisheries was the reference point for what they considered to be "natural" for the region. Each generation, thus, had a perception of what was natural based on the beginning of their fishermen lives instead of an absolute reference point farthest in time. Younger fishermen, for example, did not notice the great loss of biodiversity taking place in the region, showing themselves more at ease with the relatively small decrease in abundant fishing sites over the previous years. Only the older fishermen were able to have a broader perspective of the region's ecosystem dramatic decay in the last decades.

Brought to the business world, this result shows that we often fail to perceive the changes in our environment because they tend to occur incrementally, below the threshold of noticeable variations. What is dramatic at one point becomes reasonable later, thus creating a new "normality." Researchers Andris Zoltners, PK Sinha, and Sally Lorimer provide an example of this escalation at Wells Fargo, the US bank whose employees opened more than 3 million fake bank and credit card accounts. They envisioned the following sequence for an account manager pressured to meet a sales goal. Initially, he would push a customer to add a credit card, even though he knew it would not be in the customer's interest. Then, still short of the goal, he would ask friends and relatives to open accounts just to be closed soon. Finally, with the goal still not achieved, he would end up opening accounts without asking customers (also intending to close them shortly thereafter). As the authors point out, "As soon as the account manager gets away with the first unethical act, it was not a big step to the fraudulent ones. The justification moves from 'it's legal' to 'no one is harmed' to 'no one will notice.' When such practices are tolerated, they escalate in severity and spread throughout the organization."[40]

From a conceptual perspective, professors Blake Ashfort and Vikas Anand argue that the normalization of corruption in organizations is based on three mutually reinforcing processes: institutionalization, rationalization, and socialization.[41] During institutionalization, corrupt acts become embedded in the organization's structures and processes in a depersonalized way. In the rationalization phase, self-serving ideologies are developed and disseminated to justify corrupt practices and allow individuals to legitimize their illegal behavior. During socialization, in turn, formal and informal cooptation processes are established so that naïve newcomers are induced to view corruption as permissible, if not desirable. As summarized by Asford and Anand, "One of the most intriguing findings in the white-collar crime literature is that corrupt individuals tend not to view themselves as corrupt."[42]

There is plenty of evidence that many frauds begin with executives manipulating small numbers and making questionable day-to-day decisions over time.[43] The case of the English bank Barings is a classic example supporting this assertion. The problems started when Nick Leeson, a 28-year-old trader in charge of the Singapore office, noted that a newly hired secretary had misunderstood a purchase order of future contracts, buying 20 contracts rather than selling them. This mistake led to a loss of £20,000 for the

The Virtuous Barrel:
How to Transform Corporate Scandals into Good Businesses via Behavioral Ethics

institution, a trivial amount for day-to-day business in the financial markets. To avoid firing her, Leeson decided to hide the error from his superiors until he could find a definitive solution. He then created a fictitious account on his computer named the "88888 error account" in which he allocated the £20,000 loss. Noting the "usefulness" of this account, Leeson began using it to cover his own trading losses. The value of the losses increased over the next two years, as the trader started to bet higher amounts in pursuance of recovering the hidden deficit. As a true snowball, the losses reached stratospheric values. In 1995, Leeson fled Singapore after he could no longer roll the debts. Barings executives then discovered he had left a hidden liability of $1.3 billion, enough to drive the 233 years-old financial institution, known as the queen's bank for having the royal family among its clients, into bankruptcy.[44]

Small dubious decisions over time, therefore, can put us on a slippery slope with huge consequences. In an interview, former trader Jordan Belfort, famous after being featured in the book and movie *The Wolf of Wall Street*, shows how this takes place in practice: "You don't lose your soul on Wall Street all at once. It's a bit at each time. It's tiny and imperceptible steps. You do everything right and then you do a wrong thing. You look around and tell yourself: 'Wow, nothing bad happened because I have done it.' The next time you step over the line [of unethical practices], the line has moved. And you step a little bit farther, and farther still, farther still … All of a sudden, a couple of years have passed, and you're doing things you never thought you would do, you're associated with people you never thought you would be associated with, and everything seems just alright."[45]

Belfort's statement is in accordance with the view of three other executives who have also been involved in major scandals. The first comes from a former Enron C-level executive, who said that: "You did it once, it smelled bad. You did it again, it didn't smell as bad."[46] The second comes from Marc Dreier, the creator of a billionaire Ponzi scheme at his law firm Dreier LLP: "It's a slippery slope once you surrender to ambition. I did not set out to steal hundreds of millions of dollars but ended up doing so incrementally after crossing a line I could not retreat from ... Once I started, there seemed to be no way out other than to continue."[47] The third, in turn, comes from Brazilian Pedro Barusco, the former manager of Petrobras mentioned in the foreword who received about $100 million in grafts over many years: "Receiving bribes is a path that has no turning back. You start getting illegal money after a moment of weakness, and then it's a sword in your head ... There's no way out, there's no way out."[48]

---

[1] Source: Aristotle, book I, part 5. On the Heavens. Available at http://classics.mit.edu/Aristotle/heavens.1.i.html

[2] Source: Kahneman and Klein on strategic decisions: When can you trust your gut? 09/25/2016. Available at https://bobmorris.biz/kahneman-and-klein-on-strategic-decisions-when-can-you-trust-your-gut

[3] Darley and Batson (1973).

[4] Self-control can be defined as the ability to control our impulses in a particular situation to behave according to certain goals and standards. To a large extent, ethical decisions involve a conflict between the opportunity for short-term personal gain and a virtuous behavior with long-term gains for society.

[5] Mead et al. (2009).

[6] As a reminder, "solving the matrix" meant finding two numbers in a certain matrix that added up to ten.

[7] *Ibid*: 597.

[8] Killgore et al. (2007), Barnes et al. (2011), Christian et al. (2011) e Olsen et al. (2010).

[9] Killgore et al. (2007).

[10] The moral dilemmas presented to participants are available at http://science.sciencemag.org/content/suppl/2001/09/13/293.5537.2105.DC1

[11] These results were obtained for people who exhibited a median emotional intelligence. In the case of participants with high emotional intelligence, there was no significant reduction in the quality of moral judgments. According to Killgore et al. (2007), this suggests that some people have a cognitive "affective or emotional reserve" that enables them to make moral judgments even in case of sleep deprivation.

[12] ACP-0000342-81.2017.5.10.0011, 3ª Vara do Trabalho de Brasília – DF. The lawsuit can be accessed at https://pje.trt10.jus.br/consultaprocessual/pages/consultas/ConsultaProcessual.seam

[13] Source: MPT Notícias. 11/04/2017. Santander processado em R$460 mi por assédio e estresse. Available at http://portal.mpt.mp.br/

[14] Luyendijk (2015: 212).

[15] *Ibid*: 238.

[16] The term "moral muscle" was first used by Baumeister and Exline (1999). Muraven et al. (1998) corroborate the idea that self-control tends to succumb when tested very often.

[17] Source: Why do societies collapse? Jared Diamond at TED Talk 2003. Available at https://www.ted.com/talks/jared_diamond_on_why_societies_collapse

[18] Miller (1993: 117).

[19] Harvard Business Review. Mindfulness Isn't Much Harder than Mindlessness. January 13,

The Virtuous Barrel:
How to Transform Corporate Scandals into Good Businesses via Behavioral Ethics

2016. By Ellen Langer. Available at https://hbr.org/2016/01/mindfulness-isnt-much-harder-than-mindlessness

[20] This example comes from Soltes (2016: 154).

[21] Folha de São Paulo. 07/28/2016. Propina era custo operacional, diz ex-presidente da Andrade Gutierrez. Available at http://www1.folha.uol.com.br/poder/2016/07/1796567-propina-era-tratada-como-custo-operacional-diz-presidente-da-andrade-gutierrez.shtml

[22] Bloomberg Businessweek. 06/08/2017. No one has ever made a corruption machine like this one. Available at https://www.ft.com/content/8edf5b2c-c868-11e6-9043-7e34c07b46ef

[23] The Financial Times. 12/30/2016. A Brazilian bribery machine. Available at https://www.ft.com/content/8edf5b2c-c868-11e6-9043-7e34c07b46ef

[24] Folha de São Paulo. 03/04/2017. Única mulher entre 77 delatores da Odebrecht cuidava de setor de propina. Available at http://www1.folha.uol.com.br/poder/2017/04/1872070-unica-mulher-entre-77-delatores-da-odebrecht-cuidava-de-setor-de-propina.shtml .

[25] Folha de São Paulo. 03/07/2017. Odebrecht movimentou $3,3 bi em pagamentos ilícitos, diz delator. Available at http://www1.folha.uol.com.br/poder/2017/03/1864355-odebrecht-movimentou-us-33-bi-em-pagamentos-ilicitos-diz-delator.shtml; Estado de São Paulo. 04/05/2017. 'O meu recorde é 35 milhões em um dia', diz delator da Odebrecht sobre entregas de dinheiro. Available at http://politica.estadao.com.br/blogs/fausto-macedo/o-meu-recorde-e-35-milhoes-em-um-dia-diz-delator-da-odebrecht-sobre-entregas-de-dinheiro/

[26] Ironically, Odebrecht had received several awards, including the prestigious "Lombard Odier Global Family Business Award" as the best family business in the world in 2010 granted by the IMD Institute of Switzerland. More information on this available at http://www.globalfamilybusinessaward.com/laureates/2010-the-odebrecht-organization-brazil/

[27] This reasoning often occurs at the individual level as well: the higher we climb, the more we tend to believe we are right and the less we want to do something differently.

[28] Paduan (2016: 39;188-189).

[29] Source: Sentence of Criminal Action N° 5023135-31.2015.4.04.7000/PR. Paragraphs 274 and 275. Available at http://lavajato.mpf.mp.br/atuacao-na-1a-instancia/denuncias-do-mpf/documentos/sentenca-5023135-31-2015-404.7000

[30] Diamond (2005).

[31] Source: Harvard Business Review, July-August 1999. Why Good Companies Go Bad. Available at https://hbr.org/1999/07/why-good-companies-go-bad

[32] Source: Harvard Business Review, July 2010. How will you measure your life? Available at https://hbr.org/2010/07/how-will-you-measure-your-life

[33] Milgram's experiment, described in Chapter 4, is another example of how we can commit serious unethical deeds through small actions. It is unlikely that participants would directly apply the 450V lethal shock to another person if they were required to do so. However, about two-thirds ended up applying the lethal shock when they begin the experiment by applying low-intensity shocks.

[34] Garrett et al. (2016).

[35] *Ibid*: 1.

[36] The "boiling frog" parable describes a situation in which a frog is slowly boiled alive. The idea is based on the premise that the frog will jump out if it is put suddenly into boiling water. However, if the frog is put in warm water which is then boiled slowly, it will not perceive the danger and will be cooked to death. The fable is used as a metaphor for our inability to be aware or to react to gradual threats.

[37] Kaptein (2013: 74) describes this reasoning as follows: if behavior A is acceptable, and

behavior B somewhat less acceptable but within reasonable bounds, then B is also acceptable. If behavior C subsequently presents itself, perhaps somewhat less acceptable than B, but still within the bounds of possibility (as understood in relation to B), then C is fine, even if a single step from A to C would be unthinkable. Each step is so small that in practice it becomes something continuous in relation to the previous one: after each step, we position ourselves to give the next one.

[38] Paul (1995) has created this term by observing that people tend to perceive changes in their environment in a relative way, comparing it only to their own previous experience.

[39] Saenz-Arroyo et al. (2005).

[40] Harvard Business Review. Wells Fargo and the Slippery Slope of Sales Incentives. 09/20/2016. By Andris A. Zoltners, PK Sinha, and Sally E. Lorimer. Available at https://hbr.org/2016/09/wells-fargo-and-the-slippery-slope-of-sales-incentives

[41] Ashforth and Anand (2003). Campbell and Göritz (2014) observed that managers and employees play different

roles in the process of normalization of corruption. While managers rely primarily on institutionalization through goal setting and rewarding, employees rely primarily on rationalization and socialization mechanisms through coercion and punishment of dissenters. In a related study, Jenkins and Delbridge (2017) investigated how lying, just like corruption, can also become normalized in companies. The authors analyzed the case of VoiceTel, a market leader in virtual reception business. The company provides outsourcing services for telephone calls. Because its attendants are instructed to say that they are physically present in the offices of its customers, strategic deception was simply a cornerstone of VoiceTel's business model. After carrying out dozens of in-depth interviews over nine months, they found that receptionists overcame their initial discomfort through the steps of institutionalization, rationalization and socialization as predicted by Ashforth and Anand (2003). Over time, they gained greater recognition from their proficiency in deception and drew considerable satisfaction, self-esteem and status as employees who are "trusted to deceive".

[42] Anand et al. (2004, p. 10).

[43] Engelmann and Fehr (2016), Welsh et al. (2014), Schrand and Zechman (2012), Crocker (2011), McLean and Elkind (2003), Lerman (2001), and Stein (2000).

[44] Stein (2000) and website http://www.nickleeson.com/biography/

[45] Jordan Belfort's interview is available at https://youtu.be/G3K92uugO9o?t=49m52s

[46] McLean and Elkind (2013).

[47] Soltes (2016: 267).

[48] G1 Globo. 10/03/2015. À CPI, Barusco diz que receber propina é um 'caminho sem volta'. Available at http://g1.globo.com/politica/operacao-lava-jato/noticia/2015/03/cpi-barusco-diz-que-receber-propina-e-um-caminho-sem-volta.html

8. Ethical blind spots and the danger of rationalizations

> *"Executives live and work within an organization. Unless they make conscious efforts to perceive the outside, the inside may blind them to true reality."*
> Peter Drucker (1909–2005)[1]

As discussed earlier, we all perceive our own reality based on the frame we apply to the world surrounding us. During this process of construction of reality, we define what is inside or outside our field of vision, i.e., what should or not be considered as a feasible alternative to our decisions.

The puzzle in Fig. 5 demonstrates in a very simple way how this occurs: Try to connect the nine points of the figure using a maximum of four lines without taking the pen out of the paper. Then, see the exercise solution in the endnotes.[2]

Figure 5. A simple exercise to illustrate our framing of reality.

The framing we apply to make sense of reality is useful because it facilitates decision-making by simplifying the understanding of the complexity around us. However, as illustrated by the exercise in Fig. 5, it is difficult to be aware that we are indeed subject to a "decision frame" that bounds our perspective of the world: We always think we see the complete reality and there is no alternative to it. Thinking "outside the box" (the key to solving the puzzle above) means going beyond our personal framing of reality: We need to reflect using other paradigms.

The way we frame reality and its influence on our economic decisions were first studied by pioneer researchers Daniel Kahneman and Amos Tversky. Their "prospect theory" resulted in two main conclusions. The first is that suffering resulting from a financial loss tends to be twice as great as the pleasure of a similar gain. The second is that, in order to avoid recognizing a certain financial loss, we tend to take risks we would not accept to earn the same amount of money.

These conclusions have important implications for our ethical conduct. One is that individuals will be far more likely to circumvent rules in order to avoid accepting a certain loss than earning an equivalent gain. So, after making mistakes, people may end up doing even worse things to prevent their fault from being discovered.[3]

This behavior is frequently observed in the business world. Scandals such as the Barings, Societé Générale, and Madoff cases, for example, were a direct outcome of our tendency to take risks of an increasing magnitude in order to avoid a sure loss.[4] Let's take the case of Bernie Madoff, architect of a colossal $65 billion fraud at his asset management firm. After being arrested, he corroborated this claim by acknowledging that: "It's like a comedy of errors. To cover the losses, I decided to take in money from hedge funds. I kept taking in more money, figuring that once the market allows me to do the strategy, I would be able to fix it ... I kept on waiting for the environment to change and or course it never did ... it turned into a total fiasco."[5] This type of behavior was also observed in the case of OGX, the former oil company controlled by Eike Batista, as described in Chapter 6. According to the author of a book about the entrepreneur, "Mr. Batista was averse to bad news. When OGX forecasts announced to the market showed to be unachievable, he often acted as a card player who doubles the bets in order to avoid being caught in the bluff."[6]

The pressures of context and time described in previous chapters tend to aggravate the problems arising from our inherently limited framing of reality. On the one hand,

The Virtuous Barrel:
How to Transform Corporate Scandals into Good Businesses via Behavioral Ethics

they tend to distort our worldview. Many executives, for example, may act unethically because they are subject to a decision-making framing solely based on economic trade-offs that blind them from other perspectives. The classic case of Ford Pinto, as detailed in Appendix 1 at the end of this chapter, describes in a dramatic way how a limited framing of reality based exclusively on monetary costs and benefits can lead to making disastrous decisions in the corporate world.

In the scientific field, an important paper by researcher Jacob Rose demonstrate the risks of having a rigid framing of reality.[7] He interviewed 17 board members from Fortune 200 companies, presenting them with the following case: "You are a director who serves on the board of a corporation listed on the NYSE that manufactures plastic consumer products. The production process releases two toxic byproducts into the environment: Toxin A and Toxin B. The current plant emissions contain Toxin A and Toxin B at levels of 50 ppm each. Toxin A has just become regulated by the Environmental Protection Agency, and releases of the toxin into the environment will be limited to 25 ppm next year. Toxin B is not regulated by any government agency. Toxin A is known to be carcinogenic at levels over 25 ppm, and scientific evidence indicates that Toxin A represents a threat to the health of society. While there are no regulations that limit the release of Toxin B, recent scientific studies from University laboratories indicate that it presents as much danger to human health as Toxin A when released at levels above 25 ppm. The legal team is confident that emissions of Toxin B will not be regulated in the short-run, and they feel that emissions of Toxin B may never be regulated. As a board member, would you continue to allow this particle to be issued by your company?"

At the end, 15 out of the 17 corporate directors interviewed declared that they would authorize to keep releasing the known carcinogenic particle if it had not yet been regulated. In the post-experiment interview, directors recognized the ethical and social implications of their decisions. However, they also argued that, as corporate managers, they believed to be under the duty of maximizing shareholder value. This, in turn, would end up leading them to keep allowing the issuance of the toxin. Interestingly, in one variant of the study, directors stated that they would not allow the issuance of the same carcinogenic particle if they were acting as board members of a privately-owned company in which they were also partners.

The figure below depicts a metaphor of this situation. Many executives come to see themselves in a kind of tunnel where there is only one goal to achieve and no other possible courses of action for their decisions (e.g., "I have to act this way," "there is no other way to go," "this is my duty").

Figure 6. The "tunnel" as a metaphor for our framing of reality.

This rigid framing of reality generates "ethical blind spots" so that the implication of executives' decisions on others are simply off the radar. In the case of the tunnel metaphor, the focus on achieving professional goals (or just the quest to fulfill their alleged "role") may lead managers to do not consider options out of their "tunnel." As an example, an executive in a decision to outsource production may fail to see a serious problem involving human rights violations such as child labor or slave labor if he or she analyzes this issue from a strictly economic perspective.

The metaphor of the "tunnel" presented above is actually a mere illusion to represent the dangers of a rigid and limited framing of reality. Instead of a "tunnel," the figure is in fact a cut of a beautiful beach presented in full form in Fig. 7.

The Virtuous Barrel:
How to Transform Corporate Scandals into Good Businesses via Behavioral Ethics

Figure 7. The "beach" as a metaphor of the complete reality.

We must therefore be careful about the ethical blind spots arising from a rigid and limited framing of reality. It is this framework that often leads executives to deviate from their values and ending up in ethical blindness.

Notwithstanding, when we behave improperly, we may feel that something is wrong with our conduct. To deal with the gap between our intentions and actual behaviors (the so-called "cognitive dissonance" or "ethical dissonance"),[8] we began making use of powerful rationalizations. Rationalizations are justifications we give ourselves to accept our behavior and "go ahead with life" by maintaining a positive self-image. They help us in reinterpreting unethical behaviors to make them morally acceptable. According to the researchers, there are nine main rationalizations we systematically (consciously or unconsciously) use way to excuse our wrongful conducts.[9] They are:

1. Denial of responsibility ("it is not my fault"; "my boss told me to do that");
2. Claim of relative acceptability or normality ("everybody does it"; "this is standard business practice");
3. Appeal to higher loyalties ("I did for my company, not for me"; "I have a family to feed"; "I was just trying to maximize shareholder value");

4. Denial of injury ("no one was really harmed"; "the harm was caused to the market as whole, not to a single individual," "what they don't know will not hurt them");
5. Image of balance or the ledger metaphor ("on balance I've done more good than bad"; "I have been quite active in philanthropy"; "it's fair because I've been treated unfairly by working overtime");
6. Condemnation of those who condemn the wrongdoing ("they are hypocrites"; "they are driven by personal spite or political gain"; "they should look at themselves");
7. Social weighting ("people are worse than me"; "peers from my industry are much worst");
8. Denial of bad intentions ("it was not serious"; "I was just kidding"); and,
9. Denial of the victim ("they asked for it"; "their actions were inappropriate, so they got what they deserved").

In a study on corporate malfeasance, for instance, the researchers concluded that claim of normality, appeal to higher loyalties, and social weighting were the most frequent rationalization strategies used by employees of corrupted organizations.[10] Take, for instance, the rationalization of normality based on the argument that "everyone else is doing it." Children often use this justification when they start doing wrong things, such as lying or cheating. Although parents usually do not accept this as an excuse, it is curious to observe that many parents end up resorting to the same justification for questionable practices in their professional lives.[11]

As Jamie-Lee Campbell and Anja S. Göritz, authors of a study on corporate corruption point out, "Employees require much rationalization to reduce the cognitive and moral dissonance of their behavior ... the high amount of rationalization might explain why employees have a low level of awareness that corruption is unlawful."[12]

Rationalizations, therefore, are dangerous because they "cleanse" the conscience and legitimate the perpetuation of unethical actions. Bernie Madoff, the architect of a

The Virtuous Barrel:
How to Transform Corporate Scandals into Good Businesses via Behavioral Ethics

billionaire Ponzi scheme described in the previous chapter, exemplifies its dangers. In a series of interviews to professor Eugene Soltes when he was already serving part of his 150-year prison sentence, he said: "I sort of rationalized that what I was doing was okay – you know, that it wasn't going to hurt anybody." Throughout the interviews, Madoff also exhibited other characteristics usually associated with ethical problems pointed out throughout the book, such as overconfidence ("I built my confidence up to a level where I ... felt that ... there was nothing that ... I couldn't attain") and the time that leads to gradual and imperceptible changes ("I started to go off the tracks, and I was able to convince myself that this was, you know, a temporary situation"). According to Soltes, "The piece that's most humbling in the recording is the realization of rationalization: he recognizes now that it was all rationalization."[13]

Another practical example comes from Reinhard Siekaczek, a former accountant at Siemens who oversaw an annual bribery budget of around $50 million from 2002 to 2006 used to corrupt government officials worldwide. In an interview to investigative journalists of PBS's "Frontline," he declared: "We all knew that what we were doing was illegal. I didn't really look at it from an ethical standpoint. We did it for the company. It was about keeping the business unit alive and not jeopardizing thousands of jobs overnight ... In hindsight, I asked myself what kind of idiot I was to have shown such great loyalty toward this company. It's hard to explain. At the end of the day all I got for it was a kick in the pants ... and I am an outcast now."[14]

The complete process of ethical fading leading to ethical blindness, including the layers of contextual pressures and the time factor detailed in previous chapters, is presented in the next figure. As illustrated by the image of the prison at the bottom, executives often end up suffering the consequences of their actions at the end of the process. In some cases, it is only at this point that they become fully aware of the harm caused by their actions.

After the figure and Appendix 1 on the Ford Pinto case, the second part of the book concludes with Appendix 2 on the "AB InBev model." Considered by many market practitioners as an example of business success and even a role model to be followed by other companies, the appendix discusses this acclaimed management model from the perspective of behavioral ethics with the purpose of reflecting on its moral risks.

The Virtuous Barrel:
How to Transform Corporate Scandals into Good Businesses via Behavioral Ethics

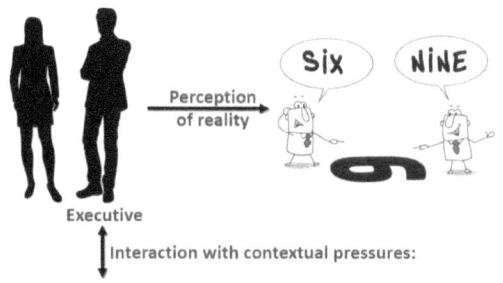

Executive

Interaction with contextual pressures:

Immediate context
- Pressure of authority
- Peer pressure
- Self-imposed pressure due to our professional role

Organizational context
- Unrealistic goals
- Unidimensional incentive systems
- Darwinian environment with winner-takes-all performance evaluation system
- Language full of euphemisms, or metaphors of war or games

Institutional context
- Culture of the country
- Dogmas or ideologies of executive education *(e.g. shareholder value, homo economicus)*
- Behavior of industry peers

The impact of time

- Time as an element of pressure that leads to thoughtless decisions
- Time as an element that cements organizational routines
- Time that leads to gradual and imperceptible changes

Narrow and rigid framing of reality creating ethical "blind spots"

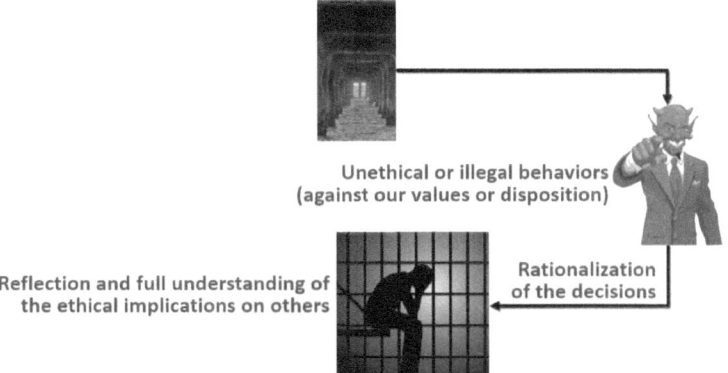

Unethical or illegal behaviors (against our values or disposition)

Rationalization of the decisions

Reflection and full understanding of the ethical implications on others

Figure 8. The process of ethical fading that leads to ethical blindness.
Source: This diagram is based on the seminal work of Palazzo, G., Krings, F. & Hoffrage, U. (2012). Ethical Blindness. *Journal of Business Ethics*. 109: 323-338.

Appendix 1. The Ford Pinto Case: The dramatic outcome of a limited framing of reality

Imagine that you are an executive of a multinational company in the automotive sector presented with the following scenario:

> *You will be in charge of the project of a new car. The vehicle is important to your company's strategy and needs to be launched in a shorter period than usual due to strong foreign competition. Market research and internal analysis show that it is highly likely that the new vehicle will manage to grab a good market share and produce positive economic value.*
>
> *The new car has an innovative design in which the gas tank is located at the rear. However, during the pre-production collision tests (when the assembly line was ready to produce the vehicle), engineers noticed an unexpected problem: Due to the unusual location of the tank, there is a reasonable likelihood that the tank would explode in the event of a rear-end collision at a given angle.*
>
> *A cost-benefit analysis shows that the cost of fixing the design problem would be $137 million. Another analysis, though, shows that the estimated costs of legal suits resulting from the damages caused by expected tank explosions would be lower than this amount. Specifically, it estimates that 180 people are expected to die and another 180 are expected to be seriously injured throughout the 10 years of sales forecasted for the vehicle.*
>
> *Because compensation for deaths and serious injuries cost around $200,000 and $67,000, respectively, total costs related to future accidents are estimated to be only around $48 million. You are also informed that the vehicle is in full compliance with current regulations, including regarding its design, as there is no prohibition of rear tanks.*

What would you do as an executive in this situation? Would you authorize the immediate production and marketing of the vehicle? Would you authorize its production only after the tank is redesigned? Or would you not authorize its production and marketing under any circumstances?

Although apparently crazy, this situation existed in reality. This is the case of the Ford Pinto launched in 1971 by Ford and produced until 1980.[15]

The Virtuous Barrel:
How to Transform Corporate Scandals into Good Businesses via Behavioral Ethics

The full story reads as follows. Under growing competition from foreign automakers during the first oil crisis, Ford rushed to put Pinto into production much faster than usual. At the time, its then CEO Lee Iacocca ordered the company to launch a model costing less than $2,000 and weighing less than 2,000 pounds. As previously described, engineers found an unexpected problem with Pinto's gas tank during its pre-production tests. Because the tank was located in the rear part of the vehicle, it could explode in the event of a rear collision such as depicted in the figure below.

Figure 9. Ford Pinto and the risks of a limited framing of reality.

An internal Ford memo estimated that the cost of damages would be less than the cost of fixing the problem (the document was found years after the launch of the vehicle, during a lawsuit in which Ford was sued after a mother died and her son was permanently disfigured by the fire resulting from a rear-end collision).[16] In order not to delay the project, the decision was simply to go ahead.

The Ford Pinto was produced with the problematic design for eight years, until the company finally opted for a recall of 1.5 million vehicles in 1978. During this time, it is estimated that at least 23 people (according to a Ford report) and up to 500 people (according to independent publications) were killed, and another dozen were seriously injured due to the tank design.[17] The case illustrates in a dramatic way the risks of framing a decision only as a "business decision" without considering its ethical implications.

Were people at Ford simply bad and insensitive? In fact, according to Professors Guido Palazzo and Ulrich Hoffrage, who analyzed the case in depth in their course on unethical decision-making,[18] a deeper understanding of Ford Pinto's episode shows that this was probably a classic example of ethical blindness.

To begin with, the event took place in the middle of the first oil crisis, a period in which US companies faced domestic recession and were under great pressure to quickly launch small, fuel-efficient cars such as the Ford Pinto. This situation, therefore, probably created a dilemma in managers' minds between keeping jobs or risking the survival of the company.

Time pressure was also present. While a new car typically used to take 43 months from design to full-scale production, Ford's senior managers established a goal for Pinto to be launched in just 25 months, the shortest production cycle in the company's history. It is likely that language was also a relevant factor. The legal department banned the use of the word "problem" in the company memos, while explosions were treated in an internal report as an "acceptable risk." In addition, the CEO Lee Iacocca used to say that "safety doesn't sell" and that Ford Pinto was his priority project. These statements may have led people to think that safety was a not a critical issue for company decisions. The company probably also discouraged employees from questioning the CEO's determination to launch the car in record time without delays.

The Ford Pinto case exposes the difference between compliance and ethics. The regulation at the time only required the tank to remain intact in collisions below 20 mph. In the tests carried out by Ford, this actually happened (explosions occurred when collision took place with slightly higher speeds, from 25 mph). Thus, the company remained in compliance with the regulations. In the case of engineers and other executives, all were focused on working hard in their daily tasks for the sake of helping the company to increase its profits. By focusing on their specific roles, however, they probably lost sight of the big picture and the wider consequences of the acts to which they were contributing.

The Virtuous Barrel:
How to Transform Corporate Scandals into Good Businesses via Behavioral Ethics

One situation worth mentioning is that of Dennis Gioia, chief of Ford's recall department (the unit responsible for alerting owners that a car has a safety-related problem and offering free repairs). His team was required to make recall decisions based on three key criteria: high frequency of the problems, unambiguous evidence that the car was defective, and clear traceability. As the tank explosions did not technically fit into these criteria, his team did not consider a recall of Ford Pinto. Later, Gioia left Ford and became a renowned business professor at Penn State University.[19] Writing about the Pinto case years later, he wondered, "Why did not I see the seriousness of the problem and its ethical implications?"[20]

The Ford Pinto case demonstrates how people often develop a moral microcosm within an organization. As a result, a decision that is viewed as irrational, unethical, and pathological to those outside this microcosm may be seen as rational, justifiable, and normal to those inside the organization.

This explanation obviously does not exempt the individuals involved in Ford Pinto decisions (or omissions) from their legal and moral responsibility. However, it is critical to have a deeper understanding of the context in which the decisions were made at Ford in order to comprehend how a rigid and distorted framing of the world can lead to disastrous consequences. Because business decisions always affect the lives of others, they all have an inherent ethical perspective that should be explicitly considered by executives in their analyses.

Appendix 2. The AB InBev model: success story or dangerous context for ethical blindness?

> *"Enterprises are paid to create wealth, not to control costs."*
> Peter Drucker (1909–2005)[21]

The "AB InBev model" refers to a set of management practices implemented by a group of companies controlled by three Brazilian entrepreneurs,[22] standing out the multinational brewer AB InBev.

At first sight, it is an indisputable case of business success. In 1989, the three entrepreneurs acquired control of Brahma, a Brazilian local brewery, for $60 million. By the end of 2016, following a series of mergers and acquisitions, the company had become AB InBev, the world's largest brewer valued at $190 billion. Other figures are impressive. From 2004 to 2016, for instance, its revenues increased fivefold (from $8.5 billion to $45.5 billion), while operating income multiplied 17 times (from $719 million to $12.8 billion).[23]

The AB InBev model makes use of a strategy based on acquisitions and relentless cost control that can be summarized as "buying and cutting the fat." As a result, the group has made five major mergers or acquisitions since 2000 in increasing order of magnitude.[24]

According to its senior executives, the key for the AB InBev's success relies in the creation of a strong culture based on the following aspects: meritocracy, owners' mentality, agility, constant attention to costs, aggressive bonuses, performance evaluation tied to the achievement of goals, full-time dedication, and retention only of the "committed" people.[25]

Correspondingly, AB InBev has a manifesto in which it lists the 10 principles of its "dream and people" culture. Among them are phrases such as "Our dream is bringing

The Virtuous Barrel:
How to Transform Corporate Scandals into Good Businesses via Behavioral Ethics

people together for a better world"; "Our greatest strength is our people"; "Leadership by personal example is at the core of our culture. We do what we say"; and "We never take shortcuts. Integrity, hard work, quality, and responsibility are key to building our company," among others.[26]

On the other hand, in spite of its apparently unquestionable success, the AB InBev model has also been subject to considerable criticism. In 2015, for example, the *Financial Times* carried out an in-depth investigation of AB InBev's management philosophy with dozens of executives, former employees, and other stakeholders. Some excerpts from this investigative report describe a much less heroic and immaculate reality:[27]

> Working for the world's largest brewer is not to everybody's taste, and that is fine with Carlos Brito, Anheuser-Busch InBev's chief executive. After Anheuser-Busch, owner of Budweiser, agreed to be taken over by InBev in 2008, Mr. Brito and his InBev colleagues arrived at the US group's St. Louis headquarters within 24 hours to start shaking up its comfortable way of working and to assess which senior people would fit in. "In any company, there's 20 percent that lead, 70 percent that follow, and 10 percent that do nothing," Mr Brito recalls. "So, the 10 percent, of course, you need to get rid of ... They're always unhappy anyway and complaining."

> The 55-year-old Brazilian, who likes to be called just "Brito," leads AB InBev by example. "My life is the company and my family." He professes to have no hobbies, and the sole pastime to which he admits is a daily 30-minute treadmill workout. The CEO's dedication to the company is typical of AB InBev managers, who, when they have time to dream, are encouraged to "dream big."

> AB InBev is a tightly run multinational... Critics allege that its steely culture is hard on a workforce increasingly managed by young graduates, whose

devotion and enthusiasm are matched only by their lack of operational experience.

For a flavor of what it is like working for AB InBev, register online to join its elite global management training program. A short game tests whether you have what it takes, as you play the role of an up-and-coming trainee preparing a presentation. One clue: When your alarm goes off at 6 a.m., and the game offers you the option of a few minutes' lie-in, do not press "snooze."

Informality and transparency are elements of its culture. For his FT interview, Mr Brito is preppily dressed in pressed jeans and blue shirt with an embroidered red Budweiser logo ... Do not confuse transparency with equality, however. Considerable rewards, in cash and equity, are available to those who hit tough targets. Miss them and bonuses vanish. Brito, for instance, received EUR250 million (around $300 million) in stocks in 2008 for integrating Anheuser-Busch and cutting deal-related debt.

Performance is constantly monitored and reviewed formally once a year, using 360-degree feedback. Underperforming staff are given six to nine months to improve. Mr Brito denies AB InBev operates a forced ranking system. Yet, he says, at some point you must say to laggards: "Look, you're a very smart guy, there are other companies out there but for us it's not working. You live only once, don't waste your time here, go somewhere else while you are young."

In 2008, after the InBev team had done its sorting of the Anheuser-Busch management, Mr Brito says he "changed the whole first tier ... Some were too rich to care, some were too old to work, some wouldn't fit the culture anyway." One senior former Anheuser-Busch executive recalls, with something like awe, how the company took tough decisions without emotion.

Others are more critical. One Belgian union official, speaking on condition of anonymity, complains about "cost-chasing," including petty approval requirements for reordering printer ink. He alludes to the rapid churn of

The Virtuous Barrel:
How to Transform Corporate Scandals into Good Businesses via Behavioral Ethics

managers, saying, "bosses are only in place for three years maximum and then they have to go somewhere else. We have a culture that's not long term — nothing is stable."

On Glassdoor, a site that allows staff and former staff to rate employers anonymously, its rating is lower than that of three main rivals — SABMiller, Molson Coors and Heineken — in every area except career opportunities and business outlook. Comments refer repeatedly to the pressure. "The workload is completely unrealistic, but they keep trimming headcount," said one person described as a "former full-time employee" in March. "Everyone is so stressed out that there is lots of fighting and tension."

The group's global HQ in Leuven, 30km east of Brussels, is decorated with poster-size reminders that AB InBev staff "pour themselves into their work." Even young and ambitious staff admit that maintaining a social life is hard. Adrien Mahieu, who joined five years ago having worked at his family business, says outsiders sometimes say AB InBev trainees have been "brainwashed": "My brother can't understand how deeply involved in the company I am because I sometimes assume more ownership for AB InBev than for my own shares in the family company."

Freddy Delvaux is emeritus professor of brewing at KU Leuven university, and now runs a small craft brewery with his sons. He, too, uses the term "brainwashed" to describe AB InBev staff he has encountered as a teacher. At first it seems positive, he says, "but I'm not so sure: they are also instilling a company view and they create an enormous internal competition." To get promotion at AB InBev, he jokes, first "you have to kill three others."

The company encourages a sense of discomfort. Mr Brito says: "We believe that people only grow when [they're] from time to time sat outside of [their] comfort zone." When smugness sets in, the group "shakes the tree" to reproduce the rush of having to learn something new quickly. Mr. Soeters, who has never worked in one role for more than two years, says: "I never get to that stage of being bored and looking elsewhere."

The profile described by the *Financial Times* is in accordance with another investigative report about the "AB InBev model" carried out by *Bloomberg Magazine* in 2013.[28] Some excerpts, portraying the main architect of the model Jorge Paulo Lemann, help to build a clearer picture of AB InBev's management philosophy.

> Lemann and his partners founded 3G (a private-equity fund) in New York in 2004 to buy US companies with the cash they'd earned from more than two decades of takeovers and turnarounds in Brazil. The name is a reference to the number to Banco Garantia, the investment bank where they developed their management philosophy.
>
> Starting in the 1970s, Lemann built Garantia into Brazil's premier financial firm. Since selling the bank to Credit Suisse in 1998, he and his partners have focused on acquisitions outside the financial industry, such as Heinz (a global food company known for its ketchup).

Their first move was to replace Heinz's long-serving chief executive officer for Bernardo Hees, a former Brazilian railroad executive who had most recently run Burger King. In August, Hees fired 600 members of Heinz's office staff in the US and Canada, or 9% of its North American workforce. About 350 of those jobs were in Pittsburgh. He also axed 11 senior executives and replaced them with young top performers from inside the company.

Much of this resembles the changes Lemann's people made at Burger King, where it's forbidden to make color copies without permission, and Anheuser, where employees no longer have access to free beer. Lemann's partner Sicupira has a favorite phrase: "Costs are like fingernails: You have to cut them constantly."

The Virtuous Barrel:
How to Transform Corporate Scandals into Good Businesses via Behavioral Ethics

Lemann was born and raised in Rio de Janeiro. The surname is Swiss — his father, a dairy entrepreneur, was born in Switzerland, as were his maternal grandparents. Lemann went to the American School of Rio de Janeiro, spending much of his time surfing and playing tennis. In 1958, he was accepted by Harvard University at a time when few Brazilians went; as he explained in a 2011 speech to a group of high school students in São Paulo, he probably got in because of his tennis game.

In the speech, Lemann said he didn't like Harvard. He hated the cold and missed the waves of Leblon Beach in Rio. So, he designed a system to get his bachelor's degree in just three years: Before signing up for a class, he gathered information on the syllabus by interviewing the professor and students who'd already taken it. He also discovered that the final exams from previous years were archived at the library and noted that they varied little from year to year, allowing for easy cramming. Harvard was mainly worthwhile, he said, because it forced him to get creative so he could finish early.

In 1971, he joined with a few other traders to take over an inconsequential brokerage known as Garantia. Lemann instituted the partnership model of Goldman Sachs, with a twist. Instead of simply awarding shares once a year for a job well done the way Goldman did, Lemann offered the best performers the chance to use their bonus to buy shares. Seniority didn't matter: To reward top performing newcomers, the bank would shrink the bonus pool for laggards.

By the 1980s, Garantia had become one of the most sought-after employers for smart young men. (There are few women in Lemann's world, even today.) Résumés didn't matter much. Candidates had to go through a gauntlet of interviews with partners who had an acronym for the profile they were looking for: PSD, for poor, smart, deep desire to get rich. Sometimes the partners posed odd or even offensive questions just to throw interviewees off balance and see how they reacted. A former executive who worked at Garantia in the early 1990s remembers being asked whether he had sex with his girlfriend.

Garantia was a place where the words fanatic and obsessive were considered compliments. The first person to go home for the day often received ironic applause. "No one came and handed anything to you on a platter," says Lerner. "A lot of people couldn't handle it."

The Garantia style was personified by Sicupira, who joined in 1973. In 1982, he led Garantia's first major foray outside finance, the acquisition of an ailing retail chain known as Lojas Americanas. Sicupira lowered executives' base salaries, cut perks, and implemented big, target-based stock incentives. Lojas Americanas' top management mutinied, calling for the return of the old system. After the executives made their demands — and went out for lunch — Sicupira fired them and locked them out of the building.

Lemann also considered General Electric's annual reports a kind of bible and adopted Jack Welch's 20-70-10 rule — promote the top 20% of your employees, maintain the middle 70%, and fire the rest. With Sam Walter, the founder of Walmart, he and Sicupira learned how to squeeze suppliers.

In 1994, Garantia cleared $1 billion in profit. Its traders got cocky. Without properly hedging itself, Garantia sold huge amounts of insurance on Brazilian government bonds, and when the Asian financial crisis exploded in 1997, sending interest rates soaring in emerging markets around the world, the bank lost hundreds of millions of dollars in a single year. It was the bank's first loss in two decades, and its aura of invincibility was ruined. The next year, Lemann and his partners sold it to Credit Suisse for $675 million, a fraction of the price they might have gotten before the losses.

Lemann's single-minded focus on cash flow explains how, after the takeover of Anheuser-Busch in 2008, AB InBev had little trouble paying down its massive debt amid the global financial crisis. It could also explain why consumers in the US have lately taken to suing the company for allegedly watering down its Budweiser.

People who know Lemann say he personally avoids the products he now peddles; he's a teetotaler who prefers a bottle of water and a salad. According to their book *Big Dream*, he ate his first Burger King hamburger only after acquiring the company and commented that he found it too big. What he liked about Burger King was how it generated cash.

These investigative reports make it clear that the "AB InBev model" is primarily characterized by relentless pressure for shareholder value maximization. It is a very dangerous management philosophy, though, from the perspective of business ethics. This concern is well-grounded on many facts. Over the years, AB InBev has been subject to several penalties arising from unethical practices toward competitors, customers, and employees.

In 2009, for instance, the Brazilian Administrative Council for Economic Defense (the equivalent of the US Federal Trade Commission Bureau of Competition) imposed an all-time record fine of BRL350 million (around $175 million at the time) on the company for employing a program that induced retail outlets to maintain sales exclusivity or reduce purchases of competing brands.[29] In 2015, an advertising campaign of the company titled "I forgot the 'no' at home" caused huge public outcry in Brazil for being accused of rape apology.[30] In the United States, longtime Budweiser consumers, one of the brands acquired by the group, filed a $5 million class-action lawsuit against AB InBev on charges of watering down the iconic US beer.[31]

The most striking unethical issues with AB InBev, however, concern the various episodes of bullying and moral harassment against its employees ("our most valuable asset," according to the company's own declared principles). Several of these episodes were brought to labor courts in Brazil, ending up in huge fines for the company.[32] Among the bizarre situations reported in these lawsuits are cases of employees subjected to several punishments in the case of not reaching their goals, such as i) doing push-ups until exhaustion with the boss stepping on their backs;[33] ii) lying in coffins while being portrayed as chickens hanged in the meeting room;[34] iii) being forced to wear skirts, lipstick, and helmets with horns;[35] iv) going through a "polish corridor" while hearing insults from their managers and peers;[36] v) being obliged to stand up during the meetings and dance in front of others while wearing t-shirts with offensive sayings[37]; and, vi) being photographed with prizes in the form of human excrement, with its subsequent exposition on the company walls for a month.[38]

Ambev's legal problems have not been confined to its unorthodox punishments. Its incentive system has also been subject to lawsuits. In one case, for instance, a former employee sued the company for being obliged to attend morning events in which prostitutes performed stripteases as part of "motivational" sessions to increase sales.[39] In another case, one of the supervisors used to gunshot its main competitor's logo for the sake of "incentivizing" employees.[40]

Another source of information on the daily practices of the AB InBev model comes from the comments posted by employees and former employees on specialized Websites such as Glassdoor. The company's overall assessment in these sites does not appear to endorse its stated values. In early 2018, AB InBev average ratings (based on around 1,000 reviews) were substantially lower than those of industry peers Heineken and MillerCoors in four out of the five criteria assessed by the Website (culture and values, work–life balance, senior management, and compensation and benefits). In addition, AB InBev CEO also had a significantly lower approval rating than his brewery peers, while only 48% of employees recommended the company to a friend.[41]

Based on an integrated assessment of employee comments on specialized websites and on other reports analyzing the AB InBev model, the company seems to exhibit a set of characteristics that causes great concern from the standpoint of behavioral ethics:

The Virtuous Barrel:
How to Transform Corporate Scandals into Good Businesses via Behavioral Ethics

- Command by young people (often recently graduated from MBAs) with great ambition but little professional experience and emotional intelligence for leadership positions;
- Excessive pressure and a highly aggressive and intimidating environment promoting a culture of fear;
- A culture that fosters prejudice against women and older people;
- A short-term focus that is likely to reduce investments and increase turnover;
- A management model similar to a financial institution in which many people feel treated as numbers; and
- Emphasis on presenting an image of meritocracy, efficiency, and quality to external audiences, not necessarily matched by the internal view of many employees.

Based on the behavioral ethics findings presented throughout the book, therefore, the AB InBev model contains a set of troubling ingredients that may lead to ethical blindness at the individual or collective level. Among these risky elements stand out the presence of a performance evaluation system based on a "winner takes it all" approach; unrealistic and unidimensional goals; highly aggressive and competitive internal environment led by "hungry" young individuals; people constantly stressed, tired, and with a poor work–life balance; an incessant pressure for hitting short-term numbers in order to remain in the company; a very strong culture to the point of creating a parallel reality; and a narrow view on the role of managers (limited to making money for shareholders).[42]

It is important, therefore, to carry out a broader and deeper evaluation of the merits of the AB InBev model well beyond the analysis of its financial outcomes.[43] This is particularly relevant today, when management models such as the one implemented by AB InBev's are widely acclaimed in business schools and in the news as success stories to be emulated by other companies.

---

[1] Source: Drucker. P. 2008. The Essential Drucker: The Best of Sixty Years of Peter Drucker's Essential Writings on Management. Ed. HarperBusiness.

² One of the possible solutions to this puzzle is:

³ Given that we are likely to doing things for the sake of not losing our reputation that we would not normally do to improve it, authors like Ariely (2012) argue that it is important for companies to create practices that give employees an opportunity to redeem their mistakes.

⁴ The Barings Bank scandal was described in the previous chapter. The scandal involving French bank Société Générale was disclosed in January 2008, when the institution announced losses of $7 billion in a single day due to derivative operations. According to the bank, all losses were caused by a junior trader named Jérome Kerviel who allegedly carried out unauthorized operations well beyond his trading limits. The scandal of Bernard Madoff's asset management fund emerged during the financial crisis of 2008. The founder had created a Ponzi scheme leading to a $65 billion fraud and causing losses to about 4,800 investors. For more on this, see Silveira (2015b).

⁵ Soltes (2016: 299).

⁶ Leo (2014: 196).

⁷ Rose (2007).

⁸ Although the term "cognitive dissonance" is widely-known in the field of psychology, some authors from the field of behavioral ethics, such as Ayal and Gino (2011), have recently coined the term "ethical dissonance" to identify the feeling of discomfort arising from the gap between our ethical behaviors and our high moral aspirations. Both terms, therefore, can be considered interchangeable in the field of behavioral ethics.

⁹ Haugh (2015), Cohen et al. (2012), Ayal and Gino (2011), Ashforth and Anand (2003), Tsang (2002), and Bersoff (1999).

¹⁰ Campbell and Göritz (2014: 304). The authors called the idea of normality or relative acceptability by the term "corruption is a matter of course" in their paper.

¹¹ This example comes from a report by mindgym. The only way is ethics: why good people do bad things and how to stop us. Consultation edition, September 2017. p. 16. Available at https://uk.themindgym.com/resources/the-only-way-is-ethics-2/

¹² Campbell and Göritz (2014: 304).

¹³ Source: Soltes (2016: 302-303) and Harvard Business School – Working Knowledge. 10/24/2009. Bernie Madoff explains himself". Available at http://hbswk.hbs.edu/item/bernie-madoff-explains-himself.

¹⁴ The New York Times, 12/20/2008. At Siemens, Bribery Was Just a Line Item. Available at https://nyti.ms/2jE03A6. Mr. Siekaczek concludes his interview with an ironic remark: "Since bribery is very common in many countries, people will only say it was bad luck and that they broke the 11th Commandment. And the 11th Commandment is: don't get caught". The video is available at https://www.nytimes.com/video/multimedia/1194836014690/at-siemens-a-paymaster-for-bribery.html

¹⁵ Several videos on YouTube detail Ford Pinto case, including the following links: https://youtu.be/3G_dt-lQVS8; https://youtu.be/PAI5T8UecEY; https://youtu.be/vVq0qCpcCoA; https://youtu.be/jltnBOrCB7I. This case has also been deeply analyzed in the academic setting, standing out the papers of Lee and Ermann (1999), Birsch and Fielder (1994), and Gioia (1992).

¹⁶ Amazingly, Ford even owned the patent of a much safer fuel tank! Source: Mother Jones, Mark Dowie. September/October 1977 Issue. Pinto Madness. Available at http://www.motherjones.com/politics/1977/09/pinto-madness

The Virtuous Barrel:
How to Transform Corporate Scandals into Good Businesses via Behavioral Ethics

[17] Sources: Mother Jones, Mark Dowie. September/October 1977 Issue. Pinto Madness. Available at http://www.motherjones.com/politics/1977/09/pinto-madness; Michael Matteson and Chris Metivier. 2017. Case: The Ford Pinto. Available at https://philosophia.uncg.edu/phi361-metivier/module-2-why-does-business-need-ethics/case-the-ford-pinto/

[18] Course "Unethical Decision Making," Coursera. Professors Guido Palazzo e Ulrich Hoffrage at the University of Lausanne. Available at https://www.coursera.org/learn/unethical-decision-making

[19] Information on Dennis Gioia are available on the website of PennState Smeal College of Business: http://www.personal.psu.edu/dag4/blogs/dennygioia/

[20] Gioia (1992: 383).

[21] Source: Drucker. P. 2008. The Essential Drucker: The Best of Sixty Years of Peter Drucker's Essential Writings on Management. Ed. HarperBusiness. Chapter 7.

[22] Jorge Paulo Lemann, Marcel Telles e Beto Sicupira. These entrepreneurs control a private equity firm named 3G Capital. 3G is widely-known for being laser-focused on maximizing earnings. According to Fortune Magazine, "the cutthroat Brazilian private-equity firm is known for swift layoffs, cost-cutting — and profits," while Financial Times emphasizes its "ruthless operating focus". Sources: Fortune Magazine. Here's what happens when 3G Capital buys your company. 03/25/2015. By Daniel Roberts. Available at http://fortune.com/2015/03/25/3g-capital-heinz-kraft-buffett/; Financial Times. Ruthless operating focus behind 3G rise. 03/25/2015. Available at http://www.ft.com/intl/cms/s/0/a7fcbc1a-d30c-11e4-a792-00144feab7de.html#axzz3YoCYtllC

[23] Source: Google Finance. Financials ADR Anheuser Busch Inbev NV; NYSE:BUD.

[24] Brahma merger with Antarctica to create Ambev in 2000 ($4.3 billion deal); merger with Belgian brewery Interbrew to create Inbev in 2004 ($11.2 billion); acquisition of US Anheuser-Busch to create AB InBev in 2008 ($52 billion); acquisition of Modelo Group from Mexico in 2012 ($20 billion); and, acquisition of SABMiller in 2015 ($106 billion).

[25] Exame magazine. 11/26/2015. Carlos Brito, da AB InBev, fala sobre a cultura da empresa. Available at http://exame.abril.com.br/revista-exame/carlos-brito-da-ab-inbev-fala-sobre-a-cultura-da-empresa/

[26] Source: http://www.ab-inbev.com/our-story/our-culture.html .

[27] Sources: Financial Times. 06/15/2015. AB InBev's hard-nosed kings of beer: The deal-thirsty brewer opens up in the first of a two-part series on its culture and ambitions; Financial Times. 06/16/2015. AB InBev: one more deal for the road? The second in a two-part series on the vast brewer's culture and ambition.

[28] Source: Bloomberg Magazine. 08/29/2013. Jorge Lemann: He Is ... the World's Most Interesting Billionaire. Article by journalist jornalista Alex Cuadros.

[29] Estado de São Paulo. 07/22/2009. Cade aplica multa recorde de R$352,7 milhões à AB-Inbev. Available at http://economia.estadao.com.br/noticias/negocios,cade-aplica-multa-recorde-de-r-352-7-milhoes-a-AB-Inbev,406688

[30] Estado de São Paulo. 02/13/2015. Cervejaria substitui campanha acusada de apologia do estupro. Available at http://economia.estadao.com.br/blogs/radar-da-propaganda/cervejaria-substitui-campanha/

[31] Business Insider. 02/26/2013. Budweiser Accused of Watering Down Beer! Available at http://www.businessinsider.com/beer-lovers-across-america-say-budweiser-watered-down-its-booze-2013-2

[32] A detailed description of these cases is available (in Portuguese) at "AB-Inbev: Assédio Moral é baluarte de estilo vitorioso" publicado pela ERA – Ética e Realidade Atual. Available at http://era.org.br/2011/10/AB-Inbev-assedio-moral-e-baluarte-de-estilo-vitorioso/

[33] In the same episode, the testimony in court claimed that it was common for the supervisor to apply "punches, slaps on the backs, and naked chokes on employees, forcing others to curse in tandem when the employee arrived late". Case AIRR 1370/2005-006-20-40.0 from 6ª Turma do Tribunal Superior do Trabalho de Sergipe. Available at http://www.conjur.com.br/2006-dez-18/ex-empregado_ambev_indenizacao_danos

[34] Case RR-32100-53.2006.5.04.0101, 2ª Turma do TST do Rio Grande do Sul. Available at http://economia.estadao.com.br/noticias/geral,ambev-tera-de-indenizar-ex-funcionario-por-dano-moral,53717e

[35] Case RR 985/2006-025-03-00.7 3ª turma Tribunal Superior do Trabalho de Minas Gerais. Available at http://www.direitonet.com.br/noticias/exibir/11479/Ambev-e-condenada-por-usar-assedio-moral-para-aumentar-produtividade

[36] A "polish corridor" is a form of punishment in which the person is obliged to go through a group of people aligned in two lines facing each so that they form a "corridor". During the passage, the person receives slaps and other forms of physical abuse from the people who formed the corridor. Case nº 00887/2003-015-04-00, 8ª Turma do Tribunal Regional do Trabalho da 4ª Região do Rio de Janeiro. Available at http://www.conjur.com.br/2004-ago-17/ambev_condenada_submeter_empregado_humilhacoes

[37] In another case, Ambev was condemned to pay BRL1 million in a collective psychological harassment case involving dozens of workers punished for not meeting their sales goals. Case TRT 6ª Reg., Proc. Nº 00340-2004-005-06-00-1. Available at http://www.conjur.com.br/2006-ago-23/ambev_pagar_milhao_assedio_moral_coletivo

[37] Case TRT 6ª Reg., Proc. Nº 00340-2004-005-06-00-1 available at http://www.conjur.com.br/2006-ago-23/ambev_pagar_milhao_assedio_moral_coletivo

[38] Case AIRR 1370/2005-006-20-40.0 from 6ª Turma do Tribunal Superior do Trabalho de Sergipe. Available at http://www.conjur.com.br/2006-dez-18/ex-empregado_AB-Inbev_indenizacao_danos

[39] According to court documents, the "employee of the month" received the right to choose one of the prostitutes for his personal pleasure as an award (all paid with company resources). The employee who sued the company claimed to suffer psychological problems due to conflicts with his religion. Case RR-3253900-09.2007.5.09.0011. 5ª turma do TST do Paraná. Available at http://www.trt4.jus.br/portal/portal/EscolaJudicial/biblioteca/noticia/info/NoticiaWindow?cod=602817&action=2&destaque=false

[40] Case AIRR 1370/2005-006-20-40.0; 6ª Turma do Tribunal Superior do Trabalho de Sergipe. Available at http://www.conjur.com.br/2006-dez-18/ex-empregado_ambev_indenizacao_danos

[41] On culture & values, for instance, AB InBev exhibited a score of 2.9 on a 1-5 scale, much lower than 4.0 of Heineken and 3.5 of MillerCoors. On work/life balance, the gap was even bigger: AB InBev scored only 2.3, against 3.4 of Heineken and 3.1 of MillerCoors. Just in the last dimension (career opportunities), AB InBev presented similar means to industry peers. Online assessment carried out on 01/14/018. Source: https://www.glassdoor.com/Reviews/Anheuser-Busch-InBev-Reviews-E428473.htm

[42] In a review of scientific papers on "corporate psychopaths," Boddy (2015) associates the presence of psychopaths in the highest echelons with the following behaviors in the business world: unnecessary layoffs of employees, over-exploitation of the workforce, lack of sense of corporate citizenship, disengaged employees, constant bullying and harassment in the workplace, political decision-making, short-term focus on corporate decisions, and tendency to go on acquisition sprees. It is remarkable – and scary – to note the presence of many of these behaviors in the criticisms coming from people closely involved with the AB InBev model.

⁴³ In addition to questioning the company's ethical behavior, the AB InBev model has also been subject to other criticisms from its business angle. Specifically, some commentators are skeptics if the AB-InBev's model: 1) will be able not only to cut costs in the short-term, but also to grow as a result of innovation and other value-creation initiatives; and, 2) if it will be sustainable in the long-term (or always dependent on periodic mergers and acquisitions). For Cuadros (2016: 209;211), the AB-Inbev's model is the product of a world with lots of cheap speculative money. According to the author, after asking 3G people to name something new they had created in their companies, he did not get a response. His conclusion is that the model is like a "creative destruction, but without the creative part."

Part 3: Core Implications of Behavioral Ethics Findings for Sound Management and Governance

9. Business scandals are not caused by a few bad apples

"If you put good apples into a bad situation, you'll get bad apples."
Philip Zimbardo (1933–)[1]

The central results of behavioral ethics described in the first two parts of the book, i.e., the tendency to overestimate our ethical behavior and the awareness that most of the wrong things are done by good people, have a very clear implication for sound business practices: large corporate scandals are usually not caused by a few "bad apples" but by dysfunctional management and governance systems that induce ordinary people to become ethically blind.

First, it is necessary to recognize that every organization obviously has some "bad apples," i.e., individuals who are willing to do anything to maximize their personal

The Virtuous Barrel:
How to Transform Corporate Scandals into Good Businesses via Behavioral Ethics

outcome in terms of money and power. To a large extent, these people have varying degrees of psychopathy, a personality disorder that can cause serious harm to the reputation and culture of organizations.[2] Some researchers, for example, relate the outbreak of the 2008 global financial crisis to the presence of psychopaths in the upper echelons of the financial world.[3] Others, in turn, claim that "corporate psychopaths" are currently the biggest threat to companies around the world.[4] As pointed out by Robert Hare, a leading authority on this field who has developed a checklist named PCL-Revised to diagnose psychopathy, "Not all psychopaths are in prison. Some are in the boardrooms."[5]

The main characteristics of psychopaths, in general, are amorality and the lack of empathy. These individuals, therefore, are not necessarily immoral because they are capable of distinguishing right from wrong. However, they ignore the ethical implications of their actions as well as the importance of upholding moral values such as respect and honesty to maximize their personal gains.

Curiously, the description of psychopaths fits perfectly into the *homo economicus* archetype, the stereotype advocated by traditional economists as the appropriate model to depict human beings. The box below describes the main features of psychopaths and the typical behaviors they manifest in the business world. This information may be useful for business leaders willing to identify and weed out such bad apples from their organizations.[6]

> *Psychopaths as the rotten apples of the business world*
>
> *Which characteristics define psychopaths, a group that most often corresponds to the "rotten apples" within organizations? The Psychopathy Checklist Revised (PCL-R) created by the psychologist Robert Hare is accepted by many as the best method to determine the presence and extent of psychopathy in a person. It evaluates 20 characteristics commonly associated with this mental disorder:*
>
> 1. *Glib and superficial charm*
> 2. *Grandiose (exaggeratedly high) estimation of self*
> 3. *Need for stimulation*

4. *Pathological lying*
5. *Cunning and manipulativeness*
6. *Lack of remorse or guilt*
7. *Shallow affect (superficial emotional responsiveness)*
8. *Callousness and lack of empathy*
9. *Parasitic lifestyle*
10. *Poor behavioral controls*
11. *Sexual promiscuity*
12. *Early behavior problems*
13. *Lack of realistic long-term goals*
14. *Impulsivity*
15. *Irresponsibility*
16. *Failure to accept responsibility for own actions*
17. *Many short-term marital relationships*
18. *Juvenile delinquency*
19. *Revocation of conditional release*
20. *Criminal versatility*

For each item, a score of 0, 1, or 2 is assigned by a qualified professional based on how well it applies to the individual. Zero means "does not apply in any way"; 1 means "partially applies"; and 2 means "fully applies." The maximum score of the index is 40. A score of 30 or above qualifies a person for a diagnosis of psychopathy (people with no criminal history usually score around 5).

In the workplace, psychopaths tend to exhibit the following unethical behaviors:

- *Public humiliation of subordinates*
- *Tendency to spread lies about colleagues to harm them*
- *Harassment and frequent bullying of peers and subordinates*
- *Systematic use of lies to reinforce their point of view*
- *Quickness in blaming others for unfinished work*
- *Tendency to sabotage or steal other people's projects*
- *Attempt to receive the credits for works carried out by teammates*
- *Establishing unrealistic goals for others to make them fail*
- *Invasion of privacy*
- *Attempt of having sexual relationships with junior or senior staff*

While it is important to recognize that there are indeed some people with malicious intent within companies, evidence shows that these bad apples constitute a tiny minority

The Virtuous Barrel:
How to Transform Corporate Scandals into Good Businesses via Behavioral Ethics

of the population. In the case of psychopaths, for example, it is estimated that about 1% of men exhibit this mental disorder (and far fewer women).[7]

It is important, though, to make a caveat on this proportion before we go ahead: Although small in general, evidence also shows that the ratio of psychopaths tends to be much higher in senior-level positions in the corporate world than in the population at large.[8] In a survey of 203 executives selected by their companies to participate in management development programs, for example, a group of researchers found that 4% of them scored 30 or more in the PCL-R test, the standard threshold for psychopathy.[9]

Another recent paper found even more frightening results: The authors concluded that the prevalence rate of psychopathy in senior management positions may be as large as the prevalence rates found in the criminal population.[10] According to the study, based on the assessment of 261 managers working in the supply chain industry, 21% of the executives were found to exhibit significant levels of psychopathic traits, a level similar to the 20% typically found in US prisons.

A third study, this time conducted in the United Kingdom, analyzed the presence of 11 different personality disorders in three groups: 317 forensic patients diagnosed with psychopathic personality disorder, 768 mentally ill patients, and 39 senior business managers from British companies in leadership positions.[11] The two first groups were comprised by individuals hospitalized at Broadmoor Special Hospital in England (all of them by definition with serious disorders). Amazingly, the authors found that the sample of senior business managers displayed significantly higher levels of histrionic personality patterns than both the mentally ill and psychopathic samples. In addition, although not statistically significant, senior business managers also exhibited greater absolute levels of narcissistic and obsessive-compulsive personality traits in relation to the two comparison groups.[12] According to the authors, managers' higher levels of histrionic, narcissist, and obsessive-compulsive personality traits bear resemblance to the typical features of psychopathy.[13]

Notwithstanding the important results of these papers, which should be seriously considered in executive selection and evaluation processes, the overwhelming majority of people working in companies obviously have good values and intentions. Thus, the existence of some bad apples such as psychopaths do not suffice to explain the extent and magnitude of the huge corporate scandals we are constantly witnessing.

Let's take the Volkswagen emissions scandal (also known as "Dieselgate") as an example. In September 2015, the US Environmental Protection Agency (EPA) announced that the German automaker had installed software in its vehicles that detected when they were being tested and artificially improved their environmental performance. Thanks to this defeat device, nitrogen oxides (NOx) emissions by VW diesel engines seemed to be within regulatory standards, when in fact they were emitting up to 40 times more toxic fumes than allowed. Initially, the EPA reported that VW had rigged tests of around 500,000 vehicles produced in the US between 2009 and 2015. Later, it was uncovered that the fraud was global, reaching 11 million cars of three brands of the company (VW, Audi and Porsche) in different countries.

It is noteworthy that the emission of NOx above legal limits does not only cause greater pollution of the environment: A scientific study concluded, for example, that Volkswagen's excess emissions are likely to have caused an estimate of 60 early deaths in the United States due to respiratory problems.[14]

A scandal of this magnitude, carried out over many years in several countries, cannot obviously be attributed to a small group of psychopaths or rotten apples. In fact, a deeper analysis of the case shows that many factors associated with collective ethical blindness were present at Volkswagen.

To begin with, the company had an extremely hierarchical culture, with very little room for dissent. In an interview with German magazine *Der Spiegel*, for example, a former employee claimed that VW was like "North Korea without labor camps" and that "You have to obey!"[15] Aggressiveness was also present. According to a senior Volkswagen executive interviewed on condition of anonymity by *The New York Times*,

The Virtuous Barrel:
How to Transform Corporate Scandals into Good Businesses via Behavioral Ethics

"They only know one way of management: be aggressive at all times!"[16] Fierce internal competition was another element of the organizational culture. In a letter published in the Italian newspaper *Corriere della Sera*, a company engineer described a workplace where highly skilled engineers competed hard for recognition and promotion. According to the executive, "In recent years here at Volkswagen, we forgot to say: 'I will not do that. I cannot. Excuse me.'"[17]

Volkswagen was run with an iron fist by two people, both engineers: its CEO Martin Winterkorn and the chairman of the supervisory board (and one of the major shareholders) Ferdinand Piëch.[18] Winterkorn was known for harshly criticizing subordinates in public as well as for not tolerating failures. The authoritarian profile applied even to other top executives. In an interview with Reuters, a former company C-level executive said he had seen presidents of different VW units being treated in an extremely disrespectful way on several occasions. In the same article, another executive described an environment full of tension: "There was always a distance, a fear, and a respect ... if he would come and visit or you had to go to him, your pulse would go up. If you presented bad news, those were the moments that it could become quite unpleasant and loud and quite demeaning."[19]

The high pressure coming from superiors has become even greater after VW leadership set extremely ambitious goals. Shortly after taking office in 2007, Winterkorn decided that the hallmark of his administration would be making VW the largest automaker in the world. The US market was key to achieve this goal: It was a market where VW had to "grow or grow" (the CEO of VW's North American operations left the company in 2013 after failing to meet aggressive sales targets).

Between 2007 and 2015, Volkswagen grew strongly, nearly doubling the number of vehicles sold to 10 million units and reaching annual revenues of $225 billion. Ironically, just before the eruption of the scandal in early 2015, VW overtook Toyota and achieved Winterkorn's goal of becoming the world's largest automaker. The joy, however, was short-lived for the CEO. Winterkorn was forced to resign right after the scandal and currently faces legal problems in the United States.[20]

Besides the strong pressure of the immediate and organizational contexts, the institutional context also contributed to VW's troubles. In an article on the scandal, Professor Guido Palazzo of the University of Lausanne remarks that the auto industry already had a long history of cheating on emission tests.[21] He points out that a number of companies in the industry had paid million dollar fines for similar frauds since 1973, including General Motors, Volvo, Renault, Honda, Ford, and Mitsubishi (the most recent case involved Fiat Chrysler in early 2017).[22] For decades, therefore, it has been customary in the auto industry to mislead regulators by developing systems to defeat emissions control systems. In addition, according to the researcher, European automakers have received the implicit support of European governments to keep these practices. In his words, "The problem of the deviation of real-world emissions from laboratory tests were well known since many years. However, many governments blocked stricter regulations on the EU level. Diesel was the technology European companies had chosen and diesel was thus the technology European governments supported with their decisions."[23]

In addition to contextual pressures, the time factor was also present. According to the investigations, Volkswagen engineers concluded in 2008 that it would be impossible to meet the stringent US environmental standards in an economically viable way after years of work and billions of investments. The enormous time pressure to find a short-term solution to enable the sale of vehicles in the United States, coupled with the idea that the defeat device would be just a quick fix no longer necessary in the near future, probably contributed to the fraud.

Slowly and gradually, therefore, the installment of deceit devices on a relatively small number of vehicles for the sake of obtaining the regulators' stamp and obtain access to a big market became a gigantic "snowball" that resulted in a fraud involving millions of

The Virtuous Barrel:
How to Transform Corporate Scandals into Good Businesses via Behavioral Ethics

cars around the world, possibly causing the premature death of hundreds or even thousands of people.

The Volkswagen scandal, therefore, only reached such a colossal scale because it obtained the tacit or explicit support from many ordinary and well-intentioned people with good values who probably came to perceive illegal practices as something justifiable or at least temporarily needed. The same reasoning applies to other scandals described in this book. In all these episodes, it becomes clear that the greatest risk does not come from a few bad apples, but from ordinary people who begin to ignore and rationalize their unethical behavior as a result of the day-to-day pressures of the business world.

In these scandals, an important concept called "motivated reasoning" or "willful blindness" is also present.[24] These terms refer to our tendency to selectively notice, encode, and retain information that is consistent with our self-serving desires. In the field of ethics, it usually involves ignoring others' people unethical behavior when it is not in our best interest to observe them.

A remarkable example of motivated reasoning comes from Brunhilde Pomsel, secretary of Joseph Goebbels, the powerful propaganda minister of the Nazi Party and one of Hitler's right-hand men. In an interview with *The Guardian* in December 2016, at the age of 105, Brunhilde said: "My job was a job like any other. I didn't do anything other than type in Goebbels' office ... I know no one ever believes us nowadays – everyone thinks we knew everything. We knew nothing, it was all kept well secret ... We believed that Jews who had been 'disappeared' had been sent to territories in need of being repopulated."[25]

Brunhilde's story exemplifies our propensity not to notice actions we prefer not to observe. This tends to be particularly true in large bureaucracies that end up separating individuals from the consequence of their actions. As noted by psychologist Robert Jackall, "Compartmentalization provides wholly acceptable rationales for not knowing about problems or for not trying to find out."[26] Our propensity to engage in willful blindness also stems from both the confirmation and the self-serving biases, as discussed in Chapter 2. As we continuously filter or edit information from the outside world to maintain our positive self-image, we end up seeing what we want and often not perceiving what we do not want.

In the business world, leaders and subordinates often resort to willful blindness. In the case of managers, we often hear arguments such as "I was not aware that something wrong was going on there." This was used, for example, as part of the defense of Jeffrey Skilling, former CEO of Enron. In response, case judge Simeon Lake instructed the jury that "You may find that a defendant had knowledge of a fact if you find that he deliberately closed his eyes to what would otherwise have been obvious to him ... knowledge can be inferred if the defendant deliberately blinded himself to the existence of a fact."[27] The judge applied a legal concept on willful blindness in effect in the United States since the nineteenth century: You are held accountable if you should have knowledge of something and, given the opportunity to know about it, you have actively preferred not to see or not to know.[28]

In the case of subordinates, the motivation to remain blind to other's people conduct is reinforced by organizational elements such as financial incentives, fear of conflict, loyalty to the organization, obedience to authority, attachment to routines, and conflicts of interest. Regarding this last issue, various studies have shown that it is virtually impossible for us to analyze a certain situation in an exempt way when we have some interest at stake.

One of the most interesting works in this field was published by a group of four neuroscientists in 2010.[29] They recruited 150 people to take part in the study. Participants were told to evaluate works of art from two galleries with fictitious names: "Third Moon" and "Wecyclers." They were also informed that the study and their payment, of $30 for the volunteers from the first group, increasing to up to $300 for those from other groups, were being generously sponsored by one of two galleries: Some were randomly told that the study was being promoted by "Third Moon," others by "Wecyclers."

The Virtuous Barrel:
How to Transform Corporate Scandals into Good Businesses via Behavioral Ethics

Individuals were placed inside a functional magnetic resonance imaging (fMRI) scanner. Sixty works of art were presented, one at a time for five seconds. In the upper-right corner, researchers exhibited the logo of the gallery that was allegedly sponsoring the experiment. Some artworks belonged to the "sponsor" while others belonged to the other gallery. Participants then evaluated the works on a scale of -4 (disliked) to +4 (liked). Participants' payment was fixed irrespective of their evaluation. What happened?

The participants assigned much better ratings to the artworks of the gallery that was allegedly sponsoring them. To see if the responses were merely the outcome of a social tendency to consciously reciprocate the benefactor's kindness, researchers looked at fMRI data. They made a remarkable observation: The presence of the logo of the fictitious sponsor substantially increased the activity of the ventromedial prefrontal cortex, an area of the brain associated with pleasure.

In other words, the gallery's courtesy in "sponsoring" the study deeply influenced the way individuals rated the works of art. When participants were questioned if they believed that the sponsor's logo had influenced their preferences, the general response was that "No, certainly there was no influence at all."

Other papers corroborate the results of this relevant research. One of them, for example, found that auditors under conflict of interest, such as providing advisory services to audited clients, are more likely to engage into motivated reasoning.[30] Another concluded that the experts expected to make neutral judgments tend to perceive the value of an asset in a biased way in favor of the party that is paying for their advice.[31]

Most of the time, these behaviors occur unconsciously. Taken to the field of business ethics, these studies reinforce the idea that governance scandals only occur when many well-intentioned people exhibit willful blindness.

The first core implication of behavioral ethics, therefore, is clear: If we really want to make companies well-managed and governed, we should focus on solving the barrel problem instead of searching for bad apples. As we shall see in Chapter 12, this means creating an organizational culture based on elements such as trust, high intrinsic motivation, psychological safety, openness to speak up, ethical leadership, and empathy.

---

[1] Source: A Conversation with Philip G. Zimbardo: Finding Hope in Knowing the Universal Capacity for Evil. The New York Times, Apr. 3, 2007.

[2] Some authors argue that psychopathy is part of the so-called "dark triad," a set of three often correlated traits that leads to unethical behavior. The other two are narcissism and machiavellianism. For more on this, see Jones (2014), Furnham et al. (2013), O'Boyle et al. (2012), and Li-Ping Tang et al. (2008).

[3] Marshall et al. (2013), Boddy (2011), Boddy et al. (2010), and Cohan (2012).

[4] Marshall et al. (2015).

[5] Hare (2002).

[6] The box was written based on the Hare Psychopathy Checklist available at: http://www.minddisorders.com/Flu-Inv/Hare-Psychopathy-Checklist.html#ixzz4VIM7V630

[7] It is estimated that the frequency of psychopathy in men is 10 to 20 higher than the presence in women (Wynn et al., 2012 and https://www.psychologytoday.com/blog/the-human-equation/201205/female-psychopaths).

[8] According to Chiaburu et al. (2013), one possible cause is that psychopaths have a greater likelihood of engaging in careerism, the propensity to achieve personal and career goals through non-performance-based activities. Based on data from 131 individuals, the authors observed that emotional stability was negatively correlated with careerism and that psychopathy was indeed an important factor in predicting careerism.

[9] Babiak et al. (2010) found that executives exhibiting high levels of psychopathic traits were positively associated with in-house ratings of charisma/presentation style (creativity, good strategic thinking and communication skills), but negatively associated with ratings of responsibility/performance (being a team player, management skills, and overall accomplishments).

[10] Fritzon et al. (2016).

[11] Board and Fritzon (2005).

[12] Histrionic personality disorder is characterized by the need to draw attention by exhibiting a pattern of excessive emotionality. A person with this disorder wants to be the center of attention of the group to which he or she belongs, and this often leads him or her to display traits such as superficial charm, falsehood, egocentrism and manipulation. Narcissism, or narcissistic personality disorder, in turn, is a mental disorder in which the person has an inflated perception of his or her own importance. The excessive focus on oneself and the exploitation of others leads to traits like lack of empathy. The narcissist's sense of grandiose, however, usually hides a very low self-esteem and vulnerability to minor criticism. The third disorder most frequently encountered in senior executives was obsessive-compulsive personality. This disorder is characterized by a constant feeling of doubt, perfectionism, scrupulosity, verifications, preoccupation with details, stubbornness, and excessive rigidity.

[13] Other papers stand out on this field, such as Boddy (2015), Mathieu et al. (2014), Smith and Lilienfeld (2013), Boddy et al. (2010), and Babiak and Hare (2006).

[14] Barrett et al. (2015). In this regard, because VW used the idea that its vehicles were

environmentally "clean" as a marketing tool, it is likely that many people more sensitive to pollution may have felt more encouraged to buy them.

[15] The New York Times. 12/13/2015. The Engineering of Volkswagen's Aggressive Ambition. Available at https://nyti.ms/2kdgjb5

[16] *Ibid.*

[17] Corriere della Sera. 10/14/2015. Carta de Emanuela Montefrancesco. Emanuela, ingegnere di Volkswagen: «Se cerchi l'auto perfetta, fai la furbata. Poteva succedere pure a me» Available at http://www.corriere.it/economia/15_ottobre_13/emanuela-ingegnere-volkswagen-se-capo-vuole-l-auto-perfetta-fai-furbata-poteva-succedere-pure-me-a81d11fe-71c7-11e5-b015-f1d3b8f071aa.shtml

[18] It is worth noting that Piëch was VW's former CEO from 1993 to 2002.

[19] Reuters. 10/10/2015. Fear and respect: VW's culture under Winterkorn. Available at http://www.reuters.com/article/us-volkswagen-emissions-culture-idUSKCN0S40MT20151010

[20] *Ibid.*

[21] Source: Palazzo, G. 2016. After the fall: Dieselgate and Corporate Responsibility. Available at https://www.alumnihec.ch/wp-content/uploads/2016/04/GuidoPalazzo.pdf .

[22] Source: The Washington Post. 01/12/2017. EPA: Fiat Chrysler software enabled emissions cheating. .

[23] Source: Palazzo, G. 2016. After the fall: Dieselgate and Corporate Responsibility. Available at https://www.alumnihec.ch/wp-content/uploads/2016/04/GuidoPalazzo.pdf .

[24] For more on this, see Heffernan (2011).

[25] Source: The Guardian. 12/30/2016. "Joseph Goebbels' 105-year-old secretary: 'No one believes me now, but I knew nothing'". Available at https://www.theguardian.com/world/2016/aug/15/brunhilde-pomsel-nazi-joseph-goebbels-propaganda-machine

[26] Jackall (1988: 194).

[27] Heffernan (2011:1). Available at http://www.ca5.uscourts.gov/opinions%5Cpub%5C06/06-20885-CR0.wpd.pdf

[28] According to Daniel (2013), the legal concept of willful blindness or motivated ignorance began with the Regina v. Sleep in the nineteenth century in the United States. In this case, the judge ruled that the defendant could not be convicted for possession of public property unless the jury concluded that he knew the origin of the property or that he "intentionally closed his eyes to this fact."

[29] Harvey et al. (2010).

[30] Moore et al. (2003). There are other interesting works on this field, such as Koch et al. (2012), Bazerman and Moore (2011), Bazerman et al. (2006), and Bazerman et al. (2002).

[31] Moore et al. (2010).

Alexandre Di Miceli da Silveira

10. Rules and controls have limited efficacy and can generate dangerous side effects

> *"The first common misuse of reports and procedures is the common belief that procedures are instruments of morality. They are not ... Problems of right conduct can never be 'proceduralized'; conversely, right conduct can never be established by procedure."*
> Peter Drucker (1909–2005)[1]

The second core implication of behavioral ethics for sound management and governance is that it is necessary to go way beyond the implementation of traditional compliance programs in order to ensure that organizations are in fact well-governed.

Currently, large companies usually spend millions of dollars per year on typical activities of a compliance program, such as publishing codes of ethics, establishing whistleblower channels, appointing chief compliance officers and ombudsmen positions, implementing compliance trainings, and so on. The result of this true "compliance arms race" to prevent and detect wrongdoings is generally poor.[2] Trust in companies did not improve over the last decade, while one study concluded that the level of observed misconducts was the same in 2015 as in the time of the 2008 global crisis.[3] Thus, there is no clear evidence that these extensive activities, which have proliferated since the 2000 decade, have indeed reduced malfeasance or made companies more principled in their relationship with society.

The Virtuous Barrel:
How to Transform Corporate Scandals into Good Businesses via Behavioral Ethics

Actually, it is worth mentioning that the vast majority of companies involved in scandals, such as Petrobras, Wells Fargo, and Volkswagen, already had control departments as well as internal policies in line with market recommendations. The existence of formal corporate governance mechanisms was even highlighted by Pedro Barusco, the former manager of Petrobras who embezzled millions to his personal account, as mentioned earlier in this book. In his testimony, he said that "Despite what happened, I think corporate governance at Petrobras was good. The problem is not in this fact, it is in the people."[4]

Why have traditional compliance programs failed to promote integrity in business? To begin with, three main problems limit the effectiveness of these programs.

The first is that they are designed from a purely legal perspective. Consequently, compliance with regulations is not treated as an intrinsically important issue ("Let's do the right thing here because this is the right thing to do") but as a series of check-the-box exercises aimed at producing reports to satisfy external audiences and reduce potential penalties by regulators. It is no coincidence that many employees see compliance programs as a series of pro forma routines and bureaucratic trainings. Three bankers from Swiss bank Credit Suisse AG went even further: From 2013 to 2015, they simply got their secretaries to do their compliance training. The case, disclosed by US Financial Industry Regulatory Authority (FINRA) earlier in 2018, showed that three heads of a unit that sells securities to investors gave their logins to administrative assistants to complete required eLearning modules on their behalf (ironically, one of the trainings was exactly about "unauthorized trading awareness").[5]

French philosopher Albert Camus used to say that "integrity has no need of rules."[6] Accordingly, honorable conduct goes well beyond the mere legal compliance with regulations. Because ethics go far beyond compliance, companies should focus on the former instead of the later. Thus, instead of creating "check-the-box" programs where employees follow procedures blindly, firms should urge them to think critically on what's the right thing to do. As summarized by a recent report, "Paradoxically, the less we focus attention on sticking to the rules, and the more on building a culture rooted in ethics, the greater the level of compliance."[7]

To promote sound ethical behavior, it is also important not to focus on the typical prohibitions emphasized by compliance programs ("This cannot be done because it goes against the rules") but on the positive aspects and virtues that everyone is required to demonstrate in the workplace ("Let's always do the right thing here!"). As pointed out by a report of the Ethics and Compliance initiative, "Workplace integrity – doing what's right in a professional context – encompasses a top-to-bottom commitment to treating others with respect, being honest and forthright and dealing fairly with those inside and outside the organization."[8]

In addition, firms should improve the way they measure the effectiveness of their compliance programs by moving from a checklist approach focusing on inputs to one focused on outcomes. One idea, proposed by expert Hui Chen and professor Eugene Soltes, is to design better models supported by richer data, so companies can objectively test what works and what doesn't in promoting the expected behaviors. As they point out, "While many firms continue to see ensuring compliance as a legal exercise, it is really much more a behavioral science."[9]

The second limitation is that the control areas created by these programs are often disconnected from the day-to-day management of the company, notably from top management. This makes these departments seen as being solely responsible for a firm's compliance with regulations, an issue that is obviously a requirement of every member of an organization. It is also worth noting that these control areas often lack the internal political power to question improper practices coming from star employees or senior managers such as those from the C-Suite. A good example comes from the financial industry. In a book about London's financial district, a veteran from the industry described that "Compliance people are always enormously intimidated by the traders. You know which ones have a huge P [profits] and L [losses] and are making a lot for the bank. Hotshot traders can be abrupt and abrasive, always under pressure … nobody ever

The Virtuous Barrel:
How to Transform Corporate Scandals into Good Businesses via Behavioral Ethics

challenges the front office. I have never seen it happen."[10] In extreme cases, a compliance program may even be designed from the outset with the intention of not working properly in order to camouflage unscrupulous acts at the top of the organization. Appendix 1 at the end of this chapter provides scientific evidence supporting this assertion.

The third problem is the most serious of all: Traditional compliance programs are designed to find defectors, that is, the value-destroying activities committed by malicious people (the so-called "bad apples" risk). They largely disregard, therefore, the systemic risk associated with the creation of a rogue culture without proper social and ethical awareness (the "barrel" risk), including the three layers of contextual pressures and the time factor, as described in part two.

Thus, compliance programs are usually focused on curbing corruption at the expense of the company – not corruption (or other unethical practices) carried out on behalf of the organization. In many recent scandals, for instance, perpetrators justified their improper behavior by saying that they were trying to protect or add value to their companies. Ethical blindness results from strong contexts that often lead people into unethical pro-organizational behaviors such as cheating society and harming stakeholders. As a result, both risks must be tackled.

In addition to these three limitations, the excessive emphasis on rules and controls has another major deficiency: It can lead to relevant side effects that can even increase the number of transgressions. In other words, traditional compliance programs may not only diminish business efficiency but also worsen the ethical behavior in the organization by fostering the bad conduct they were exactly designed to avoid. Many studies show that this may occur for two reasons.

The first is the encouragement of amoral behaviors. By removing the moral perspective from decisions, the emphasis on legal compliance motivates people to act in a strictly rational and calculated way based on the economic costs and benefits of compliance with internal policies or regulations. Tacitly, they begin to adopt the premise that "anything that is not explicitly forbidden is allowed" and stop questioning themselves about the right thing to do. As a consequence, transgressions tend to increase.

An experiment carried out by researchers Uri Gneezy and Aldo Rustichini in a group of 10 day-care centers in Israel demonstrates how this happens.[11] There, some parents used to arrive late to collect their children, forcing teachers to stay in place for hours after closing time. In order to resolve the situation, the schools introduced a monetary fine for late-coming parents. According to economic theory, applying a financial penalty would lead to a reduction in unwanted behaviors.

The establishment of the fine, however, produced the opposite result: the number of late-coming parents simply doubled. Thus, by removing the moral perspective of the situation, i.e., that parents should pick up their children on schedule to respect teachers, parents felt morally free to arrive at the time they wished, provided they paid the fine. The "financialization" of the delay served as a "free moral pass" for parents to begin viewing the situation from a strictly economic and amoral perspective.[12]

Another experiment performed by researchers Ann Tenbrunsel and David Messick came up with similar results.[13] The researchers looked at how surveillance and sanctioning systems affect cooperative behavior in situations in which participants were faced with a decision either to cooperate or to behave selfishly. The authors reached two main conclusions. The first is that implementing a sanctioning system led to less cooperation than utilizing no sanctioning system. The second is that sanctions affected the type of decision people perceived to be making, inducing them to see it as a business rather than ethical decision. Taken together, these conclusions corroborate the view that individuals tend to become increasingly amoral when organizations emphasize monitoring.

It is critical, therefore, to consider the potential side effects stemming from an emphasis on controls over people's moral motivations, including its consequences for society. Removing the moral dimension of business decisions tends create a condition of

The Virtuous Barrel:
How to Transform Corporate Scandals into Good Businesses via Behavioral Ethics

anomie in which people think of their actions only as "business" decisions.[14] Thus, the moral dimension, which is what humanizes us and binds us together, cannot be removed.

On the contrary. Leaders must reinforce the ethical perspective of every company decision by making each person responsible for reflecting and acting on what should be morally right to do. This assertion is corroborated by a former treasury director of a global financial institution. In an interview on condition of anonymity, he said that "For the financial sector ever to improve, you'd have to untangle the inherent tendency to amorality. And that tendency is embedded in the system. In an amoral environment like that, right and wrong become blurry and hard to define."[15]

Muel Kaptein, author of the book *Workplace Morality*, describes a second side effect connected to an emphasis on controls. People tend to feel resentful with their situation when they are excessively monitored. As a result, they are inclined to rebel against restrictions on their freedom, which can make them more likely to break the rules. According to Jack Brehm's theory of psychological reactance,[16] when an environment is overly monitored, individuals seek to reduce the unpleasant feeling caused by the imposed restrictions. This, is turn, may lead people to exhibit an opposite-to-expected behavior in order to reassert their freedom. As the saying goes, "Forbidden fruits taste the best because they taste of freedom...."[17]

James Pennebaker and Deborah Sanders demonstrated the effect of prohibitions on people's behavior in a curious experiment.[18] They placed placards in toilet stalls in male restrooms at a large university. The placards, affixed to the inside of each door, were situated at eye level when seated. One of them contained a high-threat message ("Do NOT Write on the Walls"), while the other had a gentle request ("Please, do not write on the walls."). In the end, the placards with more aggressive warnings were graffitied twice as much and in a more belligerent way than those with a polite appeal.

Thus, the more threatening is the prohibition order, the greater is the chance of people doing exactly the opposite. This clearly shows that imposing compliance is not effective:

The importance is to create an environment in which people are willing to stick to the rules and do not fear denouncing those who do not comply with them.

Besides these two side effects, the excessive emphasis on rules and controls can lead to other potential adverse outcomes worth mentioning, such as:

1. Fear of taking responsibility: too many rules can make people extremely fearful of violating them to such an extent that they become paralyzed.
2. Exclusive focus on compliance at the expense of the quality of work: Instead of seeing rules as a means to properly reach a greater goal, individuals can come see them as an end in themselves ("the patient has died, but at least we followed all the procedures").
3. Snowball effect on compliance costs: The greater the investment on rules and controls, the more will have to be spent in the future on monitoring because it will become increasingly difficult to restore the ethical dimension in people's minds. In this sense, Peter Drucker used to say that "Every business should regularly find out whether it needs all the reports and procedures it uses ... to 'control' everything is to control nothing."[19]

Overemphasizing controls and monitoring, therefore, can make people hesitant in a way that they end up lacking critical thinking and begin to blindly stick to the rules. They may also find ways to work around whatever standards exist, and the smarter individuals are, the more likely they are to succeed.[20] The overall results could not be more detrimental: lower productivity, increased stress, fear, and anxiety in the organization.

There is also a key issue to be discussed before concluding the debate on the negative effects of rules and controls. It concerns the premise adopted by companies regarding human nature.

Companies that believe they will solve their ethical problems through compliance systems depart from a negative or "Hobbesian" assumption about people.[21] Many organizations (if not the vast majority) believe that their employees simply cannot be trusted to make decisions and to act in the best interests of the firm. As a result, their

The Virtuous Barrel:
How to Transform Corporate Scandals into Good Businesses via Behavioral Ethics

control systems may reach such a paranoid level that they end up establishing a sort of Bentham Panopticon, i.e., a system in which all people are watched 24 hours by a central observer.[22]

The problem in adopting, implicitly or explicitly, a negative view about people is that science shows that human beings tend to respond to the way they are treated, for good or for bad. This is the so-called Pygmalion effect: the way people are viewed influences how they are treated. This, in turn, leads individuals acting according to expectations, in a true self-fulfilling prophecy.[23]

The Pygmalion effect was first studied by researchers Robert Rosenthal and Lenore Jacobson in an elementary school.[24] In their experiment, all students of a certain class initially took an intelligence test. The researchers then randomly selected 20% of the students and told teachers that these students had the highest scores on a "test for intellectual blooming," supposedly a good predictor of unusual intellectual gains in the future (teachers were intentionally misled by researchers). Eight months later, all children took once again the same intelligence test applied at the beginning of the study. Remarkably, the students whose teachers believed they had the greatest intellectual potential indeed exhibited the highest IQ increase during this period. According to the researchers, teachers began to behave differently toward these students throughout the year, listening more closely to their opinions, raising their self-esteem, and so on. This differentiated treatment led the selected children, in turn, to develop themselves more than others. At the end, the expectation that this group would perform better in fact materialized in greater intellectual advancement.

Similar to the Pygmalion effect, the self-perception theory argues that individuals change their behavior when they begin to see themselves differently.[25] A curious experiment in 2010, for example, observed that people behave more dishonestly when they took part in a test wearing fake sunglasses. According to authors, the individuals' self-view changed after using a counterfeit product: They came to see themselves as cheaters who were already doing something illegal. Consequently, the negative self-image increased their propensity to cheat.[26]

All these papers show that the expectations bosses create about their employees are often confirmed. This happens because leaders start to behave based on their premise, and employees are likely to respond accordingly. Fortunately, this process can also be used to foster good behaviors.

A good example comes from the case of FAVI, a factory specialized in copper alloys and gear forks for the automotive industry with around 500 employees located in the north of France. In 1983, a new CEO named Jean-François Zobrist took place and implemented a radical transformation in the organization.

According to Frederic Laloux, who carried out an in-depth study about FAVI for his book *Reinventing Organizations*, one of the main initiatives of the new CEO was to adopt a new set of assumptions about employees.[27] After studying the company practices and talking to people before taking over, Zobrist concluded that FAVI's previous management team assumed that employees were:

- Thieves, because all equipment had to be locked up in storage rooms;
- Lazy, because their working time had always to be controlled;
- Incapable, because the quality of their production had always to be verified by somebody else; and,
- Stupid, because managers had to think and make all decisions for them.

To change this scenario, Zobrist defined three new assumptions that, over time, became true mantras at FAVI:

1. People are systematically considered to be good, i.e., reliable, self-motivated, trustworthy, and intelligent;
2. There is no performance without happiness: to be happy, people need to be motivated. To be motivated, people need to be responsible. To be responsible people must understand "why" and "for whom" they work, and be free to decide on the "how"; and,

The Virtuous Barrel:
How to Transform Corporate Scandals into Good Businesses via Behavioral Ethics

3. Value is created on the shop floor: frontline workers craft the products; the CEO and the administrative staff at best serve to support them and, at worst, are costly distractions.

This paradigm shift broke the previous vicious circle in which fear bred more fear and established a virtuous circle in which the trust assigned to employees generated ever-increasing levels of commitment and loyalty to the organization. The positive outcome was evident in the company's remarkable performance over the long tenure of Zobrist as CEO from 1983 until his retirement in 2009.[28] FAVI's practices and results are detailed in Chapter 14. For now, suffice it to say that FAVI was the only European company in its industry to stand up to Chinese competition: Its former Europeans competitors either shut their doors or moved production to China to take advantage of cheap labor.

The Pygmalion effect, the self-perception theory, and the case of FAVI make it clear that it is crucial to wait for the best instead of the worst of people for the sake of awakening their best selves. Business leaders, therefore, should always make employees believe that they are honest. In this sense, Henry Ford used to say that "If you think you can or you think you can't, you're right."[29] This statement, though made in another context, also holds true for the image one constructs about his or her own ethics.

Biased expectations, whether coming from other people or self-generated, tend to substantially influence our ethical conduct. Bad expectations foster bad behaviors, and positive expectations encourage honorable conduct. Because our assumptions about human nature influence the ways we seek to promote ethical behavior in organizations, business leaders should be careful of the Pygmalion effect. Otherwise, they may end up having results in line with their expectations.

Appendix 1. A caveat: some companies do not want to improve ethical behavior for real

Throughout this chapter, we assumed that companies are seriously committed to improve their ethical conduct for real. However, some recent business scandals, particularly those involving corporate corruption, have shown that unfortunately this is not always the case. In practice, formal control systems, including the establishment of compliance departments, codes of conduct, internal policies, etc., may in some cases be designed with the intention of camouflaging improper practices. There is scientific evidence that a conscious option for the "ethical washing" to promote the impression of compliance with laws and regulations is relatively common in the business world.

A study by three US researchers with the provocative title of "A Wolf in Sheep's Clothing," analyzed the annual reports of 1,500 companies for 12 years searching for terms related to "ethics" and "social responsibility." Subsequently, the study found that companies that most frequently used these expressions in their public reports exhibited worse governance practices, were subject to more class-action suits, and belonged to industries that caused more damage to the environment.[30] According to the authors, the study results show that executives seeking to emphasize their companies' ethical conduct in their annual reports have a greater chance of doing so to deceive stakeholders.

Another investigation, also conducted in the United States over the same period, evaluated the codes of ethics of S&P500 index companies through text analysis techniques. In conclusion, the researchers noted that companies tend to plagiarize each other's content. The sample companies had, for example, an average of 37 phrases from their code of ethics identical to the other 499 companies of the S&P index. In addition, more than half of the companies exhibited a correlation of over 75% between the texts of their codes of ethics. In some cases, the authors even found a complete duplication of codes, a particularly unethical deed given that they were exactly analyzing the contents of codes of ethics.[31]

---

[1] Source: Drucker. P. 2008. The Essential Drucker: The Best of Sixty Years of Peter Drucker's Essential Writings on Management. Ed. HarperBusiness.

[2] The term "compliance arms race" comes from Azish Filabi, CEO of Ethical Systems, in her article "Are We in a Compliance Arms Race?". Available at https://wp.nyu.edu/compliance_enforcement/2017/07/20/are-we-in-a-compliance-arms-race/

[3] Mindgym. The only way is ethics: why good people do bad things and how to stop us. Consultation edition, September 2017. p. 5. Available at https://uk.themindgym.com/resources/the-only-way-is-ethics-2/

[4] G1/Globo. 03/10/2015. "À CPI, Barusco diz que receber propina é um 'caminho sem volta'". Available at http://g1.globo.com/politica/operacao-lava-jato/noticia/2015/03/cpi-barusco-diz-que-receber-propina-e-um-caminho-sem-volta.html .

[5] The Street. 02/14/2018. Credit Suisse Bankers Got Secretaries to Do Their Compliance Training. Available at https://www.thestreet.com/story/14488740/1/credit-suisse-bankers-pawned-off-compliance-training-on-secretaries.html

[6] Albert Camus. 1942. The Myth of Sisyphus. The Absurd Man. Available at https://en.wikiquote.org/wiki/Albert_Camus

[7] Mindgym. The only way is ethics: why good people do bad things and how to stop us. Consultation edition. September 2017. p. 11. Available at https://uk.themindgym.com/resources/the-only-way-is-ethics-2/

[8] Ethics and Compliance Initiative. 2016 Global Business Ethics Survey™. p. 4. Available at https://www.ethics.org/wp-content/uploads/2018/09/GBESFinal-1.pdf

[9] Harvard Business Review. March-April 2018. Why Compliance Programs Fail – and How to Fix Them. By Hui Chen and Eugene Soltes. Available at https://hbr.org/2018/03/why-compliance-programs-fail

[10] Luyendijk (2015:75-76). In addition, a compliance officer at a major bank noticed that "bankers look at the compliance department the way footballers look at linesmen: losers running back and forth along a line, stopping players from scoring or doing great things".

[11] Gneezy and Rustichini (2000).

[12] Interestingly, authors observed that no reduction occurred in the number of late-coming parents after the fine was removed a few weeks before the end of the 20-week experiment. This suggests that, once you remove the moral perspective of a decision, it is very difficult to restore it.

[13] Tenbrunsel and Messick (1999).

[14] Anomie can be defined as a condition in which society provides little moral guidance to individuals, ending up in a lack of social ethic. The word was popularized by French sociologist Émile Durkheim.

[15] Luyendijk (2015: 237).

[16] Brehm (1966), Miron and Brehm (2006), and Brehm and Brehm (2013).

[17] This saying is quoted by Kaptein (2013: 34) on his discussion about reactance theory.

[18] Pennebaker et al. (1976).

[19] Source: Drucker. P. 2008. The Essential Drucker: The Best of Sixty Years of Peter Drucker's Essential Writings on Management. HarperBusiness.

[20] mindgym. The only way is ethics: why good people do bad things and how to stop us. Consultation edition, September 2017. p. 11. Available at

https://uk.themindgym.com/resources/the-only-way-is-ethics-2/

[21] Allusion to the English philosopher of century XVII Thomas Hobbes. In Leviathan, his most famous book, Hobbes describes a situation of selfish and savage competition among people. The term is usually used to describe a negative view about the nature of human beings.

[22] For Jeremy Bentham (1748-1832), this concept would constitute a rational solution to social problems and could be employed in prisons, schools, hospitals, etc. For more on this, see Bentham, J. (1791). Panopticon or the inspection house (Vol. 2) or https://en.wikipedia.org/wiki/Panopticon

[23] Eden (1990) and Livingston (2009).

[24] Rosenthal and Jacobson (1968).

[25] Bem (1972).

[26] Gino et al. (2010) make an interesting teaser at the end of their paper: What should we expect from executives who often lie about their resumés?

[27] This case was built based on Frederic Laloux's book "Reinventing organizations". Source: Laloux (2014, p. 108-109).

[28] After leaving the company, Zobrist detailed FAVI's story in his book with the suggestive title of "The company that believed that man is good". Source: Zobrist, J. F. (2014). La belle histoire de Favi: l'entreprise qui croit que l'homme est bon. Humanisme & Organisations.

[29] Source: https://en.wikiquote.org/wiki/Talk:Henry_Ford. For some authors, this quote is apocryphal.

[30] Loughran et al. (2009).

[31] Forster et al. (2009). There are other related studies worth mentioning, such as Bodolica and Spraggon (2015), and Holder-Webb and Cohen (2012).

Part 4: Solutions to Promote Ethics in Business

11. What can I do to avoid becoming ethically blind? Defensive strategies at the personal level

> *"If people want to change their environment, they need to change themselves and their own actions – not someone's else."*
> Karl Weich (1936–)[1]

One of the key messages of this book is that the power of context of which we are part of can drive us to thoughtless decisions contrary to our values and principles. It is critical, therefore, to reflect on how we can minimize the likelihood of becoming ethically blind at the personal level. We can apply eight main personal strategies to defend ourselves from ethical blindness:

1. Recognizing our vulnerability;
2. Knowing our values;
3. Being aware that ethical conflicts are inevitable and that we are always capable of making choices;
4. Adopting techniques to put our values into practice;

5. Preparing for both the objections of other people and to our own rationalizations;
6. Being capable of getting away from routine and freeing ourselves from fear;
7. Developing our "moral imagination"; and,
8. Exercising the "moral muscle."

Recognizing our vulnerability

> "If we humbly recognize that we might not always even notice the choices that will lead us astray, we are more likely to develop ways to identify and control those decisions."
> Eugene Soltes[2]

The first and probably the most important step to avoid ethical blindness is simply to acknowledge that we are fallible. This means being humble to accept that we are also one of the people who can succumb to the forces of the circumstances and end up doing things contrary to our principles.

Taking this first step is more difficult than it seems. As we have seen in Chapter 1, we generally have an inflated perception of ourselves in all areas of life, particularly in the moral sphere. We tend to believe that we are "morally invincible," in the sense that we will not commit ethical lapses because we are individuals of good character. Thinking that "I'll never do it" or that "I know I will be able to do the right thing at the right moment" is usually a sign of overconfidence and the root of many problems.

What was your opinion, for example, when you read about Milgram's experiment described in Chapter 4? If you are like most people, then you plausibly accepted the scientific validity of the experiment and its empirical results from the rational standpoint. At the same time, though, you probably still firmly believe that the pressure of the "scientist" would never lead you to apply the lethal shock on other human being. That's where the problem is: Milgram's study shows that about two-thirds of people eventually would apply the lethal shock, although the vast majority of individuals are sure they would not act this way even after reading about it.

The Virtuous Barrel:
How to Transform Corporate Scandals into Good Businesses via Behavioral Ethics

The numerous experiments presented throughout the book demonstrate that we are more vulnerable to powerful contexts than we assume. The hard reality, hence, is that we simply do not know in advance how we would behave in certain circumstances.

It is also critical to realize that having a high IQ or relevant academic degrees does not prevent us from ethical blindness. We can be analytically intelligent and even aware of the contextual pressures that lead to improper behaviors. Unfortunately, though, this does not eradicate the risk of forgetting these lessons at critical moments.[3]

We must, therefore, be constantly vigilant about both the contextual forces and the cognitive biases that may impair our ethical judgments (especially the overconfidence, narcissism, egocentricity, and favoritism biases described in Chapter 2). People in leadership positions should also remind that power is as an additional source of concern for ethical judgments. As shown in Chapter 4, feeling powerful induces us to think that the rules apply to others, but not to ourselves.

Knowing our values

> *"It's not hard to make decisions when you know what your values are."*
> Roy E. Disney *(1930–2009)*[4]

Values can be defined as the principles or motivators that we consider important to guide our choices and conduct.[5] Thus, the key to behave ethically is to create awareness of the values that form our "moral compass," which we would not give up under any circumstances. As pointed out by Insead professors Ian Woodward and Samah Shaffakat, "Really knowing and being able to articulate our values can give us rich insights into our behaviors, our interaction with others, and our frames through which we make decisions."[6]

On the other hand, failing to reflect on our values can lead us to be unconsciously overpowered by questionable values and routines of the organization in which we work.[7] This is the conclusion of Joris Luyendijk, the author of a book on the inner workings of global financial institutions: "The point is that delusional bankers have stopped responding rationally to incentives. They were not so much lying to others as to themselves. How do you reach someone living in the midst of self-delusion and addiction?"[8]

Implicitly, our values are already reflected in the things we like, in the way we interact with others, and in our personal concept of "success."[9] On the other hand, it is rare to allocate a reasonable amount of time to reflect on this issue more deeply. What would you answer, for example, if a person asked you right now what are your core values?

Some questions can help us in identifying and articulating our values in a more structured way. In this sense, it is worth to regularly reflect on issues such as:

- What is really important to me?
- What do I want to achieve? What am I working for?
- What kind of flexibility am I willing to accept? What is non-negotiable?
- Am I happy with my ethical conduct and the decisions I have been making as an executive? Have I acted as a good example of ethics and integrity? If not, why not?
- What are the core values that should guide my professional and personal conduct?
- What are the personal values I must honor or a part of me will die out? Am I "selling my soul" in my current job?
- Who inspires me the most? Which qualities in these people inspire me?
- What impact do I want to cause? On whom? In which way?
- If you could give a message to a large group of people, who would be those people? What would be your message?
- What do I want to learn in life? How do I want to evolve professionally and as a human being?
- What will make my professional life worthwhile? What do I want to be proud of when I'm older?

The Virtuous Barrel:
How to Transform Corporate Scandals into Good Businesses via Behavioral Ethics

- What would I regret not doing, being or having in my life?
- What kind of legacy do I want to leave?

These questions are not easy to answer. One needs time to ponder them with due depth in order to answer them appropriately. Unfortunately, we are often prone to postpone this reflection when we are immersed in the routines of our personal and professional lives. Consequently, this lack of self-reflection and self-awareness is exactly what gives rise to a behavior contrary to our intentions. Actually, many authors consider the lack of self-knowledge as the major driver behind our ethical crisis.[10]

It is vital for all of us to identify our values and to cultivate them before ethical conflicts occur. Thus, becoming "insightfully aware" of our values should be viewed as a key element of the leadership development of everyone.[11] Another important issue is to check the level of congruence between our personal values and the values of the organization we work for. If there is a structural values' conflict, then severe ethical issues are likely to arise.

In this sense, although each organization may have different values, research shows that some values are deemed as important by most human beings. Research conducted in over 70 nations with more than 200 samples around the world, for instance, has concluded that there are 56 universal values that can be grouped into 10 distinct categories.[12] Among the values that tend to be common to all human communities are honesty, respect, responsibility, justice, empathy, equality, friendship, humility, and solidarity.[13]

Knowing ourselves is also crucial for being able to realize to what extent we would resist temptations. An apocryphal anecdote attributed to Abraham Lincoln shows the importance of knowing what is our "price."[14] Before becoming president, Lincoln enjoyed a successful career as a lawyer in Illinois. One day, a well-known criminal came to his office saying he would like Lincoln to defend him. Lincoln then asked him "Are you guilty?" receiving in response: "Of course, I'm guilty, that's why I want to hire you. For you to avoid my condemnation!" Lincoln, in turn, replied, "Well, if you are admitting that you are guilty to me, then I cannot defend you." The criminal then reacted angrily: "I do not think you are understanding me: I'm willing to pay you a thousand dollars for you to defend me!" A thousand dollars was a small fortune at the time, but Lincoln refused the offer resolutely. The criminal then proceeded: "Mr. Lincoln, I'll pay you two thousand dollars!" Lincoln declined again, showing to be resolute on his decision. Desperate, the criminal told him, "Mr. Lincoln, you're the best lawyer in the area, and I did not come all the way here to get a negative answer. I'll pay you four thousand dollars!" At that moment, Lincoln flew from his chair, grabbed the criminal by the collar, dragged him to the door of his office, and threw him into the street. After recovering, the criminal asked: "Why did you throw me out of your office when I offered you four thousand dollars?" to which Lincoln replied: "Because every man has his price, and you were getting close to mine!"

As pointed out by Erasmus University Professor Muel Kaptein, this story shows that the central issue is often not whether or not people are honest, but for how long, under what conditions, and under what temptations they will be able to resist to the point they would relinquish their integrity.[15]

Being aware that ethical conflicts are inevitable and that we are always capable of making choices

> *"Unfortunately, the world is not black and white. Senior managers spend most of their life in the gray regardless of their responsibility and that can be a dangerous place to be."*
> Stephen Richards *(1965–)*[16]

Among the main rationalizations people use to justify unethical behavior in the business world are the arguments that "I did not expect to end up facing this ethical conflict" and that, once exposed to it, "I had no choice under that situation."

To begin with, we must accept that sooner or later during our professional life there will be conflicts between what we believe to be the right thing to do and questionable requests from superiors, peers, or other members of an organization. Because the

The Virtuous Barrel:
How to Transform Corporate Scandals into Good Businesses via Behavioral Ethics

"temptations" tend to be bigger in the top echelons of the corporate world, these ethical conflicts are more even likely to happen as we climb into higher positions.

As pointed out by Professor Mary Gentile, professor of business ethics at the University of Virginia, preparing ourselves to act ethically is at least as important as getting updated with the technical issues of our professional field. As a result, it is important to "normalize" ethical conflicts, which means seeing them as an inevitable part of our professional journey and not as exceptional events.[17]

Still, according to Professor Gentile, when faced with an ethically challenging situation, it is easy to think that we have no choice but to compromise our personal values. Each one has his or her own justification: Young people, for example, tend to say that they have a career ahead of them and that they cannot hurt their professional perspectives; older people, in turn, tend to say that they have worked hard to get where they are, and that, at this point of their career, they have "much to lose."[18]

The reality is that we always have some free will to make our choices, however difficult they may seem. In all corporate scandals depicted throughout this book, the idea that one was "forced" to participate in certain practices or to omit oneself about them is in fact nothing more than a rationalization. After all, the world goes far beyond the borders of any company.

To prepare ourselves for the ethical dilemmas we will inevitably face, it is necessary to ponder periodically about questionable requests coming from leaders or peers that we are likely to face as a result of our position.

Thinking about these issues will help us to better prepare ourselves for the ethical challenges that will sooner or later arise. This will aid us to exhibit a less emotional reaction to these situations, thus increasing the chance of exhibiting a better response to them. The idea, in short, is always to anticipate all the problems, including the ethical ones.

Adopting methods to put our values into practice

The overwhelming majority of people have good values and want to put them into practice when ethical conflicts appear in the workplace. To do so, there are specific techniques that can support us in finding the motivation, ability, and confidence to manifest our values in such decisive moments.

One of the most useful approaches is the Giving Voice to Values (GVV) business curriculum created by Professor Mary Gentile.[19] The GVV offers executives several practical techniques to employ when they are exposed to questionable requests or witness improper behaviors in their organizations. The following are five specific tactics adapted from Gentile's program:

1. *Framing decisions according to values that most people will tend to agree and support*

    Honesty, respect, responsibility, fairness, empathy, and solidarity. Most people tend to agree that these are sound values that should serve as the basis for everyone's conduct. Thus, relying on common values like these is a good way to earn the support of other members of the organization when facing an ethical conflict in the workplace.[20]

    As an example, imagine a situation in which you are part of a group that intends to approve an initiative that, in your view, is ethically questionable (e.g., a product that will likely mislead customers). In this case, it is worth framing the decision based on a value shared by all.

    One possibility would be to raise the following question: "The bulk of our customers will not understand the financial costs associated with the purchase of this product. I am convinced that we would not like to be treated in the same way if we were on the other side. Do you really think we should go ahead with this decision?"

    Because most people want to do the right thing, clearly explaining the impact of their decisions on others based on common values tends to help us get the support and build coalitions with like-minded colleagues.

The Virtuous Barrel:
How to Transform Corporate Scandals into Good Businesses via Behavioral Ethics

2. *Thinking in advance on the factors that enable us to put (or not) our values into practice*

There are factors that help us give voice to our values and others that make it more difficult. The former are the so-called "facilitators" or "enablers." Examples of these are the existence of a boss who is open to discuss ethical issues or of coworkers aligned with our values. The latter are the so-called "disablers." Examples of these are the time pressure to make decisions and the lack of savings that make us financially dependent on the company.[21]

It is important to previously reflect on the factors that enable or disable our ethical conduct. By doing so, we will be able to maximize the use of enablers and think about the ways to overcome the obstacles represented by disablers.

3. *Finding the approach that makes us more comfortable to put our values into practice based on our personality and preferred style of communication*

Having good self-awareness of our personality and preferred style of communication can help us to find a more comfortable way to speak up when faced with an ethical conflict.[22] Shy people, for example, may be more likely to report objections by crafting a compelling memo. Extroverts with better oral communication, in turn, may find it easier to raise their concerns verbally.

Another important recommendation is to frame our ethical dilemmas from a perspective that maximizes the chance of having the courage to put our values into practice. Individuals who are strongly risk-averse, for example, can frame their conflict by thinking that the greatest risk in such situation is to omit themselves and accept the unethical practice. Risk-lovers, in turn, may frame the same situation by questioning themselves about taking the risk of doing the right thing.

Thus, it is essential to be aware of our profile so that we can use the most effective strategy to speak up when ethical issues arise. By knowing ourselves, we will manage to align our strengths to our values and to make decisions in accordance to our ethical expectations.

4. Rehearsing

Practice is the basis of good performance in any activity. Consequently, in order to develop moral competence in the professional life, it is important to practice the behavior we intend to have. One way is to present the concerns we intend to raise in our organization to trusted people in our inner circle. Another possibility is to write about the ethical dilemmas we face. This will make it easier to reflect on the various aspects involved in difficult situations and help us to come up with better arguments to support our point of view.

5. Having financial savings

Putting our values into practice when we are subject to questionable requests is obviously risky. Ultimately, if things do not go as planned, we may be forced to leave a workplace plagued with unethical practices.[23] It is much easier to show moral courage when we have financial peace of mind than when we are in debt and completely dependent on the organization to pay short-term bills. Therefore, it is critical to build a safety net, i.e., the so-called "go to hell funds," which will allow us to maintain our standard of living for a reasonable period until finding another job.

Preparing for both the objections of other people and to our own rationalizations

Expressing our opposition to questionable requests through the techniques presented in the previous topics is a necessary but not sufficient condition to "win the battle" against improper practices in the workplace.

Equally important is preparing ourselves for the objections and criticisms that are likely to arise from superiors or colleagues after we manifest our disapproval to unethical actions. In general, people use the same justifications everywhere for questionable behaviors, such as: "everyone in our industry is doing it," "that's the way we have always done things here," "it's an order from the top," and "I do not want to harm my colleagues."[24]

It is critical, therefore, to anticipate these justifications and criticisms by previously thinking on how to respond to them. A useful option is to express opposition to questionable requests by offering an alternative course of action to what is being proposed. This will show others that it is possible to act in another way within ethically acceptable boundaries.

Having ready answers to possible objections by superiors and colleagues is paramount to persuade others to do the right thing. This strategy is also useful to prevent us from falling into our own rationalizations. After all, accepting rationalizations like those presented in Chapter 8 is often the easier path instead of keeping true to our values. We should be careful, therefore, to do not self-sabotage ourselves.

Being capable of getting away from routine and freeing ourselves from fear

> *"Their [the Bankers] answer to the question of why they continue with business as usual is not 'greed' but 'fear'. If you press them, they say: I'm stuck."*
> Joris Luyendijk (1971–)[25]

If a rigid and distorted framing of reality is what leads to ethical blindness, then we must be able to apply a more flexible and holistic perspective to our worldview to avoid it.

To do this, it is critical to periodically free ourselves from our organizational routines loaded with endless e-mails, meetings, and travels. This means creating "spaces of reflection" where we can slow down and develop our capacity for self-assessment, introspection, and personal scrutiny. As Harvard Professor Eugene Soltes observes in his analysis on the causes of white-collar crimes, "If these executives had been yanked out of their offices at those moments and exposed to alternative perspectives and a careful consideration of the consequences, I suspect they would have made different choices."[26]

A research with the suggestive title "Honesty Requires Time" demonstrates the importance of these moments of reflection to avoid thoughtless decisions.[27] The authors recruited hundreds of individuals for a simple experiment: Participants were asked to roll the dice three times and anonymously report the outcome of the first roll to determine their pay. They were informed that their pay would be proportional to the number reported (the highest pay would be for those reporting six). They were separated into two groups. The first was called "high time pressure." In this group, individuals had up to 20 seconds to roll the dice three times in an isolated room and report the result in a computer. The second group was called "low time pressure." In this case, participants could use the time they wanted to play the dice and inform the outcome. The results showed that participants with little time to declare their numbers, who tended to act on the "impulse," turned out to behave much more dishonestly than those who had more time to ponder on what they would report. While the high-pressure group reported an average outcome of 4.56, the second group on average reported only 3.87. The researchers also noted that the figures reported by the high-pressure group were consistent with the likelihood of these people reporting the highest roll out of the three rolls (instead of the result of the first roll as instructed).[28] According to the authors, their results show that the "dark side" of people's automatic self-serving tendency may be overcome when time to decide is ample.

Developing the habit of practicing mindfulness is one of the best ways to improve our self-knowledge and consciousness as well as to have a clearer comprehension of our environment. A recent study with 232 volunteers corroborates this argument.[29] Researchers conducted two experiments. In the first, they observed that individuals with high scores on mindfulness are more likely to value upholding ethical standards and to use a principled approach to ethical decision-making. In the second, they noticed that individuals high in mindfulness cheated substantially less in an exercise than those low in mindfulness.

The ability to remain aware and focused in the present moment can also be stimulated by breathing techniques or contemplative practices. In the case of contemplative practices, dozens of researches have demonstrated the beneficial effects of meditation on our ability to understand and control our emotions (both critical aspects to enable us to act according to our values).[30] One of these papers, for instance, concluded that individuals with the habit of regularly meditating for 10 to 90 minutes had larger gray matter volumes in the areas of the brain associated with emotional regulation and response control.[31]

Another way to stay open and aware is to participate in leadership programs based on a holistic approach dedicated to the development of the individual in its wholeness instead of only focusing on professional competencies. One such program, developed by a group coordinated by Professor Richard Boyatzis, aims at developing "resonant leaders."[32] The method, based on the theory of intentional change and anchored in the principles of emotional intelligence and quality of life, aims to make business leaders in tune or in sync with others. It is composed of five stages. The first is to discover your "ideal self," whom you would like to be in a few years. The second is to discover your "real self," who you actually are today. The third is to outline a "learning agenda," a set of goals and activities with the purpose of getting closer to your personal vision. The fourth consists of the experimentation and practice of the new behaviors, thoughts, and feelings acquired. The last stage of the process, in turn, focuses on building and maintaining a network of trusted relationships that will support us throughout the process of change.

In addition to the lack of moments for reflection and the development of a narrow framing for our life, fear is the other element that leaves us vulnerable to ethical blindness. We often fail to do the right thing because we are afraid of many things, such as being dismissed, ridiculed, marginalized by peers, humiliated, suffering retaliations, or not meeting others' expectations, etc. As remarked by Russian writer Fyodor Dostoyevsky, "Nowadays, almost all capable people are terribly afraid of being ridiculous and are miserable because of it."[33]

Usually, though, fear is an imaginary feeling linked to the future instead of a concrete issue of the present. Thus, the best way to know what to do in situations of ethical dilemmas is to ask ourselves how we would decide if we were not afraid.[34] By asking ourselves this way, we will be free from the pressures of context and be able to do what is right for us.

Developing our "moral imagination"

Amid so many corruption scandals, the business world often seems to send an implicit message that it is necessary to choose between being ethical or succeeding. Many people begin to agree that this false dichotomy is indeed true. As a result, they tend to view an honest conduct as a sort of "superfluous" option that they cannot afford to progress in their careers.

Some people manage to break with this way of thinking even in difficult circumstances. These individuals have the so-called "moral imagination": the ability to identify ways to behave ethically and at the same time to succeed. Moral imagination, therefore, is the ability to find creative and morally acceptable solutions to a particular situation involving ethical conflicts.

The importance of moral imagination was demonstrated in a 2017 study by Professor Bobby Parmar.[35] He analyzed over 1,000 pages of audio transcriptions from the original 1960s Stanley Milgram experiment described in Chapter 4. At the time, Milgram had found no demographic pattern (e.g., age, gender, education) associated with greater resistance to follow the scientist's order to apply lethal shocks of 450V. Professor Parmar found that participants who succeeded in challenging the scientist's authority and giving up before the lethal shock exhibited a distinctive speech pattern to express their concerns. They tested their assumptions, exercised moral imagination, speculated out loud about the consequences of their actions, and realized that they had control over those outcomes. Specifically, resistors were able to personalize the issue and made more "I" statements ("I don't want to be part of this any longer"). They also asked more about the

The Virtuous Barrel:
How to Transform Corporate Scandals into Good Businesses via Behavioral Ethics

consequences of the study ("Suppose he gets all these wrong and I get up to a level where it's going to be extremely painful. What happens if I do this?"). Questioning the consequences and expressing their personal preferences out loud, therefore, allowed resistors to exhibit a moral imagination superior to those who succumbed to unethical orders of authority.

Developing moral imagination is critical not only because it helps people in dealing with ethical conflicts in their workplace, but also because it can help companies find ways to make a profit while serving society.

How can we develop our moral imagination? The first step is to eliminate from our minds the false dichotomy between "being ethical and having a mediocre career" or "being unethical and succeeding." In the case of entrepreneurs, there is often a false dichotomy between "if I'll be ethical, I will go bankrupt" and the idea of "I have to be unethical for the company to survive."

The second step is to find "out of the box" solutions for ethical conflicts through reflection, creativity, and hard work. One way to discover new alternatives for a particular decision is to brainstorm with people who share the same values and also want to find morally acceptable solutions. Another way is to listen to people outside the organization, such as experts, clients, suppliers, public authorities, communities, etc.

A third way to develop moral imagination is to apply a broader temporal perspective to decisions by questioning ourselves something akin to "What are the long-term implications of what I am doing for myself, my company, and society?"

The more openness we have to get in touch with other realities and the longer the time horizon of our reflection, the greater will be our ability to develop moral imagination and to behave in an ethical way.

Exercising the "moral muscle"

"I count him braver who conquers his desires than him who conquers his enemies; for the hardest victory is the victory over self."

Aristotle (384BC–322BC)[36]

There is no use in reflecting on the ethical consequences of our decisions and having the best values in the world if we are not able to put them into practice at the decisive moment. As highlighted throughout the book, almost all people have good intentions in the planning phase of our decision-making. The challenge is to stick with them in the moment of temptation. To do so, we must exercise our "moral courage."[37]

This is an old issue. Aristotle used to say that, while intellectual virtue derives from study, "moral excellence comes about as a result of habit." He also said that the ultimate goal of ethics is not only "to know what virtue is, but to become good."[38] So, just as we do with our muscles, we must also exercise our moral courage constantly (especially when we are subject to dangerous contexts).

The analogy with a muscle is useful. Just like our muscles weaken from lack of physical exercise, our virtue can also weaken over time. This leads many well-meaning people, for example, to say things such as "I could not resist the temptation," "I succumbed to pressure," or "I had a moment of weakness" after behaving badly.

One way to exercise the moral muscle is to resist the small pressures and temptations of everyday life, as these little "victories" give us the confidence and determination to resist great offerings. Moreover, because many large unethical conducts usually start with minor transgressions, it is critical to stick to the rules even when the transgression seems innocuous. As the adage goes, "It is easier to be honest with a small amount than with a large one."

Another way to increase our moral courage is to share with a person we admire the ethical dilemmas we face and what we intend to do about them. This will strengthen our will and increase our commitment to do the right thing.

Benjamin Franklin, one of the founding fathers of the United States, provides one of the best examples of how we can cultivate virtue and train our character constantly. At age 20, Franklin built a life plan based on 13 virtues: temperance, silence, order,

The Virtuous Barrel:
How to Transform Corporate Scandals into Good Businesses via Behavioral Ethics

resolution, frugality, work, sincerity, justice, moderation, cleanliness, tranquility, simplicity, and humility.[39]

To maintain his adherence to these virtues, Franklin created a card with a matrix in which the columns corresponded to the days of the week and the lines corresponded to these 13 virtues. Each card lasted a week. During this period, he spotted every "mistake" he had made on any of these virtues with a dot in the cell corresponding to the day of the week and the breached virtue.[40] His goal was to systematically reduce the number of "dots" on his cards. If he managed to do this, then he would manage to live an increasingly virtuous life.

Throughout his life, Franklin observed that the number of "mistakes" in his cards indeed decreased. Although he acknowledged never being able to achieve "moral perfection," the practice seems to have helped him a lot. Franklin had a full life, dying at age 85 in 1790 after achieving great prominence in many fields of life. Among other things, he was a renowned writer, diplomat, inventor, politician, scientist, civic activist, and manager.

Franklin's example makes it clear that exercising virtue on a daily basis helps us to strengthen our "moral muscle," which in turn gives us the necessary strength to do the right thing at critical moments. Possessing ethical behavior, therefore, is not just a matter of intention and disposition: self-control, training, and discipline are necessary to resist our impulses and inevitable temptations.

---

[1] Source: Weick, K. E. (1995). Sensemaking in organizations. Thousand Oaks, CA: Sage.
[2] Soltes (2016: 330).
[3] As detailed in Chapter 3, our decision-making process in comprised by three stages. The option that leads to the best immediate personal gain (what "I want to do") tends to remain silent during the stage of planning on how we would like to act (what "I ought to do"). It is at the moment of decision-making, however, that this self-interested option tends to dominate our choices.
[4] Source: https://www.goodreads.com/author/show/439861.Roy_Disney
[5] This definition is based on Woodward and Shaffakat (2016). Alternatively, Schwartz and Bilsky (1987: 551) present a more formal definition on this construct. For them, values are (a)

concepts or beliefs (b) about desirable behaviors or end results (c) that transcend specific situations, (d) that guide the evaluation or selection of behaviors and events and that (e) are ordered in terms of relative importance. Values, therefore, represent the criterion of importance that people use to evaluate and select behaviors and events.

[6] Woodward and Shaffakat (2016: 2).

[7] This definition comes from Woodward and Shaffakat (2016).

[8] Luyendijk (2015: 240).

[9] Our values are even reflected in the way we decorate our workplace and on how we dress. Everything we do sends messages to others about who we are and what we enjoy.

[10] Arvidsson and Peitersen (2013), Scherer and Palazzo (2008), and Sen (1999).

[11] The term "insightfully aware" comes from Woodward and Shaffakat (2016).

[12] Schwartz (1992). The categories of values are: achievement, power, hedonism, self-direction, stimulation, universalism, benevolence, tradition, security, and, conformity.

[13] The psychologist Shalom H. Schwartz, formulator of the theory of basic human values is a leading researcher in this area. Among his papers, stand out Schwartz (1992), Schwartz (1994), Smith et al. (1997), Schwartz and Bardi (2001), Smith et al. (2002), Schwartz (2005), Fischer e Schwartz (2011), and Schwartz (2012).

[14] This anecdote is presented by Kaptein (2013: 8).

[15] Kaptein (2013: 9).

[16] Source: Soltes (2016: 197). Stephen Richards was a senior manager at Computer Associates. In 2006, he was sentenced to 84 months in jail on fraud charges.

[17] Gentile (2010: 73).

[18] These examples come from Gentile (2010: 161-163).

[19] According to Gentile (2010), GVV aims to enable individuals to put their values into practice through seven pillars: values, choice, normalization, purpose, self-knowledge and alignment, voice, reason and rationalization. More information on it is available at http://www.givingvoicetovaluesthebook.com/

[20] Gentile (2010: 29-30).

[21] *Ibid*: 53.

[22] *Ibid*: 108.

[23] *Ibid*: 211.

[24] *Ibid*: 170.

[25] Source: Luyendijk, J. (2015: 183). Swimming with Sharks: My Journey into the World of the Bankers. Guardian Faber Publishing.

[26] Soltes (2016: 314).

[27] Shalvi et al. (2012).

[28] This result corroborates the self-concept maintenance theory, since it allowed people to cheat while at the same time keeping a positive self-image of themselves. The researchers performed variants of this experiment, including a situation in which participants of the "high pressure" group were required to roll the dice only once and report its outcome in only up to eight seconds. The results remained qualitatively the same in conditions such as this one. Another curious result was that the people who reported the greatest numbers (probably dishonestly) were those who reported feeling in worse mood at the end of the experiment. This also reinforces the idea that lying makes us feel bad.

[29] Ruedy et al. (2010).

[30] Goyal et al. (2014), Shonin et al. (2013), Sedlmeier (2012), Chu (2010), and Monk-Turner (2003).

[31] The areas of the brain with the largest volume were the hippocampus, the orbitofrontal cortex, the thalamus, and the inferior temporal gyrus. The study by Luders et al. (2009) also noticed that meditators exhibited larger volumes of gray matter in the brain.

[32] A "resonant leader" is a leader who is attuned to herself and to the people around her around towards a common vision. She uses her emotional intelligence to build hope, compassion, mindfulness, and joy in her relationships. For more on this program, see Boyatzis and McKee (2013), Boyatzis et al. (2013), and Boyatzis et al. (2006).

[33] Source: https://quotes.thefamouspeople.com/fyodor-dostoevsky-1441.php

[34] Palazzo and Hoffrage (2014).

[35] Parmar (2017).

[36] Source: https://www.uky.edu/~eushe2/quotations/aristotle.html

[37] In general, decisions involving ethical dilemmas can be divided into four stages: 1) ethical awareness: recognizing the ethical dilemma before us; 2) moral decision: having the ability to form a judgment on what is the right thing to do; 3) moral intention: having the will to do the right thing; and, 4) moral action: having the ability to act in line with our moral intention. Moral courage, thus, corresponds to the fourth stage of this process.

[38] "*Moral excellence [i.e. virtue] comes about as a result of habit,*" and "*the present inquiry does not aim at theoretical knowledge like the others (for we are inquiring not in order to know what virtue is, but in order to become good, since otherwise our inquiry would have been of no use).* Source: Aristotle. Habit and Virtue in The Nicomachean Ethics. Book II of *Nicomachean Ethics*. Available at http://classics.mit.edu/Aristotle/nicomachaen.mb.txt .

[39] For more on this, see http://www.thirteenvirtues.com/

[40] Each week, Franklin concentrated on meeting one specific virtue. In the week dedicated to frugality, for example, he made every possible effort not to commit a "mistake" on this virtue.

12. What should be done to avoid ethical blindness in my organization? The role of culture

> *"The only thing of real importance that leaders do is to create and manage culture. If you do not manage culture, it manages you, and you may not even be aware of the extent to which this is happening."*
> Edgar Schein (1928–)[1]

Establishing a healthy culture – based on elements such as trust, transparency, accountability, high intrinsic motivation, psychological safety, cooperation, empathy, and solidarity – is the key to prevent unethical behaviors in any organization. After all, as noted by a group of scholars, "Business not only produces goods and services, they produce people."[2]

Before exploring this issue, it is important to make a brief digression into the concept of "organizational culture." Culture comprises the behavioral patterns shared by members of a community primarily relying on socially transmitted information.[3] These behavioral patterns, in turn, reflects the prevailing values, beliefs, habits, assumptions, vocabulary, rituals, styles, and tacit rules that generate the unique social and psychological environment of an organization ("the way things are done here").[4] Culture, in short, provides the behavioral norms considered to be accepted or not by the organization which are manifested in its daily operations and relationship with stakeholders.[5]

According to Edgard Schein, a leading authority in this field, organizational culture is defined by three layers.[6] The first layer is composed of the company's artifacts and

The Virtuous Barrel:
How to Transform Corporate Scandals into Good Businesses via Behavioral Ethics

rituals. These are easily observable through the company's facilities, offices, the way employees dress and behave, myths, and corridor stories. The second layer consists of the espoused beliefs and values. They reflect the organization's formal aspirations such as its mission, vision, and value statements. The third layer, in turn, corresponds to the organization's underlying assumptions, i.e., the "unspoken rules" that are simply taken for granted and rarely discussed. These include, for instance, the premises about human nature, the concept of success, and the way decisions should be made and communicated.

In recent years, the term "ethical culture" has been increasingly used to describe the slice of the overall organizational culture concerning ethical issues. This concept includes the formal and informal systems that should promote sound ethical judgment and action in organizations. According to EthicalSystems,[7] an initiative that brings together leading business ethics researchers, "If the organizational culture represents 'how we do things around here,' the ethical culture represents 'how we do things around here in relation to ethics and ethical behavior in the organization.'"

The culture of a company is the product of its history, strategy, industry, region, country, and personality of key shareholders and executives, among other things. It also stems from its organizational practices on issues such as hiring, pay, performance appraisal, communication, promotion, and dismissal. Culture, thus, is an invisible but powerful force that strongly drives people's behavior for better or worse.

In a huge 2016 survey with nearly 1,900 CEOs and CFOs of over 1,300 US firms, more than 90% of them said that culture is important or very important, while 92% believe that improving culture would increase firm value. Moreover, 85% of top executives believe that a poor culture increases the chance of an employee acting illegally, while only 16% reported that their firm's culture is exactly where it should be.[8]

If poorly managed, the culture of a company can become so pernicious that people end up failing to assign any meaning to formal norms and laws. In fact, the vast majority of recent governance scandals were not caused by the absence of governance documents but by toxic cultures that have driven ordinary people to unethical behaviors.

On the other hand, promoting a strong and healthy culture is a vital competitive advantage for the creation of long-term value. This asset is even more important in a world in which business value increasingly depends on its intangibles and engagement of its members.

The idea of cultivating a strong culture relates to the concept of "moral capital" developed by psychologist Jonathan Haidt. He defines this term as "the resources [such as values, norms and practices] that sustain a moral community" in a way that its members are able to restrain individual selfishness for the advancement of the collective good.[9] Thus, a well-run company will manage to avoid unethical behavior through a high moral capital.[10]

Haidt notices, though, that a highly cohesive group can also carry out unethical deeds on behalf of its members more effectively. One example comes from the Mafia, an institution with a strong culture and high moral capital in a technical sense that pursues standards contrary to laws and society's accepted norms.[11] Thus, in the quest for self-preservation, highly cohesive groups can promote its interests by violating the interests of society and other stakeholders through harm and cheating. As Haidt and two colleagues point out, "Some of the most unethical things people do in organizations are done not to advance the self-interest of the individual actor but to promote or protect the collective entity. This can especially be the case when individuals strongly identify with the organization."[12]

This claim is corroborated by a study based on interviews with experts on corporate corruption. Authors Jamie-Lee Campbell and Anja Göritz concluded that employees of corrupt organizations see themselves as a so-called "community of fate." This community requires its members to rely on each other to secure its own continuity. The interdependence of the group, in turn, increases both the commitment to its values and norms as well as the pressure for all employees to tolerate corruption and support the organization.[13]

The Virtuous Barrel:
How to Transform Corporate Scandals into Good Businesses via Behavioral Ethics

That's why it is critical for culture to be not only strong but also healthy, in the sense that employees are committed to behave in accordance to ethical standards of society and to abide to the law even when it comes at the expense of the best outcome for their organization. As Haidt and his colleagues conclude, "A group that maintains high moral capital while respecting common norms of business practice is likely to be a boon to society, generating value in a sustainable way."[14]

Five initiatives should be prioritized to establish a healthy organizational culture and foster sound ethical judgment in employees:

1. Provide people with psychological safety to express their views;
2. Encourage divergent thinking;
3. Strengthen mutual trust to bring out the best instead of the worst out of people;
4. Make people accountable not only for their actions but also for their omissions; and
5. Foster open discussions about ethical dilemmas faced in day-to-day business.

Provide people with psychological safety to express their views

> *"A person reaches out to the environment in wonder and interest, and expresses whatever skills he has, to the extent that he is not crippled by fear, to the extent that he feels safe enough to dare."*
> Abraham Maslow (1908–1970)[15]

If there is a single word that summarizes the cause of current business scandals, this word is "fear." When a climate of terrorism is created within an organization, people become defensive and afraid to express their points of view, including on issues involving ethical dilemmas. Writer Steve Ross resumed this situation by saying that "You can't operate a company by fear, because the way to eliminate fear is to avoid criticism. And the way to avoid criticism is to do nothing."[16] Environments where fear prevails, therefore, are the most prone to ethical blindness.

Implementing a system of "zero job security" in which waves of people are regularly fired is one of the main ways to install an atmosphere of fear in an organization. This toxic hire-and-fire culture seems to be particularly true at large financial institutions. As one banker pointed out: "The fear factor is very strong in finance. People are very defensive. Ass-covering is a major element if you want to survive ... every day you're getting closer to getting fired."[17] This also the conclusion of the author of *Swimming with Sharks*, a book on the inner workings of the City of London: "There is always the sword of Damocles hanging over everyone's head: what you end up is the law – or rather the lawlessness – of the jungle. How realistic is it to expect 'internal controls' to do their jobs in such a context?"

Outside the financial world, the case of Petrobras, the Brazilian oil company involved in a massive bribery scandal, perfectly illustrates the dangers of fostering a climate of fear. Throughout its history, Petrobras had developed a culture of nondismissal of its employees. On the other hand, it also established a practice of ostracizing people considered "inconvenient" for a particular management team (being a federal state-owned company, Petrobras' leadership used to change completely after presidential elections). These bothersome employees were often sent to a specific floor in a building outside the headquarters of the company ironically called CREO (a Portuguese acronym for "Center for the Recovery of Idle Executives"). There, they were placed in complete ostracism, often without tasks to be performed and treated by many as true ghosts inside the organization. Although their salaries were reduced by half due to the loss of their managerial status, most of these employees opted to remain for years in this true psychological torture for the sake of not losing corporate benefits and their retirement plan. Everyone obviously feared ending up in that position. As a result, the best thing to do for most people was simply to accept unethical practices that, under normal circumstances, they would speak out against.[18]

In order to reduce fear, it is critical to provide a humanized and psychologically safe workplace in which employees feel respected and protected to take risks.[19] When we feel

The Virtuous Barrel:
How to Transform Corporate Scandals into Good Businesses via Behavioral Ethics

psychologically secure, we become less concerned with retaliation, social ostracism, or other negative consequences resulting from views which are different from our group.[20]

The benefits of a climate with high psychological safety go beyond an improvement in the organization's ethical behavior. Numerous scientific evidences shows that working in such environments generates a higher level of productivity and innovation.[21] This happens because psychological safety increases intrinsic motivation on employees to engage in activities requiring critical thinking and creativity such as giving and receiving feedback, challenging the status quo, asking difficult questions, being opened to new views, not having a defensive posture, and having the courage to try new things.

One of these studies, carried out with hundreds of employees from 30 organizations, concluded that a climate of high psychological safety is associated with lower levels of bullying and harassment in the workplace as well as to a higher level of meritocracy and employee engagement.[22] According to the authors, in companies with a high level of psychological safety, top management takes a zero-tolerance stance toward any attempts at intimidation and disrespect. A similar conclusion was found at Google. After carrying out a massive two-year study based on around 200 interviews and extensive data analysis, the company concluded that psychological safety was the key distinguishing factor among its high-performing teams.[23]

Harvard Business School Professor Francesca Gino, a leading researcher in behavioral ethics, corroborates this view by asserting that "When you give people the opportunity to be authentic and show what they really are, the evidence shows that they bring their best selves to the workplace."[24]

Top management is responsible for creating a workplace with high psychological safety through policies and procedures that foster tolerance and pluralism instead of fundamentalism and dogmatism. Business leaders, therefore, must be (really!) opened to criticism in order to ensure a democratic and constructive atmosphere for decision-making in their organizations.

Encourage divergent thinking

The pressure to behave in conformity with the group and reach a consensus at any cost tends to drive people to act on autopilot without questioning established practices and routines. Consequently, it is essential to actively encourage divergent thinking in an organization. As pointed out by Harvard Professor Cass Sunstein and University of Chicago Professor Reid Hastie, this means creating a culture in which being a "team person" does not necessarily mean going along with the group but rather contributing with new information and different perspectives.[25]

According to Francesca Gino, it is necessary to encourage people to exhibit a "constructive nonconformity," i.e., behaviors that deviate from organizational norms, others' actions, or common expectations to the benefit of the organization. Gino argues that this is rare nowadays. In one of her surveys, conducted with over 1,000 executives of US companies, less than 10% said they work in companies that regularly encourage divergent thinking.[26]

An episode at Brazilian oil company Petrobras shows how constraining different viewpoints is an invitation to ethical blindness.[27] At a senior management team meeting to discuss a gas pipeline bid, a manager of the gas and power department, named Rafael Frazao, was called to represent his C-level boss who was travelling abroad. After analyzing the issue with other colleagues from his department, Frazao argued during the meeting that the best thing to do would be to cancel the bidding process due to the excessive price asked by private national contractors invited to execute the project (subsequent investigations showed that these contractors were acting on a cartel). In his view, it was necessary to start a new bidding process from scratch, preferably with the invitation of international contractors. A C-level executive in charge of the services and purchasing department, named Renato Duque (later arrested in the Operation Car Wash), intervened, arguing that they should insist in hiring one of the national contractors without a new bidding process. Duque's view was supported by two other C-level executives, Paulo Roberto Costa and Nestor Cervero (both also imprisoned afterward for taking bribes) and his position finally prevailed. Days later, Frazao was summoned by the

The Virtuous Barrel:
How to Transform Corporate Scandals into Good Businesses via Behavioral Ethics

CEO Sérgio Gabrielli. Right after showing up at his office, the CEO asked him: "Some people told me that you've been willing to affront the executive board, Frazao ... is it true?" Frazao answered that he did not intend to confront anyone but simply disagreed with the decision about the bidding process. Weeks later, Frazao was ousted from his managerial role and thrown into the typical ostracism at Petrobras, as described in the previous section. When Frazao was informed of this decision, his boss told him that the other C-level executives did not like his "defiant" stance in the meeting and that the CEO had "asked for his head."

The importance of fostering alternative views to make better decisions was already highlighted by Alfred Sloan Jr., the legendary CEO of GM from the early twentieth century considered by many as the archetype of the first professional executive in history. In a famous quote, he said: "Gentlemen, I take it we are all in complete agreement on the decision here. Then, I propose we postpone further discussion of this matter until the next meeting to give ourselves time to develop disagreement and perhaps gain some understanding of what the decision is all about."[28]

Divergent thinking can be promoted in different ways. One is to increase the diversity of backgrounds and profiles in key positions as well as in the composition of the main governance bodies of the company, such as committees, executive boards, and boards of directors. Among the dimensions of diversity to be enhanced stand out the gender, cultural, generational, and expertise aspects. Extensive research has shown that diversity is a particularly relevant element for the performance of working groups performing tasks that require high creativity and innovation.[29]

Having people with different psychological profiles also tends to increase divergent thinking. This means having group members who are risk-averse and risk-lovers, anxious and relaxed, optimistic and pessimistic, creative and analytical, etc. In group decisions, there is usually a stage of "opening" in which courses of action are created and another of "closing" in which options are evaluated. More relaxed and creative people, for instance, can be more useful in the first stage, while more anxious and analytical people can be more valuable in the second.[30]

Another important initiative is to ensure fair division of speech time in meetings so that authoritative people do not end up monopolizing the time for discussions. Oftentimes, leaders and experts tend to think that their information is more important and that it should be prioritized by the group.

In this sense, a series of experiments conducted with hundreds of people by MIT researchers found that groups whose members speak in the same proportion of time tend to have greater "collective intelligence" (the so-called "c" factor) leading these groups to perform better on a wide variety of tasks.[31]

Still, according to these experiments, the other two factors leading to greater collective intelligence are the average social sensitivity of members and the proportion of women in the group. To a large extent, the proportion of women has proved to be a significant element of collective intelligence because women usually score higher on social sensitivity tests.[32] Additionally, it is also worth noting that, surprisingly, the average analytical intelligence of group members did not prove to be a strong predictor of group performance.

A third way to encourage divergent thinking is by adopting innovative decision-making techniques. There are a number of techniques available to maximize the contribution of each member of a working group, such as the "devil's advocate," the nominal group, the step-ladder decision-making, and the "six thinking hats" method. The text below details the "devil's advocate," one of the most recommended practices.

> *The decision-making technique of the "devil's advocate"*
>
> *Formalizing the role of the "devil's advocate" is a simple solution to help working groups substantially improve their decision-making. The term refers to the role of "advocatus diabolic," a position created by the Catholic church in 1587 aimed at increasing the credibility of its then discredited canonization process.*

The Virtuous Barrel:
How to Transform Corporate Scandals into Good Businesses via Behavioral Ethics

The appointed person was required to evaluate the candidates for canonization with skepticism. He questioned the personal conduct of the candidates and tried to identify frauds in the miracles attributed to them.

Evidence shows that the idea worked very well. Suffice it to say that about 500 people were canonized between the extinction of this position by Pope John Paul II in 1983 and the end of the twentieth century, five times more than the 98 canonized by all his predecessors in the previous 80 years.

Bringing this concept to the business context, the devil's advocate is a person formally tasked with criticizing a given proposal. He or she should identify weaknesses and inconsistencies in the assumptions underlying it as well as potential adverse outcomes in case of approval. This person would help in ensuring that the premises of an important subject are deeply analyzed, the opposing arguments are heard, that conflicts of interest are manifested, and the poor explanations are made salient.

The formalization of the devil's advocate facilitates the institutionalization of corporate dissent, leaving other group members freer to express their opinions and question the views of powerful group members. When the person assigned as devil's advocate raises questions, other members also feel more comfortable in criticizing ideas without fear of being labeled negatively. This would arguably increase the level of critical thinking of the group and prevent the monopolization of the decision by its most powerful or knowledgeable member.

Intellectual independence and seniority are two important attributes of the profile of a good devil's advocate. Regarding the specific activities to perform this task, the individual should identify the central premises behind the proposed courses of action and critically evaluate the less defensible assumptions, obtain information from external experts on aspects of which group members do not have much expertise, talk to people within the organization who may have different views, and prepare a report containing counterarguments, contradictory data, and alternative courses of action.

To succeed, the devil's advocate depends on three fundamental factors. First, the group leader must believe in the value of dissent by encouraging criticism and alternative views. Second, there must be a rotation of the members appointed to the role. If the same person acts as the devil's advocate continuously, then she may suffer a process of resistance within the group with her criticism being taken less and less seriously. Third, the role of the devil's advocate should be only used for the most relevant and complex subjects, especially those in which there seems to be a greater initial tendency for consensus.

To conclude this section, it is important to make an important caveat: divergent thinking does not mean treating others in an offensive and disrespectful way. Let's take, for example, the case of Amazon. One of its 14 management principles is to "disagree and to engage." Although seemingly positive at first glance, a *New York Times* investigative report showed that, in practice, executives often are encouraged to destroy their colleagues' ideas in such a hard way that finding people desolate after the meetings became commonplace in the company.[33] As one former Amazon executive told the newspaper, "You walk out of a conference room, and you'll see a grown man covering his face ... Nearly every person I worked with, I saw cry at their desk." It is crucial that dissenting thinking is not achieved at the expense of the harmony and respect that must exist within the organization. In this sense, training in nonviolent communication techniques can substantially help people make criticisms without disrespecting their colleagues or humiliating subordinates.[34]

Strengthen mutual trust to bring out the best – not the worst – of people

"Trust comes on foot and leaves on horseback."
Dutch proverb[35]

Strengthening trust within an organization is another key element to help foster better ethical conduct.[36] Reciprocity is the base for trust, and the premise for reciprocity is honesty and integrity that bring about mutual benefit.[37] Trust must be strengthened both horizontally among peers as well as vertically across individuals from different hierarchical levels.

Brazilian oil company Petrobras offers another bad example to illustrate this important issue. According to the book *Petrobras: A History of Pride and Shame*, its former CEO Graca Foster was an extremely centralizing person who distrusted everyone without exception. The book describes the testimony of an employee who shows the climate of distrust reigning in the organization: "I witnessed a very embarrassing situation. She called one manager to confirm information passed by another executive. It

The Virtuous Barrel:
How to Transform Corporate Scandals into Good Businesses via Behavioral Ethics

turns out that the manager she was asking about was at her side, listening to the call on the speakerphone."[38]

The example of Petrobras shows how difficult it is to promote a healthy climate of trust with negative behaviors like this, especially when they come from a leader who serves as the role model for everybody in the organization. Thus, a management style that emphasizes distrust reduces people's intrinsic motivation, which in turn increases the chance of unethical behaviors.

On the other hand, leaders who succeed in creating a high-trust environment end up increasing employees' commitment as well as encouraging everyone to reflect on the consequences of their actions. Therefore, it is paramount to treat employees with respect and involve them in a higher purpose: This will motivate employees to exhibit behaviors more aligned with the long-term success of the company. Indeed, a broadened focus on business purpose connected to the common good is critical to develop a healthy culture.

One of the prime ingredients to raise trust in organizations is to always expect the best – not the worst – from people. As described in Chapter 10, the Pygmalion effect shows how individuals tend to behave according to the way they are treated.

If employees are seen as trustworthy human beings, they will tend to receive more responsibilities, which in turn will induce them to behave more responsibly. Positive expectations – even in regard to ethical behavior – tend to generate positive responses.

Make people accountable not only for their actions, but also for their omissions

> *"A person may cause evil to others not only by his action but by his inaction, and in either case he is justly accountable to them for the injury!"*
> John Stuart Mill (1806–1873)[39]

Creating a culture in which people understand that silence means tacit agreement and that they will be held accountable for failing to take reasonable steps to prevent wrongdoings is another critical step to promote better ethical behavior.

According to Elizabeth Morrison, a professor at New York University, there are two main reasons why employees often fail to report unethical behavior in the workplace. The first is the sense of futility, that is, the perception that voicing will not change anything and that no one has genuine interest in listening to them. The second is the fear that this action will lead to retaliation by superiors or others involved.[40]

Unfortunately, this fear is backed by solid evidence. A 2014 survey conducted in the United Kingdom, for example, found that more than 50% of people who reported unethical practices in their workplace were dismissed or resigned. Another 28% have been bullied by their co-workers or were punished by their bosses. Only 16% reported that blowing the whistle had a positive outcome.[41] In early 2017, the English bank Barclays provided a concrete case justifying the fear of potential whistleblowers: its CEO Jes Staley admitted using the bank's internal security team to hunt for a whistleblower who had sent two anonymous letters to the board questioning the conduct of a senior manager he had brought to the bank.[42] Another bad example took place at US bank Wells Fargo. According to the *New York Times*, several employees were fired for internally reporting the existence of abusive, and in some cases fraudulent, practices at the bank before the emergence of the scandal in 2016.[43] This has been confirmed by an internal investigation at the bank following the crisis. It revealed that there had been 885 calls to its ethics hotline from 2011 to 2016 in which employees identified themselves by name and were subsequently subject to "corrective" actions.[44]

Companies can also actively discourage whistleblowing by granting financial incentives to employees who could play an important role in the uncovering of corporate malfeasances. There is scientific evidence on this. After analyzing 663 companies subjected to shareholder litigation, three researchers concluded that firms granted more stock options to rank-and-file employees (ordinary workers occupying lower-level positions) while they were committing fraud compared with a benchmark sample of 663 similar firms that were not under investigation for financial misreporting.[45] According to

The Virtuous Barrel:
How to Transform Corporate Scandals into Good Businesses via Behavioral Ethics

the authors, these company efforts were effective because misreporting firms that granted more stock options to employees were less likely to be exposed by a whistleblower.[46]

From the behavioral perspective, there are at least two other reasons why many people do not blow the whistle when they witness improper behaviors in the workplace. The first is due to the "status quo" bias, which is our tendency to go with the default and maintain the current state of affairs. The second is due to a phenomenon called "the bystander effect," a situation of collective passivity in which the presence of others in an environment discourages individuals from taking initiative to intervene in a problem.[47] The term "bystander effect" was coined after a dramatic episode taking place in the United States in 1964. Right after arriving at her home in the Queens (New York), 28-year-old Catherine Genovese was attacked by a psychopath named Winston Moseley. For about 30 minutes, the aggressor stabbed her 14 times, raped, and finally killed her. During this period, Kitty (as Catherine was known) shouted twice for help and even managed to momentarily drive the assailant away. Although several people in the neighborhood listened her screams, and some turned on the lights to see what was going on, none intervened. The case created huge outcry at the time as a symbol of the apathy and callousness of urban dwellers in the United States.[48]

The episode also stimulated several studies in the field of psychology.[49] These papers have shown that the larger the group, the greater the propensity to passivity of its members due to three main reasons: diffusion of responsibility (no one is individually responsible for resolving the situation), social pressure for conformity (a social norm is developed is which no one should interfere in what is happening), and fear of sanctions or condemnation by the group in case of interference on the situation.

This collective inertia may also occur in cases of widespread organizational corruption: the bigger and more complex the company, the less likely it will be for someone to act and the greater the chance of ending up with the bystander effect ("if everyone knows, then no one speaks"). In short, the increasing difficulty of breaking the silence encourages corruption.

Foster open discussions about ethical dilemmas faced in day-to-day business

"Improving ethics often requires altering the type of situation a person is in, not simply altering the type of people in a given situation."
Nicholas Epley and David Tannenbaum[50]

To a large extent, we become more knowledgeable on ethics by talking systematically about concrete ethical conflicts with others. Thus, allowing people to frankly discuss the dilemmas they face on a day-to-day basis and the consequences of their decisions on stakeholders and society is another crucial factor to improve ethical behavior. Many companies, however, do the opposite: They create a feeling that talking about ethics or questioning current practices of the organization is a sign of naiveté or personal weakness.

A study, based on interviews with experts on corporate scandals, for instance, concluded that people in corrupt organizations usually engage into an "organizational silence" on work problems.[51] Thus, avoiding discussions on ethical dilemmas or disqualifying them as a sign of frailty indicates that the organization is in a very dangerous terrain.

Companies should also avoid restricting ethics discussions to annual events designed to symbolize that it cares about the subject. As pointed out by Professor Robert Jackall in his analysis of the inner workings of large corporations: "Managers do not generally discuss ethics, morality, or moral rules-in-use in a direct way with each other, except perhaps in seminars organized by ethicists. Such seminars, however, are unusual, and, when they do occur, they are often strained, artificial, and often confusing even to managers because they frequently become occasions for the solemn public invocation, particularly by high-ranking managers, of conventional moralities and traditional shibboleths."[52]

The Virtuous Barrel:
How to Transform Corporate Scandals into Good Businesses via Behavioral Ethics

Thus, it is important to engage in authentic conversations addressing concrete situations instead of discussing ethics in an abstract way. Values and principles are obviously important, but the key during these exchanges is to provide clear guidance on practical situations ("if I face situation X, I should act in a Y-way").

Promoting positive examples from the day-to-day business is also important. This will demonstrate that there is room for virtuous behavior in an organization and that this conduct should be seen as the benchmark for all. The more space people have to talk on ethical issues and the more they are exposed to good examples, the better they will tend to behave.

The background: The clash between the formal and informal value systems

According to Professors Linda Treviño and Katherine Nelson, authors of a conceptual model on ethical culture, organizations have two value systems at work: a formal and an informal one. The formal or tangible system is represented by what is stated in its documents (e.g., code of ethics, by-law, mission statement) and procedures (e.g., hiring practices, training systems, performance indicators, criteria for promotion).[53]

The informal or intangible system is defined by the culture of the organization, including the company's social norms, role models, rituals, myths, and language. As pointed out in the beginning of this chapter, culture sends strong signals to people about expected behaviors, including from an ethical point of view. It is through these unofficial messages, therefore, that people learn what the company really values and what distinguishes it from other firms.

To a large extent, the level of alignment between the formal and informal systems determines the quality of an organization's ethical culture. In the case of recent governance scandals, for example, the informal value system of the companies involved was clearly distorted, becoming completely detached from its explicit norms. As one study concluded, "Corrupt organizations provide contradictory information to their employees along the lines of 'We follow ethical values, but in fact, we do not care.'"[54]

When there is such a discrepancy between the two systems, then cynicism, unspoken rules and everyday habits prevail.

This claim is corroborated by a 2015 book on the behavior of bankers after the 2008 financial crisis.[55] Based on interviews with 200 executives from global banks working in the financial district of London, Dutch journalist Joris Luyendijk concluded that changes in regulations and the tightening of internal policies have hardly affected the culture of the world of finance and that "A few years on, the city seemed to be behaving more and more as if it were 'business as usual' again."[56]

The sale of financial products continues to be made based on a widespread amoral perspective in which everything that is not expressly forbidden is allowed. The enormous pressure to reach short-term goals, the transactional perspective in all relationships, and the high executive turnover also remain the norm. As one banker declared, "If you can be out of the door in five minutes, your horizon becomes five minutes."[57]

Discussions on ethics remain nonexistent. According to Luyendijk, people at these financial institutions never ask if an idea such as a new product is right or wrong. They just ask if it is profitable and if it will be able to get the stamp of approval by the compliance department. If the "boxes" are successfully checked, then the initiative goes on.

A culture of "no error" also contributes to the wrongdoings. If a trader makes a mistake, for instance, it will be unlikely for him to admit he got something wrong. As result, "Rogue trading is often not about greed. It is about despair and it is a direct consequence of how the banks are now organized."[58] The overall message of his book *Swimming with Sharks* is bleak. It indicates that amorality at financial institutions is endemic and the outcome of a dysfunctional value system. Consequently, it will probably be just a matter of time before these institutions experience relevant wrongdoings once again.[59]

The Virtuous Barrel:
How to Transform Corporate Scandals into Good Businesses via Behavioral Ethics

Actually, the overall conclusion of Luyendijk's 2015 book is not that new. An extremely short-term oriented culture war already observed by Robert Jackall in his classic 1988 study of ethics in large US corporations. At that time, he'd already noticed that short-term results were what managers are judged by and that a strong past performance was quickly forgotten as the focus moved not to next month but to tomorrow.

In his view, this goes to the heart of the ethics problem in business: "Managers think in the short-run because they are evaluated by both their superiors and peers on their short-term results. Those who are not seen to be producing requisite short-run gains come to be thought of as embarrassing liabilities."[60] Jackall also observed that managers feel that the long-run hardly matters if they do not survive the short-run. As a result, executives are constantly buying time for the future by hitting to short-term goals. As summarized by one interviewee, "Our horizon is today's lunch."[61]

Jackall also recognized that the focus on short-term outcomes was strongly related to the frequent turnover of executives in different jobs at the organization. Because executives were not tracked from one assignment to the next, they were constantly fixated on "milking" the resources under their direction while postponing the liabilities for their successor in the position. As one senior manager explained, "One way of looking at success patterns in the corporation is that the people who are in high positions have never been in one place long enough for their problems to catch up with them. They outrun their mistakes. That's why to be successful in a business organization, you have to move quickly."[62]

The overall conclusion of both books validates a recent study aimed at investigating the major causes of corporate corruption.[63] According to the report, published in 2016 by the Center for the Advancement of Public Integrity at Columbia University, corruption seems most likely in organizations where growth is a fetish, insecurity is rampant, and high performance goes unquestioned.

The overemphasis on growth generates a culture based on a permanent sense of urgency in which the ends justify the means. The feeling of insecurity contributes to an atmosphere of fear in which people become reluctant to expose their concerns. The pressure to meet high financial targets through rewards and penalties that disregard ethical considerations, in turn, contributes to the escalation of misbehavior because the adoption of improper practices by one person ends up putting pressure on peers to cut corners in the same way. Taken together, these characteristics make the "rules and processes put in place to promote integrity to be practiced selectively and to be easily evaded."[64] The report concludes by compiling the main cultural traits of a corrupt organization:

- Strategy: only driven by competition, with growth as the exclusive goal;
- Leadership: complacent leaders who hoard information, disperse accountability, avoid taking responsibility, and create plausible rationalizations. High performers are venerated and unquestioned;
- Decision-making and authority: opaque, myopic, and strongly hierarchical structures based on top-down "command and control";
- Incentives: discretionary bonus based on hitting unrealistic goals set without regard to market conditions or employee behavior;
- Values and beliefs: permanent feeling of urgency, insecurity, powerlessness and rivalry. In-group language that relies on humor and metaphors of war and sport; and,
- Norms and behaviors: low transparency, secrecy, fear, and lack of pride in the organization.

The solution to large-scale cases of corporate corruption, therefore, will not arise from governance documents but rather from a complete overhaul of the identity and informal value system of the organizations.

The Virtuous Barrel:
How to Transform Corporate Scandals into Good Businesses via Behavioral Ethics

Companies truly committed to high ethical standards must have a single set of formal and informal norms, all pointing in the same direction. They should also strive to achieve a balance between the use of controls and the personal responsibility of each employee.

In this sense, all employees should be required to reflect on the consequences of their decisions and to respond based on sound ethical principles. This is what will make each member vigilant about the behaviors of coworkers and allow an organization to self-regulate itself.

In addition to senior managers, who should promote fairness in the workplace and provide the necessary resources to build an effective ethical culture, the board of directors also plays a key role in promoting a sound culture that lead to successful compliance with regulations and ethical decisions. The box below details the role of the board on this issue.

> *The critical role of the board of directors in fostering a strong and healthy culture*
>
> *Despite being a key issue for any organization, the role of the board in setting the right culture is seldom explored. Literature generally focuses on discussing its role on strategy. However, quoting Peter Drucker, "culture eats strategy for breakfast."*
>
> *One of the key roles of a board is to ensure that the company has a culture that draws the best out of people. There are five main ways a board can shape and promote a healthy culture:*
>
> *Leading by example: The consistency between what the board does and communicates is critical. The board must adopt a "zero tolerance" stance for unethical behaviors. In addition, board members must demonstrate the elements of a sound culture – trust, transparency, accountability, integrity, collaboration, and empathy – in board meetings and in its interactions with executives.*
>
> *Defining a higher purpose and the values that should guide the behavior of everyone: A strong and healthy culture begins with a clear statement of a greater purpose to be pursued beyond profits. Having a higher purpose unites and motivates all stakeholders as well as establishes the values to be used as a benchmark for assessing the behavioral performance of executives and employees.*

Selecting, managing, and even replacing a CEO based on his or her ability to embody and implement the desired culture: The CEO is the main driver of the company's culture; he or she should encourage the desired behaviors and serve as a role model for everyone's conduct. Choosing the right person for the CEO position, therefore, is the most effective way for the board to ensure a healthy culture.

Periodically discussing the company's culture, values, and behaviors in board meetings: It is important to discuss culture, values, and behaviors periodically. These topics can be discussed as standalone issues or can be integrated into other topics related to the company's culture, such as indicators of customer satisfaction or employee surveys.

Developing tools to evaluate and monitor culture: Having a good understanding of the company's current culture is a complex task that depends on information from a wide range of sources. Specifically, boards can evaluate and monitor culture by: assessing culture indicators from different areas (e.g., human resources, internal audit, risk, compliance); visiting operations and having conversations with employees and focus groups; conducting anonymous surveys with employees to assess the level of convergence between the formal and informal value systems; interviewing executives and employees who have quit the organization; talking to key stakeholders, such as clients, suppliers, and regulators, to see how they are treated by the organization; carrying out reputational analysis in the media and social networks; and assessing employees comments on specialized websites such as www.glassdoor.com through data analysis techniques.

---

[1] Source: Edgar H. Schein, Organizational Culture and Leadership: A dynamic view. Jossey-Bass. 1992. p. 20.

[2] Hollensbe et al. (2014: 1229).

[3] Scientific American. September 1st 2018. What Made Us Unique – How we became a different kind of animal. By Kevin Laland. Available at https://www.scientificamerican.com/article/what-made-us-unique/

[4] Deal and Kennedy (2000).

[5] It is important to note that the word "culture" comes from the Latin word "cultura", which means cultivate. Thus, as highlighted by Treviño et al. (2017: 60), "the agricultural origin of the word conveys the sense of shaping or nurturing something over time. Like plants, people are rooted in a particular place, and they are shaped by the norms of that place."

[6] Schein (2010). According to Schein (2010: 18) the culture of a group is "a pattern of shared basic assumptions learned by a group as it solved its problems of external adaption and internal integration, which has worked well enough to be considered valid and, therefore, to be taught to new members as the correct way to perceive, think, and feel in relation to those problems."

[7] Source: http://www.ethicalsystems.org/content/corporate-culture

[8] Graham et al. (2017). Still according to this research, C-level executives linked culture especially to ethical choices, innovation, and productivity at their firms.

[9] Haidt (2012: 292). The author offers an expanded definition of moral capital as "the degree to

which a community possesses interlocking sets of values, virtues, norms, practices, identities, institutions, and technologies that enable the community to suppress or regulate selfishness and make cooperation possible."

[10] Kluver et al. (2014: 155-156) describe three ways by which companies can enhance their moral capital. The first is by creating meaningful work which people view as a calling, in contrast to a more transactional-oriented workplace: to the extent that people see themselves as part of a larger group working together with a shared fate to create virtuous outcomes, they can be expected to suppress self-interest because they are a "part of a whole." The second is by building group-level identities and shared values: employees who feel that their managers share their moral values are more internally motivated to act morally. The third is by promoting a view of organizations as "hives," rather than silos: fear of bad gossip in the workplace, for instance, can promote moral capital by motivating everyone to be better citizens.

[11] *Ibid*: 154.
[12] *Ibid*: 155.
[13] Campbell, J. L., & Göritz (2014: 303).
[14] Kluver et al. (2014: 154).
[15] Source: Maslow, A. (1998). Toward a Psychology of Being. 3 ed. Wiley, p. 65.
[16] Source: The Ultimate Book of Quotations. Compiled and Arranged by Joseph Demakis. 2012, p. 42. ed. Lulu Enterprises.
[17] Luyendijk (2015: 94, 87).
[18] Paduan (2016: 248-249).
[19] According to Law et al. (2011), a workplace with psychological security is one in which senior management implements policies, practices and procedures that ensure the protection of the psychological health of employees.
[20] Oftentimes, the concept of psychological safety is mistakenly confused with the concept of trust. While psychological safety refers to behavior regarding the norms of the group where the person is inserted, trust is focused on one's safety as a result of others' behavior.
[21] Carmeli et al. (2010), Baer and Frese (2003), Edmondson (1999), and Brown and Leigh (1996).
[22] Law et al. (2011).
[23] The five keys to a successful Google team. Julia Rozovsky. November 17, 2015. Available at https://rework.withgoogle.com/blog/five-keys-to-a-successful-google-team/
[24] Source: The Harvard Gazette. 11/28/2016. Think different, maybe. Available at http://news.harvard.edu/gazette/story/2016/11/harvard-business-school-francesca-gino-office-nonconformity/
[25] Sunstein and Hastie (2014).
[26] Source: Harvard Business Review. 24/10/2016. "Let your workers Rebel". Article by Francesca Gino. Available at https://hbr.org/cover-story/2016/10/let-your-workers-rebel
[27] Paduan (2016: 243-246).
[28] Source: Sloan, A. P. (1964). My years with general motors. Crown Business.
[29] Van Knippenberg and Schippers (2007), and Williams and O'Reilly III (1998).
[30] Sunstein and Hastie (2014), Aggarwal et al. (2015), and Kozhevnikov et al. (2014).
[31] These experiments analyzed the performance of groups of 2-5 people in tasks requiring creative brainstorming, negotiation, solution of mathematical puzzles and ethical dilemmas, among other activities. In these exercises, the three factors that make up the "c" factor were responsible for about 50% of the performance variance between the groups. For more on this, see Woolley et al. (2015), and Woolley et al. (2010).

³² Social sensitivity has been measured in these studies through the "Reading the Mind in the Eyes" test, developed by Cambridge University researcher Simon Baron-Cohen. The test assesses the ability to identify mental states of other people by viewing photos of their eyes. In a very interesting paper, Engel et al. (2014) showed that social sensitivity is a key factor for group performance even in tasks in which people collaborated online, thus without any visual contact! For more, see Engel et al. (2014) and Baron-Cohen et al. (2001).

³³ Source: The New York Times. 08/15/2015. Inside Amazon: Wrestling Big Ideas in a Bruising Workplace. Available at https://nyti.ms/2k1fqlS .

³⁴ For more on nonviolent communication techniques, see https://www.cnvc.org/

³⁵ Free translation of "*Vertrouwen komt te voet en vertrekt te paard*". Source: https://en.wikiquote.org/wiki/Dutch_proverbs

³⁶ According to the 2012 publication "Where has all trust gone" of the Chartered Institute of Personnel and Development, "trust" means having security in depending on a person, group or organization in a situation where there is uncertainty and risk. The report highlights that trust is even more important in periods of uncertainty like present times. The report also provides many evidence on the strong relationship between trust and several positive outcomes, such as higher employee engagement and motivation, lower absenteeism, lower costs with controls, higher productivity, and higher rate of innovation. Available at https://www.cipd.co.uk/knowledge/culture/ethics/has-trust-gone-report

³⁷ Hollensbe et al. (2014: 1231).

³⁸ Paduan (2016: 297). Still according to the book, a former employee mentioned that "she (the former CEO Graca Foster) does not only say that your work is awful. She says that the employee is dumb, stupid, and asshole… and she does this shouting in front of others!".

³⁹ Source: Mill, J. S. 1859. On Liberty. Chapter I. I.11 http://www.econlib.org/library/Mill/mlLbty1.html

⁴⁰ Harvard Business Review. 12/12/2016. Why Ethical People Make Unethical Choices. By Ron Carucci (the interview is cited as part of the article).

⁴¹ Financial Times. 10/14/2015. What to do if you discover your company is corrupt. By Michael Skapinker. Available at https://www.ft.com/content/ba176c22-71a1-11e5-9b9e-690fdae72044

⁴² The Guardian. 04/26/2017. Barclays boss used bank's security team to hunt for whistleblower. Available at https://www.theguardian.com/business/2017/apr/10/barclays-boss-jes-staley-may-lose-bonus-over-bid-to-expose-whistleblower

⁴³ The New York Times. 05/04/2017. Wells Fargo Whistle-Blowers' Fate Becomes Just a Footnote. Available at https://nyti.ms/2pLFYh4

⁴⁴ *Ibid.*

⁴⁵ Call et al. (2016). Specifically, the authors found that misreporting firms granted 14% more stock options to employees when they were allegedly misreporting its financial statements, but the number of options they granted decreased by 32% after stop misreporting.

⁴⁶ *Ibid.* The rationale to justify this strategic incentive is quite straightforward. The value of stock options is directly tied to the value of the firm's stock. On the other hand, whistleblowing allegations result in an immediate decline in the firm's stock price. Thus, employees stand to lose financially if they decide to blow the whistle. According to the authors, approximately 10% of the sample firms were subject to a whistleblowing allegation, and companies that avoided a whistleblower granted 78% more stock options than those that did not.

⁴⁷ The video at https://youtu.be/z4S1LLrSzVE?t=1m30s shows an impressive example of how the bystander effect can manifest itself in everyday life.

The Virtuous Barrel:
How to Transform Corporate Scandals into Good Businesses via Behavioral Ethics

[48] Initially, it was estimated that 38 people had ignored the call for help. Subsequently, the investigations showed that this number had been substantially lower. The criminal was initially sentenced to the electric chair and later had his sentence commuted to life imprisonment. He died in 2016 after spending 52 years in prison. The New York Times. 04/04/2016. Winston Moseley, Who Killed Kitty Genovese, Dies in Prison at 81. Available at https://nyti.ms/2k1ijTS; The New York Times. 27/03/1964. 37 Who Saw Murder Didn't Call the Police. Available at https://nyti.ms/2jALhNk

[49] The seminal papers on this field were written by Darley and Latane (1968), and Latane and Darley (1968). Fischer et al. (2011) present a recent review of this literature.

[50] Source: Epley and Tannenbaum (2017: 76).

[51] Campbell and Göritz (2014: 306).

[52] Jackall (1988: 6).

[53] Treviño and Nelson (2016).

[54] Campbell and Göritz (2014: 295).

[55] Luyendijk (2015).

[56] *Ibid*: 3.

[57] *Ibid*: 98.

[58] *Ibid*: 144.

[59] In the words of Luyendijk (2015: 154): "…vast trading floors where mercenaries survive in a haze of complexity and *caveat emptor* (let the buyer beware); an atmosphere of deep mutual distrust; a relentless and amoral focus on profit and 'revenue responsibility'; a brutal hire and fire culture… why would people on a trading floor worry about the risks or ethics of the complex financial products they were selling, let alone about the long-term financial health of their own bank? Why would they even think about it as 'their' bank, knowing they could be out of the door in five minutes? Why would a risk manager or compliance officer in such an environment sound the alarm? This was almost like a blueprint for short-termism".

[60] Jackall (1988: 84). The author also observes that managers obviously know that today's minor issues can quickly become tomorrow's major crises. However, "the pressure for annual, quarterly, monthly, daily, and even hourly results crowds out reflection about the future."

[61] *Ibid*: 84.

[62] *Ibid*: 90-91.

[63] Center for the Advancement of Public Integrity/Trustees of Columbia University. (2016). What Do Corrupt Firms Have in Common? Red Flags of Corruption in Organizational Culture. Available at http://web.law.columbia.edu/sites/default/files/microsites/public-integrity/files/what_do_corrupt_firms_have_in_common_-_capi_issue_brief_-_april_2016.pdf

[64] Center for the Advancement of Public Integrity/Trustees of Columbia University. (2016). What Do Corrupt Firms Have in Common? Red Flags of Corruption in Organizational Culture. Available at http://web.law.columbia.edu/sites/default/files/microsites/public-integrity/files/what_do_corrupt_firms_have_in_common_-_capi_issue_brief_-_april_2016.pdf

13. What should be done to avoid ethical blindness in my organization? The role of leadership

> *"A fruit grower's task is not only to prevent rotting, but to cultivate apples of a high quality."*
> Muel Kaptein[1]

Leadership is the most critical factor in shaping an ethical culture.[2] In order to build a healthy organizational context that avoids ethical blindness, the first requisite is to have business leaders who authentically believe in the value of integrity. After all, while it is true that senior managers are influenced by their environments, they are obviously the most responsible for the actions that proliferate in their organizations. Thus, just as there will be no ethical business with leaders whose money is the primary value, ethical blindness will not thrive in environments in which senior managers exhibit a virtuous conduct.

To a large extent, the basic role of business leaders is to create an environment that encourages aspired behaviors. Their task is not to monitor everything with the purpose of preventing a certain employee from misbehaving (which is obviously impossible) but rather to ensure that everyone works in a place in which they can show their best selves and flourish as human beings. As pointed out by Professor Muel Kaptein's quote opening this chapter, the role of a good leader is similar to that of a farmer. Some rotten fruits will unfortunately sprout, but the leader's function is to create a fertile ground so that the vast majority of fruits will reach the highest possible quality.

The Virtuous Barrel:
How to Transform Corporate Scandals into Good Businesses via Behavioral Ethics

To this end, leaders should combine the traditional control-based approach designed to smoke out the bad apples with a trust-based approach focused on creating a healthy context that activates people's consciousness. Both approaches can be viewed as a sort of "continuum" that should be moved over time to the trust side in order to bring the best out of people.[3]

In the case of companies that have experienced scandals, changing the current atmosphere depends on a broad overhaul to embed a completely new mindset. In addition to the traditional skills associated with leadership such as organization, dynamism, courage, proactivity, etc., business leaders need to be attuned to the world of the twenty-first century by combining ten primary qualities:

1. Ability to be attuned with themselves (self-awareness) and connected to the others (social-awareness);
2. Sense of purpose and capacity to inspire people by creating an emotionally positive environment;
3. Willingness to serve, not to be served;[4]
4. Readiness to take responsibility when things go wrong;
5. Opening to receive criticism and to encourage divergent opinions;
6. Willingness to attend places in which people have different views, including regular conversations with representatives of all stakeholders;
7. Competence to create a culture of trust, care, fairness, transparency, accountability, integrity, and cohesion in which employees show their best selves;
8. Capacity to build bridges among people with different worldviews and create a highly diverse workplace;
9. Genuine desire to care for each member of the organization and capacity of exhibiting high empathy;
10. Courage to go against the opinion of the majority by "paddling against the tide" in certain situations.

Gathering these qualities – all related to high emotional and moral maturity – is essential for an effective leader nowadays. This will inspire employees and decisively contribute to the creation of a workplace that fosters ethical behavior.

For leaders interested in improving the ethical culture of their organizations, a useful step is to assess to what extent managers are indeed exhibiting social sensitivity and integrity daily. There are many instruments to carry out such assessment. Appendix 1 at the end of this chapter, for instance, provides the excerpt of a questionnaire that assesses the degree of ethical leadership.[5]

In the following topics, I describe the main ways by which business leaders can cultivate a culture that minimizes the chance of ethical blindness in their organizations. They include the ability to:

1. Lead by example;
2. Send clear (never ambiguous!) signals on the expected behavior of everyone;
3. Allow people to bring their whole selves to the workplace;
4. Ensure constant communication and dialogue on ethical blindness;
5. Periodically evaluate the informal value system of the organization;
6. Periodically assess the level of convergence (or coherence) between formal and informal value systems through anonymous surveys with employees;
7. Reinforce the importance of ethics in the hiring process;
8. Reward employees who display good conduct as well as sanction transgressors irrespective of their performance;
9. Ensure that everyone explicitly reflects on the ethical implications of each company decision; and
10. Enlarge people's perspective about their role as executives.

Lead by example

By far, leading by example is the primary means by which managers can instill ethical behavior in their organizations. Their values and conducts are learned and emulated all

The Virtuous Barrel:
How to Transform Corporate Scandals into Good Businesses via Behavioral Ethics

the time, and the so-called "tone at the top" is a key determinant of their subordinates' level of integrity. This is particularly true when employees observe how leaders react in challenging situations, such as when they are contradicted, subjected to ethical dilemmas, or receive bad news.

The notion that being exposed to people of high moral stature makes a difference in employee behavior is validated by scientific evidence. A recent survey of 659 employees and 217 managers of a large company concluded, for instance, that having an ethical role model throughout the executive's career was positively related to subordinated-rated ethical leadership.[6] Interestingly, the researchers noted that the reference person who is most relevant to the executive's ethical behavior tends to change with age. For younger managers, having had childhood ethical role models was more strongly related to ethical leadership. For older managers, in contrast, having had career mentors or superiors as role models was the most important aspect related to ethical leadership.[7] The research corroborates the argument that having leaders acting as ethical role models generate a positive "cascade effect" in organizations that fosters the development of other virtuous leaders below in the hierarchy.

It is critical, thus, to have people in leadership positions who truly believe in the value of ethics and who exhibit daily conduct in line with this view. Otherwise, subordinates will perceive the presence of "moral hypocrisy" and, consequently, the formal rules will not lead people to proper behavior. This is corroborated by many studies showing that unethical behaviors by leaders tend to be copied more quickly by subordinates than ethical doings.[8]

One of these papers, conducted through experiments with 850 people, found that individuals who imitate their superiors' unethical attitudes have a lower chance of being punished by their organizations.[9] According to the authors, transgressions committed by leaders change the way employees view the issue of blame in these situations, making them more tolerant of offenders. For companies, the study shows that having unethical leaders encourages their subordinates to act in the same way, thus creating a dangerous spiral toward ever-increasing violations.[10]

Being an ethical role model is a greater challenge for people in leadership roles compared with employees. There are at least three main reasons for this assertion. First, as shown in Chapter 4, human beings tend to exhibit less empathy and more moral hypocrisy as they become more powerful. Second, being promoted to key positions tends to increase the monetary temptations to act unethically as well as the pressure to behave in a questionable way to maintain this more privileged position. And third, reaching the top echelons of an organization may lead to the so-called "stress power," which can bring about side effects from the ethical standpoint.[11]

It is important for leaders, therefore, not to fall into the temptation of having a "master of the universe" attitude. On the contrary, they must see themselves as good examples to be followed by others. Again, legendary former GM CEO Alfred Sloan offers a good lesson by stating that "Leadership is not charisma. It is not public relations. It is not showmanship. It is consistent behavior, trustworthiness. The professional manager is a servant. Rank does not confer privilege. It does not give power. It imposes responsibility."[12]

Send clear (never ambiguous!) signals on the expected behavior of everyone

In addition to being role models, it is crucial for leaders to make clear what are the rules of the game and the behavior expected of everyone in the company. The clearer the expectations on how each employee should behave, the more people will tend to act accordingly.

The case of Siemens shows the importance of clarity about having a clearly expected conduct. Back in 2007, a joint investigation by German and US prosecutors discovered that the huge multinational with presence in 190 countries and 372,000 employees disbursed around $1.4 billion in briberies to secure contracts in emerging countries between 2000 and 2006. As a result, the company paid fines of $1.6 billion to settle

The Virtuous Barrel:
How to Transform Corporate Scandals into Good Businesses via Behavioral Ethics

charges in both countries in 2008. In May 2007, Siemens hired Peter Löscher to be its new CEO. A former pharmaceuticals industry executive, he was the first CEO hired outside the company since its foundation in 1847. Without links to former executives, Löscher carried out a complete overhaul at Siemens.

To begin with, all members of the management board – used to the old way of doing business – were dismissed, as well as 80% of all first-level executives and 70% of second-level managers. The compliance department gained prominence, with its head becoming one of the eight members of the company's powerful management board.[13] Diversity has also become a priority issue. Shortly after taking office, Löscher caused uproar by saying that Siemens was "too male, white and German." For the first time in history, women were appointed to the management board. According to the CEO, this "made women suddenly realize that there was no glass ceiling at the company."[14] Another key change took place in the ethical tone at the top. In the annual ethics and compliance trainings, which he usually attended, Löscher emphatically pointed out to employees that "There is a red line, and the red line is uniform across the organization. If you cross this line, you will suffer the consequences, immediately!" The results obtained by Siemens since the outbreak of the scandal show that having a genuine concern for ethics and compliance is fully compatible with healthy profits. From 2006 to 2016, its revenues grew from EUR 64 billion to EUR 79 billion, while its net profit grew from EUR 4.0 billion to EUR 5.5 billion.

The clear message sent by Siemens' CEO to employees is a good example to be followed by other business leaders, particularly those who inadvertently issue contradictory signals such as "You have to follow the code of conduct" and "You have to secure this contract at any cost" or "Don't tell me how you are going to make it, I just want to see the outcome!" Sending ambiguous messages such as these, which at the same time mean "Comply with the code and violate the code" is an invitation to misconducts.

In fact, because leaders are co-responsible for the actions incited on subordinates, these mixed signals can be seen as unethical behaviors. It is much easier to accept questionable conduct when it is performed by someone else due to the division of labor than when it is performed directly by ourselves. This is unfortunately very common in the business world.

In his classic 1988 book *Moral Mazes*, sociologist Robert Jackall analyzed the moral consciousness of US executives based on several years of fieldwork. He noticed that, although power in large corporations is concentrated at the top in the hands of the CEO, it is simultaneously decentralized in the sense that responsibility for decisions and profits is pushed as far down in the organizational line as possible. According to Jackall, this has serious ethical implications because "Too much knowledge is a dangerous thing for a CEO. It's much better to have a subordinate take the blame for things which go wrong and to know nothing of the details."[15] He also observes that "Superiors do not like to give detailed instructions to subordinates ... pushing down details relieves superiors of the burden of too much knowledge, particularly guilty knowledge ... it creates great pressure on middle managers not only to transmit good news but, precisely because they know the details, to act to protect their corporations, their bosses, and themselves in the process."[16]

Many leaders, therefore, intentionally delegate questionable decisions to subordinates or prompt them to do whatever it takes to achieve a particular outcome. That is why business leaders must be legally and morally accountable for their subordinates' actions when there is evidence that the organization tolerates or implicitly encourages improper behavior.

Business leaders should never put people in a "survival mode" nor make them think that they will have to choose between integrity or success in the company. On the contrary. Those genuinely interested in promoting ethical behavior should reinforce the role of employee autonomy with proper accountability, making it clear that each one is responsible for his or her own decisions and consequences.

It is also important to emphasize that blame should never be attributed to the market. One study found, in this sense, that employees of corrupt organizations feel trapped by the power of competitors and market conditions.[17] Because of this submissive relationship to market conditions, they did not see a chance of changing the system and ended up abiding to illicit practices. Encouraging people to develop their own inner reflections and the power of choice, thus, is critical to avoid employees becoming ethically blind.

Allow people to bring their whole selves to the workplace

Creating an environment in which employees feel they can behave authentically and don't need to put on a "professional mask" when they check in at the office generates many benefits, such as greater engagement, innovation, and productivity. Research has shown, for example, that employees who feel they can bring their "whole selves" to the day-to-day business are 16% more committed than those who feel they need to hide who they really are.[18]

Usually, there is an opposite relationship between the pressure to conform and the feeling of authenticity: The more people feel that they can be themselves, the less likely they are to submit to peer pressures and accept questionable practices. This, in turn, will decrease the chance of unethical behaviors. As referred by Maryam Kouchaki, a professor at Northwestern University's Kellogg School of Management, "We have multiple identities that we could be at any moment. When our identities are integrated, they are in sync. When our identities are segmented, we feel like our various selves are in conflict."[19]

Therefore, it is up to leaders to actively foster the sense of wholeness among employees, so they can take their whole selves to the workplace instead of leaving their values and ideals at home. This includes, among other things, allowing individuals to expose not only their "rational" side but also their intuitive, emotional, and even spiritual sides.

Frederic Laloux's book *Reinventing Organizations* describes many practices to foster a sense of wholeness.[20] One is to start every meeting – an occasion in which people tend to exacerbate their ego and behave inauthentically – with a minute of silence. This helps participants to connect with themselves and focus on the present moment. Another is the practice of carrying out periodic meetings in which employees share their life histories so colleagues can connect with them as human beings (according to evolutionary psychology, storytelling is one of the most effective ways to build trust and mutual appreciation).

A third option is establishing moments of joint self-reflection. At Heiligenfeld (a German healthcare company), for example, about 350 employees meet every week for about an hour to carry out a joint rumination on an issue not necessarily linked to the day-to-day running of the business, including topics such as personal health, conflict resolution or dealing with failures.

Even the physical space can be used to enhance the feeling of authenticity. At FAVI, a French automotive company, production teams are encouraged to paint the machines of their area and to decorate the factory floor with plants and aquariums. At Patagonia, a US outdoor clothing company, employees are encouraged to take their small children to a childhood center attached to the office, so they can go to their parents' desks from time to time. Other companies, in turn, have created a space for contemplative practices, such as joint meditation rooms. Still according to author Frederic Laloux, no firm has gone as far as Sounds True, a North American media company. There, employees are encouraged to take their dogs to the office and even to the meetings.

Ensure constant communication and dialogue on ethical blindness

As we saw in Part 1 of this book, most people believe to be "immune" to ethical problems because they have an intrinsically good character and believe to have full control of their moral boundaries. As demonstrated throughout this book, though, this thinking is very dangerous. As Harvard Professor Eugene Soltes points out, after interacting with dozens of executives condemned for white-collar crimes, "The errors made by executives are ones that we are all susceptible to. We are all susceptible to making the same mistakes as these former executives."[21]

The Virtuous Barrel:
How to Transform Corporate Scandals into Good Businesses via Behavioral Ethics

It is up to the leaders, therefore, to disseminate among employees the key findings of behavioral ethics and the organizational factors that may lead ordinary people to make unethical or even illegal decisions. This will "raise our guard" that we are all subject to make decisions contrary to our values from which we may regret.

As described in Part 2, the fast pace and pressures of corporate life make it particularly easier for executives to become ethically blind. This was one the conclusions of sociologist Robert Jackall in his classical account of how managers think the world works. After showing to several executives a case in which a fictitious officer called Brady faced an ethical dilemma after discovering wrongdoings committed by his superiors, he noticed that managers simply could not see the moral dimension of the situation. According to the sociologist, "The corporate managers to whom I presented this case see Brady's dilemma as devoid of moral or ethical content. In their view, the issues that Brady raises are simply practical matters."[22] In managers' view, compromise about anything and everything is simply an inevitable fact of organizational life. After all, "bureaucracy transforms all moral issues into immediately practical concerns... and managers do not want evangelists working for them."[23]

An important activity for leaders authentically committed to avoid ethical blindness, therefore, is to hold periodic events to communicate, discuss, and reinforce practical aspects of the values and principles of the organization. It is essential for key leaders to actively participate in these events, especially the CEO and other C-level executives.

A good example comes from the French company L'Oreal, one of the leading cosmetics companies in the world. Every year, the company celebrates the "ethics day," an event in which its global CEO answers questions directly from employees based everywhere (in 2014, the workforce sent more than 3,900 questions).[24] On the same date, CEOs of more than 60 countries where L'Oreal has business units also carry out this exercise with local employees.[25]

The "corridor stories" are also an important form of communication. Valuing "company legends" that reinforce good examples, such as situations in which individuals confronted their superiors to avoid improper acts is also important, as it strengthens the idea that ethical choices should be the norm in the company.

Periodically evaluate the informal value system of the organization

Because a toxic culture is the main factor driving unethical behaviors, it is imperative for leaders to have an in-depth understanding of the informal value system of their organizations.

One way to get a better grasp of the prevalent culture is by talking periodically with people about the factors that may lead to ethical blindness, such as an atmosphere of aggressiveness and fear, the use of euphemistic or warlike language, the adoption of inadequate incentive systems, excessive pressure for consensus and conformity, unethical practices by industry peers, and so on.

The following are examples of questions that can be asked on such occasions:

- What are the main pressures people feel in the organization?
- What is the profile of those who make it to the top here? (e.g., are they goal-oriented or thoughtful and principle-oriented?)
- What kinds of decisions are rewarded by the organization? What is really incentivized?
- Are there known episodes of individuals who stood up to their leaders on ethical issues? What happened to them?
- Which are the most discussed and not discussed topics in an organization? (e.g., money, power, safety, society, customers, etc.)
- What are the main "corridor stories" or legends of the organization? What values do these stories promote?
- Do employees feel that their opinions can change current practices at the organization or is there a feeling that "it will always be like this"?

The Virtuous Barrel:
How to Transform Corporate Scandals into Good Businesses via Behavioral Ethics

- Which group has "the president's ear" and is more powerful in the company? (e.g., financiers, salesmen, engineers, control people, etc.)
- Which departments have little power or are ostracized ("the dead zones")?

Answering these questions based on private conversations with individuals from different areas and ranks will enable business leaders to have correct understanding of their company's informal value system, including the factors that can encourage wrongdoings.

Periodically assess the level of convergence (or coherence) between formal and informal systems of values through anonymous surveys with employees

One point emphasized in the previous chapter is that many business scandals occur when the formal and informal value systems diverge substantially. In such cases, people tend to simply disregard what policies say by behaving according to the unwritten rules of everyday life.

Thus, business leaders should periodically assess the level of convergence (or coherence) between the organization's formal and informal value systems. This can be done through anonymous surveys with employees aiming to assess how they agree with statements that cue a healthy ethical culture, such as:

- I feel safe and comfortable to express my views, even when they are different from the opinion of my superiors;
- Top leaders of my organization behave ethically and lead by their example;
- The people in my organization are very motivated by its values and purpose, not only by financial rewards or by the threat of being fired;
- In my organization, it is not only important to reach the goals, but to achieve them ethically and within the norms;
- The pressure to achieve the goals is NOT excessive.

Appendix 2 at the end of this chapter contains an excerpt of an instrument designed to measure the degree of ethical culture of organizations.[26] In addition, EthicalSystems, a collaboration of top researchers in the field of business ethics has developed a tool to measure the ethical culture of businesses.[27] The tool is divided in ten areas of assessment that clarify the do's and don'ts companies must focus to build an effective ethical culture. Five areas, called "disqualifiers", capture the minimum requirements business need to address before developing a strong ethical culture: organizational unfairness, abusive manager behavior, selfish orientation, lack of awareness, and fear of retaliation. The other five areas, called "qualifiers" represent the qualities companies need to focus to foster a strong ethical orientation: organizational trust, ethical leadership, benevolent orientation, empathy, and efficacy & speaking out.[28]

This exercise is important to see if the company is indeed promoting a healthy environment for employees or if its policies are only being used to satisfy external audiences.[29]

Reinforce the importance of ethics in the hiring process

To show that ethics is important for real, business leaders should prioritize this issue in the company's hiring process. New executives and employees, therefore, should not be hired solely based on their ability to perform well from the financial standpoint but also by careful evaluation of their ethical behavior in both their prior organizations and their personal lives (a recent paper found, for instance, that an executive's past reckless behavior as a driver is correlated with subsequent financial reporting risk).[30]

According to David de Cremer, one of the leading authorities on ethical leadership, there are six main traits related to better ethical conduct that should be emphasized in hiring processes:[31]

1. *Conscientiousness*: Individuals exhibiting this trait tend to be more careful, reflective, and reliable, which is positively associated with higher levels of moral reasoning.
2. *Moral attentiveness*: This characteristic describes the extent to which individuals are aware of the various ethical dilemmas present in their personal

and professional lives. As a result, they tend to see ethical conflicts where others may see none.
3. *Duty orientation*: Individuals with a strong sense of duty tend to be more loyal and oriented to the organization's mission as well as motivated to take action when they perceive a problem.
4. *Customer orientation*: Individuals who are more motivated to prioritize the needs of customers tend to adopt more ethical attitudes in their work due to their higher empathy.
5. *Assertiveness*: Individuals with a more assertive personality are important in building an ethical culture because they are more likely to prevent groupthink by standing up to the pressures of group conformity.
6. *Proactivity*: More proactive individuals tend to feel less constrained by situational forces, making them more likely to engage more quickly in acts of whistleblowing.

Assessing the candidates based on the parameters above, therefore, is an important step toward building a culture where people are more likely to point out wrongdoings.

Reward employees who display good conduct as well as sanction transgressors irrespective of their performance

Proper conduct will only get reinforced on a daily basis if leaders reward and punish based on the adherence to ethical values. Take the case of rewards, for example. Celebrating individuals or teams whose high performance may come from questionable conduct send a message that the end justifies the means in the organization. On the other hand, making people aware that those who violate the rules will certainly face negative consequences irrespective of the financial outcome is an obvious way to show that integrity is a priority for the company.

In particular, it is imperative for leaders to ensure that the rules are applicable to everyone, regardless of rank or the profits they bring to the company.[32] As discussed in

Chapter 7, ethical problems tend to occur incrementally over time. In addition, people tend to replicate others' behaviors. Thus, observing colleagues who breach the policies going unpunished induce others to do the same.

To prevent transgressions from proliferating in an organization, it is important to address violations quickly and in a visible way for all. This should be done even when the misconduct is considered small and with no significant harm. By cutting off evil at the root, business leaders avoid sending wrong signals to everyone.

The importance of establishing a "zero tolerance" policy for unethical behavior relates to the "broken windows theory."[33] This concept, elaborated by two American researchers in the 1980s, has been corroborated over the years by substantial scientific evidence.[34] Its name comes from the observation that when a window is broken in a certain neighborhood, the chance of another one also being broken increases. This bad signaling effect of disorder, in turn, increases the frequency of transgressions and even of crimes in the area. This happens because people come to see social and physical disorder as a sign that authority is absent and that everything is allowed, leading to a decrease of the moral constraints and social barriers to illegal behaviors. The key message of the broken windows theory is clear: small ethical deviations cannot be tolerated because they increase the risk that we will not be able to manage the deterioration of transgressions over time. As the adage goes, "the first cut is the deepest."

Ensuring effective sanctions for misconduct is particularly important in the case of people who hold senior positions or are considered high performers. These situations constitute the true "acid test" for organizations willing to adopt a culture of integrity because not punishing transgressors in these cases sends a dangerous message to other employees that the end justifies the means, and it is worth imitating them.

In many cases, companies avoid punishing executives who are considered financially valuable. A classic example took place with Enron in 1987. Its internal audit found that two oil traders who had generated big profits in the previous two years were diverting resources from the company to their personal accounts. Upon being informed, the then-

The Virtuous Barrel:
How to Transform Corporate Scandals into Good Businesses via Behavioral Ethics

CEO Kenneth Lay decided not only to avoid firing the high-performers but also to conceal auditors' findings from the board of directors. At the end, he sent a handwritten message to the two transgressors asking them to "keep making us millions ...."[35]

A more recent example took place with Uber, a global taxi technology company. Earlier in 2017, a former software engineer named Susan Fowler published an article in which she described a culture of harassment in the company where top performers always went unpunished.[36] Soon after her induction training, she described suffering sexual harassment from her immediate superior. Embarrassed, the former employee sent screenshots of the improper messages to the company's human resources department asking for some kind of punishment to the harasser. To her surprise, the HR department reported that it was not going to apply any penalty based on the argument that it was his first offense and that he was a "high-performer" with stellar reviews from his superiors. Fowler then moved to another area to avert remaining subordinate to the aggressor. Later, after talking with colleagues, she discovered that several other women had already been sexually harassed at the company, some even by her same former superior. In all cases, she discovered that the HR area had sent the same message to the victims arguing that it was their "first offense." In addition to harassment, Fowler described details of a highly hostile, sexist, and misogynist environment at Uber.[37] The case caused huge repercussions, leading to the resignation of its CEO, the dismissal of 20 employees, and the appointment of a C-level officer in charge of diversity issues.[38]

It is important to emphasize that sanctions should also be applied when the unethical behavior harms not only the organization but also its stakeholders such as customers and suppliers. This will show that the company is seriously committed to take an ethical stance in all its relationships.

Although leaders often focus on punishing wrongdoings, it is no less important to reward employees who demonstrate behavior consistent with the company's values and "do the right thing."[39] Although it is obvious that ethical behavior should be an integral part of any professional activity, publicly recognizing examples of sound ethical conduct as part of performance reviews and promotion sends a strong message that encourages similar behaviors.

One suggestion is to ask how goals have been achieved during performance appraisals and promotion decisions, instead of only focusing on the numbers achieved. This practice will make employees see that the firm has a strong commitment to the so-called "principled performance."

Another recommendation, in the case of companies who are truly devoted in putting customers' interests first is to reward employees who, in certain situations, have placed the interests of customers above commercial interests.

A third idea is to disclose at corporate events the cases in which the company opted to stop doing business with suppliers suspected of violating its ethical principles, such as those involving human and workers' rights. Implementing initiatives like these will help a lot in raising the ethical standards of an organization.

Ensure that everyone explicitly reflects on the ethical implications of each company decision

Executives often tend to frame their decisions exclusively as "business decisions." This is, in fact, an illusion. All decisions taken at companies affect the lives of others. They all have an inherent ethical dimension, even if executives try to categorize them only as "business decisions."

Thus, it is crucial to ensure that all executives, employees, and governance bodies (such as committees and boards) systematically reflect on the ethical consequences of their decisions. One way to make this happen is by explicitly including ethical questionings in all corporate decisions. According to Professors Guido Palazzo and Ulrich Hoffrage, a useful idea is to establish the practice of evaluating each decision based on the following parameters:[40]

- Is this a good business decision?
- Is this a good legal decision?

The Virtuous Barrel:
How to Transform Corporate Scandals into Good Businesses via Behavioral Ethics

- Is this a good technical decision?
- Is this a good <u>ethical</u> decision?

Applying these criteria in a sequential way will lead to a more integrated view of the topics under discussion and produce more balanced and well-thought decisions. In this regard, one of the key findings of behavioral ethics is that people are more likely to make sound ethical judgments when their moral standards are "activated" just before their actions.[41]

One of the most interesting examples come from a research by Nina Mazar, On Amir, and Dan Ariely.[42] In this experiment, participants were required to solve "matrix tasks" similar to those described in Chapter 4.

In one of its variants, the authors divided participants into two groups. One was asked to write the 10 Commandments before doing the matrix tests. The other was told to write the names of 10 books they had read. In the jargon of psychologists, the first group had been "primed" to act ethically, while the second group (the control group) had received a neutral priming.[43]

The results were impressive. The group in charge of naming the books they had read cheated the test in a similar way to the individuals who had been tested without any priming (people generally claimed to have solved about 15% more matrices than they actually did). On the other hand, the group asked to recall the 10 Commandments simply did not cheat at all: all reported solving the exact number of matrices they had indeed solved. Curiously, this outcome was achieved despite none of the participants perfectly remembering the 10 Commandments (actually, this group even contained some atheists).

The researchers found similar results in a "secular" variant of the experiment. In this case, they asked participants – MIT and Yale students – to sign a document declaring that "the experiment should be conducted within the ethical standards defined by the MIT/Yale code of honor." The result was similar to the effect of the 10 Commandments, i.e., no one cheated the experiment. Curiously, it is noteworthy that none of the universities had the alleged code of honor. (Once again, the researchers only created a fiction in order to activate participants' "ethical capital.")

In a related work, a team of researchers asked individuals to report how many matrix tasks they had solved in a document formatted to look like a typical business expense report.[44] Half the participants were told to attest the veracity of the information by signing at the very end of the document (after entering the number of matrices they claimed to have solved). The other half, in turn, were required to sign at the beginning of the document, before reporting the number of matrices solved. According to the researchers, the act of signing a document brings the attention on ourselves. Thus, signing before entering the data could lead people to think on their morality right before conducting the tests, which would increase the likelihood of behaving honestly.

The results were remarkable. The mere action of signing at the beginning of the document reduced dishonesty substantially: While 64% of those who signed at the beginning of the report inflated the number of matrices they had actually solved, only 37% of those who signed at the beginning cheated on the test. For the authors, the results demonstrate that signing before reporting something helps to emphasize the morality aspect at the time of temptation. On the other hand, they argue that when the signature is required at the end of the report, "The morality train has passed...."

The activation of people's moral standards is effective not only when it is conscious but also when it is done unconsciously. One study found, for example, that simply exposing people to "green" products can increase their ethical behavior.[45] Another research asked participants to rearrange random words in order to construct phrases with some ethical content (e.g., "Mary to charity gave" becoming "Mary gave to charity").[46] The mere exposure to this unconscious priming produced remarkable results. While 48% of participants behaved dishonestly in the control situation, only 7% behaved dishonestly when they were unconsciously primed by this exercise.[47]

These experiments show the importance for leaders to create "moral reminders" that keep ethics top of mind by triggering people's conscience at the very time of their

The Virtuous Barrel:
How to Transform Corporate Scandals into Good Businesses via Behavioral Ethics

deliberations. A simple recommendation, for example, is to leave the code of ethics visible during meetings. Another suggestion, already adopted by some companies, is to leave an empty chair in meetings. This chair would symbolically represent the collective interest of the organization or of its customers, two parties to be remembered in all decisions.[48]

A further initiative to make people reflect on the ethical implications of their acts is to increase the empathy regarding all stakeholders of the company. This is important because executives are usually physically, emotionally, and temporally distant from the people impacted by their decisions. As this distance grows, customers, investors, and fellow citizens become an anonymous mass that reduces our ability to empathize with them.

One way to increase executives' ability to empathize with stakeholders is through a story-telling process describing the concrete impacts of company decisions on the lives of others through specific examples. The more employees feel the magnitude of the impact of their actions on the lives of others, the more their gut feelings will be triggered and the more likely they will positively adjust their behaviors.

Finally, as we saw in Chapter 7, it is worth remembering that many unethical deeds are the result of thoughtless decisions motivated by time pressure. Thus, it is up to leaders to avoid creating an environment characterized by constant rushing as well as reminding employees that they should develop the habit of pressing the "pause button" before making decisions. As pointed out by Dov Seidman, founder of the Legal Research Network (LRN), "When you press the pause button on a machine, it stops. But when you press the pause button on human beings, they start."[49]

This will enable employees to assess the implications of their behaviors on other people. One possibility is to encourage the creation of regular "time gaps" without specific tasks. Another is to hold periodic sessions designed to jointly reflect on the outcomes of past decisions from different perspectives.

Enlarge people's perspective on their role as executives
As we have seen throughout this book, our ethical judgment critically depends on how we frame reality. Therefore, one last – but not least – role of business leaders is to enlarge people's perspective about their professional duties as executives.

Each member of an organization must understand that his or her role is not only to make money but also to contribute to society in an ethical way. Peter Drucker, a management guru of the twentieth century, validates this assertion by remembering that "One is responsible for one's impact, whether they are intended or not. This is the first rule. There is no doubt regarding management's responsibility for the social impacts of its organization. They are management's business."[50]

One way to broaden corporate managers' conception of business is to emphasize that the organizational boundaries extend far beyond the walls of its office and that the company should be viewed as an interdependent system made up of all its stakeholders, including society at large. As pointed out by an editorial of the *Academy of Management Journal*, the role of business in society should be "Founded on the premise that business is *part* of society and not *apart* from society ... a business that succeeds in a society that fails becomes self-defeating."[51]

Extending the boundaries of a company reduces the likelihood that the organization in question develops a microcosm with a unique and "parallel reality" which is often an invitation to ethical blindness. In the case of companies involved in corruption scandals, it is worth remembering another message from Drucker, who argued that "Since any institution can exist only within the social environment, it is indeed an organ of society ... (Thus), a healthy business cannot exist in a sick society."[52]

Another way to make executives see their role more broadly is to remind them that they are accountable to all stakeholders not just to shareholders. Actually, the laws in most countries are in accordance with this expanded view of the role of business and management.

The Virtuous Barrel:
How to Transform Corporate Scandals into Good Businesses via Behavioral Ethics

In this sense, the idea that executives should solely focus on profits must be viewed as an outdated idea from the twentieth century. The modern concept from the twenty-first century is that managers have a noble and decisive role for promoting a healthier society. Good executives should understand and be proud of this enlarged responsibility. This will make them voluntarily interested in connecting their companies to the communities of which they are part.

Appendix 1. Excerpt of the Ethical Leadership at Work by Kalshoven, Hartog, and De Hoogh[53]

Statements should be rated on a 1 to 5 scale from "fully disagree" to "fully agree"

#	Please rate your level of agreement with the following statements
	Dimension 1: People orientation – My leader:
1	Is interested in how I feel and how I am doing.
2	Is genuinely concerned about my personal development.
3	Cares about his/her followers.
	Dimension 2: Fairness – My leader:
1	DOES NOT hold me accountable for problems over which I have no control.
2	DOES NOT pursues his/her own success at the expense of others.
3	IS NOT focused mainly on reaching his/her own goals.
	Dimension 3: Power sharing – My leader:
1	Seeks advice from subordinates concerning organizational strategy.
2	Will reconsider decisions on the basis of recommendations by those who report to him/her.
3	Delegates challenging responsibilities to subordinates.
	Dimension 4: Concern for Sustainability – My leader:
1	Would like to work in an environmentally friendly manner.
2	Shows concern for sustainability issues.
3	Stimulates recycling of items and materials in our department.
	Dimension 5: Ethical Guidance – My leader:
1	Explains what is expected from employees in terms of behaving with integrity.
2	Ensures that employees follow codes of integrity.
3	Stimulates the discussion of integrity issues among employees.
	Dimension 6: Role clarification – My leader:
1	Indicates what the performance expectations of each group member are.
2	Explains what is expected of each group member.
3	Clarifies priorities and who is responsible for what.
	Dimension 7: Integrity – My leader:
1	Keeps his/her promises.
2	Can be trusted to do the things he/she says.
3	Always keeps his/her words.

Appendix 2. Excerpt of an Indicator to Measure the Degree of Ethical Awareness of the Organization

Statements should be rated on a 1 to 5 scale from "fully disagree" to "fully agree"

#	Please rate your level of agreement with the following statements
1	I feel safe and comfortable to express my views, even when they are different from the opinion of my superiors.
2	Our leaders often highlight the importance of hearing dissonant opinions in order to improve decisions.
3	Top leaders of my organization behave ethically and lead by their example.
4	Senior leaders always make clear the ethical behavior accepted by the organization and expected from each one.
5	I feel safe to present contrary views against a formed majority of peers in committees, boards, and other collegiate bodies.
6	People frequently discuss concrete cases involving ethical dilemmas they face.
7	I'm sure that people would report unethical actions if they saw them.
8	I did not see any unethical or illegal behavior in my work environment last year.
9	The people in my organization are motivated by its values and purpose and not only by financial rewards or by the threat of being fired.
10	People are promoted not only for performance but also for their ethical behavior and compliance with our rules and principles.
11	People who behave in an unethical or illegal way suffer the necessary sanctions here.
12	In my organization, it is not only important to reach the goals but to achieve them ethically and within the norms.
13	In my organization, failure to report unethical behaviors means being co-responsible for them.
14	I feel that the values and principles of my organization are widely incorporated by people on a daily basis.
15	My organization rewards and values people who behave ethically.
16	The pressure to achieve the goals is NOT excessive.
17	People are NOT constantly tired and stressed.
18	I feel that, over the years, we are constantly evolving in relation to ethics and integrity.
19	Our organizational routines do not lead people to make questionable decisions on "autopilot" mode.
20	We always explicitly evaluate the ethical implications of our decisions (this is part of our decision-making process).

[1] Source: Kaptein, M. (2013). Workplace morality: Behavioral ethics in organizations. Emerald Group Publishing.
[2] BSR – The of a Better World. The Five Levels of an Ethical Culture. March 2017, p. 16. Available at https://www.bsr.org/reports/BSR_Ethical_Corporate_Culture_Five_Levels.pdf
[3] Charles Munger, vice-chairman of Berkshire Hathaway, is a supporter of the trust-based approach. In a recent interview, he said that "a lot of people think if you just had more process and more compliance – checks and double-checks and so forth – you could create a better result in the world. Well, Berkshire has had practically no process. We had hardly any internal auditing until they forced it on us. We just try to operate in a seamless web of deserved trust and be careful whom we trust". Source: Corporate Governance According to Charles T. Munger. Stanford Closer Look Series. March 2014. By David F. Larcker, Brian Tayan. Available at https://www.gsb.stanford.edu/faculty-research/publications/corporate-governance-according-charles-t-munger
[4] According to Viktor Frankl, renowned Austrian psychiatrist who dedicated his life to studying the issue of human happiness, "the more one forgets one's self and begins to serve a greater cause or to love one's neighbor, the more human and happy he is". Source: Frankl (2006).
[5] The excerpt comes from the ethical leadership at work questionnaire (ELW) created by Kalshoven et al. (2011). It is worth mentioning that the concept of ethical leadership includes attributes other than honesty, such as empathy, respect for people, the ability to communicate clearly the expected behaviors by the organization, the effectiveness in punishing unethical behavior, etc.
[6] Brown and Treviño (2014).
[7] In other words, the widely-used argument that "ethics comes from home-based education" is more likely to be applicable in the case of young executives who are starting their careers. Afterwards, what counts most are the examples of their superiors throughout their professional lives.
[8] Bauman et al. (2016), Brown and Treviño (2014), Mawritz et al. (2012), Litzky et al. (2006), and Treviño and Brown (2005).
[9] Bauman et al. (2016).
[10] In one variant of the study, researchers informed participants that superiors who had committed unethical doings imitated by subordinates had been subsequently punished. In this case, the participants applied the standard penalty to the offender. This result is very interesting, because it shows that the "advantage" of imitating superiors' bad behaviors was completely eliminated when it was reported that the high-ranked individuals have been punished.
[11] The term "stress power" was created by researcher Richard Boyatzis. He says that leaders can avoid the stress power through practices that foster mindfulness, hope, and compassion. For more on this, see Boyatzis and McKee (2013).
[12] Source: Alfred Sloan. 1964. My Years with General Motors.
[13] The case of Siemens shows how a bad example can turn into a benchmark in terms of compliance. Nowadays, Siemens has about 600 full-time employees dedicated to compliance. Its program is based on the tripod "prevent-detect-remedy," ranging from continuous educational activities to independent mechanisms for investigations of suspected transgressions. Compliance metrics have been included in the variable compensation of key executives. And, most importantly, ethics and compliance have become central issues for the its CEO.
[14] Source: Harvard Business Review. November 2012. The CEO of Siemens on Using a Scandal to Drive Change. Available at https://hbr.org/2012/11/the-ceo-of-siemens-on-using-a-

scandal-to-drive-change .

[15] Jackall (1988: 17).

[16] *Ibid*: 20.

[17] Campbell and Göritz (2014).

[18] Cable and Kay (2012).

[19] Interview for strategy+business. Why Good Employees Do Bad Things. January 30, 2017. Summer 2017. Issue 87. Available https://www.strategy-business.com/article/Why-Good-Employees-Do-Bad-Things?gko=f472c

[20] Laloux (2014).

[21] Soltes (2016: 9).

[22] Jackall (1988: 109).

[23] *Ibid*: 110.

[24] El País. 02/16/2015. El que lleva las riendas tiene un deber de actuar éticamente. Available at http://cincodias.com/cincodias/2015/02/14/empresas/1423874090_355791.html

[25] It is worth mentioning that, although events like this are important, talking about ethics should be a continuous activity in the organization instead of something restricted to an annual compliance training.

[26] For more information on the complete indicator, go to www.direzione.com.br

[27] Details about the ethical culture measurement tool are available at https://www.ethicalsystems.org/content/our-approach-culture-measurement

[28] Source: A Two-Factor Model of Ethical Culture: A Conceptual Frame for Ethical Systems' Culture Survey. By Caterina Bulgarella. Available at www.ethicalsystems.org

[29] As highlighted by Treviño et al. (2017: 64), employees are likely to complete such surveys and do so honestly if they trust their responses will not be traced back to them and if they believe that the results will be used for a good purpose. As a result, the authors argue that it is extremely important to have a trusted third part to collect and manage the data, as well as to deliver results to management that do not identify individuals.

[30] Davidson et al. (2015). In the same vein, Mironov (2015) found that Russian CEOs with worse records of driving violations divert more money from their companies and pay more money under the table.

[31] Harvard Business Review. 12/22/2016. Six Traits That Predict Ethical Behavior at Work. By David De Cremer. Available at https://hbr.org/2016/12/6-traits-that-predict-ethical-behavior-at-work

[32] The behaviors that should lead to sanctions go way beyond fraud and corruption. They also include intimidation, bullying, hostility, discrimination, and moral and sexual harassment, among other improper acts.

[33] Broken window theory: J. Q. Wilson, G. L. Kelling, "Broken windows," Atl. Mon. (March 1982), p. 29.

[34] Cerdá et al. (2009), Keizer et al. (2008), Messner et al. (2007), and Harcourt and Ludwig (2006).

[35] This episode is described in the book of McLean and Elkind (2013).

[36] Susan Fowler. 19/02/2017. Reflecting on one Very, Very Strange Year at Uber. Available at https://www.susanjfowler.com/blog/2017/2/19/reflecting-on-one-very-strange-year-at-uber

[37] According to The New York Times, it is likely that the wrong "tone at the top" has echoed in Uber's workplace. In 2014, for instance, the then CEO Travis Kalanik referred to his company as "Boob-er" given the ease with which it helped him attracting women. The New York Times. 02/22/2017. Inside Uber's Aggressive, Unrestrained Workplace Culture. Available at

https://nyti.ms/2lx4TRC; GQ Magazine. 02/27/2014. Uber Cab Confessions. Available at http://www.gq.com/story/uber-cab-confessions?currentPage=1

[38] The New York Times. 02/22/2017. Inside Uber's Aggressive, Unrestrained Workplace Culture. Available at https://nyti.ms/2lx4TRC; CNN. 03/02/2017. The real story behind Uber CEO. Available at http://edition.cnn.com/2017/03/01/opinions/real-story-behind-uber-sims-opinion/; Quartz Magazine. 02/19/2017. A female engineer's account of working at Uber alleges rampant sexism repeatedly ignored by execs and HR. Available at https://qz.com/914946/a-female-engineers-account-of-working-at-uber-alleges-rampant-sexism-repeatedly-ignored-by-execs-and-hr/

[39] Fichter (2016).

[40] Course "Unethical Decision Making," Coursera. Professors Guido Palazzo and Ulrich Hoffrage. Available at https://www.coursera.org/learn/unethical-decision-making

[41] Welsh and Ordóñez (2014).

[42] Mazar et al. (2008).

[43] The process of "priming" increases the sensitivity of the subject to certain issues right before experiments. This priming can be conscious (e.g., asking participants to read a code of conduct) or unconscious (e.g., asking them to rearrange words to construct a sentence that has an ethical connotation). Conscious priming operates through our deliberative processes (system 2), while subconscious priming operates through our automatic and intuitive processes (system 1).

[44] Shu et al. (2012).

[45] Mazar and Zhong (2010).

[46] Welsh and Ordóñez (2014).

[47] Interestingly, researchers found that this subconscious priming substantially reduced unethical behavior even when people were subjected to a variant of the study setting ambitious goals (a practice that tends to increase dishonesty in participants).

[48] The practice is detailed at http://www.reinventingorganizationswiki.com/Listening_to_Purpose .

[49] This quote comes from the book "Thank you for being late: An optimist's guide to thriving in the age of accelerations," by Thomas Friedman (Farrar, Straus and Giroux publisher, 2016). It is also important to note that imposing a permanent time pressure on employees is usually a sign that the company has not been able to set proper targets or to allocate adequate resources for its execution.

[50] Source: Drucker. P. 2008. The Essential Drucker: The Best of Sixty Years of Peter Drucker's Essential Writings on Management. Ed. HarperBusiness.

[51] Hollensbe et al. (2014: 1228-1229).

[52] *Ibid.*

[53] The excerpt comes from the ethical leadership at work questionnaire (ELW) created by Kalshoven et al. (2011).

Part 5: A Final Message

14. Toward a new paradigm for sound organizations: culture, leadership, and purpose as the foundation for business success in the twenty-first century

> *"You can't take on twenty-first century tasks with 20th century tools and hope to get the job done."*
> Cathy Davidson (1949–)[1]

My main motivation for writing this book was to help organizations become more accountable, sustainable and transparent as a result of a process of human development of its leaders centered on ethics. With this goal in mind, the first two parts were devoted to describing the results of the emerging field of behavioral ethics, the most promising area to understand how wrongdoings proliferate in organizations. The third part, in turn, was dedicated to exploring the main implications of this field for management and governance, while the fourth part provided provide concrete solutions to avoid ethical blindness at both the individual and organizational levels.

In this final part, I analyze the corporate misconducts we have been recently witnessing from a broader perspective with the aim of providing new views for twenty-first century organizations. My point is that, although apparently heterogeneous, these scandals have a common thread: The adoption of a wrong approach to management and corporate governance based on the belief that the sole role of managers is to maximize the financial outcome to a single stakeholder, i.e., the shareholders.

This narrative, usually encouraged by business schools, sees companies as economic entities disconnected from society whose success must be exclusively measured by the returns produced to shareholders.

As shown throughout the book, the widespread misconduct currently observed in the business world has not been caused by a few "bad apples" or by our supposedly "selfish nature." Actually, it is a consequence of an outdated mentality on the role of business in society and, consequently, about the correct way to manage and govern companies.

What these scandals show, in fact, is a situation in which many firms – managed as if they were still in the twentieth century – are finding it increasingly difficult to continue succeeding in the world of the twenty-first century with the same business practices of the past. Thus, most companies need structural changes in the way they are managed and governed so they can be aligned with the society of the twenty-first century.

These profound changes will lead to a new paradigm of what it means to be a well-run company. In this sense, alternative perspectives have emerged in the past few years to improve the way companies are managed, such as the "conscious capitalism," the "benefit corporation," and the "reinventing organizations" movements.

These new views, in full growth with the adhesion of a growing number of companies around the world, indicate that the emerging paradigm for sound governance will be based on three central elements: ethical culture, conscious leadership, and higher purpose.

The adoption of a broader paradigm for healthy management and governance will be a critical aspect for business success in the twenty-first century. In the following sections, I describe these ideas in detail aiming (and above all hoping) to inspire business leaders

The Virtuous Barrel:
How to Transform Corporate Scandals into Good Businesses via Behavioral Ethics

making their organizations increasingly ethical, conscious and attuned to the new values of a more evolved society.

Our world is going through structural changes and moving toward a new zeitgeist in this transition to the twenty-first century

The first thing to do in order to rethink the current paradigm for business practices is to recognize that our world is going through structural changes and moving toward a new zeitgeist in this transition to the twenty-first century. Among these major shifts, stand out the following issues:

- We are living in an increasingly transparent world

There is less and less room for opacity. In the Operation Car Wash in Brazil, for example, prosecutors managed to identify the Swiss bank accounts from the individuals and companies involved in the bribes with the cooperation of Swiss authorities, something that would have been simply impossible 10 or 20 years ago. Sooner or later, therefore, the way companies really behave will be of public knowledge.

- Change is taking place at high-speed in an increasingly volatile world:

Another element of this "new normal" is the speed of the changes in the external environment. Although we now possess a huge amount of information, we live in a so connected and complex system that it is impossible to predict what is going to happen in the next years. The high volatility and unpredictability of our contemporary world makes adaptability a key element for business success, thus replacing the traditional quest for maximum efficiency through an attempt to control all variables impacting the organization.

- People everywhere are increasingly connected and empowered due to the access to new technologies

Anyone using a small device can collect and disseminate sensitive information in real time to all over the world. Moreover, there are small groups of stakeholders who closely monitor what businesses are doing and exert a strong pressure for better practices. A recent survey called them "stakebrokers," in the sense that these highly engaged influencers look at companies from a 360-degree perspective and are willing to act to defend the interests of all their traditional audiences simultaneously.[2] As pointed out in the report, "Stakebrokers' activism across multiple channels and their power as influencers make them a formidable force in the global market." One example comes from the Volkswagen emissions scandals (described in Chapter 9) that may end up costing around $45 billion for the company.[3] The whole process began with an independent investigation carried out by a small team of five researchers at West Virginia University with just $70,000 funded by a nonprofit environmental organization.[4] People everywhere, therefore, have more access to resources and much more power to change things than in the past.

- We are facing megatrends whose consequences are impossible to estimate in the coming decades, such as climate change, the development of AI, sustainability issues, demographic, and social shifts.

Let's take the case of artificial intelligence, for instance. We are approaching the era of the smart machine age that will result in dramatic shifts in the job market. One of the best studies done so far on this topic was carried out by researchers from Oxford University.[5] It estimates that up to 47% of the jobs in the United States (a sophisticated market) can be replaced until 2030. Although this is still a conjecture at this point, it exemplifies how we are living in an increasingly volatile, uncertain, complex, ambiguous, and fragmented world.

On top of these changes, we are seeing the emergence of a new set of values and beliefs that is particularly pronounced in the new generations such as the millennials and centennials (people born between the early 1980s and the 2000s and after the 2000s, respectively).[6] Both generations will make up 75% of the workforce in developed countries by 2025, while millennials already comprise the largest share of the labor market and the generation with the biggest spending power in the United States.[7]

The Virtuous Barrel:
How to Transform Corporate Scandals into Good Businesses via Behavioral Ethics

Research shows that these generations, especially those with access to better education, have greater environmental and social awareness. One survey with 7,700 millennials from 29 countries, for instance, concluded that around 50% try to buy products from companies that support the causes they care about.[8] Another survey, in turn, observed that the main values defended by this generation are transparency, sustainability, participation, sharing, collaboration, and social commitment.[9]

The younger generations also show a greater preference for experiences over stability and routines. In a 2016 survey, 56% of millennials interviewed said they expect to leave their organization by the end of 2020 to join a new organization or to do something different.[10] When asked why, they usually responded that they do not feel motivated or do not think their skills are being fully developed in their current companies.

This leads us to two other aspects of this new Zeitgeist, which is the greater emphasis on intrinsic motivators, e.g., autonomy, mastery, and purpose, and on a concept of personal success more related to work-life balance (the "quality of life") than to financial rewards. A survey of 19,000 millennials in 25 countries found, for example, that 90% consider free time and time flexibility as priorities in their job choice. Another study observed that 56% of millennials ruled out ever working for an organization because of its values or standards of conduct.[11]

The overall message from these reports is that people nowadays, particularly from younger generations, are increasingly looking for a sense of meaning and for a work that makes a positive difference in the world.

The implication of this change of values to the business world has been well summarized by a recent report from the Legal Research Network. It argues that companies hired hands in the nineteenth century (of the industrial economy), brains in the twentieth century (of the knowledge economy) and will have to hire hearts in the twenty-first century (of the human economy).[12]

These structural changes are driving stakeholders to have increasingly higher expectations on the role of companies in tackling society's problems

These structural changes, in turn, are driving stakeholders to ever-greater expectations on the role of business in society. Some CEOs are already aware of this. A 2016 survey with 1,409 CEOs from 83 countries, for instance, concluded that[13]

- 55% of the CEOs are concerned about the lack of trust in business today; three years before, only 37% expressed such concern;
- 59% believe top talent wants to work with firms with whom they share social values; 67% believe this will be the case in five years' time;
- 37% believe investors already seek ethical investments, while 45% of the CEOs believe this will be the case five years later; and
- 76% agree that business success in twenty-first century will be defined by more than profits, while only 13% disagree.

This report shows, therefore, that most CEOs agree with the view that customers, employees, and other stakeholders are increasingly judging companies based on how they help society and live up to their values.

These results have been corroborated by another 2016 study based on interviews with 400 senior executives from more than 50 countries. In this case, 89% of business leaders agreed with the idea that companies need to shift their focus by widening their perspective in order to create value for all their stakeholders.[14]

Many companies, though, still did not realize these sweeping changes and continue to be run as if they were in the twentieth century

Despite the awareness of some senior executives, the reality is that many companies still have not realized these structural changes in society. As a result, they continue to be run as if they were in the twentieth century. This old way of managing companies – based on the so-called "business as usual" – is characterized by

- The focus on deal-making at any cost without any ethical considerations;

The Virtuous Barrel:
How to Transform Corporate Scandals into Good Businesses via Behavioral Ethics

- The bottom line as the only measure of success;
- Opacity, both inside and outside the company, seen as a competitive advantage;
- Highly hierarchical structures led by autocratic "military" leaders or by "mercenary" leaders only focused on the reaching the numbers to maximize their wealth; and,
- A business culture based on fear, aggressiveness, pressure, and stress.

There will be increasingly less room for companies with this narrow, transactional, amoral, and myopic view in the twenty-first-century society. Actually, profits will increasingly derive from a company's ability to create value for all its stakeholders in an ethical and sustainable way.

Structural changes require structural solutions: it is necessary to revisit fundamental business issues with the aim of adopting a new paradigm for sound corporate governance

Because structural changes require structural rather than incremental solutions, the answer to today's scandals goes far beyond strengthening control areas or replacing a few executives. It is necessary to go to the root of the problem.

This means revisiting key issues with the sake of reshaping not only governance, but the way companies are managed in the twenty-first century. Five central questions stand out in this regard:

- What should be the purpose of companies? How a higher purpose aligned with the common good can be instilled in all businesses?
- What should be the role of managers?
- Which assumptions about people's behavior should serve as the basis for management and governance models?
- What incentive systems should be prioritized so that people feel motivated and engaged to their organizations?
- What is a successful company? How should we measure business success?

A new paradigm for sound governance should emerge, based on an ethical culture that brings the best out of people, conscious leadership, and the pursuit of an a higher purpose

Revisiting these fundamental issues will lead to a new paradigm for business based on an ethical culture that brings the best out of people, conscious leadership, and a higher purpose.

Ten key attributes are likely to characterize this new paradigm and hence form the basis for successful company of the twenty-first century:[15]

1. A higher purpose as the driving force of the company, so that profits are the product of purposeful work in the service of society rather than an end in itself.
2. The embedment of ethics in the business agenda, so that it becomes an explicit and relevant aspect of all business decisions.
3. A broader concept of business success based on the creation of long-term value for all stakeholders.
4. Business leaders focused on aligning the interests of all stakeholders through the continual pursuit for mutually beneficial solutions (win–win solutions instead of viewing business relationships as a zero-sum game).
5. Management based on trust, authenticity, and care (and not on pressure and fear) in order to create high levels of intrinsic motivation among all employees.
6. Commitment to principled performance, so that the way by which performance is achieved becomes more important than the bottom line.
7. Companies managed as a web of relationships with an emphasis on cooperation (not on competition) both within the firm as well as between the company and its stakeholders.
8. Continuous effort to improve transparency and dialogue with key stakeholders, particularly on business impacts and nonfinancial issues.

9. Voluntary willingness of managers in estimating and bearing the costs of the firm's externalities instead of trying to conceal and avoid them.
10. External environment and regulations viewed as an opportunity to innovate and improve standards instead as of enemies to be fought or manipulated.

The attributes above still seem far away from the prevailing mindset in most of the business world. Nonetheless, they should be used as a benchmark for companies genuinely interested in being attuned to what lies ahead in a very near future. After all, companies displaying such qualities will earn the loyalty of stakeholders and the public trust, being better placed to withstand the major forthcoming social, political, and environmental changes coming ahead.

Fortunately, two movements have emerged in the past few years as new proposals for sound management and governance: "conscious capitalism" and the "reinventing organizations"

Many people around the world, including some business leaders, have already realized that the current approach to healthy management and governance needs deep reformulation. As a result, two movements have recently emerged with new proposals for improving the way companies are run: the "conscious capitalism" and the "reinventing organizations."

Conscious Capitalism

The first movement is called "conscious capitalism." Its seeds were sown in the 1980s based on the work of Edward Freeman, the father of stakeholder theory. In 2013, the movement came to fruition with the release of an eponymous book written by John Mackey, founder of the US retailer Whole Foods Market, and Professor Raj Sisodia of Babson College.[16]

The main aspiration of conscious capitalism is to motivate companies to operate from a broader perspective than shareholders' financial interests so as they create long-term value for all its stakeholders. The movement is based on four tenets or pillars:

- Higher purpose

Profits are viewed as the means to a greater end, but not as the primary reason for a business to exists. Thus, having a larger purpose transcending profit maximization is the starting point for becoming a conscious company, i.e., it gives meaning, motivation, and energy to people. The purpose should be viewed as a clear statement on the difference that the company seeks to make in the world. Consequently, each organization should ask itself questions such as: Why does our company exist? Why do we need to exist? Which contribution our company intend to make? What would the world miss if we disappear? These are some of the questions firms should make to craft a genuine and higher purpose. Having a high purpose facilitates decision-making and helps in keeping all stakeholders together, especially in times of difficulty. Starting from a greater purpose is part of conscious capitalism vision that profit is the end product when the company has a sense of meaning and the business is built based on care and solidarity. The relevance of purpose was already highlighted by Peter Drucker, who argued that "Every enterprise requires commitment to common goals and shared values. Without such commitment there is no enterprise; there is only a mob."[17]

- Stakeholder Orientation:

A conscious company strives to meet the legitimate needs of its stakeholders (or multiple constituencies) as an end in itself, instead of as a means to make the most money. The concept of value, in turn, goes beyond its financial aspect, by including the perspective of creating intellectual, social, cultural, emotional, and ecological value for all stakeholders. This goes in line with Henry Ford's statement that "A business that makes nothing but money is a poor business."[18] In the current paradigm prevalent in the business world, a good manager is viewed as one who can make the most favorable trade-offs for shareholders. This trade-off mentality represents a "zero sum" mindset: if someone wins, someone has to lose. According to conscious capitalism advocates, the

The Virtuous Barrel:
How to Transform Corporate Scandals into Good Businesses via Behavioral Ethics

problem is that when you privilege a single stakeholder, all other participants become defensive and begin to act in a short-sighted way by putting their personal interest first. For them, it is true that we will find trade-offs if we look for them, but it is also true that we will find synergies if we aim for them. So, instead of extracting the most out of the stakeholders for the sake of maximizing profits, executives should always strive to find win–win solutions through dialogue, creativity, and innovation. This is what allows the organization having loyal customers, inspired employees, collaborative suppliers, and a supportive community. As summarized by professors Edward Freeman and Heather Elms, "The winning business models of the 21st century figure out how to get these interests going in the same direction, with as few trade-offs as possible."[19] Stakeholder orientation, in short, means focusing on finding ways to "expand the pie" instead of concentrating on how to divide it in the most advantageous way for shareholders at the expense of other stakeholders.

- Conscious Culture

The third tenet is a healthy culture that provides a strong sense of community. For conscious capitalism advocates, it is critical to create a TACTILE culture, an acronym standing for trust, accountability, transparency, care, integrity, loyalty and egalitarianism. In addition to aspects already present in the recommendations of corporate governance codes, such as transparency, accountability, and integrity, conscious capitalism innovates by emphasizing the importance of less observed issues, such as the willingness to care. The movement criticizes the prevalent view in the business world that love, affection, and endearment undermine people's performance in the real world. To conscious capitalism advocates, these feelings are not fragile virtues. On the contrary, they are the strongest human attributes. As a result, the opposite should be true: Companies operating based on fear and punishment should be the ones on the road for extinction. The combination of the seven elements that constitute a TACTILE culture will, therefore, create a healthy environment in which people feel psychologically safe to point out what is wrong and make better decisions.

- Conscious Leadership

The fourth principle is having a conscious leadership in the sense that C-level executives become servant leaders rather than egocentric celebrities. Most companies with the twentieth century mindset are characterized by military or mercenary leaders. The first archetype is based on an authoritarian model with no room for questioning. The second is typified by managers solely focused on meeting short-term numbers with no passion for the business. For conscious capitalism advocates, it is critical to evolve toward missionary leaders who possess high emotional, moral, and systemic intelligence, in addition to the traditionally required analytical intelligence. These mature leaders must see themselves as trustees of their organizations. That is, as individuals who must nurture and protect them for future generations. Missionary leaders understand that they have a noble duty to turn over their organization healthier than they have received it. To accomplish this, they must exhibit qualities traditionally associated to women, such as empathy, compassion, communion, and a more intuitive view. Their main motivation, in short, should be the desire to serve and to leave a positive legacy for society. John Mackey, one of the creators of the conscious capitalist movement, described how critical it is for business leaders to achieve a higher level of personal development in order to raise the level of consciousness of their organizations by stating that "More than once in the history of Whole Foods Market, the company was unable to collectively evolve until I myself was able to evolve – in other words, I was holding the company back. My personal growth enabled the company also to evolve!".[20]

Reinventing organizations

The second emerging approach to sound management and governance comes from a movement named "reinventing organizations." This approach is based on the premise that humanity has been evolving through successive stages of development or levels of awareness.[21]

The Virtuous Barrel:
How to Transform Corporate Scandals into Good Businesses via Behavioral Ethics

Each stage corresponds to a paradigm or way of seeing the world. When we leap into a new level, society undergoes profound changes, including in the ways in which people work together. These transitions throughout history have allowed us to reach increasingly higher levels of prosperity.

For advocates of this movement, a new level of awareness is coming about nowadays. It should lead, in turn, to radically different companies attuned to the new times. The following table summarizes the organizational types associated with each evolutionary paradigm according to reinventing organizations. To ease the understanding, each group is depicted by a specific color.

Type of Organization / Color / Metaphor / Examples	Key Characteristics	Innovations	Weaknesses
Impulsive Red Wolfpack *(e.g. Mafia, street gangs, tribal militias)*	Alpha male retains power by force (fear as the "glue" of the organization); Impulsive top-down decisions derived by the chief's personality; Reactive and short-term oriented group; Thrives in chaotic environments.	Division of labor within the group. Command authority.	Difficulty to reach big size; Succession problems difficult long-term stability.
Conformist Ambar Army *(e.g. Military, church, government agencies, "old style" firms)*	Stability as the major value of the organization; Rigorous processes and controls so the future is like the past; Highly formal roles within a rigid hierarchical pyramid; Top down decisions based on "command and control"; Position occupied by correspondence with certain criteria; Fixed compensation based on the position.	Formal roles allow for scalable hierarchies; Clear processes and power associated with the position (not the person) ensure long-term survival.	Rigidity hinders adjustments to changes in the external environment; Dogmatism and pressure for conformity difficult a correct reading of reality; Aversion to innovation.
Industrial / Achiever Orange Machine *(e.g. Multinationals, banks, most of the companies)*	Focus on maximizing profits and growth; Competition as the key value of the organization; Innovation as a key element to beat competitors; Less rigid pyramid (e.g., multidisciplinary teams and matrix reporting); Top-down decisions based on management by objectives (senior managers define strategy; people	Innovation as key element to staying ahead of competitors, Accountability associated with the achievement of goals; Meritocracy: rise in organization possible for anyone and associated with	Exclusive profit motivation generates lack of meaning and disengagement on employees Indifference to environmental impacts; Systematic ethical failures; Collective unhappiness

The Virtuous Barrel:
How to Transform Corporate Scandals into Good Businesses via Behavioral Ethics

Type of Organization / Color / Metaphor / Examples	Key Characteristics	Innovations	Weaknesses
	below have some freedom to achieve the goals); "Heroic" leaders with high ability to hit the targets; Individual variable compensation associated with the achievement of personal goals.	ability, intelligence and dedication.	among stakeholders resulting from a materialistic and machine-like view of the firm.
Post-industrial / Pluralistic Green Family (e.g. Patagonia, Southwest Airlines, Ben & Jerry's, Zappos.com, The Container Store, Wegmans, Trade Joe's, Toms)	Focus on culture and values to enchant customers and achieve extraordinary levels of employee motivation; Culture of empowerment of front-line teams as a key element to foster engagement; Cooperation as the key value of the organization; Broader perspective of the firm, including its role in the world and its social responsibility; Consensus-oriented decisions; "Humble" leaders dedicated to serve and leave a positive legacy; Collective variable compensation associated with the achievement of team goals.	Strong culture and decisions genuinely guided by shared values; Consensus-oriented decisions; "Empowered" pyramid with more power for front-line teams; Management focused on balancing the interests of all stakeholders.	Potential slowness in group decisions and pitfalls associated with consensus-seeking; Potential conflict between people's desire for greater autonomy and the maintenance of a hierarchical structure.
Integral / Evolutive Teal Living Organism	Self-management replaces hierarchical pyramid (flat organizational structure based on fully autonomous teams); Substitution of job titles for fluid roles; Fully distributed leadership: absence	Self-management: anyone can make any decision, provided she seeks the advice of everyone who will be affected by it;	Instability of the model in case of crises or leadership changes (constant pressure to

Type of Organization / Color / Metaphor / Examples	Key Characteristics	Innovations	Weaknesses
(e.g. FAVI, Buurtzorg, The Morning Star, Holacracy, Sun Hydraulics, Heilingenfeld)	of managerial positions eliminates power disputes; Almost lack of controls: premise of trusting in people; Self-fulfilment and sense of purpose as the main motivators and measures of performance; Wholeness (people allowed to take their "whole selves" to the workplace, including their emotional and spiritual sides) viewed as essential for high engagement and motivation; Organization seen as a living entity with its own evolutionary purpose ("sense and respond" to instead of trying to "predict and control" the future).	Wholeness: practices designed to help people be themselves at work; Evolutionary purpose: purpose is not defined by a single person. It evolves as the organization develops and learn.	return to traditional paradigms that provide a greater sense of control for the top management).

Table 1. Organizational types according to "Reinventing Organizations"

According to the reinventing organizations movement, the vast majority of companies currently operates under the industrial/orange paradigm. The problem is that this paradigm, i.e., materialistic and solely motivated by financial outcomes, has increasingly shown signs of exhaustion as demonstrated by the extremely high levels of disengagement among employees and the constant wrongdoings by corporations.

As a result, the advocates of this movement argue that success in the twenty-first century will increasingly depend on the ability of companies to migrate to more evolved stages of organizational consciousness, particularly to the so-called "evolutionary/teal" paradigm.[22]

The Virtuous Barrel:
How to Transform Corporate Scandals into Good Businesses via Behavioral Ethics

To demonstrate that the "reinventing organizations" movement is based on concrete ideas, its author Frederic Laloux published a homonym book in 2014 in which he presents the results of a three-year research with 12 companies already operating under the teal paradigm.[23]

These organizations, from different industries and countries, exhibit a set of revolutionary practices that can be summarized into three groups:[24] self-management, wholeness, and evolutionary purpose. Self-management means operating effectively with a system based on peer relationships, without the need for either hierarchy or consensus. Wholeness means practices that invite people to reclaim their inner wholeness and bring all of who they are to work, instead of with a narrow "professional" self. Evolutionary purpose means organizations are seen as having a life and a sense of direction of their own. As a result, members of the organization are invited to listen and understand what the organization wants to become and what purpose it wants to serve.[25]

As a consequence of these practices, teal companies typically do not have a hierarchical pyramid. This means there are no fixed roles, bosses, or managerial positions. Each member of the organization can make any decision, provided he or she first seek the advice of everyone who will be affected by it (the member is not obliged to follow the advices received). All work is carried out by self-organizing teams will full autonomy, such as to hire people, services, etc. There is also no central strategic planning nor monitoring of budgeted versus performed indicators. Nobody receives variable compensation. All information is made available in real-time for everyone, including those about company financials and compensation. There are virtually no controls, as these organizations depart from the assumption that employees are trustworthy and responsible human beings who will seek to do their best if they are free to act based on their own convictions at work.[26]

The results of the businesses portrayed by Frederic Laloux in his book *Reiventing Organizations* show that this model, completely opposite to the orange paradigm adopted today by most companies, is not only feasible but also tends to produce better performance in all dimensions, including from the financial standpoint. By way of illustration, two business cases explored in depth by Laloux are described here.

The first is FAVI, the French brass foundry specialized in supplying gearbox forks for the automotive industry, as described in Chapter 10.[27] This family-owned business started adopting innovative practices in 1983, after a CEO named Jean-François Zobrist took over. He divided employees into 21 teams made up of 15 to 35 people called "mini factories." Each mini factory was dedicated to a specific customer or customer type (e.g., the VW team, the FIAT team). The new model established that there would be virtually no rules or procedures other than those that the teams would decide by themselves (the human resources, procurement, planning, and even sales departments have all been simply shut down).

FAVI has achieved remarkable results after adopting these self-management practices. The company was the only one in its industry to remain in Europe in the face of the Chinese competition (all former European competitors have shut their doors and moved production to China). FAVI not only survived, it has expanded from around 80 to more than 500 employees and holds a 50% stake in the gearbox forks market, its main product. Its quality and on-time delivery are considered legendary: The firm did not deliver a single order late in over 25 years.

Despite strong Chinese competition, FAVI has produced net profit margins quite satisfactory for its sector of around 5% to 7% in the last decades. It has also managed to pay salaries well above the market average, while the turnover rate of its employees is virtually zero (workers exposed to FAVI's self-management model hardly want to return to work in traditional factories). Its philosophy has proved particularly robust in times of difficulty. During the global financial crisis of 2008, for example, its orders suddenly dropped by 30%. In line with its values, the firm was able to emerge from the recession without firing a single employee and still make a positive profit margin at the height of the crisis.

The Virtuous Barrel:
How to Transform Corporate Scandals into Good Businesses via Behavioral Ethics

The second example comes from a Dutch home care firm called Buurtzorg.[28] Until the mid-2000s, dozens of companies in the country provided nursing services. All operated under the industrial/orange paradigm. Nurses received a daily itinerary with the homes they were supposed to go to, the procedures to be followed, and the exact time (timed in minutes and seconds) they should spend on each residence (there was even a bar code on clients' doors to validate the times of entry and exit). Junior nurses were given the simplest procedures, such as applying an injection, while older and more expensive nurses received the more complex ones. Everything was highly organized and planned to maximize economic efficiency.

The only "minor" problem of this model was that nurses and patients were very unhappy. Nurses could not do a high-quality job or develop any relationship with patients because they had to go as fast as possible from one place to the other as if they were dealing with objects. Patients, in turn, used to receive dozens (or even hundreds) of different nurses per year, leaving them with no human reference for treatment.

In 2007, Jos de Blok, a nurse who worked at one of these companies got tired of this bleak scenario and tried to create a new model. He resigned and founded Buurtzorg ("neighborhood care" in Dutch) with a small team of four nurses, including himself, and under two central mottos: "humanity above bureaucracy" and "trust instead of control." The management model was very simple: each team, comprised of eight to 12 professionals, would have complete autonomy to make whatever decisions they wanted, including who would care for each patient and how long they would stay in each household. As an example, one common practice quickly adopted throughout the teams was having a cup of coffee or tea with each patient before starting medical procedures in order to establish a personal connection.

Buurtzorg results have been impressive. Nurses had their sense of purpose and professional pride restored, while patients were amazed at how they are treated and cared for. Its business model is considered so efficient and superior that the organization has reached 75% of the Dutch market share in just eight years, growing to 9,500 nurses. As a consequence of this self-management system, its administrative staff is comprised of only 45 people located in a modest building in the north of Holland. This makes Buurtzorg with only 8% of overhead costs, against 25% of industry peers.

Surveys conducted by the Dutch government show that its customer satisfaction far exceeds that of industry peers. As a result, patients regain their autonomy faster. It is estimated that Buurtzorg spends only about 40% of the time prescribed by doctors for treatments, generating an estimated $2 billion in savings for Dutch society.[29] Buurtzorg also achieved the highest employee satisfaction ratings among organizations with more than 1,000 employees in The Netherlands, being awarded for five consecutive years as the "best national employer" (ironically, without having a HR department).

According to its CEO Jos de Blok, this has led nurses from competitors to simply resign and "knock on Buurtzorg's door" wishing to be part of this new organizational mindset. Nowadays, the Buurtzorg model is being studied by several countries willing to replicate it in their health systems. One of these independent studies, sponsored by the British government, concluded that "the main factor in Buurtzorg's success seems to be trusting more, controlling less and focusing on clinical and personal outcomes as main measure of quality."[30]

For the advocates of the "reinventing organizations," the success of companies operating under the teal paradigm is quite natural. They argue that these organizations manage to release an enormous amount of energy from people that was being wasted under the old paradigm. This includes the energy spent on trying to please superiors, showing to be efficient, defending silos, complying with controls, strengthening themselves politically to increase the chances of promotion, etc.[31]

The roots underlying the idea of teal organizations are not new. One of the pioneer organizations in this practice was the Brazilian Semco, nowadays an equity investment firm with a diversified portfolio of dozens of companies under its umbrella. In the 1980s, its CEO and controlling shareholder Ricardo Semler implemented an innovative managerial model with major repercussions in the business world.[32] Among them, he

The Virtuous Barrel:
How to Transform Corporate Scandals into Good Businesses via Behavioral Ethics

implemented an extremely participatory decision-making process in which employees set their working hours, compensation, and even voted on who was going to be their bosses. In a 1994 article in *Harvard Business Review*, for example, Semler anticipated many practices to be adopted decades later by teal firms by saying that:

> I believe in responsibility but not in pyramidal hierarchy. I think that strategic planning and vision are often barriers to success. I dispute the value of growth. I don't think a company's success can be measured in numbers, since numbers ignore what the end user really thinks of the product and what the people who produce it really think of the company. I question the supremacy of talent, too much of which is as bad as too little. I'm not sure I believe that control is either expedient or desirable. I don't govern Semco – I own the capital, not the company – but on taking over from my father, I did try to reconstruct the company so that Semco could govern itself on the basis of three values: employee participation, profit sharing, and open information systems.[33] (Semler 1994)

Almost 25 years later, as of early 2018, Semco had equity stakes in more than 20 successful companies and an impressive annual return rate of 46% on the invested capital throughout its history.[34]

The organizations we see today, therefore, are simply a reflection of our worldview and stage of consciousness. As the world increasingly moves away from the mechanistic, industrial, and materialist paradigm that forms the basis of the "orange machines" characteristic of our current business environment, radically different organizational forms are likely to arise. This emergence will presumably lead to the creation of more genuine and humanized workplaces, filled with authenticity, communion, passion, and purpose.

Migrating to a more complex paradigm depends fundamentally on the organization's key leader, usually the founder or CEO. According to Frederic Laloux, creator of the reinventing organizations movement, the general rule is that the level of consciousness of a company cannot exceed the level of consciousness of its leaders as human beings.[35] Thus, the stage of development of business leaders determines to a large extent the success of the transformation toward higher stages of organizational awareness.

There is growing evidence that implementing a new paradigm for management and governance is rewarding... even from the financial point of view

Although inspiring, the "conscious capitalism" and the "reinventing organizations" movements presented in the previous section are still met with skepticism by many executives. Are they realistic alternatives for most companies? Is it feasible to implement a new paradigm for robust management and governance based on ethical culture, conscious leadership, and higher purpose?

The good news is that a growing number of recent research has shown that the answer is yes. That is, managing companies based on their values is not only realistic but also advantageous from a financial point of view.

One of the main studies in this field was conducted by three researchers who analyzed data from 1,000 American companies between 2007 and 2011.[36] About 400,000 employees evaluated their own companies through 58 statements related to different aspects of their workplace. The key result, very simple and powerful, was the following: the level of employee agreement with two statements related to the integrity of their leaders proved to be strong predictors of corporate performance years later.[37]

Specifically, the more employees agreed with two very simple statements, the better was their companies' performance years later in different dimensions. Both statements were related to the integrity of business leaders. The first was "management's actions match its words," while the second was "management is honest and ethical in its business practices."

The more employees perceived top managers as trustworthy and ethical, the greater was the firm value and the better was its operational profitability afterwards. These companies also exhibited better relationships with employees (measured by the number of conflicts with unions), as well as were more attractive to prospective job applicants (more qualified people applied for new jobs).

The results of this study are remarkable because they show that two very simple questions related to the employees' perceptions of the leaders' ethical behavior sufficed to predict better performance years later.[38]

The second has been published by Legal Research Network (LRN) in 2016.[39] Similarly to the previous study, the network asked 16,000 employees from 17 countries to anonymously assess their own firms through 69 questions related to corporate governance, culture, and leadership. Based on the employees' responses, companies were segregated in three organizational archetypes:

- "Blind Obedience": power-based, task-driven organizations that operate through command-and-control, and which places little emphasis on building enduring relationships among colleagues, with companies, or within society. In other words, these are the outdated firms from earlier the twentieth century.
- "Informed Acquiescence": rules-based, process-driven organizations that operate through hierarchy, policy, and "good management" practices from late twentieth century. Although more formalized and structured than the previous type, these companies are still run based on the traditional carrot-and-stick approach. Employees are motivated by performance-based rewards and monitored by strong controls.
- "Self-Governance": purpose-inspired, values-based organizations that are led with moral authority and operate with a set of core principles. Employees are inspired by a desire for significance and encouraged to act as leaders regardless of role. Namely, these are firms attuned with the zeitgeist of the twenty-first century with a strong culture of shared values focused on long-term legacy.

After segregating the companies in these three archetypes, researchers compared the outcomes of these groups in several different dimensions related to corporate performance.

One of the dimensions, for example, was based on financial results. In this case, "self-governing" companies increased their market share and profitability substantially more than the other two groups, particularly when compared to "blind obedience" firms. Employees at these self-governing values-based organizations were also less likely to experience misconduct at work and more likely to report any transgressions to do occur. In addition, self-governing companies also exhibited significantly better performance in the other dimensions related to innovation, employee engagement, and sustainability.

These two researches are good examples of a growing body of evidence showing that adopting a broader approach to management and governance based on integrity and value creation for all stakeholders pay off and is an important source of competitive advantage.

Business success in the twenty-first century will depend on the adoption of a new paradigm for management and governance: This will lead to more ethical and evolved organizations

Irrespective of the label, the emerging movements described in this chapter make it clear that sound management and governance practices must be viewed as an integrated and inseparable element of conscious leadership and a strong culture that bring out the best in people. It is this integration, in turn, that will enable organizations to pursue a greater purpose beyond profits that serves the common good. The figure below summarizes this key concept today for virtuous corporate governance.

The Virtuous Barrel:
How to Transform Corporate Scandals into Good Businesses via Behavioral Ethics

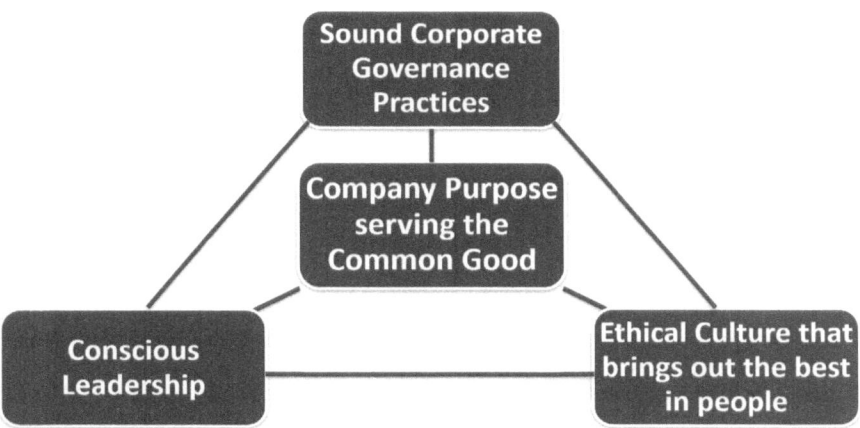

Figure 10. Governance, Leadership and Culture as Inseparable Elements to Achieve a Higher Purpose

The business scandals we have witnessed in the past years validate the concept illustrated in the figure above: Without an ethical culture and principled leadership, corporate governance becomes hollow, and no higher purpose will be achieved. Thus, for the business world to become part of the solution instead of the problem to society's pressing needs, these three elements need to be integrated and enhanced in all organizations.

Over the next few years, it will become increasingly clear that business success in the twenty-first century will depend on the adoption of a new paradigm for corporate governance that is more holistic, humanized, and attuned to the ideas, values, and generations of these new times.

More than a prediction, this is a mere deduction. After all, a more evolved society will require more evolved organizations.

---

[1] Source: Now You See It: How the Brain Science of Attention Will Transform the Way We Live, Work, and Learn. 2011.

[2] University of Virginia, Darden Ideas to Action. 03/16/ 2015. What makes a champion brand? Ten champion brand survey insights every business leader needs to know. By Bidhan L. Parmar and Laura Hennessey Martens. Available at https://ideas.darden.virginia.edu/2015/03/what-makes-a-champion-brand-ten-champion-brand-survey-insights-every-business-leader-needs-to-know/

[3] Financial Times. 17/04/2016. VW faces looming deadline as potential costs of scandal mount.

[4] Fortune. 07/03/2016. Hoaxwagen. Available at http://fortune.com/inside-volkswagen-emissions-scandal/. The New York Times. 07/24/2016. Researchers Who Exposed VW Gain Little Reward from Success. Available at https://nyti.ms/2jBh6pm

[5] Frey and Osborne (2017).

[6] Millenials are also known as Generation Y, while Centennials are also called Generation Z or iGen. A Bank of America Merrill Lynch report called Centennials them "millennials with steroids" due to their strong use of technology. Source: Bank of America Merrill Lynch. 08/30/2016. New Kids on the Block – Millennials & Centennials Primer.

[7] Time. 05/11/2015. Millennials Now Largest Generation in the US Workforce. Available at http://time.com/3854518/millennials-labor-force/; CNBC. 08/17/2015. How trillion-dollar millennials are spending their cash. Available at http://www.cnbc.com/2015/08/17/how-trillion-dollar-millennials-are-spending-their-cash.html

[8] The Deloitte Millennial Survey 2016. Available at https://www2.deloitte.com/gz/en/pages/about-deloitte/articles/millennialsurvey.html

[9] Lumesse White Paper. Survey 2016. Corporate Social Responsibility is a Key in Attracting Millennials. Available at http://www.lumesse.com/sites/default/files/corporate-social-responsiblity-attracting-millenials-white-paper.pdf

[10] The Deloitte Millennial Survey 2016. Available at https://www2.deloitte.com/gz/en/pages/about-deloitte/articles/millennialsurvey.html

[11] ManPower Group. 2016. Carreras profesionales de los Millennials: Horizonte 2020; The Deloitte Millennial Survey 2016.

[12] The How Report 2016. Available at http://howmetrics.lrn.com/

[13] PWC 19th Annual Global CEO Survey 2016. Available at http://www.pwc.com/gx/en/ceo-survey/2016/landing-page/pwc-19th-annual-global-ceo-survey.pdf

[14] Association of International Certified Professional Accountants, Black Sun, and the IIRC. 2016. (Beyond) Value of Value: Board-level Insights. Available at http://integratedreporting.org/wp-content/uploads/2016/12/2016-Value-of-Value-Board-Level-Insights-1.pdf

[15] Some attributes are inspired on Professor R. Edward Freeman principles described in his Coursera course "New Models of Business in Society". Available at https://www.coursera.org/learn/uva-darden-business-society

[16] Mackey and Sisodia (2013). The non-profit organization "Conscious Capitalism" had been founded by Mackey, Sisodia and other enthusiasts a few years earlier in 2008.

[17] Drucker. P. 2008. The Essential Drucker: The Best of Sixty Years of Peter Drucker's Essential Writings on Management. Ed. HarperBusiness.

[18] Source: Ford Motor Company Fund and Community Services. Available at http://corporate.ford.com/our-company/community/ford-fund/presidents-message-401p?releaseId=1244754314736.

[19] MIT Sloan Management Review. 04/01/2018. The Social Responsibility of Business is to Create Value for Stakeholders. By Edward Freeman and Heather Elms. Available at https://sloanreview.mit.edu/article/the-social-responsibility-of-business-is-to-create-value-for-stakeholders/

[20] Mackey and Sisodia (2013: 195).

[21] These stages would be: tribal or archaic (about 10,000 years ago): world seen as a dangerous place where power is the only way to have security; agrarian or traditional (about 5,000 years ago): world ruled by immutable laws represented by the church and aristocracy; industrial or modern (about 500 years ago): world seen as a complex machine that can be understood through science; information or postmodern (about 50 years ago): relationships as the central aspect that governs the world; and, integral (emerging now): world seen as a place destined for personal or collective fulfillment or revelation.

[22] In the evolutionary scale of reinventing organizations, the companies that are part of the conscious capitalism movement would fit in the post-industrial/green paradigm.

[23] Laloux (2014).

[24] The twelve companies surveyed were the following (in brackets the industry, country of operation and number of employees): Buurtzorg (home care, Holland, 9,500 employees); Favi (foundry industry, France, 500); Patagonia (outdoor clothing, US, 1,350); Sun Hydraulics (hydraulic components, Global, 900); RHD Human Services (health services, US, 4,000); BSO/Origin (IT consulting, Global, 10,000); Heiligenfeld (hospital, Germany, 600); Holacracy (consulting, US, 50); ESBZ (education, Germany, 1.500); Morning Star Food (tomatoes processing, US, 2,400); Sounds True Media (mental health, US, 90); AES Energy (Energy, US, 40.000). In the case of AES Energy, Laloux points out that its pioneering practices lasted only until the 1990s when the company was run by its founder. After the transition to a new CEO and listing on the stock exchange, AES started operating with typical practices of the orange paradigm.

[25] Among the main self-management practices, stand out: self-organizing teams; meetings mostly *ad hoc* when needs arise; minimum (or no) plans and budgets; fluid roles; fully decentralized decision-making based on advice process; all information available in real-time to all, including about company financials and compensation; well-structured multi-step conflict resolution process based on a set of guidelines and ground rules; focus on team performance; peer-based processes for individual appraisals; self-set salaries with peer calibration for base pay; no bonuses, but equal profit sharing. Among the main wholeness practices, stand out: values of the organization translated into concrete day-to-day ground rules; group-based contemplative practices, including meditation; no status markers in the workplace; coaching by peers; storytelling practices to support self-disclosure and build community; no job titles, fluid and granular roles instead of fixed job descriptions; honest discussion about individual time commitment to work vs. other meaningful commitments in life; regular time devoted to bring to light and address conflicts; specific meeting practices to keep ego in check and ensure everybody's voice is heard; hiring interviews by future colleagues, focus on fit with organization and with purpose; personal freedom and responsibility for training; recruitment, training, and appraisals used to explore juncture of individual calling and organizational purpose; Among the main evolutionary purpose practices, stand out: strategy emerges organically from the collective intelligence of self-managing employees; practices to listen into the organization's purpose (e.g., everyone a sensor, large group processes); concept of competition is irrelevant ("competitors" are embraced to pursue purpose), growth and market share only relevant if they help achieving the company purpose; profit as a lagging indicator and mere consequence of a well-done job; absence of budgeted vs. performed monitoring; constant search to "sense and respond" to the external environment instead of trying to "predict and control" the future; absence of specific goals; suppliers based on their alignment with the purpose of the organization.

[26] According to Laloux (2014), work engagement and the willingness to do the best in these organizations derive from a combination of three factors: intrinsic motivation, peer pressure and

market pressure.

[27] Laloux (2014: 58, 73-83, 85, 111, 115, 153, 175, 183, 252, 255, 267, 274-275, 319).

[28] Laloux (2014: 57, 62-73, 102, 115, 121, 127, 244, 249, 274, 319).

[29] Gray et al. (2015).

[30] *Ibid.*

[31] There is scientific evidence on this. Ryan and Deci (2008), for example, find that individuals' perception of autonomy increases their degree of motivation and the energy with which they pursue a goal.

[32] Ricardo Semler became a visiting professor at MBA courses of Harvard Business School and the MIT. He wrote articles on his innovative management model at Harvard Business Review and his books became international bestsellers in fourteen different languages. In 1990 and 1992, the Wall Street Journal elected him Brazil's businessman of the year after conducting a poll with more than 52,000 executives. For more on his innovations, see Semler (1988), Semler (1994), Semler (2001), and Semler (2004).

[33] Semler (1994).

[34] Source: http://www.semco.com.br/en/

[35] To a large extent, leaders implement organizational structures, practices and cultures that match their worldview. It is worth noting that, just like societies and companies, people also operate under different levels of awareness. Each color, for example, can be associated with a sentence summarizing its central value, such as: red: "immediate satisfaction of my needs"; amber: "conformity with social rules and standards"; orange: "efficiency, success and selfish ambitions"; green: "harmony and feeling of belonging"; Teal: "inner righteousness, service to the world, vocation and purpose".

[36] Guiso et al. (2015).

[37] Employees were asked to express a measure of the strength of their experience on a scale from 1 (almost always untrue) to 5 (almost always true). Researchers then averaged the employees' responses to a company-year level.

[38] It is also worth mentioning that researchers also observed that the mission and values advertised by companies on their websites proved to be completely irrelevant to predict their future performance. This result reinforces the view that what really matters for business ethics is how things happen on a daily basis, not what documents say.

[39] LRN – Legal Research Network. 2016. The How Report. Available at http://howmetrics.lrn.com/

References

Aggarwal, I., Woolley, A. W., Chabris, C. F., & Malone, T. W. (2015). Cognitive diversity, collective intelligence, and learning in teams. Proceedings of Collective Intelligence.

Akaah, I. P. (1996). The influence of organizational rank and role on marketing professionals' ethical judgments. Journal of Business Ethics, 15(6), 605-613.

Anand, V., Ashforth, B. E., & Joshi, M. (2004). Business as usual: The acceptance and perpetuation of corruption in organizations. The Academy of Management Executive, 18(2), 39-53.

Anderson, M. C., & Hanslmayr, S. (2014). Neural mechanisms of motivated forgetting. Trends in cognitive sciences, 18(6), 279-292.

Andre, J. (1991). Role morality as a complex instance of ordinary morality. American Philosophical Quarterly, 28(1), 73-80.

Aquino, K., & Reed II, A. (2002). The self-importance of moral identity. Journal of personality and social psychology, 83(6), 1423.

Ariely, D. (2012). The (honest) truth about dishonesty. Harper Audio.

Aristóteles (2015). Ética a Nicômaco, tradução de Luciano Ferreira de Souza. Ed. Martin Claret.

Arnold, D. F., Bernardi, R. A., Neidermeyer, P. E., & Schmee, J. (2007). The effect of country and culture on perceptions of appropriate ethical actions prescribed by codes of conduct: A Western European perspective among accountants. Journal of Business Ethics, 70(4), 327-340.

Arvidsson, A., & Peitersen, N. (2013). The ethical economy: Rebuilding value after the crisis. Columbia University Press.

Asch, S. E. (1955). Opinions and social pressure. Readings about the social animal, 193, 17-26.

Asch, S. E. (1956). Studies of independence and conformity: I. A minority of one against a unanimous majority. Psychological monographs: General and applied, 70(9), 1.

Ashforth, B. E., & Anand, V. (2003). The normalization of corruption in organizations. Research in organizational behavior, 25, 1-52.

Ayal, S., & Gino, F. (2011). Honest rationales for dishonest behavior. The social psychology of morality: Exploring the causes of good and evil. Washington, DC: American Psychological Association, 149-66.

Babiak, P., & Hare, R. D. (2006). Snakes in suits: When psychopaths go to work. New York, NY: Regan Books.

Babiak, P., Neumann, C. S., & Hare, R. D. (2010). Corporate psychopathy: Talking the walk. Behavioral sciences & the law, 28(2), 174-193.

Baer, M., & Frese, M. (2003). Innovation is not enough: Climates for initiative and psychological safety, process innovations, and firm performance. Journal of organizational behavior, 24(1), 45-68.

Bakshy, E., Messing, S., & Adamic, L. A. (2015). Exposure to ideologically diverse news and opinion on Facebook. Science, 348(6239), 1130-1132.

Bandura, A. (1969). Social-learning theory of identificatory processes. Handbook of socialization theory and research, 213.

Bandura, A. (1990). Selective activation and disengagement of moral control. Journal of Social Issues, 46(1), 27-46.

Bandura, A., & Walters, R. H. (1963). Social learning and personality development (Vol. 14). New York: Holt, Rinehart and Winston.

Bandura, A., & Walters, R. H. (1977). Social learning theory.

Banuri, S., & Eckel, C. (2012). Chapter 3 Experiments in Culture and Corruption: A Review. In New advances in experimental research on corruption (pp. 51-76). Emerald Group Publishing Limited.

Barnes, C. M., Schaubroeck, J., Huth, M., & Ghumman, S. (2011). Lack of sleep and unethical conduct. Organizational Behavior and Human Decision Processes, 115(2), 169-180.

Baron-Cohen, S., Wheelwright, S., Hill, J., Raste, Y., & Plumb, I. (2001). The "Reading the Mind in the Eyes" test revised version: A study with normal adults, and adults with Asperger syndrome or high-functioning autism. Journal of child psychology and psychiatry, 42(2), 241-251.

Barr, A., & Serra, D. (2010). Corruption and culture: An experimental analysis. Journal of Public Economics, 94(11), 862-869.

Barrett, S. R., Speth, R. L., Eastham, S. D., Dedoussi, I. C., Ashok, A., Malina, R., & Keith, D. W. (2015). Impact of the Volkswagen emissions control defeat device on US public health. Environmental Research Letters, 10(11), 114005.

Barsky, A. (2008). Understanding the ethical cost of organizational goal-setting: A review and theory development. Journal of Business Ethics, 81(1), 63-81.

Bauman, C. W., Tost, L. P., & Ong, M. (2016). Blame the shepherd not the sheep: Imitating higher-ranking transgressors mitigates punishment for unethical behavior. Organizational Behavior and Human Decision Processes, 137, 123-141.

Bauman, Y., & Rose, E. (2011). Selection or indoctrination: Why do economics students donate less than the rest?. Journal of Economic Behavior & Organization, 79(3), 318-327.

Baumeister, R. F., & Juola Exline, J. (1999). Virtue, personality, and social relations: Self-control as the moral muscle. Journal of personality, 67(6), 1165-1194.

Bazerman, M. H., & Moore, D. (2011). Is it time for auditor independence yet? Accounting, Organizations and Society, 36(4), 310-312.

Bazerman, M. H., & Tenbrunsel, A. E. (2011). Blind spots: Why we fail to do what's right and what to do about it. Princeton University Press.

Bazerman, M. H., Loewenstein, G., & Moore, D. A. (2002). Why good accountants do bad audits. Harvard business review, 80(11), 96-103.

Bazerman, M. H., Moore, D. A., Tetlock, P. E., & Tanlu, L. (2006). Reports of solving the conflicts of interest in auditing are highly exaggerated. Academy of Management Review, 31(1), 43-49.

Bazerman, Max H., and Francesca Gino. (2012). Behavioral ethics: Toward a deeper understanding of moral judgment and dishonesty. Annual Review of Law and Social Science 8: 85-104.

Becker, G. S. (1968). Crime and punishment: An economic approach. In The economic dimensions of crime (pp. 13-68). Palgrave Macmillan UK.

Bem, D. J. (1972). Self-perception theory. Advances in experimental social psychology, 6, 1-62.

Bennett, R. J., & Robinson, S. L. (2000). Development of a measure of workplace deviance. Journal of applied psychology, 85(3), 349.

Benhabib, J., Bisin, A., & Schotter, A. (2010). Present-bias, quasi-hyperbolic discounting, and fixed costs. Games and Economic Behavior, 69(2), 205-223.

Bersoff, D. M. (1999). Why good people sometimes do bad things: Motivated reasoning and unethical behavior. Personality and social psychology bulletin, 25(1), 28-39.

Bickerton, D. (2017). Language and human behavior. University of Washington Press.

Birsch, D., & Fielder, J. (1994). The Ford Pinto case: A study in applied ethics, business, and technology.

Board, B. J., & Fritzon, K. (2005). Disordered personalities at work. Psychology, crime & law, 11(1), 17-32.

Boddy, C. R. (2011). The corporate psychopaths theory of the global financial crisis. In Corporate Psychopaths (pp. 163-166). Palgrave Macmillan UK.

Boddy, C. R. (2015). Organisational psychopaths: a ten-year update. Management Decision, 53(10), 2407-2432.

Boddy, C. R., Ladyshewsky, R., & Galvin, P. (2010). Leaders without ethics in global business: Corporate psychopaths. Journal of Public Affairs, 10(3), 121-138.

Bodolica, V., & Spraggon, M. (2015). An examination into the disclosure, structure, and contents of ethical codes in publicly listed acquiring firms. Journal of Business Ethics, 126(3), 459-472.

Boyatzis, R. E., Smith, M. L., & Blaize, N. (2006). Developing sustainable leaders through coaching and compassion. Academy of Management Learning & Education, 5(1), 8-24.

Boyatzis, R. E., Smith, M. L., Van Oosten, E., & Woolford, L. (2013). Developing resonant leaders through emotional intelligence, vision and coaching. Organizational Dynamics, 42(1), 17-24.

Boyatzis, R., & McKee, A. (2013). Resonant Leadership: Renewing Yourself and Connecting with Others Through Mindfulness, Hope and Compassion. Harvard Business Press.

Brehm, J. W. (1966). A theory of psychological reactance.

Brehm, J., & Festinger, L. (1957). Pressures toward uniformity of performance in groups. Human Relations, 10(1), 85–91.

Brehm, S. S., & Brehm, J. W. (2013). Psychological reactance: A theory of freedom and control. Academic Press.

Brendl, C. M., Chattopadhyay, A., Pelham, B. W., & Carvallo, M. (2005). Name letter branding: Valence transfers when product specific needs are active. Journal of Consumer Research, 32(3), 405-415.

Brief, A. P., Buttram, R. T., Elliott, J. D., Reizenstein, R. M., & McCline, R. L. (1995). Releasing the beast: A study of compliance with orders to use race as a selection criterion. Journal of Social Issues, 51(3), 177-193.

Brooks, N., Fritzon, K., & Croom, S. (2016). The Emergence of noncriminal psychopathy. The Australian Psychological Society 2016. In Press.

The Virtuous Barrel:
How to Transform Corporate Scandals into Good Businesses via Behavioral Ethics

Brown, M. E., Treviño, L. K., & Harrison, D. A. (2005). Ethical leadership: A social learning perspective for construct development and testing. Organizational behavior and human decision processes, 97(2), 117-134.

Brown, M. E., & Treviño, L. K. (2014). Do role models matter? An investigation of role modeling as an antecedent of perceived ethical leadership. Journal of Business Ethics, 122(4), 587-598.

Brown, S. P., & Leigh, T. W. (1996). A new look at psychological climate and its relationship to job involvement, effort, and performance. Journal of applied psychology, 81(4), 358.

Brown, S., Gray, D., McHardy, J., & Taylor, K. (2015). Employee trust and workplace performance. Journal of Economic Behavior & Organization, 116, 361-378.

Bzdok, D., Schilbach, L., Vogeley, K., Schneider, K., Laird, A. R., Langner, R., & Eickhoff, S. B. (2012). Parsing the neural correlates of moral cognition: ALE meta-analysis on morality, theory of mind, and empathy. Brain Structure and Function, 217(4), 783-796.

Cable, D. M., & Kay, V. S. (2012). Striving for self-verification during organizational entry. Academy of Management Journal, 55(2), 360-380.

Cain, D. M., Loewenstein, G., & Moore, D. A. (2011). When sunlight fails to disinfect: Understanding the perverse effects of disclosing conflicts of interest. Journal of Consumer Research, 37(5), 836-857.

Call, A. C., Kedia, S., & Rajgopal, S. (2016). Rank and file employees and the discovery of misreporting: The role of stock options. Journal of Accounting and Economics, 62(2-3), 277-300.

Campbell, J. L., & Göritz, A. S. (2014). Culture corrupts! A qualitative study of organizational culture in corrupt organizations. Journal of business ethics, 120(3), 291-311.

Carmeli, A., Reiter-Palmon, R., & Ziv, E. (2010). Inclusive leadership and employee involvement in creative tasks in the workplace: The mediating role of psychological safety. Creativity Research Journal, 22(3), 250-260.

Carter, J. R., & Irons, M. D. (1991). Are economists different, and if so, why?. The Journal of Economic Perspectives, 5(2), 171-177.

Caruso, E., Epley, N., & Bazerman, M. H. (2006). The costs and benefits of undoing egocentric responsibility assessments in groups. Journal of personality and social psychology, 91(5), 857.

Cerdá, M., Tracy, M., Messner, S. F., Vlahov, D., Tardiff, K., & Galea, S. (2009). Misdemeanor policing, physical disorder, and gun-related homicide: a spatial analytic test of "broken-windows" theory. Epidemiology, 533-541.

Chiaburu, D. S., Muñoz, G. J., & Gardner, R. G. (2013). How to spot a careerist early on: Psychopathy and exchange ideology as predictors of careerism. Journal of Business Ethics. 118(3), 473-486.

Christian, M. S., & Ellis, A. P. (2011). Examining the effects of sleep deprivation on workplace deviance: A self-regulatory perspective. Academy of Management Journal, 54(5), 913-934.

Chu, L. C. (2010). The benefits of meditation vis-à-vis emotional intelligence, perceived stress and negative mental health. Stress and Health, 26(2), 169-180.

Chugh, D., Bazerman, M. H., & Banaji, M. R. (2005). Bounded ethicality as a psychological barrier to recognizing conflicts of interest. Conflicts of interest: Challenges and solutions in business, law, medicine, and public policy, 74-95.

Cikara, M., Jenkins, A. C., Dufour, N., & Saxe, R. (2014). Reduced self-referential neural response during intergroup competition predicts competitor harm. NeuroImage, 96, 36-43.

Cipriani, G. P., Lubian, D., & Zago, A. (2009). Natural born economists? Journal of Economic Psychology, 30(3), 455-468.

Cohan, W. (2012). This is how Wall Street psychopaths caused the financial crisis. Disponível em www.businessinsider.com/bill-cohan-an-academic-describes-how-wall-street-psychopaths-caused-the-financial-crisis-2012-1

Cohen, J., Ding, Y., Lesage, C., & Stolowy, H. (2012). Corporate fraud and managers' behavior: Evidence from the press. In Entrepreneurship, governance and ethics (pp. 271-315). Springer Netherlands.

Cohn, A., Fehr, E., & Maréchal, M. A. (2014). Business culture and dishonesty in the banking industry. Nature, 516(7529), 86-89.

Colquitt, J. A. (2001). On the dimensionality of organizational justice: a construct validation of a measure. Journal of applied psychology, 86(3), 386.

Costa, A., Foucart, A., Hayakawa, S., Aparici, M., Apesteguia, J., Heafner, J., & Keysar, B. (2014). Your morals depend on language. PloS one, 9(4), e94842.

Côté, S., Piff, P. K., & Willer, R. (2013). For whom do the ends justify the means? Social class and utilitarian moral judgment. Journal of Personality and Social Psychology, 104(3), 490.

Crocker, J. (2011). The road to fraud starts with a single step. Nature, 479(7372).

Cuadros, A. (2016). Brazillionaires: Wealth, Power, Decadence, and Hope in an American Country. Spiegel & Grau, p. 46-47.

Cullen, J. B., Victor, B., & Bronson, J. W. (1993). The ethical climate questionnaire: An assessment of its development and validity. Psychological reports, 73(2), 667-674.

Cumming, D., Leung, T., & Rui, O. (2012). Gender diversity and securities fraud. Available at http://dx.doi.org/10.2139/ssrn.2154934

Curtis, M. B., Conover, T. L., & Chui, L. C. (2012). A cross-cultural study of the influence of country of origin, justice, power distance, and gender on ethical decision making. Journal of International Accounting Research, 11(1), 5-34.

Damasio, A. R. (1994). Descartes' error: Emotion, rationality and the human brain. New York: Putnam.

Daniel, A. R. (2013). Willful Blindness: The Hazards of an Evolving Standard of Knowledge.

Darley, J. M., & Batson, C. D. (1973). "From Jerusalem to Jericho": A study of situational and dispositional variables in helping behavior. Journal of personality and social psychology, 27(1), 100.

Darley, J. M., & Latane, B. (1968). Bystander intervention in emergencies: Diffusion of responsibility. Journal of personality and social psychology, 8(4), 377-383.

Davidson, R., Dey, A., & Smith, A. (2015). Executives' "off-the-job" behavior, corporate culture, and financial reporting risk. Journal of Financial Economics, 117(1), 5-28.

Dawson, L. M. (1997). Ethical differences between men and women in the sales profession. Journal of Business Ethics, 16(11), 1143-1152.

De Cremer, David, David M. Mayer, and Marshall Schminke. (2010). Guest Editors' Introduction: On Understanding Ethical Behavior and Decision Making: A Behavioral Ethics Approach. Business Ethics Quarterly 20, no. 01: 1-6.

Deal, T. E., & Kennedy, A. A. (2000). Corporate cultures: The rites and rituals of corporate life. Da Capo Press.

DeBacker, J., Heim, B. T., & Tran, A. (2015). Importing corruption culture from overseas: Evidence from corporate tax evasion in the United States. Journal of Financial Economics, 117(1), 122-138.

Decety, J. (2016) How Evolutionary Theory and Neuroscience Contribute to Understanding the Development of Prosociality: Commentary. Encyclopedia on Early Childhood Development.

Decety, J., Michalska, K. J., & Kinzler, K. D. (2011). The Developmental Neuroscience of Moral Sensitivity. Emotion Review, 3(3), 305-307.

Deci, E. & Ryan, R. (1985). Intrinsic Motivation and Self-Determination in Human Behavior (Perspectives in Social Psychology).

Detert, J. R., Treviño, L. K., & Sweitzer, V. L. (2008). Moral disengagement in ethical decision making: a study of antecedents and outcomes. Journal of Applied Psychology, 93(2), 374.

De Hoogh, A. H., & Den Hartog, D. N. (2008). Ethical and despotic leadership, relationships with leader's social responsibility, top management team effectiveness and subordinates' optimism: A multi-method study. The Leadership Quarterly, 19(3), 297-311.

Diamond, J. (2005). Collapse: How societies choose to fail or succeed. Penguin.

Diekmann, A., Jungbauer-Gans, M., Krassnig, H., & Lorenz, S. (1996). Social status and aggression: A field study analyzed by survival analysis. The Journal of social psychology, 136(6), 761-768.

Diekmann, K. A., Tenbrunsel, A. E., & Galinsky, A. D. (2003). From self-prediction to self-defeat: Behavioral forecasting, self-fulfilling prophecies, and the effect of competitive expectations. Journal of Personality and Social Psychology, 85(4), 672.

Dimant, E., & Schulte, T. (2016). The nature of corruption: An interdisciplinary perspective. German LJ, 17, 53.

Eden, D. (1990). Pygmalion in management: Productivity as a self-fulfilling prophecy. Lexington Books/DC Heath and Com.

Edmondson, A. (1999). Psychological safety and learning behavior in work teams. Administrative science quarterly, 44(2), 350-383.

Egan, M. L., Matvos, G., & Seru, A. (2017). When Harry fired Sally: The double standard in punishing misconduct (No. w23242). National Bureau of Economic Research.

Engel, D., Woolley, A. W., Jing, L. X., Chabris, C. F., & Malone, T. W. (2014). Reading the mind in the eyes or reading between the lines? Theory of mind predicts collective intelligence equally well online and face-to-face. PloS one, 9(12), e115212.

Engelmann, J. B., & Fehr, E. (2016). The slippery slope of dishonesty. Nature Neuroscience, 19(12), 1543-1544.

Epley, N., & Tannenbaum, D. (2017). Treating ethics as a design problem. Behavioral Science & Policy, 3(2), 72-84.

The Virtuous Barrel:
How to Transform Corporate Scandals into Good Businesses via Behavioral Ethics

Espinoza (2009). Ética, tradução de Tomaz Tadeu. Ed. Autêntica; Furrow, D. (2005). Ethics: Key concepts in philosophy. Bloomsbury Publishing.

Etzioni, A. (2015). The moral effects of economic teaching. Sociological Forum, 30(1), 228-233.

Fast, N. J., & Chen, S. (2009). When the boss feels inadequate power, incompetence, and aggression. Psychological Science, 20(11), 1406-1413.

Fichter, R. (2016). Do the Right Thing! Developing Ethical Behavior in Financial Institutions. Journal of Business Ethics, 1-16.

Fischer, R., Callander, R., Reddish, P., & Bulbulia, J. (2013). How do rituals affect cooperation?. Human Nature, 24(2), 115-125.

Fischer, P., Krueger, J. I., Greitemeyer, T., Vogrincic, C., Kastenmüller, A., Frey, D., ... & Kainbacher, M. (2011). The bystander-effect: a meta-analytic review on bystander intervention in dangerous and non-dangerous emergencies. Psychological bulletin, 137(4), 517.

Fischer, R., & Schwartz, S. (2011). Whence differences in value priorities? Individual, cultural, or artifactual sources. Journal of Cross-Cultural Psychology, 42(7), 1127-1144.

Fisman, R., & Miguel, E. (2007). Corruption, norms, and legal enforcement: Evidence from diplomatic parking tickets. Journal of Political economy, 115(6), 1020-1048.

Forster, M., Loughran, T., & McDonald, B. (2009). Commonality in codes of ethics. Journal of Business Ethics, 90, 129-139.

Frank, B., & Schulze, G. G. (2000). Does economics make citizens corrupt? Journal of economic behavior & organization, 43(1), 101-113.

Frank, R. H., Gilovich, T., & Regan, D. T. (1993). Does studying economics inhibit cooperation? The Journal of Economic Perspectives, 7(2), 159-171.

Frey, B. S. (1994). How intrinsic motivation is crowded out and in. Rationality and society, 6(3), 334-352.

Frey, B. S., & Jegen, R. (2001). Motivation crowding theory. Journal of economic surveys, 15(5), 589-611.

Frey, B. S., & Meier, S. (2003). Are political economists selfish and indoctrinated? Evidence from a natural experiment. Economic Inquiry, 41(3), 448-462.

Frey, B. S., & Oberholzer-Gee, F. (1997). The cost of price incentives: An empirical analysis of motivation crowding-out. The American economic review, 87(4), 746-755.

Frey, C. B., & Osborne, M. A. (2017). The future of employment: how susceptible are jobs to computerisation? Technological forecasting and social change, 114, 254-280.

Friedman, M. 1970. The Social Responsibility of Business is to Increase its Profits. The New York Times Magazine. 13/09/1970.

Fritzon, K., Bailey, C., Croom, S., & Brooks, N. (2016). Problem personalities in the workplace: Development of the corporate personality inventory. In P.-A. Granhag, R. Bull, A. Shaboltas, & E. Dozortseva (Eds.), Psychology and law in Europe: When west meets east. CRC Press.

Furnham, A., Richards, S. C., & Paulhus, D. L. (2013). The Dark Triad of personality: A 10 year review. Social and Personality Psychology Compass, 7(3), 199-216.

Gächter, S., & Schulz, J. F. (2016). Intrinsic honesty and the prevalence of rule violations across societies. Nature.

Garrett, N., Lazzaro, S. C., Ariely, D., & Sharot, T. (2016). The brain adapts to dishonesty. Nature Neuroscience.

Geipel, J., Hadjichristidis, C., & Surian, L. (2015). How foreign language shapes moral judgment. Journal of Experimental Social Psychology, 59, 8-17.

Gentile, M. C. (2010). Giving Voice to Values: How to Speak Your Mind When You Know What's Right. Yale University Press. Prefácio.

Ghoshal, S. (2005). Bad management theories are destroying good management practices. Academy of Management learning & education, 4(1), 75-91.

Gibson, K. (2003). Contrasting role morality and professional morality: Implications for practice. Journal of Applied Philosophy, 20(1), 17-29.

Gino, F. (2013). Sidetracked: Why our decisions get derailed, and how we can stick to the plan. Harvard Business Review Press.

Gino, F., Ayal, S., & Ariely, D. (2009). Contagion and differentiation in unethical behavior the effect of one bad apple on the barrel. Psychological science, 20(3), 393-398.

Gino, F., Norton, M. I., & Ariely, D. (2010). The counterfeit self the deceptive costs of faking it. Psychological science.

Gioia, D. A. (1992). Pinto fires and personal ethics: A script analysis of missed opportunities. Journal of Business Ethics, 11(5), 379-389.

Gneezy, U., & Rustichini, A. (2000). A fine is a price. Journal of Legal Studies, 29, 1.

The Virtuous Barrel:
How to Transform Corporate Scandals into Good Businesses via Behavioral Ethics

Goyal, M., Singh, S., Sibinga, E. M., Gould, N. F., Rowland-Seymour, A., Sharma, R., ... & Ranasinghe, P. D. (2014). Meditation programs for psychological stress and well-being: a systematic review and meta-analysis. JAMA internal medicine, 174(3), 357-368

Graham, J. R., Harvey, C. R., Popadak, J. A., Rajgopal, S. (2017). Corporate Culture: Evidence from the Field. Duke I&E Research Paper No. 2016-33; Columbia Business School Research Paper No. 16-49. Disponível em https://ssrn.com/abstract=2805602

Grant, A. (2013). Give and take: Why helping others drives our success. Penguin.

Gray, B. H., Sarnak, D. O., & Burgers, J. S. (2015). Home care by self-governing nursing teams: the Netherlands' Buurtzorg model.

Greene, J. D. (2014). Beyond Point-and-Shoot Morality: Why Cognitive (Neuro)Science Matters for Ethics. Ethics, 124(4), 695-726.

Greene, J. D., & Cohen, J. (2004). For the Law, Neuroscience Changes Nothing and Everything. Philosophical Transactions of the Royal Society London B, 359(1451), 1775-1785.

Greene, J. D., Sommerville, R. B., Nystrom, L. E., Darley, J. M., & Cohen, J. D. (2001). An fMRI investigation of emotional engagement in moral judgment. Science, 293(5537), 2105-2108.

Guenther, C. L., & Timberlake, E. A. (2012). The motivated self: self-affirmation and the better-than-average effect. Personality and Social Psychology Bulletin.

Guiso, L., Sapienza, P., & Zingales, L. (2015). The value of corporate culture. Journal of Financial Economics. 117(1), 60-76.

Haidt, J. (2001). The emotional dog and its rational tail: a social intuitionist approach to moral judgment. Psychological review, 108(4), 814-834.

Haidt, J. (2006). The Happiness Hypothesis: Finding Modern Truth in Ancient Wisdom. Basic Books.

Haidt, J. (2012). The Righteous mind: Why good people are divided by politics and religion. Vintage.

Haidt, J. (2013). The Righteous Mind: Why Good People are Divided by Politics and Religion. Vintage.

Hall, G. B., Dollard, M. F., & Coward, J. (2010). Psychosocial safety climate: Development of the PSC-12. International Journal of Stress Management, 17(4), 353.

Haney, C., Banks, C., & Zimbardo, P. (1972). Interpersonal dynamics in a simulated prison (No. ONR-TR-Z-09). Stanford University Department of Psychology.

Haney, C., Banks, W. C., & Zimbardo, P. G. (1973). A study of prisoners and guards in a simulated prison. Naval Research Review, 30, 4-17.

Harari, Y. N. (2014). Sapiens: A brief history of humankind. Random House.

Hare, R. D. (2002). The predators among us. In Keynote address. Canadian Police Association Annual General Meeting, St. John's, Newfoundland and Labrador.

Harcourt, B. E., & Ludwig, J. (2006). Broken windows: New evidence from New York City and a five-city social experiment. The University of Chicago Law Review, 271-320.

Hart, W., Albarracín, D., Eagly, A. H., Brechan, I., Lindberg, M. J., & Merrill, L. (2009). Feeling validated versus being correct: a meta-analysis of selective exposure to information.

Harvey, A. H., Kirk, U., Denfield, G. H., & Montague, P. R. (2010). Monetary favors and their influence on neural responses and revealed preference. Journal of Neuroscience, 30(28), 9597-9602.

Haselhuhn, M. P., & Wong, E. M. (2011). Bad to the bone: facial structure predicts unethical behaviour. Proceedings of the Royal Society of London B: Biological Sciences, rspb20111193.

Haucap, J., & Just, T. (2010). Not guilty? Another look at the nature and nurture of economics students. European Journal of Law and Economics, 29(2), 239-254.

Haugh, T. (2015). Overcriminalization's new harm paradigm. Vand. L. Rev., 68, 1191.

Heal, G. (2005). Corporate social responsibility: An economic and financial framework. The Geneva papers on risk and insurance Issues and practice, 30(3), 387-409.

Hofling, C. K., Brotzman, E., Dalrymple, S., Graves, N., & Pierce, C. M. (1966). An experimental study in nurse-physician relationships. The Journal of nervous and mental disease, 143(2), 171-180.

Holder-Webb, L., & Cohen, J. (2012). The cut and paste society: Isomorphism in codes of ethics. Journal of Business Ethics, 107(4), 485-509.

Hollensbe, E., Wookey, C., Hickey, L., George, G., & Nichols, C. V. (2014). Organizations with purpose. Academy of Management Journal, 57(5), 1227-1234.

Huang, M., Li, P., Meschke, F., & Guthrie, J. P. (2015). Family firms, employee satisfaction, and corporate performance. Journal of Corporate Finance, 34, 108-127.

Invernizzi, A. C., Menozzi, A., Passarani, D. A., Patton, D., & Viglia, G. (2017). Entrepreneurial overconfidence and its impact upon performance. International Small Business Journal, 35(6), 709-728.

Irlenbusch, B., & Villeval, M. C. (2015). Behavioral ethics: how psychology influenced economics and how economics might inform psychology? Current Opinion in Psychology, 6, 87-92.

Jackall, Robert. (1988). Moral Mazes: The World of Corporate Managers. New York: Oxford University Press.

Jehn, K. A. (1995). A multimethod examination of the benefits and detriments of intragroup conflict. Administrative science quarterly, 256-282.

Jenkins, S., & Delbridge, R. (2017). Trusted to deceive: A case study of 'strategic deception' and the normalization of lying at work. Organization Studies. 8(1): 53-76.

Jensen, M. (2001). A Theory of the Firm: Governance, Residual Claims, and Organizational Forms. Harvard University Press. Cambridge, Massachusetts.

Jensen, M., Meckling, W. (1976). Theory of the Firm: Managerial Behavior, Agency Costs and Ownership Structure. Journal of Financial Economics. 3: 305-360.

Jia, Y., Lent, L. V., & Zeng, Y. (2014). Masculinity, testosterone, and financial misreporting. Journal of Accounting Research, 52(5), 1195-1246.

Jondle, D., Ardichvili, A., & Mitchell, J. (2014). Modeling ethical business culture: Development of the ethical business culture survey and its use to validate the CEBC model of ethical business culture. Journal of Business Ethics, 119(1), 29-43.

Jones, D. N. (2014). Risk in the face of retribution: Psychopathic individuals persist in financial misbehavior among the Dark Triad. Personality and individual Differences, 67, 109-113.

Jones, J. T., Pelham, B. W., Carvallo, M., & Mirenberg, M. C. (2004). How do I love thee? Let me count the Js: implicit egotism and interpersonal attraction. Journal of personality and social psychology, 87(5), 665.

Kahane, G., Everett, J. A., Earp, B. D., Farias, M., & Savulescu, J. (2015). 'Utilitarian' judgments in sacrificial moral dilemmas do not reflect impartial concern for the greater good. Cognition, 134, 193-209.

Kahneman, D. (2011). Thinking, fast and slow. Macmillan.

Kahneman, D., & Tversky, A. (1979). Prospect theory: An analysis of decision under risk. Econometrica: Journal of the econometric society, 263-291.

Kalshoven, K., Den Hartog, D. N., & De Hoogh, A. H. (2011). Ethical leadership at work questionnaire (ELW): Development and validation of a multidimensional measure. The Leadership Quarterly, 22(1), 51-69.

Kang, C., Germann, F., & Grewal, R. (2016). Washing away your sins? Corporate social responsibility, corporate social irresponsibility, and firm performance. Journal of Marketing, 80(2), 59-79.

Kant, I. (1998). Critique of Pure Reason (traduzida por Paul Guyer & Allen W. Wood). Ed. Cambridge University Press.

Kaptein, M. (2008). Developing and testing a measure for the ethical culture of organizations: The corporate ethical virtues model. Journal of Organizational Behavior, 29(7), 923-947.

Kaptein, M. (2008). Developing a measure of unethical behavior in the workplace: A stakeholder perspective. Journal of Management, 34(5), 978-1008.

Kaptein, M. (2011). Understanding unethical behavior by unraveling ethical culture. Human relations, 64(6), 843-869.

Kaptein, M. (2013). Workplace morality: Behavioral ethics in organizations. Emerald Group Publishing.

Keizer, K., Lindenberg, S., & Steg, L. (2008). The spreading of disorder. Science, 322(5908), 1681-1685.

Killgore, W. D., Killgore, D. B., Day, L. M., Li, C., Kamimori, G. H., & Balkin, T. J. (2007). The effects of 53 hours of sleep deprivation on moral judgment. Sleep-New York Then Westchester-, 30(3), 345.

Koellinger, P., Minniti, M., & Schade, C. (2007). "I think I can, I think I can": Overconfidence and entrepreneurial behavior. Journal of economic psychology, 28(4), 502-527.

Kluver, J., Frazier, R., & Haidt, J. (2014). Behavioral Ethics for Homo economicus, Homo heuristicus, and Homo duplex. Organizational behavior and human decision processes, 123(2), 150-158.

Koch, C., Weber, M., & Wüstemann, J. (2012). Can auditors be independent? experimental evidence on the effects of client type. European Accounting Review, 21(4), 797-823.

Kohlberg L. (1969). Stage and Sequence: The Cognitive-Developmental Approach to Socialization. In D. A. Goslin (Ed.), Handbook of Socialization Theory and Research (pp. 347-480). Chicago: Rand McNally.

Kosfeld, M., Heinrichs, M., Zak, P. J., Fischbacher, U., & Fehr, E. (2005). Oxytocin increases trust in humans. Nature, 435(7042), 673-676.

Kotchen, M. (2012). Corporate Social Responsibility for Irresponsibility. The BE Journal of Economic Analysis & Policy, 12(1), 1-23.

Kouchaki, M., & Gino, F. (2016). Memories of unethical actions become obfuscated over time. Proceedings of the National Academy of Sciences, 113(22), 6166-6171.

Kozhevnikov, M., Evans, C., & Kosslyn, S. M. (2014). Cognitive style as environmentally sensitive individual differences in cognition: A modern synthesis and applications in education, business, and management. Psychological Science in the Public Interest, 15(1), 3-33.

Laloux, F. (2014). Reinventing organizations. Nelson Parker.

Lama, D. (2000). Uma ética para o novo milênio / Sua Santidade, o Dalai Lama, tradução de Maria Luiza Newlands. Ed. Sextante.

Lammers, J., Stoker, J. I., & Stapel, D. A. (2010). Power and behavioral approach orientation in existing power relations and the mediating effect of income. European Journal of Social Psychology, 40(3), 543-551.

Langevoort, D. C. (2015). Behavioral Ethics, Behavioral Compliance.

Latane, B., & Darley, J. M. (1968). Group inhibition of bystander intervention in emergencies. Journal of personality and social psychology, 10(3), 215.

Law, R., Dollard, M. F., Tuckey, M. R., & Dormann, C. (2011). Psychosocial safety climate as a lead indicator of workplace bullying and harassment, job resources, psychological health and employee engagement. Accident Analysis & Prevention, 43(5), 1782-1793.

Lee, M. T., & Ermann, M. D. (1999). Pinto "madness" as a flawed landmark narrative: An organizational and network analysis. Social Problems, 46(1), 30-47.

Leo, Sergio. (2014). Ascensão e Queda do Império X. Editora Nova Fronteira. p. 207-208.

Lerman, L. G. (2001). The slippery slope from ambition to greed to dishonesty: Lawyers, money, and professional integrity. Hofstra L. Rev., 30, 879; 151.

Levine, J. M. (1999). Solomon Asch's legacy for group research. Personality and Social Psychology Review, 3(4), 358-364.

Liberman, V., Samuels, S. M., & Ross, L. (2004). The name of the game: Predictive power of reputations versus situational labels in determining prisoner's dilemma game moves. Personality and social psychology bulletin, 30(9), 1175-1185.

Lie, E. (2005). On the timing of CEO stock option awards. Management Science, 51(5), 802-812.

Li-Ping Tang, T., Chen, Y. J., & Sutarso, T. (2008). Bad apples in bad (business) barrels: The love of money, Machiavellianism, risk tolerance, and unethical behavior. Management Decision, 46(2), 243-263.

Litzky, B. E., Eddleston, K. A., & Kidder, D. L. (2006). The good, the bad, and the misguided: How managers inadvertently encourage deviant behaviors. The Academy of Management Perspectives, 20(1), 91-103.

Livingston, J. S. (2009). Pygmalion in management. Harvard Business Review Press.

Loughran, T., McDonald, B., & Yun, H. (2009). A wolf in sheep's clothing: The use of ethics-related terms in 10-K reports. Journal of Business Ethics, 89(1), 39-49.

Luders, E., Toga, A. W., Lepore, N., & Gaser, C. (2009). The underlying anatomical correlates of long-term meditation: larger hippocampal and frontal volumes of gray matter. Neuroimage, 45(3), 672-678.

Luyendijk, J. (2015). Swimming with Sharks: My Journey into the World of the Bankers (Vol. 4). Guardian Faber Publishing.

Mackey, J., & Sisodia, R. (2013). Conscious capitalism, with a new preface by the authors: Liberating the heroic spirit of business. Harvard Business Review Press.

Marshall, A. J., Ashleigh, M. J., Baden, D., Ojiako, U., & Guidi, M. G. (2015). Corporate psychopathy: can 'search and destroy' and 'hearts and minds' military metaphors inspire HRM solutions? Journal of Business Ethics, 128(3), 495-504.

Marshall, A., Baden, D., & Guidi, M. (2013). Can an ethical revival of prudence within prudential regulation tackle corporate psychopathy? Journal of business ethics, 117(3), 559-568.

Marwell, G., & Ames, R. E. (1981). Economists free ride, does anyone else?: Experiments on the provision of public goods, IV. Journal of public economics, 15(3), 295-310.

Mathieu, C., Neumann, C. S., Hare, R. D., & Babiak, P. (2014). A dark side of leadership: Corporate psychopathy and its influence on employee well-being and job satisfaction. Personality and Individual Differences, 59, 83-88.

Mawritz, M. B., Mayer, D. M., Hoobler, J. M., Wayne, S. J., & Marinova, S. V. (2012). A trickle-down model of abusive supervision. Personnel Psychology, 65(2), 325-357.

Mazar, N., & Zhong, C. B. (2010). Do green products make us better people? Psychological science.

Mazar, N., Amir, O., & Ariely, D. (2008). The dishonesty of honest people: A theory of self-concept maintenance. Journal of marketing research, 45(6), 633-644.

McDonald, D. (2017). The Golden Passport: Harvard Business School, the limits of capitalism, and the moral failure of the MBA elite. HarperCollins.

McLean, Bethany, Elkind, Peter. 2004. The Smartest Guys in the Room: The Amazing Rise and Scandalous Fall of Enron. Penguin Books.

McLeod, S. A. (2008). Hofling hospital experiment. Retrieved from www.simplypsychology.org/hofling-obedience.html

McLeod, S. A. (2016). Zimbardo – Stanford Prison Experiment. Available at www.simplypsychology.org/zimbardo.html

Mead, N. L., Baumeister, R. F., Gino, F., Schweitzer, M. E., & Ariely, D. (2009). Too tired to tell the truth: Self-control resource depletion and dishonesty. Journal of experimental social psychology, 45(3), 594-597.

Meier, S., & Sprenger, C. (2010). Present-biased preferences and credit card borrowing. American Economic Journal: Applied Economics, 2(1), 193-210.

Merritt, A. C., Effron, D. A., & Monin, B. (2010). Moral self-licensing: When being good frees us to be bad. Social and personality psychology compass, 4(5), 344-357.

Messick, D. M., & Bazerman, M. H. (1996). Ethics for the twenty-first century: A decision making approach.

Messick, D. M., Bloom, S., Boldizar, J. P., & Samuelson, C. D. (1985). Why we are fairer than others. Journal of Experimental Social Psychology, 21(5), 480-500.

Messner, S. F., Galea, S., Tardiff, K. J., Tracy, M., Bucciarelli, A., Piper, T., ... & Vlahov, D. (2007). Policing, drugs, and the homicide decline in New York City in the 1990s. Criminology, 45(2), 385-414.

Milgram, S. (1963). Behavioral Study of obedience. The Journal of abnormal and social psychology, 67(4), 371.

Milgram, S. (1965). Some conditions of obedience and disobedience to authority. Human relations, 18(1), 57-76; Milgram, S., & Gudehus, C. (1978). Obedience to authority.

Miller, D. (1993). The architecture of simplicity. Academy of Management Review, 18: 116-138.

Miller, D. T., Downs, J. S., & Prentice, D. A. (1998). Minimal conditions for the creation of a unit relationship: The social bond between birthdaymates. European Journal of Social Psychology, 28(3), 475-481.

Miron, A. M., & Brehm, J. W. (2006). Reactance theory-40 years later. Zeitschrift für Sozialpsychologie, 37(1), 9-18.

Mironov, M. (2015). Should one hire a corrupt CEO in a corrupt country? Journal of Financial Economics, 117(1), 29-42.

Monk-Turner, E. (2003). The benefits of meditation: experimental findings. The Social Science Journal, 40(3), 465-470.

Moore, D. A., Loewenstein, G., Tanlu, L., & Bazerman, M. H. (2003). Auditor independence, conflict of interest, and the unconscious intrusion of bias. Division of Research, Harvard Business School.

Moore, D. A., Tanlu, L., & Bazerman, M. H. (2010). Conflict of interest and the intrusion of bias. Judgment and Decision Making, 5(1), 37.

Moore, D. A., Tetlock, P. E., Tanlu, L., & Bazerman, M. H. (2006). Conflicts of interest and the case of auditor independence: Moral seduction and strategic issue cycling. Academy of Management Review, 31(1), 10-29.

Muraven, M., Tice, D. M., & Baumeister, R. F. (1998). Self-control as a limited resource: Regulatory depletion patterns. Journal of personality and social psychology, 74(3), 774.

Nisan, M. (1990). Moral balance: A model of how people arrive at moral decisions. The moral domain, 283-314.

North, D. C. (1990). Institutions, institutional change and economic performance. Cambridge University Press.

Nowak, M. A. (2006). Five rules for the evolution of cooperation. science, 314(5805), 1560-1563.

Nowak, M. A. (Ed.). (2013). Evolution, games, and god. Harvard University Press.

Nowak, M., & Highfield, R. (2011). Supercooperators: Altruism, evolution, and why we need each other to succeed. Simon and Schuster.

O'Boyle Jr, E. H., Forsyth, D. R., Banks, G. C., & McDaniel, M. A. (2012). A meta-analysis of the dark triad and work behavior: A social exchange perspective. Journal of Applied Psychology, 97(3), 557.

Olsen, O. K., Pallesen, S., & Eid, J. (2010). The impact of partial sleep deprivation on moral reasoning in military officers. Sleep, 33(8), 1086-1090.

Ones, D. S., Dilchert, S., Viswesvaran, C., & Judge, T. A. (2007). In support of personality assessment in organizational settings. Personnel psychology, 60(4), 995-1027.

Ordóñez, L. D., Schweitzer, M. E., Galinsky, A. D., & Bazerman, M. H. (2009). Goals gone wild: The systematic side effects of overprescribing goal setting. The Academy of Management Perspectives, 23(1), 6-16.

Orlitzky, M. (2016). How cognitive neuroscience informs a subjectivist-evolutionary explanation of business ethics. Journal of Business Ethics, 1-16.

Paduan, Roberta. (2016). Petrobras: Uma História de Orgulho e Vergonha. Editora Objetiva.

Palazzo e Hoffrage. (2014). Unethical Decision Making in Organizations. Course MOOC Course, setembro 2014. Available at www.coursera.org

Palazzo, G., Krings, F., & Hoffrage, U. (2012). Ethical blindness. Journal of Business Ethics, 109(3), 323-338.

Parmar, B. L. (2017). Disobedience of Immoral Orders from Authorities: An Issue Construction Perspective. Organization Studies.

Pauly, D. (1995). Anecdotes and the shifting baseline syndrome of fisheries. Trends in ecology and evolution, 10(10), 430.

Pelham, B. W., Mirenberg, M. C., & Jones, J. T. (2002). Why Susie sells seashells by the seashore: implicit egotism and major life decisions. Journal of personality and social psychology, 82(4), 469.

Pennebaker, J. W., & Sanders, D. Y. (1976). American graffiti: Effects of authority and reactance arousal. Personality and Social Psychology Bulletin, 2(3), 264-267.

Petersen, L. E., & Dietz, J. (2000). Social Discrimination in a Personnel Selection Context: The Effects of an Authority's Instruction to Discriminate and Followers' Authoritarianism1. Journal of Applied Social Psychology, 30(1), 206-220.

Piff, P. K. (2014). Wealth and the inflated self-class, entitlement, and narcissism. Personality and Social Psychology Bulletin, 40(1), 34-43.

Piff, P. K., Stancato, D. M., Côté, S., Mendoza-Denton, R., & Keltner, D. (2012). Higher social class predicts increased unethical behavior. Proceedings of the National Academy of Sciences, 109(11), 4086-4091.

Pink, D. (2011). Drive: The Surprising Truth About What Motivates Us. Riverhead Books Plenum Press.

Poortvliet, P. M., & Darnon, C. (2010). Toward a more social understanding of achievement goals. The interpersonal effects of mastery and performance goals. Current Directions in Psychological Science, 19(5), 324–328.

Prentice, R. (2014). Teaching behavioral ethics. Journal of Legal Studies Education, 31(2), 325-365.

Qin, Z., Johnson, D. W., & Johnson, R. T. (1995). Cooperative versus competitive efforts and problem solving. Review of educational Research, 65(2), 129-143.

Radtke, R. R. (2008). Role Morality in the Accounting Profession–How do we Compare to Physicians and Attorneys? Journal of business ethics, 79(3), 279-297.

Rand, D. G., & Nowak, M. A. (2013). Human cooperation. Trends in cognitive sciences, 17(8), 413-425.

Robertson, D. C., Voegtlin, C., & Maak, T. (2016). Business Ethics: The Promise of Neuroscience. Journal of Business Ethics, 1-19.

Rose, J. M. (2007). Corporate directors and social responsibility: Ethics versus shareholder value. Journal of Business Ethics, 73(3), 319-331.

Rosenthal, R., & Jacobson, L. (1968). Pygmalion in the classroom: Teacher expectation and pupils' intellectual development. New York: Holt, Rinehart & Winston.

Ross, M., & Sicoly, F. (1979). Egocentric biases in availability and attribution. Journal of personality and social psychology, 37(3), 322-336.

Ross, M., McFarland, C., Conway, M., & Zanna, M. P. (1983). Reciprocal relation between attitudes and behavior recall: Committing people to newly formed attitudes. Journal of Personality and Social Psychology, 45(2), 257.

Rubinstein, A. (2003). "Economics and psychology"? The case of hyperbolic discounting. International Economic Review, 44(4), 1207-1216.

Rubinstein, A. (2006). A Sceptic's Comment on the Study of Economics. The Economic Journal, 116(510), C1-C9.

Ruedy, N. E., & Schweitzer, M. E. (2010). In the moment: The effect of mindfulness on ethical decision making. Journal of Business Ethics, 95, 73-87.

Rupp, D. E., Wright, P. M., Aryee, S., & Luo, Y. (2011). Special issue on 'behavioral ethics, organizational justice, and social responsibility across contexts'. Management and organization review, 7(02), 385-387.

Rust, J., & Schwitzgebel, E. (2013). Ethicists' and Nonethicists' Responsiveness to Student E-mails: Relationships Among Expressed Normative Attitude, Self-Described Behavior, and Empirically Observed Behavior. Metaphilosophy, 44(3), 350-371.

Ryan, L. V. (2016). Sex differences through a neuroscience lens: Implications for business ethics. Journal of Business Ethics, 1-12.

Ryan, R. M., & Deci, E. L. (2000a). Intrinsic and extrinsic motivations: Classic definitions and new directions. Contemporary educational psychology, 25(1), 54-67.

Ryan, R. M., & Deci, E. L. (2000b). Self-determination theory and the facilitation of intrinsic motivation, social development, and well-being. American psychologist, 55(1), 68.

Ryan, R. M., & Deci, E. L. (2008). From ego depletion to vitality: Theory and findings concerning the facilitation of energy available to the self. Social and Personality Psychology Compass, 2(2), 702-717.

Sachdeva, S., Iliev, R., & Medin, D. L. (2009). Sinning saints and saintly sinners the paradox of moral self-regulation. Psychological science, 20(4), 523-528.

Saenz-Arroyo, A., Roberts, C., Torre, J., Cariño-Olvera, M., & Enríquez-Andrade, R. (2005). Rapidly shifting environmental baselines among fishers of the Gulf of California. Proceedings of the Royal Society of London B: Biological Sciences, 272(1575), 1957-1962.

Salvador, R., & Folger, R. G. (2009). Business ethics and the brain. Business Ethics Quarterly, 1-31.

Sansone, C., & Harackiewicz, J. M. (2000). Intrinsic and extrinsic motivation: The search for optimal motivation and performance. Academic Press.

Schein, E. H. (2010). Organizational culture and leadership (Vol. 2). John Wiley & Sons.

Scherer, A. G., & Palazzo, G. (2008). Globalization and corporate social responsibility.

Schrand, C. M., & Zechman, S. L. (2012). Executive overconfidence and the slippery slope to financial misreporting. Journal of Accounting and Economics, 53(1), 311-329.

Schwartz, M. S. (2005). Universal moral values for corporate codes of ethics. Journal of Business Ethics, 59(1), 27-44.

Schwartz, S. H. (1992). Universals in the content and structure of values: Theoretical advances and empirical tests in 20 countries. Advances in experimental social psychology, 25, 1-65.

Schwartz, S. H. (1994). Are there Universal Aspects in the Structure and Contents of Human Values? Journal of Social Issues, 50 (4): 19–45.

Schwartz, S. H. (2012). An overview of the Schwartz theory of basic values. Online readings in Psychology and Culture, 2(1), 11.

Schwartz, S. H., & Bardi, A. (2001). Value hierarchies across cultures taking a similarities perspective. Journal of cross-cultural Psychology, 32(3), 268-290.

Schwartz, S. H., & Bilsky, W. (1987). Toward a universal psychological structure of human values. Journal of personality and social psychology, 53(3), 550.

Schweitzer, M. E., Ordóñez, L., & Douma, B. (2004). Goal setting as a motivator of unethical behavior. Academy of Management Journal, 47(3), 422-432.

Schwieren, C., & Weichselbaumer, D. (2010). Does competition enhance performance or cheating? A laboratory experiment. Journal of Economic Psychology, 31(3), 241-253.

Schwitzgebel, E. (2009). Do ethicists steal more books?. Philosophical Psychology, 22(6), 711-725.

Schwitzgebel, E., & Rust, J. (2009). The moral behaviour of ethicists: Peer opinion. Mind, fzp108.

Schwitzgebel, E., & Rust, J. (2010). Do ethicists and political philosophers vote more often than other professors?. Review of Philosophy and Psychology, 1(2), 189-199.

Schwitzgebel, E., & Rust, J. (2014a). The moral behavior of ethics professors: Relationships among self-reported behavior, expressed normative attitude, and directly observed behavior. Philosophical Psychology, 27(3), 293-327.

Schwitzgebel, E., & Rust, J. (2014b). The Behavior of Ethicists. Blackwell Companion to Experimental Philosophy.

Schwitzgebel, E., Rust, J., Huang, L. T. L., Moore, A. T., & Coates, J. (2012). Ethicists' courtesy at philosophy conferences. Philosophical Psychology, 25(3), 331-340.

Sedikides, C., Meek, R., Alicke, M. D., & Taylor, S. (2014). Behind bars but above the bar: Prisoners consider themselves more prosocial than non-prisoners. British Journal of Social Psychology, 53(2), 396-403.

Sedlmeier, P., Eberth, J., Schwarz, M., Zimmermann, D., Haarig, F., Jaeger, S., & Kunze, S. (2012). The psychological effects of meditation: A meta-analysis. Psychological bulletin, 138(6), 1139.

Semler, R. (1994). Why my former employees still work for me. Harvard Business Review, 72(1), 64.

Semler, R. (2001). Maverick!: the success story behind the world's most unusual workplace. Random House.

Semler, R. (2004). The seven-day weekend: Changing the way work works. Penguin.

Semler, R. F. (1988). Virando a própria mesa. Ed. Rocco.

Sen, A. (1999). On ethics and economics. OUP Catalogue.

Shalvi, S., Eldar, O., & Bereby-Meyer, Y. (2012). Honesty requires time (and lack of justifications). Psychological science, 23(10), 1264-1270.

Shonin, E., Van Gordon, W., & Griffiths, M. D. (2013). Meditation as medication: are attitudes changing? Br J Gen Pract, 63(617), 654-654.

Shu, L. L., Gino, F., & Bazerman, M. H. (2011). Dishonest deed, clear conscience: When cheating leads to moral disengagement and motivated forgetting. Personality and Social Psychology Bulletin, 37(3), 330-349.

Shu, L. L., Mazar, N., Gino, F., Ariely, D., & Bazerman, M. H. (2012). Signing at the beginning makes ethics salient and decreases dishonest self-reports in comparison to signing at the end. Proceedings of the National Academy of Sciences, 109(38), 15197-15200.

Silveira, A. M., Donaggio, A. R., Sica, L. P., Ramos, L. (2014). Women's Participation in Senior Management Positions: Gender Social Relations, Law and Corporate Governance. Available at SSRN: https://ssrn.com/abstract=2508929

Silveira, Alexandre Di Miceli da. (2015a) Ten Adverse Outcomes When Managers Focus on Creating Shareholder Value: A Review (July 8, 2015). Available at SSRN: https://ssrn.com/abstract=2614752

Silveira, Alexandre Di Miceli da. (2015b). Corporate Scandals of the twenty-first century: Limitations of Mainstream Corporate Governance Literature and the Need for a New Behavioral Approach. Available at SSRN: https://ssrn.com/abstract=2181705

Silveira, Alexandre Di Miceli da. (2015). Governança corporativa no Brasil e no mundo: teoria e prática. Elsevier.

Silveira, Alexandre Di Miceli. (2014). Governança Corporativa: O Essencial para Líderes. Elsevier. 232 p.

Smith, C. A., Organ, D. W., & Near, J. P. (1983). Organizational citizenship behavior: Its nature and antecedents. Journal of applied psychology, 68(4), 653.

Smith, P. B., & Schwartz, S. H. Values. In Poortinga, Y. H., & Pandey, J. (Eds.). (1997). Handbook of cross-cultural psychology: Social behavior and applications (Vol. 3).

Smith, P. B., Peterson, M. F., & Schwartz, S. H. (2002). Cultural values, sources of guidance, and their relevance to managerial behavior: A 47-nation study. Journal of cross-cultural Psychology, 33(2), 188-208.

Smith, S. F., & Lilienfeld, S. O. (2013). Psychopathy in the workplace: The knowns and unknowns. Aggression and Violent Behavior, 18(2), 204-218.

Soltes, E. (2016). Why they do it: inside the mind of the white-collar criminal. PublicAffairs.

Sommer, M., Meinhardt, J., Rothmayr, C. Dohnel, K., Hajak, G. Ruppercht,R., & Sodian, B. (2014) Me or You? Neural Correlates of Moral Reasoning in Everyday Conflict situations in Adolescents and Adults. Social Neuroscience, 9(5), 452-470.

Steffensmeier, D., Schwartz, J., & Roche, M. (2013). Gender and Twenty-First-Century Corporate Crime: Female Involvement and the Gender Gap in Enron-Era Corporate Frauds. American Sociological Review. 78(3): 448-476.

Stein, M. (2000). The risk taker as shadow: A psychoanlytic view of the collapse of Barings Bank. Journal of Management Studies, 37(8), 1215-1230.

Steinhage, A. L., Cable, D., & Wardley, D. P. (2015). Winning Through Cheating or Creativity: How Emotions Influence Behavioral Choice in Competition. In Academy of Management Proceedings (1): 16796. Academy of Management.

Stout, L. (2010). Cultivating conscience: How good laws make good people. Princeton University Press.

Stout, L. (2012). The Shareholder Value Myth. Berret-Koehler Publishers.

Sunstein, C. R., & Hastie, R. (2014). Wiser: Getting beyond groupthink to make groups smarter. Harvard Business Press.

Tappin, B. M., & McKay, R. T. (2016). The Illusion of Moral Superiority. Social Psychological and Personality Science.

Taylor, S. E., & Brown, J. D. (1988). Illusion and well-being: a social psychological perspective on mental health. Psychological bulletin, 103(2), 193.

Tenbrunsel, A. E., & Messick, D. M. (1999). Sanctioning systems, decision frames, and cooperation. Administrative Science Quarterly, 44(4), 684-707.

Tenbrunsel, A. E., & Messick, D. M. (2004). Ethical fading: The role of self-deception in unethical behavior. Social Justice Research, 17(2), 223-236.

Tetlock, P. E., Kristel, O. V., Elson, S. B., Green, M. C., & Lerner, J. S. (2000). The psychology of the unthinkable: taboo trade-offs, forbidden base rates, and heretical counterfactuals. Journal of personality and social psychology, 78(5), 853.

Thomas, K. (2009). Intrinsic Motivation at Work: What Really Drives Employee Engagement. Berrett-Koehler Publishers.

Touré-Tillery, M., & Fishbach, A. (2012). The end justifies the means, but only in the middle. Journal of Experimental Psychology: General, 141(3), 570.

Treviño, L. K., Butterfield, K. D., & McCabe, D. L. (1998). The ethical context in organizations: Influences on employee attitudes and behaviors. Business Ethics Quarterly, 8(03), 447-476.

Treviño, L. K., & Brown, M. E. (2005). The role of leaders in influencing unethical behavior in the workplace. Managing organizational deviance, 69-87.

Treviño, L. K., Weaver, G. R., Reynolds, S. J. (2006). Behavioral ethics in organizations: A review. Journal of management 32.6: 951-990.

Treviño, L. K., Haidt, J., & Filabi, A. E. (2017). Regulating for ethical culture. Behavioral Science & Policy, 3(2), 56-70.

Treviño, L. K., & Nelson, K. A. (2016). Managing business ethics: Straight talk about how to do it right. John Wiley & Sons.

Tsang, J. A. (2002). Moral rationalization and the integration of situational factors and psychological processes in immoral behavior. Review of General Psychology, 6(1), 25.

Tversky, A., & Kahneman, D. (1973). Availability: A heuristic for judging frequency and probability. Cognitive psychology, 5(2), 207-232.

Van der Zwan, N. (2014). Making sense of financialization. Socio-Economic Review, 12, 99-129.

Van Kleef, G. A., Oveis, C., Van Der Löwe, I., LuoKogan, A., Goetz, J., & Keltner, D. (2008). Power, distress, and compassion: Turning a blind eye to the suffering of others. Psychological science, 19(12), 1315-1322.

Van Knippenberg, D., & Schippers, M. C. (2007). Work group diversity. Annu. Rev. Psychol., 58, 515-541.

Victor, B., & Cullen, J. B. (1988). The organizational bases of ethical work climates. Administrative science quarterly, 101-125.

Welsh, D. T., & Ordoñez, L. D. (2014). Conscience without cognition: The effects of subconscious priming on ethical behavior. Academy of Management Journal, 57(3), 723-742.

Welsh, D. T., & Ordoñez, L. D. (2014). The dark side of consecutive high-performance goals: Linking goal setting, depletion, and unethical behavior. Organizational Behavior and Human Decision Processes, 123(2), 79-89.

Welsh, D. T., Ordoñez, L. D., Snyder, D. G., & Christian, M. S. (2014). The slippery slope: How small ethical transgressions pave the way for larger future transgressions. Journal of Applied Psychology, 100(1), 114.

Werhane, P. H., & Freeman, R. E. (1999). Business ethics: the state of the art. International Journal of Management Reviews, 1(1), 1-16.

Westen, D., Blagov, P. S., Harenski, K., Kilts, C., & Hamann, S. (2006). Neural bases of motivated reasoning: An fMRI study of emotional constraints on partisan political judgment in the 2004 US presidential election. Journal of cognitive neuroscience, 18(11), 1947-1958.

Williams, K. Y., & O'Reilly III, C. A. (1998). A review of 40 years of research. Res Organ Behav, 20, 77-140.

Wilson, D. S. (1975). A theory of group selection. Proceedings of the national academy of sciences, 72(1), 143-146.

Wilson, D. S. (2010). Darwin's cathedral: Evolution, religion, and the nature of society. University of Chicago Press.

Woodward, I., & Shaffakat, S. (2016). Understanding Values for Insightfully Aware Leadership. INSEAD Working Paper No. 2016/05/OBH. Available at SSRN: https://ssrn.com/abstract=2471492

Woodzicka, J. A., & LaFrance, M. (2001). Real versus imagined gender harassment. Journal of Social Issues, 57(1), 15-30.

Woolley, A. W., Aggarwal, I., & Malone, T. W. (2015). Collective intelligence and group performance. Current Directions in Psychological Science, 24(6), 420-424.

Woolley, A. W., Chabris, C. F., Pentland, A., Hashmi, N., & Malone, T. W. (2010). Evidence for a collective intelligence factor in the performance of human groups. science, 330(6004), 686-688.

Wynn, R., Høiseth, M., & Pettersen, G. (2012). Psychopathy in women: theoretical and clinical perspectives.

Zell, E., & Alicke, M. D. (2011). Age and the Better-Than-Average Effect. Journal of Applied Social Psychology, 41(5), 1175-1188.

Zhong, C. B., & Liljenquist, K. (2006). Washing away your sins: Threatened morality and physical cleansing. Science, 313(5792), 1451-1452.

Zhong, C. B., Liljenquist, K. A., & Cain, D. M. (2009). Moral self-regulation. Psychological perspectives on ethical behavior and decision making, 75-89.

Zimbardo, P. G. (2007). Lucifer Effect. Blackwell Publishing Ltd.

Zingales, L. (2015). The "cultural revolution" in finance. Journal of Financial Economics, 1(117), 1-4.

Zobrist, J. F. (2014). La belle histoire de Favi: l'entreprise qui croit que l'homme est bon. Humanisme & Organisations.

Annex. Behavioral business ethics measuring instruments

Construct	Source and Definition	Full instrument
Ethical Culture	Kaptein (2008) "The perceived conditions in the organizational context that stimulate employees to behave ethically."	58 items divided into 8 dimensions. *Dimension 1: Clarity* 1. In my immediate working environment, it is sufficiently clear how we are expected to conduct ourselves in a responsible way. The organization makes it sufficiently clear to me how I should: 2. Conduct myself appropriately toward others within the organization. 3. Obtain proper authorizations. 4. Use company equipment responsibly. 5. Use my working hours responsibly. 6. Handle money and other financial assets responsibly. 7. Deal with conflicts of interests and sideline activities responsibly. 8. Deal with confidential information responsibly. 9. Deal with external persons and organizations responsibly. 10. Deal with environmental issues in a responsible way. *Dimension 2: Congruency of supervisors* My supervisor: 11. Sets a good example in terms of ethical behavior. 12. Communicates the importance of ethics and integrity clearly and convincingly. 13. Would never authorize unethical or illegal conduct to meet business goals. 14. Does as he says. 15. Fulfils his responsibilities. 16. Is honest and reliable. *Dimension 3: Congruency of management* 17. The conduct of the Board and Senior Management reflects a shared set of norms and values. 18. The Board and Senior Management sets a good example in terms of ethical behavior.

Construct	Source and Definition	Full instrument
		19. The Board and Senior Management communicates the importance of ethics and integrity clearly and convincingly.
20. The Board and Senior Management would never authorize unethical or illegal conduct to meet business goals.
Dimension 4: Feasibility
21. In my immediate working environment, I am never asked to do things that conflict with my conscience.
22. In order to be successful in my organization, nobody has to sacrifice his or her personal norms and values.
23. I have sufficient time at my disposal to carry out my tasks responsibly.
24. I have sufficient information at my disposal to carry out my tasks responsibly.
25. In my organization, employees have adequate resources at their disposal to carry out their tasks responsibly.
26. In my immediate working environment, employees are never put under pressure to break the rules.
Dimension 5: Supportability
In my immediate working environment:
27. Everyone is totally committed to the (stipulated) norms and values of the organization.
28. An atmosphere of mutual trust prevails.
29. Everyone has the best interests of the organization at heart.
30. A mutual relationship of trust prevails between employees and management.
31. Everyone takes the existing norms and standards seriously.
32. Everyone treats one another with respect.
Dimension 6: Transparency
33. If a colleague does something which is not permitted, my manager will find out about it.
34. If a colleague does something which is

Construct	Source and Definition	Full instrument
		not permitted, I or another colleague will find out about it.
35. If my manager does something which is not permitted, someone in the organization will find out about it.
36. If I criticize other people's behavior, I will receive feedback on any action taken as a result of my criticism.
37. In my immediate working environment, there is adequate awareness of potential violations and incidents in the organization.
38. In my immediate working environment, adequate checks are carried out to detect violations and unethical conduct.
39. Management is aware of the type of incidents and unethical conduct that occur in my immediate working environment.
Dimension 7: Discussability
In my immediate working environment:
40. Reports of unethical conduct are handled with caution.
41. I have the opportunity to express my opinion.
42. There is adequate scope to discuss unethical conduct.
43. Reports of unethical conduct are taken seriously.
44. There is adequate scope to discuss personal moral dilemmas.
45. There is adequate scope to report unethical conduct.
46. There is adequate ample opportunity for discussing moral dilemmas.
47. If someone is called to account for his or her conduct, it is done in a respectful manner.
48. There is adequate scope to correct unethical conduct.
49. If reported unethical conduct does not receive adequate attention, there is sufficient opportunity to raise the matter

Construct	Source and Definition	Full instrument
		elsewhere in the organization. *Dimension 8:* Sanctionability. 50. If necessary, managers are disciplined in my organization if they behave unethically. 51. The people that are successful in my immediate working environment stick to the norms and standards of the organization. 52. If I reported unethical conduct to management, I believe those involved would be disciplined fairly regardless of their position. In my immediate working environment: 53. People are accountable for their actions. 54. Ethical conduct is valued highly. 55. Only people with integrity are considered for promotion. 56. Ethical conduct is rewarded. 57. Employees will be disciplined if they behave unethically. 58. Employees who conduct themselves with integrity stand a greater chance to receive a positive performance appraisal than employees who conduct themselves without integrity.
	Trevino, Butterfield, and McCabe (1998) "A subset of organizational culture, representing a multidimensional interplay among various formal and	14 items (unidimensional): 1. Management in this organization disciplines unethical behavior when it occurs. 2. Employees in this organization perceive that people who violate the ethics code still get formal organizational rewards. 3. Penalties for unethical behavior are strictly enforced in this organization. 4. Unethical behavior is punished in this organization. 5. The top managers of this organization represent high ethical standards. 6. People of integrity are rewarded in this organization. 7. The ethics code serves as "window dressing" only in this organization.

Construct	Source and Definition	Full instrument
	informal systems of behavioral control that are capable of promoting either ethical or unethical behavior."	8. Top managers of this organization regularly show that they care about ethics. 9. Top managers of this organization are models of unethical behavior. 10. Ethical behavior is the norm in this organization. 11. Top managers of this organization guide decision making in an ethical direction. 12. The ethics code serves only to maintain the organization's public image. 13. Ethical behavior is rewarded in this organization. 14. Ethics code requirements are consistent with informal organizational norms.
	Jondle, Ardichvili, and Mitchell (2014) "It is based on an alignment between formal structures, processes, policies, training and development programs, consistent value-based ethical behavior of top leadership, informal	10 items associated with the five characteristics of an ethical culture: *Values-Driven:* 1. The organization strives to build relationships of trust and respect with its stakeholders (e.g., customers, suppliers, employees, owners and community). 2. The organization's values form the basis for all aspects of how the organization conducts its business. *Stakeholder Balance* 3. The organization balances the drive for profit with the need for delivering customer value. *Leadership Effectiveness* 4. Senior leaders lead by example of personal integrity. 5. Senior leaders expect ethical conduct at every level of the company. *Process Integrity* 6. There is a dedication to the quality process that leads to quality products and services. 7. The every-day execution of business processes and functions reflect the organization's values.

Construct	Source and Definition	Full instrument
	recognition of heroes, stories, and the use of rituals, metaphors and language that inspire organizational members to behave in a manner consistent with high ethical standards."	*Long-term Perspective* 8. Business decisions are based on the organization's values, not just profit. 9. The long-term perspective is favored over the short-term perspective. 10. Senior leaders emphasize that they are building/sustaining a company that will be around for the long-term.
Ethical Climate	Victor and Cullen (1988) & Cullen et al. (1993) "Those aspects of work climate that determine what constitutes ethical behavior at work or the prevailing perceptions of typical organizational practices and procedures that	36 items divided into five dimensions: 1. In this company, people are mostly out for themselves. 2. The major responsibility for people in this company is to consider efficiency first. 3. In this company, people are expected to follow theft own personal and moral beliefs. 4. People are expected to do anything to further the company's interests. 5. In this company, people look out for each other's good. 6. There is no room for one's own personal morals or ethics in this company. 7. It is very important to follow strictly the company's rules and procedures here. 8. Work is considered sub-standard only when it hurts the company's interests. 9. Each person in this company decides for himself what is right and wrong. 10. In this company, people protect their own interest above other considerations. 11. The most important consideration in

Construct	Source and Definition	Full instrument
	have ethical content."	this company is each person's sense of right and wrong. 12. The most important concern is the good of all the people in the company. 13. The first consideration is whether a decision violates any law. 14. People are expected to comply with the law and professional standards over and above other considerations. 15. Everyone is expected to stick by company rules and procedures. 16. In this company, our major concern is always what is best for the other person. 17. People are concerned with the company's interests—to the exclusion of personal interests. 18. Successful people in this company go by the book. 19. The most efficient way is always the right way, in this company. 20. In this company, people are expected to strictly follow legal or professional standards. 21. Our major consideration is what is best for everyone in the company. 22. In this company, people are guided by theft own personal ethics. 23. Successful people in this company strictly obey the company policies. 24. In this company, the law or ethical code of theft profession is the major consideration. 25. In this company, each person is expected, above all, to work efficiently. 26. It is expected that you will always do what is right for the customer and public. 27. People in this company view team spirit as important. 28. People in this company have a strong sense of responsibility to the outside community. 29. Decisions here are primarily viewed in

Construct	Source and Definition	Full instrument
		terms of contribution to profit. 30. People in this company are actively concerned about the customer's, and the public's, interest. 31. People are very concerned about what is generally best for employees in the company. 32. What is best for each individual is a primary concern in this organization. 33. People in this company are very concerned about what is best for themselves. 34. The effect of decisions on the customer and the public are a primary concern in this company. 35. It is expected that each individual is cared for when making decisions here. 36. Efficient solutions to problems are always sought here.
Ethics program	Kaptein (2011) "The formal or tangible organizational control systems designed to create an ethical culture and to, directly or indirectly, impede unethical conduct and promote ethical conduct."	Knowledge of respondents on the existence of nine different components of an ethics program in their organization. For each component, the response scale is 0 = not at all, 1 = informally, 2 = formally, 3 = unsure/no opinion, and 4 = not applicable: 1. A code of ethics. 2. An ethics officer or ethics office, also called compliance office(r), ombudsperson or ethics committee. 3. Formal ethics training and other types of information and communications. 4. A dedicated telephone system to raise ethical issues, usually called ethics hotline or ethics helpline. 5. Policies to hold management and employees accountable for unethical behavior. 6. Policies on investigating allegations of unethical behavior. 7. Policies that create incentives and rewards for ethical behavior. 8. Internal monitoring systems and ethics audits.

Construct	Source and Definition	Full instrument
		9. Pre-employment screenings of the ethics and integrity of applicants.
Ethical Leadership	Brown, Trevino, and Harrison (2005) "The demonstration of normatively appropriate conduct through personal actions and interpersonal relationships, and the promotion of such conduct to followers through two-way communication, reinforcement, and decision-making."	10 items (unidimensional): my department manager: 1. Listens to what employees have to say. 2. Disciplines employees who violate ethical standards. 3. Conducts his/her personal life in an ethical manner. 4. Has the best interests of employees in mind. 5. Makes fair and balanced decisions. 6. Can be trusted. 7. Discusses business ethics or values with employees. 8. Sets an example of how to do things the right way in terms of ethics. 9. Defines success not just by results but also the way that they are obtained. 10. When making decisions, asks "what is the right thing to do?".
	De Hoog and Den Hartog (2008) & Kalshoven, Hartog, and De Hoogh (2011)	38 items divided into seven dimensions: *Dimension 1 – People orientation:* 1. Is interested in how I feel and how I am doing. 2. Takes time for personal contact. 3. Pays attention to my personal needs. 4. Takes time to talk about work-related emotions.

Construct	Source and Definition	Full instrument
	"The process of influencing in a social responsible way others' activities toward goal achievement through seven behaviors: fairness, people orientation, role clarification, ethical guidance, environment orientation, power sharing and integrity."	5. Is genuinely concerned about my personal development. 6. Sympathizes with me when I have problems. 7. Cares about his/her followers. *Dimension 2 – Fairness:* 8. Holds me accountable for problems over which I have no control. 9. Holds me responsible for work that I gave no control over. 10. Holds me responsible for things that are not my fault. 11. Pursues his/her own success at the expense of others. 12. Is focused mainly on reaching his/her own goals. 13. Manipulates subordinates. *Dimension 3 – Power sharing:* 14. Allows subordinates to influence critical decisions. 15. Does not allow others to participate in decision making. 16. Seeks advice from subordinates concerning organizational strategy. 17. Will reconsider decisions on the basis of recommendations by those who report to him/her. 18. Delegates challenging responsibilities to subordinates. 19. Permits me to play a key role in setting my own performance goals. *Dimension 4 – Concern for sustainability:* 20. Would like to work in an environmentally friendly manner. 21. Shows concern for sustainability issues. 22. Stimulates recycling of items and materials in our department. *Dimension 5 – Ethical guidance:* 23. Clearly explains integrity related codes of conduct. 24. Explains what is expected from employees in terms of behaving with integrity.

Construct	Source and Definition	Full instrument
		25. Clarifies integrity guidelines. 26. Ensures that employees follow codes of integrity. 27. Clarifies the likely consequences of possible unethical behavior by myself and my colleagues. 28. Stimulates the discussion of integrity issues among employees. 29. Compliments employees who behave according to the integrity guidelines. *Dimension 6 – Role clarification:* 30. Indicates what the performance expectations of each group member are. 31. Explains what is expected of each group member. 32. Explains what is expected of me and my colleagues. 33. Clarifies priorities. 34. Clarifies who is responsible for what. *Dimension 7 – Integrity:* 35. Keeps his/her promises. 36. Can be trusted to do the things he/she says. 37. Can be relied on to honor his/her commitments. 38. Always keeps his/her words.
Organizational Citizenship Behavior (OCB)	Smith, Organ, and Near (1983) "Extra-role behavior that promotes organizational effectiveness but is not explicitly recognized by an	16 items (unidimensional): respondents asked to think of an employee who worked or had worked for them and to rate, on a 5-point scale, how characteristic each statement was of the employee. 1. Helps others who have been absent. 2. Punctuality. 3. Volunteers for things that are not required. 4. Does not takes undeserved breaks. 5. Orients new people even though it is not required. 6. Attendance at work is above the norm. 7. Helps others who have heavy workloads. 8. Does not coasts towards the end of the day.

Construct	Source and Definition	Full instrument
	organization's reward system. It reflects prosocial, voluntary behavior that is beneficial to the organization."	9. Gives advance notice if unable to come to work. 10. Does not spend a great deal of time with personal phone conversations. 11. Does not take unnecessary time off work. 12. Assists supervisor with his or her work. 13. Makes innovative suggestions to improve department. 14. Does not take extra breaks. 15. Attend functions not required but that help company image. 16. Does not spend time in idle conversation.
Organizational justice	Colquitt (2001) "Interpersonal Justice: The degree to which people are treated with politeness, dignity, and respect by authorities or others involved in executing procedures or determining outcomes. Informational Justice: Explanations provided to	20 items divided into four dimensions. All items on a 5-point scale with anchors of 1 = to a small extent and 5 = to a large extent. *Interpersonal Justice – The following four items refer to (the authority figure who enacted the procedure). To what extent:* 1. Has he/she treated employees in a polite manner? 2. Has he/she treated employees with dignity? 3. Has he/she treated employees with respect? 4. Has he/she refrained from improper remarks or comments? *Informational Justice – The following five items refer to (the authority figure who enacted the procedure). To what extent:* 5. Has he/she been candid in communications with employees? 6. Has he/she explained the procedures used to make job decisions thoroughly? 7. Were his/her explanations regarding the procedures used to make job decisions reasonable? 8. Has he/she communicated details in a timely fashion? 9. Has he/she seemed to tailor his/her communications to individuals' specific needs?

Construct	Source and Definition	Full instrument
	people that convey information about why procedures were used in a certain way or why outcomes were distributed in a certain fashion. Procedural justice: the fairness of the procedures used to determine outcome distributions or allocations. Distributive justice: the fairness of outcome distributions or allocations."	*Procedural justice – The following items refer to the procedures used to arrive at your (outcome). To what extent:* 10. Have you been able to express your views and feelings during those procedures? 11. Have you had influence over the (outcome) arrived at by those procedures? 12. Have those procedures been applied consistently? 13. Have those procedures been free of bias? 14. Have those procedures been based on accurate information? 15. Have you been able to appeal the (outcome) arrived at by those procedures? 16. Have those procedures upheld ethical and moral standards? *Distributive justice – The following items refer to your (outcome). To what extent:* 17. Does your (outcome) reflect the effort you have put into your work? 18. Is your (outcome) appropriate for the work you have completed? 19. Does your (outcome) reflect what you have contributed to the organization? 20. Is your (outcome) justified, given your performance?
Employee trust	Brown, Gray, McHardy, Taylor (2015) "The extent to which employees trust their	4 items (unidimensional): Employees asked to indicate their degree of agreement with the statements. 1. Managers here can be relied upon to keep their promises. 2. Managers here deal with employees honestly. 3. Managers here treat employees fairly. 4. Managers here are sincere in attempting to understand employees' views.

Construct	Source and Definition	Full instrument
	managers will treat them honestly and fairly."	
Unethical Behavior	Kaptein (2008) "Behavior in and by organizations that violates generally accepted moral norms of behavior."	38 items (unidimensional): respondents express their level of agreement with the following general sentence "In the past 12 months, I have personally seen or have first-hand knowledge of employees or managers in my work group:" *Unethical behavior towards financiers:* 1. Falsifying or manipulating financial reporting information. 2. Falsifying time and expense reports. 3. Stealing or misappropriating assets (e.g., money, equipment, materials). 4. Breaching computer, network, or database controls. 5. Abusing or misusing confidential or proprietary information of the organization. 6. Violating document retention rules. 7. Providing inappropriate information to analysts and investors. 8. Trading securities based on inside information. 9. Engaging in activities that pose a conflict of interest (e.g., conflicting sideline activities, favoritism of family and friends, use of working hours for private purposes, executing conflicting tasks). 10. Wasting, mismanaging, or abusing organizational resources. *Unethical behavior towards customers:* 11. Engaging in false or deceptive and marketing practices (e.g., creating unrealistic expectations). 12. Submitting false or misleading invoices to customers. 13. Engaging in anticompetitive practices (e.g., market rigging, quid pro quo

Construct	Source and Definition	Full instrument
		deals, offering bribes or other improper gifts, 14. favors, and entertainment to influence customers). 15. Improperly gathering competitors' confidential information. 16. Fabricating or manipulating product quality or safety test results. 17. Breaching customer or consumer privacy. 18. Entering into customer contracts relationships without the proper terms, conditions, or approvals. 19. Violating contract terms with customers. *Unethical behavior towards employees:* 20. Discriminating against employees (on the basis of age, race, gender, religious belief, sexual orientation, etc.). 21. Engaging in (sexual) harassment or creating a hostile work environment (e.g., intimidation, racism, pestering, verbal abuse, and physical violence). 22. Violating workplace health and safety rules or principles. 23. Violating employee wage, overtime, or benefits rules. 24. Breaching employee privacy. *Unethical behavior towards suppliers:* 25. Violating or circumventing supplier selection rules. 26. Accepting inappropriate gifts, favors, entertainment, or kickbacks from suppliers. 27. Paying suppliers without accurate invoices or records. 28. Entering into supplier contracts that lack proper terms, conditions, or approvals. 29. Violating the intellectual property rights or confidential information of suppliers. 30. Violating contract or payment terms with suppliers.

Construct	Source and Definition	Full instrument
		31. Doing business with disreputable suppliers. *Unethical behavior towards society:* 32. Violating environmental standards or regulations. 33. Exposing the public to safety risk. 34. Making false or misleading claims to the public or media 35. Providing regulators with false or misleading information. 36. Making improper political or financial contributions to domestic or foreign officials. 37. Doing business with third parties that may be involved in money laundering or are prohibited under international trade restrictions and embargos. 38. Violating international labor or human rights.
Unethical Behavior	Akaah (1996) "Behavior in and by organizations that violates generally accepted moral norms of behavior."	17 items divided into six dimensions: employees rate their departments' unethical behavior in a 7-point scale with descriptive anchors ranging from "never" to "frequently." "To what extent do department employees:" *Personal use of company resources:* 1. Use company services for personal use? 2. Do personal business on company time? 3. Pilfer company materials and supplies? 4. Take extra personal time (lunch hour, breaks, personal departure)? *Passing blame on others:* 5. Conceal one's errors? 6. Pass blame for errors to an innocent coworker? 7. Claim credit for someone else's work? *Bribery:* 8. Give gifts/favors in exchange for preferential treatment? 9. Accept gifts/favors in exchange for preferential treatment? *Falsification:* 10. Falsify time/quality/quantity reports?

Construct	Source and Definition	Full instrument
		11. Call in sick to take a day off? 12. Authorize a subordinate to violate company rules? *Padding expenses:* 13. Pad an expense account up to 10%? 14. Pad an expense account more than 10%? *Deception:* 15. Take longer than necessary to do a job? 16. Divulge confidential information? 17. Not report others' violations of company policies and rules?
Organizational Deviant Behavior	Bennett and Robinson (2000) "Voluntary behavior that violates significant organizational norms and, in so doing, threatens the well-being of the organization or its members, or both. It refers to voluntary behavior in that employees either lack motivation to conform to, and/or become	12 items (unidimensional): employees rate the extent to which employees, as a whole, engaged in various deviant behaviors within the past year on a seven-point response format from never to daily. *To what extent did they see people from their organizations engaging in each of the behaviors in the last year.* 1. Taken property from work without permission. 2. Spent too much time fantasizing or daydreaming instead of working. 3. Falsified a receipt to get reimbursed for more money than you spent on business expenses. 4. Taken an additional or longer break than is acceptable at your workplace. 5. Come in late to work without permission. 6. Littered your work environment. 7. Neglected to follow your boss's instructions. 8. Intentionally worked slower than you could have worked. 9. Discussed confidential company information with an unauthorized person. 10. Used an illegal drug or consumed alcohol on the job. 11. Put little effort into your work. 12. Dragged out work in order to get

Construct	Source and Definition	Full instrument
	motivated to violate, normative expectations of the social context."	overtime.
Relationship conflict	Jehn (1995) "The amount and type of conflict in work units. Conflict is defined as the perceived incompatibilities or perceptions by the parties involved that they hold discrepant views or have interpersonal incompatibilities."	8 items (unidimensional): employees rate the amount of relationship conflict in their departments using a 5-point Likert scale from "strongly disagree" to "strongly agree." 1. There is a lot of friction among employees in my department. 2. There are a lot of personality conflicts in my department. 3. There is a lot of tension among employees in my department. 4. There is a lot of emotional conflict among department employees. 5. People in my department often disagree about opinions regarding the work being done. 6. There are frequent conflicts about ideas in my department. 7. There is a lot of conflict about my work in my department. 8. There is a lot of differences of opinion in my department.

About the Author

Alexandre Di Miceli da Silveira, Ph.D.

Prof. Dr. Alexandre Di Miceli is a professional speaker, consultant, researcher and columnist entirely devoted to corporate governance and business ethics since 2000. He is a full professor of corporate governance at Alvares Penteado School of Business in Sao Paulo and founder of Direzione Management Consulting.

Dr. Alexandre is the author of several best-selling books on these topics in Brazil, including Corporate Governance in Brazil and in the World, Behavioral Business Ethics: Solutions for Management in the 21st Century, and Corporate Governance: The Essentials for Leaders.

He is a consultant for the IFC (International Finance Corporation, World Bank Group) in projects and trainings related to corporate governance around the world and is a member of the committee that prepared the Brazilian Code of Best Practices issued by the IBGC (Brazilian Institute of Corporate Governance). He was also a professor at the University of Sao Paulo (2005-2016), independent consultant for the OECD (Organisation for Economic Cooperation and Development), and vice-president of the Brazilian Society of Finance.

Dr. Alexandre holds a Ph.D. and M.S. degrees in management from the University of São Paulo and has been a visiting professor at Cornell University and Université Catholique de Louvain. He has published more than 25 papers on peer-reviewed journals and presented more than 50 papers at international conferences. For his contributions to corporate governance and business ethics in Brazil, Dr. Alexandre is the recipient of several awards.

alexandre@direzione.com.br

www.ingramcontent.com/pod-product-compliance
Lightning Source LLC
Chambersburg PA
CBHW020627220526
45464CB00001B/54